DESIGNING YOUR BUSINESS

DESIGNING YOUR BUSINESS

STRATEGIES FOR INTERIOR DESIGN PROFESSIONALS

GORDON T. KENDALL, J.D., M.B.A.

FAIRCHILD PUBLICATIONS, INC.
New York

This text is dedicated to Michael J. Regier.

Executive Editor: Olga T. Kontzias
Development Editor: Sylvia L. Weber
Art Director: Adam B. Bohannon
Production Manager: Ginger Monaco
Associate Production Editor: Elizabeth Marotta
Manuscript Editor: Sheila Friedling
Interior Design: Andrew Katz
Associate Development Editor: Suzette Lam
Assistant Acquisitions Editor: Jaclyn Bergeron
Cover Design: Adam B. Bohannon

Library of Congress Catalog Card Number: 2005920620

ISBN: 1-56367-326-6

GST R 133004424

Printed in the United States of America

CONTENTS

PREFACE

A career in interior design means a career in business.

HARRY SIEGEL AND ALAN SIEGEL

Welcome to the world of interior design professional practices. As important as creativity and design knowledge are for designers, other skills are necessary to prosper. Generally known as *professional practices*, these skills and the knowledge that goes with them are predominantly business-oriented. Whether your goal is to have your own studio or combine design work with management at a large firm or in a team with other designers, you will need a knowledge of business: what being in business really involves; how businesses are organized and operated; and, most important, how business skills may be applied to the practice of interior design. With this knowledge, you can form step-by-step plans, known as strategies, in order to design your own interior design business that meets your own professional and personal goals.

This text is organized in five parts, each intended to provide information that will help you make sound decisions about working with clients and others as well as about the operation of any interior design business. In short, each part is about you and enhancing your ability to make sound professional and business decisions.

Each part presents an overview of the topics discussed in its chapters, which address key issues of professional practice. Part 1, "You and Your Work," discusses the development of professionalism and standards of business ethics in an interior design practice. Part 2, "You and Your Business," considers the four basic business components required to operate or to participate in an interior design business. Meaningful, responsive interior design work depends on a designer's ability to develop and maintain strong client relationships. Part 3, "You and Your Clients," explores how you might handle this responsibility. Part 4, "You and Your Resources" shows you how to access suppliers of merchandise and services and develop strong working relationships with them. Part 5, "You and Your Career," shows you how to acquire and build the professional skills necessary for developing your practice.

To assist you in applying strategies for the professional practice of interior design, each chapter presents information in a consistent, accessible manner. The chapter projects, unique among professional practices texts, reinforce your newly acquired knowledge with memorable real-world situational problems that you help to resolve. With these thoughts in mind, you can expect each chapter to contain the following features to guide you:

- *Why This Chapter Is Important To You* Most students ask why they should devote time and energy to learning a particular subject. This first section of every chapter answers that question for you.
- *Professional Practices Portfolio* This section serves two purposes. First, it is a review resource that solidifies your knowledge of key topics by posing questions that are addressed within the chapter. Its other important purpose is to compile a ready reference by maintaining in one portfolio your responses to the questions in every chapter.
- *Strategies-in-Action Projects* Three projects that conclude each chapter introduce you to three aspects of the practice of interior design. Each type of project will usually require for its completion the use of business forms and documents contained in the chapters, which are also featured on the accompanying CD-ROM.
  - The first project asks you to build incrementally your business plan for your own interior design business or ideal work situation. Then you will develop a career action plan, in which you document the additional education and experience you will need before you can achieve your professional goals.
  - The second end-of-chapter project can help you to apply professional practice skills throughout the life of a specific project. In the Residential Interior Design Project Simulation, you are introduced to Lee, a young interior designer who is working on a project that could launch her career. The diary in which she has recorded the progress of this first project is available for you to read. You may be asked to complete various practices-related tasks for her or to answer some questions. By suggesting solutions to the problems that arise in the simulation, you are preparing yourself to handle the same situations, should you face them in real-world practice.

◆ The third project takes you into the world of nonresidential, or contract, interior design. This series of case studies is written to resemble the special case studies used by businesspeople to analyze problematic situations. From case studies, decision makers learn to identify problems and consider alternative ways to resolve them. The cases in this text expose you to a variety of commercial and institutional settings in which contract design specialists practice.

One educator has observed that design students are usually not motivated to understand professional practices. While the study of business and related concerns may seem removed from the aspects of interior design that attract most students, remember that as you encounter clients throughout your career, they will expect, in the words of American designer Billy Baldwin (1903–1984), "the same kind of same" from you: That is, you are always a competent business professional who happens to be an interior designer. This book is here to help you devise ways of becoming just that.

ACKNOWLEDGMENTS

Despite pursuing other career options, I have always been fascinated by the interior design profession. It was, therefore, with delight I learned in 2002 of an opportunity to use my legal and business education and experience to write a textbook for interior design students under the Fairchild banner. The result is before you. Introducing and explaining to interior design students the variety of subjects that make up professional practices in ways that might be both approachable and interesting were the touchstones of this project. I am grateful to Olga T. Kontzias, executive editor of Fairchild Books, for working with me to focus and shape this text to accomplish such a worthy goal.

The early support from colleagues in the Family and Consumer Sciences Department of Texas State University (formerly Southwest Texas State University) was much appreciated, especially that of Drs. B. J. Friedman, Beth Wuest, and Karol Blaylock; and Jene T. Laman, M.F.A.

This text is result of my own research, observations, and interviews of a great many interior design educators and professionals. I would specifically like to acknowledge Lynn Grey, a practicing interior designer in the Austin and Houston areas for over twenty years for sharing with me her business practices and for alerting me to many of the issues now appearing in this text. I have been fortunate to be privy to a great many recounts by practitioners, clients, vendors, and service providers of their interior design experiences, many of which were adapted for use in this text to illustrate topics and concepts presented.

Throughout the writing (and rewriting) of this text, the assistance of all members of the Fairchild staff was much appreciated and needed. The contributions made by both Sylvia Weber, development editor, and Elizabeth Marotta, associate production editor, to the text are significant. I am grateful for their help and their friendship throughout this process. I acknowledge with admiration the assistance of Sheila Friedling, a superb wordsmith, who worked with the editors to make valuable improvements to the manuscript. My thanks also go to Adam Bohannon, art director, and Ginger Monaco, production manager, for their contributions.

The input from family and friends during the preparation of this book were also motivating. I would like to thank my parents, Diana and Terry Kendall, both experienced with writing and publishing, for their many suggestions and comments as this work progressed. Other family and friends whose encouragement was much appreciated include that of Virginia Regier, an able journalist and former newspaper editor in her own right, Dr. Susan K. Adler, Gene Brenek, Carla Cox, and Michael Helferich (including his parents and sister). Finally, a special thanks to Michael J. Regier for his unwavering support for this project and belief in me.

The following interior design educators, selected by the publisher, provided valuable feedback in their reviews of the text: Ann Black, University of Cincinnati; Phyllis Harbinger, Fashion Institute of Technology; Gera King, Scottsdale Community College; Robert Krikac, Washington State University; LuAnn Nissen, University of Nevada, Reno; and Celeste Stone, Scottsdale Community College.

To the instructors and students using this book, I would like to acknowledge the importance your contributions in the form of thoughtful comments and suggestions can make to future editions. This input will allow *Designing Your Business* to remain a relevant and useful source of information.

PART ONE

YOU AND YOUR WORK

"You have to start somewhere!" Undoubtedly you heard that before when you started a course of study. Your course in professional and business practices is probably quite different from other subjects you may have encountered in the field of interior design. What then, might be a logical focus for your initial encounter with this unfamiliar topic?

Perhaps first exploring what comprises the domain of professional interior design might be of benefit, including topics such as the goals sought by the organized practice of interior design and the basic fields of interior design specialization. Furthermore, defining some of the specific disciplines that contribute to interior design professional and business practices might be helpful as you identify those other professionals with whom interior designers frequently interact. Chapter 1, "Introduction to Professional Practices," seeks to provide this sense of context and purpose for your work. As you will soon learn in greater detail, interior design professionals employ a regular, methodical process to organize and execute their work. That systematic approach is described here in overview fashion so that you can get a first impression of the tasks performed by interior design professionals when working and describing a project.

The practice of interior design as a professional endeavor has a fascinating developmental history, a surprisingly inconsistent present status, but, more importantly for a young practitioner like you, an exciting future filled with infinite possibilities.

Chapter 2, "Becoming a Professional," takes this multifaceted approach when describing these topics. As you may suspect from the title of this part, you and your work in interior design will be influenced by the past, present, and future of the field. By identifying these influences at this early stage of your study, you gain important insights about what is required to begin your work in a particular location; what areas of interior design practice appear poised to offer future professional opportunities to practitioners; and how you and your work will ultimately fit into and maybe even influence the larger history of the profession. If you have ever wondered what it means to be a professional as well as an interior designer, this chapter addresses these primary concerns, while later chapters identify specific career options among which interior designers may choose.

Earning a profit from your professional work is important if you are to maintain an interior design practice. But at what cost to others and to society at large? Chapter 3, "Working Ethically," seeks to reach a practical understanding of the meaning, application, interpretation, and enforcement of professional standards of ethics in the practice of interior design.

CHAPTER ONE

INTRODUCTION TO PROFESSIONAL PRACTICES

The interior design professional provides services encompassing research, development, and implementation of plans and designs of interior environments to improve the quality of life, increase productivity, and protect the health, safety, and welfare of the public. NCIDQ definition of Interior Design

HARRY SIEGEL AND ALAN SIEGEL

WHY THIS CHAPTER IS IMPORTANT TO YOU

From this chapter you will gain an initial sense of what comprises the professional and business practices of interior designers. This knowledge will enable you to complete the three chapter projects and to understand the expanded description of concepts and terms found in later chapters. This chapter will explain the following basic principles of the interior design profession:

1. Where the organized practice of interior design may be classified among other occupations, as well as distinguishing aspects of the interior design profession
2. The various disciplines from which an interior designer's professional and business practice skills derive

3. The commonly used process by which interior designers organize and manage projects

PROFESSIONAL PRACTICES PORTFOLIO

By now you have devoted a great deal of time to the development of your creative portfolio. While not nearly so exhaustive as that effort undoubtedly was and will continue to be throughout your career, this chapter begins your creation of another kind of portfolio, your professional practices portfolio. Think for a moment why putting together a concise written document describing professional practice issues and problem-solving skills might be important.

Envision yourself as busy with one of your first interior design projects when a question arises, one related to project organization. For example, you cannot recall what steps a designer should take to formally *close out* a project. You think for a moment but just cannot recall a detail that seemed so straightforward in school. Then, it occurs to you to check what you wrote in your professional practices portfolio. Referring to that portfolio, you quickly determine the steps to take after project installation and, breathing a sigh of relief, go about your work. What could be easier than to take the time now, while you are studying professional practices, to make your own helpful reference portfolio?

With that thought in mind, write down the following questions with your responses in a convenient notebook or journal. You will build this portfolio throughout this text, and at the end of your course you will have developed your own primer for referral as you begin your work as an interior designer.

1. Can you define the term *professional practices* as it applies to interior design? Describe components of the definition.
2. Can you articulate several reasons why the study of professional practices is important for interior designers?
3. What are some characteristics of a *professional* and of an *entrepreneur?*
4. Can you describe the components of strengths, weaknesses, opportunities, and threats (SWOT) analysis and explain the circumstances in which it is used?
5. Can you name three ways by which professional practice decisions are monitored and controlled?
6. How can you develop and enhance professional practice skills?

INTRODUCTION TO INTERIOR
DESIGN PROFESSIONAL PRACTICES

How will your clients and other professionals describe their experience after working with you? Will you develop good working relationships with those who provide merchandise and services to you? Do you know how to remain in good standing with professional organizations of which you are a member? The answer to these and many other questions will reflect how well you understand and apply professional practice skills in your interior design work. Are there any further reasons to devote special consideration to this topic?

You might note that professional practices–based questions are included on standardized certification exams, which are used by a growing number of accrediting agencies to license interior design professionals within their jurisdiction. While this text is not intended as a study guide for such exams, it serves as an introduction to the material included on those exams. Also, think practically about the uniquely interpersonal, one-on-one nature of interior design work. Throughout your study of interior design, you have come to realize how much sensitive information you must learn about your clients to mesh their functional goals for the project with your proposed design concept. As one famous Hollywood designer recounted, "you have to know if (the client) eat(s) chocolate at 2 A.M. for breakfast" (Mann 1999). In addition to knowing how to handle sensitive and personal information, shouldn't you also have sufficient business knowledge to be entrusted with the large sums of money typically required to complete interior design projects? Your study of professional practices aims to make tasks such as these manageable as you carry out your work.

You probably realize by now you cannot function as an interior designer without assistance. After all, you are not an architect, carpenter, painter, general contractor, or any of a host of others on whom you will come to rely in your practice. You are, however, the link, sometimes the only link, between these professionals and your clients. As the interior designer "of record" on a project, you have prescribed responsibilities to clients and to various others to make working relationships as efficient, as beneficial, and as ethically imbued as possible (see National Council for Interior Design Qualification [NCIDQ] definitions, Box 1.1). You might also note that other programs of professional study, such as those for architects, attorneys, accountants, and physicians, also include required

BOX 1.1. DEFINITION OF INTERIOR DESIGN

SHORT DEFINITION

The professional interior designer is qualified by education, experience, and examination to enhance the function and quality of interior spaces.
For the purpose of improving the quality of life, increasing productivity, and protecting the health, safety, and welfare of the public, the professional interior designer:

- analyzes the client's needs, goals, and life and safety requirements;
- integrates findings with knowledge of interior design;
- formulates preliminary design concepts that are appropriate, functional, and aesthetic;
- develops and presents final design recommendations through appropriate presentation media;
- prepares working drawings and specifications for non-load bearing interior construction, materials, finishes, space planning, furnishings, fixtures, and equipment;
- collaborates with licensed practitioners who offer professional services in the technical areas of mechanical, electrical, and load-bearing design as required for regulatory approval;
- prepares and administers bids and contract documents as the client's agent;
- reviews and evaluates design solutions during implementation and upon completion.

LONG DEFINITION (SCOPE OF SERVICES)

The interior design profession provides services encompassing research, development, and implementation of plans and designs of interior environments to improve the quality of life, increase productivity, and protect the health, safety, and welfare of the public. The interior design process follows a systematic and coordinated methodology. Research, analysis, and integration of information into the creative process result in an appropriate interior environment. Practitioners may perform any or all of following services:

PROGRAMMING. Identify and analyze the needs and goals. Evaluate existing documentation and conditions. Assess project resources and limitations. Identify life, safety, and code requirements. Develop project schedules, work with their experience and knowledge of interior design. Determine the need, make recommendations, and coordinate with consultants and other specialists when required by professional practice or regulatory approval.

(continued)

BOX 1.1 (continued)

CONCEPTUAL DESIGN. Formulate for client discussion and approval preliminary plans and design concepts that are appropriate and describe the character, function, and aesthetic of a project.

DESIGN DEVELOPMENT. Develop and present for client review and approval final design recommendations for: space planning and furnishings arrangements; wall, window, floor, and ceiling treatments; furnishings, fixtures, and millwork; color, finishes, and hardware; and lighting, electrical, and communications requirements. Develop art, accessory, and graphic/signage programs. Develop budgets. Presentation media can include drawings, sketches, perspectives, renderings, color and material boards, photographs, and models. Contract documents. Prepare working drawings and specifications for non-load bearing interior construction, materials, finishes, furnishings, fixtures, and equipment for client's approval. Collaborate with specialty consultants and licensed practitioners who offer professional services in the technical areas of mechanical, electrical, and load-bearing design as required by professional practice or regulatory approval. Identify qualified vendors. Prepare bid documentation. Collect and review bids. Assist clients in awarding contracts.

CONTRACT ADMINISTRATION. Administer contract documents as the client's agent. Confirm required permits are obtained. Review and approve shop drawings and samples to assure they are consistent with design concepts. Conduct on-site visits and field inspections. Monitor contractors' and suppliers' progress. Oversee on the clients' behalf the installation of furnishings, fixtures, and equipment. Prepare lists of deficiencies for the client's use.

EVALUATION. Review and evaluate the implementation of projects while in progress and upon completion as representative of and on behalf of the client.

Adapted from the National Council for Interior Design Qualification.

courses of a similar nature. It seems logical for interior design professionals to be offered such a course as well.

A compelling reason to embark on a study of professional practices, finally, stems from the current status of interior design as well as its future. Interior designers now play a critical role in advising clients about much more than surface decoration details. Designers work to realize both residential and commercial projects in a physical environment made increasingly more complicated by technology and regulation (Coleman 2002). To continue to play this role, designers need to know about those complex constraints and how to work best within their parameters to complete a client's projects. Furthermore, designers must be willing and able to continue learning long after their formal education is completed (Knackstedt 2002). Particularly, designers need to be aware of how best to work with sophisticated clients and a wide variety of equally sophisticated consultants and trade resources. To do so, designers must have enough knowledge to establish credibility and engender trust in their business dealings.

If, indeed, the practice of interior design and designer practitioners are at a "crossroad," as one writer has suggested, between merely providing "beautiful and useful contributions" and abject extinction, then it seems reasonable that whatever relevance the profession and even designers themselves will have in the future will come from how adroitly knowledge of professional practices is applied in obtaining and carrying out creative work (Coleman 2002). Still, the most obvious reason for studying professional practices is the pride in accomplishment for a job well done and the satisfaction of having clients describe you and your work as truly professional. In this context, what specific objectives should you consider as you begin your study of professional practices for interior designers?

OBJECTIVES TO CONSIDER

You may wonder what this text has in store for you—what it's all about, in other words. You would be correct to assume that business-related topics such as accounting, commercial law, finance, and marketing will be included. After all, you will become both an interior designer and a businessperson once you begin your work. As you look through this book, you will encounter chapters devoted to both interior design and business. As important as they are, however, the study of professional practices involves much more than acquiring business information. This text explores many other topics, including personal career development.

With so many subjects to cover, you may wonder where this discovery process will begin. First, it would be useful to understand where interior design, its practice, and its practitioners fit in the larger world of work. To provide that context, this chapter identifies several objectives for you to consider. These include classifying the professional practice of interior design within the business world; identifying the disciplines from which the components of interior design professional practices derive; describing the process an interior designer may implement to make informed professional decisions; and, lastly, introducing the systematic procedures by which interior design projects are planned and managed. Although interior design project management is more thoroughly detailed in chapter 6, it is important you have a working knowledge of this process since its terminology is so basic to this text. This chapter acquaints you with that terminology, along with the skills necessary for successfully navigating the earliest stages of an interior design project-to-be. Understanding this last objective should be of great assistance to you in your study of the first Residential Interior Design Project Simulation.

DEFINING PROFESSIONAL PRACTICES

How would you classify the practice of interior design in relation to other occupations? Which trends in the business community would be particularly applicable to interior designers? Sociologists, who study interactions among groups of people, have noted a marked increase since World War II in the numbers of occupations now considered *professions* (Brint 1994). This trend has affected the practice of interior design. Previous generations of consumers largely considered the occupation to fall in the domain of *decorators*, or populated by "imaginative, magnetic amateurs high on the social scale" (Siegel and Siegel 1982). Contrast that view with the rigorous education now required to obtain credentials as an interior designer. This extensive, specialized education together with the sophisticated management skills required, among other characteristics, suggest that interior design is now considered a profession. Some have argued this trend toward professional status for interior designers is not yet complete, noting that "to date, interior design has not been adequately acknowledged as a profession that requires a distinct set of core competencies that extend well beyond simple decoration; nor has the broad social and economic impact of the profession been recognized" (Coleman 2002).

9

THE ENTREPRENEURIAL PROFESSION

In addition to their acknowledgment as professionals, many interior designers may also be considered entrepreneurs, who are distinguished by a willingness to take business-related risks, such as assuming responsibility for business ownership, as well as an interest in pursuing new opportunities (Norman 1999). Entrepreneurship is a hallmark of most practicing interior designers whether they work for themselves or are formally employed by others. A solo designer operating a home-based studio is a good example of a designer pursuing an entrepreneurial venture. So, too, would be an interior designer who is a shareholder (partial owner) in a large architecture/interior design firm. Both practitioners, to varying degrees, have assumed business ownership risks, and both rely on obtaining new clients or capitalizing on new opportunities to earn their income and advance their professional interests.

Although employees generally do not, by definition, assume risks of business operations, choosing to work instead in a salary-based position under the direction and supervision of others, there is a trend toward entrepreneurial thinking among them. These employees identify and, with their employer's consent, individually pursue new opportunities on behalf of their companies (Pinchot 1985; Bellman 2001). In this way, even an interior designer employed by someone else has become a new breed of business entrepreneur.

WHAT A DESIGNER NEEDS TO KNOW ABOUT BUSINESS

With this understanding of the context of the business environment in which interior design functions, is it possible to arrive at a working definition of the all-encompassing term *professional practices* that you may conveniently use in your study? In this text, professional practice skills include an understanding of the subjects and processes necessary for the competent and profitable completion of services rendered by an interior designer to a client.

Consider the components of this definition. You must have a sound, basic knowledge of certain subjects to begin your work. For interior design students, these subjects include aspects of business such as accounting, commercial law, finance, and marketing; each is a separate discipline with its own core of concepts and terminology necessary for the successful conduct of any business. Your knowledge of these fields will grow as you proceed in your work. Right now, however, as daunting as the prospect of learning "all that stuff" may seem, there are ways—interesting ways—to introduce you to the application of these subjects in your work.

This book is organized so that the objectives an accountant, lawyer, marketer, salesperson, or other professional might seek on behalf of an interior designer are listed first. These objectives are then followed by applications of these aspects of business to interior designers and their practice. For example, many interior designers sell products to clients in the course of their business. Objectives related to that sales activity include evaluating records of the purchase and sale of those items (accounting); drafting effective agreements for the sale of goods (law); and assessing client satisfaction with the goods (marketing). This approach enables you to appreciate the relevance of business topics because they are directly applied to the very tasks you will undertake as an interior designer. Interior designers can and should also develop processes that enable them to operate efficiently; this means maintaining accurate financial records and drafting useful, up-to-date written business forms. Knowing how to apply these business-related skills in your work and how to implement related processes are two important components of the definition of professional practices for interior designers.

The study of professional practices does not address or evaluate the creative and technical aspects of an interior designer's work. Instead, this discussion of professional practices considers the idea of competent completion as accomplishing design tasks in a rational, accurate manner. For example, a completed project may be entirely acceptable to a client but will need to be modified or even entirely redone because the designer submitted faulty specifications that did not comply with applicable building codes. Other examples of questionable competency occur when a designer fails to adhere to budget guidelines or orders products without client consent. Understanding the interplay of the variety of rules, laws, and expectations that apply to each project is an important measure of a designer's professional competency.

All businesses, including interior design firms, must be organized and run with the objective of earning more in revenue than is needed for the operation of the business. As a result, you must complete every project you undertake profitably. It is only partially true that "it takes money to make money." It is more accurate to say that it takes a professional's knowledge to know when agreeing to a project will cost the designer more in time and resources than the client could ever be expected to pay.

Gauging accurately the potential for profit (or financial headache) is part of the ability to thoroughly assess the requirements that will be placed on you, the designer, to complete a project. How might you make such assessments? First, think about what it is that an interior designer offers.

EXPERTISE IN A SERVICE PROFESSION

Interior design is a service profession. Unlike the making and selling of tangible products, or goods, you will become a professional whose stock in trade is the specialized knowledge and expertise you bring to design projects. Accordingly, professional services practices means understanding the unique challenges involved when working with clients who may have different ideas about what knowledge and expertise they want to buy. For this reason, one of the most important professional practices designers can develop is the ability to define the scope of services they will perform for any client on any particular project. Defining a set of services offered in this way and making the client aware of what those services will be are central to the work of an interior designer and to a definition of the designer's professional practices.

The NCIDQ defines, in short form, a professional **interior designer** as being one who "is qualified by education, experience, and examination to enhance the function and quality of interior spaces" (see Box 1.1). Once you become a professional, however, you must maintain that status. The professional practices of an interior designer include keeping abreast of the rules and regulations required to maintain those qualifications, usually through formal continuing education. Finally, you must have clients and the revenue generated from their projects to remain an actively practicing interior designer. To obtain these clients, your professional practices skills include marketing and promotion of yourself and your services. Clients also need to connect with you personally. Understanding the interpersonal nature of interior design work and working to enhance your abilities to communicate with a variety of people constitute a professional practice skill arguably as important as any business skill.

This text has identified the following as skills necessary to enhance a designer's professional practice abilities:

1. Understanding the context for interior design within the business community

2. Understanding ways in which businesses, including those focused on interior design, are organized and why
3. Knowing the ethical obligations and implications of interior design work
4. Having a working knowledge of basic business law and its application to interior design
5. Knowing the basics of business finance and how it applies to the practice of interior design
6. Understanding basic principles of management and how they relate to interior design businesses
7. Realizing the importance of marketing and promotion activities for interior designers
8. Providing quality professional services to your clients by first defining your services
9. Knowing how to use a description of your services to determine an effective way to charge clients for the work you do
10. Implementing effective project management techniques and processes
11. Using contracts incorporating elements that define your relationship with the client
12. Working with vendors
13. Working with contractors and other service providers
14. Becoming and maintaining your status as an interior design professional
15. Planning a meaningful and rewarding career

This chapter will discuss in detail each set of skills and knowledge itemized in this list.

KNOWLEDGE OF BUSINESS ORGANIZATION

Consider for a moment the objectives listed here, among them the knowledge of how businesses are organized. Businesses appear differentiated to many students by only the products or services they offer. In fact, the ways in which commercial ventures are formed vary greatly according to the financial and other objectives their founders wish to achieve. Besides making money, what might be other business objectives formulated by businesspeople, interior designers included? To get yourself thinking about these objectives, consider that you and a friend wish to open an interior design practice together. In what ways might you organize that business to establish a clear understanding between you and your friend about how the business is to be run and what responsibilities each of you has?

The various methods of business formation are described in laws that address these concerns of ownership and responsibility not only between operators of a venture but also between them and *outsiders*, such as creditors, those to whom the business owes money. Considerations about which business formation to utilize are, or should be, the first commercially oriented decisions made regarding any new business; they comprise a professional practice skill set required of interior designers.

Ethics, especially in the highly competitive world of business, are both elusive to define and, if in recent reports the media are to be believed, equally elusive to apply. No text or course can teach anyone to be ethical. Ethics must personally be understood as a necessary component of one's working life and practiced accordingly. What can be explored are the ways in which ethical challenges appear in the practice of interior design and how practitioners may recognize and resolve them. The study of ethics, no matter how brief, and suggestions for resolving ethical concerns highlight an important fact: failure to work within ethical bounds may result in serious consequences, even preventing a designer from working as an accredited professional.

Your professional practices course may offer you your only exposure to general business topics during your study of interior design. An entrepreneurial interior designer wishing to become involved in business ownership will first be called upon to comply with laws regarding the ways in which businesses are organized. In fact, laws and the legal system control virtually every aspect of modern business, and some knowledge of their application is a practical requirement. Savvy businesspeople, however, do not need to know as many details of business law as an attorney. They do need to know enough to operate their business within the requirements of the law; and, equally important, they need to learn to recognize legal problems to prevent their occurrence. Interior designers routinely enter into agreements, purchase and resell products, and work as their clients' agent as they execute projects. Awareness of general business law principles is therefore a professional practice skill required of interior designers. A competent businessperson needs to also know the limits of his or her knowledge of business law and recognize when to seek the advice of a professional.

The study of finance may seem daunting or uninteresting to innovative young design professionals who intend to make their mark creatively. Nevertheless, most viable businesses rely on gathering correct financial information and interpreting it to make decisions. Not all finance information is used for the same purposes, however; some of it is gathered and interpreted with the aim of disclosure to others outside the business. For example, financial accounting practices include interpreting the monetary activities of a business for the purpose of tax reporting. Other information is gathered and used to make decisions about the way in which the business is operated. Managerial accounting interprets financial data primarily for the internal use of the company to make decisions about such issues as how best to attain profitability. Pricing goods and services offered to consumers are examples of managerial accounting concerns. These financial professional-practice skills are necessary for interior designers who want to be both creative and profitable.

Management skills are important if you work in a design firm and, especially, if you own a firm. While general management skills are certainly important professional practice skills, in the practice of interior design employment policies should be considered less in terms of large-scale corporate, standardized applications and more as an integral part of the creative vision for the design firm. Developing and implementing management policies in this context may help to ensure a shared vision of the business among employees and management.

Marketing and related forms of promotional activities, such as personal selling, are necessary professional practice skills. After all, how will potential clients even know of your existence without some planned effort on your part to make them aware of you and the services you offer? Unique to the marketing function is the close relationship marketing can have with the creative vision of the designer or the design firm: Through marketing you may define a unique business niche distinguishing you and your work from other designers. When you create such an identity through the use of marketing techniques, it can cost a designer both time and money. Marketing requires the careful allocation of these resources so that other business goals are not jeopardized.

The 1998 "Analysis of the Interior Design Profession" concluded, among other things that "the skills that competent interior designers demonstrate include the ability to . . . manage contracts, money, data, people, and projects." Central to the management of "people and projects," which encompasses the majority of an interior designer's professional practice skills, is the scope-of-services analysis that an interior designer must perform before taking on any project. Quite simply, before a project is started it must be detailed in writing. Thoroughly describing the many tasks required for project completion is one facet of this professional practice skill; another facet is describing these steps to clients who are unfamiliar with interior design processes and terminology.

Determining what to charge your clients for the work you perform is linked to that definition of services. The profitability or insolvency of a designer or design venture results from how well informed this decision is. In this respect, understanding when and how various methods of charging clients are applicable is a critical professional practices skill. Both defining the scope of services you will perform for a client and detailing the method, or methods, by which you will be monetarily compensated for carrying out those services involves the understanding and careful use of written agreements. Many of these agreements exist in the form of prepared, fill-in-the-blank documents. Using these forms correctly is one of the processes inherent in professional practices.

As a professional interior designer, you will wear many hats and serve clients in many different capacities, not the least of which will be your function as an agent. Understanding how this agency relationship affects the handling of your client's money and project are related professional practice skills.

The buying and selling of goods is a business function designers undertake as a routine part of their work. Understanding the set of laws related to agreements involving the sale of goods is a professional practice skill; its mastery will help to ensure that products destined for use in a project arrive as specified and in a timely manner. Again, laws and rules related to buying and selling goods require not only memorization but also an ability to explain to clients and relevant trade sources how they apply and affect the delivery of goods.

ADVANCING THE PROFESSION AND YOUR CAREER

You are in the process of becoming a professional, a member of an occupational group with a long, colorful history and expansive possibilities for future growth. Understanding that history as well as reasons for advancing the professional status of designers and the practice of interior design is an important professional practice skill. Perhaps the strongest way to grow the professional status of interior designers is through advocacy or advancing their interests through political processes. Knowledge of the story of interior design and an awareness pursuant to the industry's agendas are different from business skills, but equally important.

Finally, professional practices skills are also personal in nature. You have already expended considerable effort, time, and resources in the pursuit of your design education. Does it surprise you to know that you may have to devote large amounts of time to keeping abreast of relevant changes in the profession and future career opportunities for yourself? Learning does not stop after leaving school. Career development is therefore a personal professional practice skill, which is necessary to develop plans for a successful, fulfilling future. As you can see, the professional and entrepreneurial nature of interior design work requires a great many business and personal career development skills. How might you learn to make effective decisions about professional practice matters using the information you know and will come to learn?

DECISION MAKING IN PROFESSIONAL PRACTICE

At the very heart of learning about professional practices is learning how to make decisions. Suppose, for example, an interior designer with a thriving practice wishes to develop and market new products. That is, to be sure, a professional practice decision of great consequence. How might the designer determine whether to pursue such interests? This chapter has identified specific areas of knowledge that play a part in professional decision making, but more than knowledge of these topics alone is necessary to make informed professional decisions.

A SWOT ANALYSIS

One method of business decision making used to assess a problem or issue is known as a **SWOT analysis**. You will recall that SWOT is an acronym that stands for strengths, weaknesses, opportunities, and threats. Businesspeople first determine the objective or outcome to be accomplished and then employ the SWOT evaluative approach to reach a conclusion. Referring to our earlier example, the designer might state as a business objective the development, manufacture, and introduction into the market by a certain date of a new line of furniture bearing his or her name. A SWOT analysis might first reveal issues internal to the designer's business in the form of the firm's strengths as they relate to the objective (Persus 2003). For example, the designer might note as strengths the facts that he or she enjoys tremendous name recognition in the community and has previously won awards for product design. However, related weaknesses might also be discovered, such as the fact that the designer is less well-known outside of the community as well as the great expenses associated with developing new products. By applying the SWOT analysis, the designer might ascertain an opportunity and thus a demand for the proposed new products since they would be unlike others currently available. Yet, they face a clear threat since they might easily be cheaply copied once introduced.

This brief summary shows how a SWOT analysis is applied. Most businesspeople are familiar with it and employ it in some form when making their decisions. It remains, however, the businessperson's task to accurately assess the actual situation surrounding the proposed business objective; and he or she must rely on a realistic and honest determination as to whether the facts really do support a desired outcome or are merely hopeful justifications for action. More thorough methods of business analyses are introduced and explored in later chapters. The Strategic Planning Project at the end of each chapter, for example, asks you to perform a personal SWOT analysis as you brainstorm about your ideal interior design venture.

CONSEQUENCES OF BUSINESS DECISION MAKING

You now have some sense of the scope of information that influences professional practice decisions. Ask yourself next about those decisions. As you know, consequences result from any decision. The business and professional decisions an interior designer makes are no exception. The consequences of some erroneous decisions may result in merely minor inconveniences, while other errors may result in substantial financial loss or even physical injury. In the example of the entrepreneurial designer wishing to develop new products, he or she may enjoy very beneficial results from a decision or he or she may not be so fortunate. The next stage in considering the role of professional practice–based decisions in a designer's working life is to understand how and by whom those practices are controlled and what consequences they may impose.

Perhaps the most obvious controls placed on decisions are those imposed by laws. Civil and criminal laws provide what are referred to as *remedies* to either aggrieved private individuals, by way of civil law, or to governmental units seeking enforcement of criminal statutes. These remedies are one way in which professional practices are enforced and, in general, are usually available to those who seek accountability for an interior designer's actions. A more complete description of the legal environment surrounding the practice of interior design is set out in chapter 4.

Voluntary associations also play an active role in the enforcement of professional practices of interior designers. Organizations such as the **American Society of Interior Designers (ASID)** and many others promulgate rules relating to professional practices and ethics. These professional organizations are a potent source of supervision and enforcement of professional practices among their members, since they make available grievance or complaint procedures to those who feel that a designer's actions were in some way harmful to them. These groups also provide for reprimands and membership revocations as ways of enforcing professional practices.

DEVELOPING FURTHER
PROFESSIONAL PRACTICE SKILLS

Innovation, new ideas and concepts, and new things! These are probably some characteristics of the practice of interior design that attracted you to the profession in the first place. Although you may not eagerly await or seek out new business publications with the same gusto as a new furniture catalog, there is also much innovation and excitement in the practices side of the profession. New business technologies help to ensure that clients are correctly charged and billed, and new laws are passed that directly affect how designers will interact with clients and the built environment. Examples of new developments in professional practices occur daily and almost endless. You must keep abreast of these new ideas but, more importantly, also be willing to adopt them in your work. *Hidebound* should apply only to the furniture you specify, not to you!

What are some ways by which you might respond to these new ideas? First, you should simply accept change as a fact of business life. Although that may seem obvious, think how easy it is to fall into a routine. Although it may feel comfortable and familiar, it may also make you appear *dated*, or out of touch, in the estimation of potential clients. Keeping up with changes in your industry and picking up professional practice tips from other designers through formal continuing-education seminars and meetings is one way of staying up-to-date; it is required of designers with licenses and professional group affiliations. Informal *networking* can also help. Reading business publications on a frequent basis is another way to keep up with issues related to professional practices, as is asking advice of professionals such as attorneys and accountants. Listening to your clients and understanding how best your business and professional practices can meet their needs is another way to be responsive to the need for change. Currently, there are many books available addressing the need to keep abreast of change and be willing to accept its challenges. As one of these authors has expressed: "If you do not change, you become extinct" (Johnson 1998).

PROCEDURES AND PROCESSES FOR
MANAGING INTERIOR DESIGN PROJECTS

"The interior design process follows a systematic and coordinated methodology (definition of interior design, NCIDQ)." Interior design does not just happen. It comes about through planning and organization, skills you will begin to acquire in this chapter. Have you thought about how your projects will proceed from conversations with clients to actual completion? Although you are creative and likely have a thorough knowledge of decorative styles and products, as well as building codes and standards, do you also know what formal steps designers take to turn such knowledge into completed, usable installations? Because project management tasks will encompass a large part of your work, this chapter's final objective is to introduce the commonly accepted sequence in which interior design work is carried out. This method is inherent in the definition of interior design provided by the NCIDQ and cited here for your reference. Furthermore, its terminology is used in discussions throughout this book. Project management issues are fundamental to many of the problems you will address in your studies of professional practices and as a working interior designer.

As you will learn in subsequent chapters, particularly chapter 10, "Managing Your Client's Project," this "systematic and coordinated methodology" is detailed and lengthy since it comprises many separate sets of interrelated procedures. The focus of this chapter's discussion, however, is to acquaint you with the terminology and sequence of constituent phases in the project management process and to provide a basic description for each phase (see Box 1.2). In fact, the names of phases in the process become so familiar among professionals that they sometimes employ only phase names as a shortcut to denote the kinds of tasks on which they are working. Interior design clients, however, may not be as familiar with either the process or its related terminology. In this chapter's Contract Interior Design Case Study, you can apply your knowledge of the phases of project management to inform your clients about the steps required to complete their projects.

Finally, this section focuses on the beginning stage in a designer's association with a prospective client. A stage so early, in fact, that a formal project may not really be said to have begun. What should occur as both designer and prospective client come to know one another and discuss what lies ahead? The practical implications of this exciting phase are explored further in the Residential Interior Design Project Simulation. Understanding the role of this phase and its application in the simulation will enable you, as a young interior designer, to form a useful strategy for handling project details from their outset.

How do you think the formal stages of managing an interior design project might be described? Interior design professionals have commonly identified five unique phases through which projects advance: programming, schematic design, design development, contract documents, and contract administration. In your later practice, you may find these phases may be less demarcated and in actuality may blend into each other. The circumstances of some projects may also result in their developing according to slightly different sequences. As your own expertise develops, your way of sequencing project management tasks may vary. That said, however, learning the names of these phases and the order in which they appear should give you a better understanding of how the sequencing of interior design tasks defines the work to be done (Piotrowski 2004).

1. **Programming Phase** Once designer and client have entered into an agreement to work together, this phase begins. It can be thought of as the stage in which project information is obtained and assessed by the designer. During programming, designer and client consult with one another about project goals through interpersonal communication, as in residential work; or designers conduct interviews with

BOX 1.2. PROJECT MANAGEMENT OUTLINE

Programming Phase
Associated Tasks
Consult/review initial project requirements
Document project requirements
Prepare project budget/schedule
Determine physical/budgetary feasibility
Provide written program of requirements

Schematic Design Phase
Associated Tasks
Prepare preliminary functional diagrams
Review alternative approaches to project
Prepare space allocations/utilizations
Prepare design concept studies
Submit preliminary cost estimates

Design Development Phase
Associated Tasks
Prepare documents to fix/describe final project
Complete documents with final appearance/function
Recommend colors/materials/finishes as necessary
Prepare presentation boards, related materials
Advise on cost-of-work adjustments

Contract Documents Phase
Associated Tasks
Prepare final working drawings/specs
Advise on further cost adjustments
Obtain necessary approvals/permits
Qualify vendors/suppliers/contractors
Assist client in assessing bids for project
Assist in preparing/awarding FF&E bids

Contract Administration Phase
Associated Tasks
Assist with final bids
Job-site management
Procure furniture/furnishings with orders
Maintain project management records
Visit job site periodically for correct completion
Supervise installation
Assist in determing substantial completions payments/releases
Post-occupancy evaluations/adjustments

those affected by or required to function in the completed space, as occurs in nonresidential interior design work. Designers of both residential and nonresidential projects may inventory and evaluate items for possible use in the new installation. Client preferences are noted extensively throughout this stage, and designers frequently provide feedback concerning their feasibility. A designer will research possible project constraints by considering applicable building codes or other standards that may apply. For example, a designer must understand what design solutions will be required to make public spaces compliant with laws such as the Americans with Disabilities Act (ADA).

2. **Schematic Design Phase** Once the designer obtains project information from the client and any relevant consultants, that knowledge is translated into the project design concept during the schematic design phase. This phase is the stage in which the designer prepares the first round of design, budget, and schedule considerations for client review. The designer prepares preliminary space and adjacency plans and selects project merchandise; he or she also prepares a preliminary budget and work schedule for the project. After client review and approval of these efforts, the next project phase usually begins.

3. **Design Development Phase** In this phase, designer and client finalize details such as space configurations, merchandise selections, and other specifications needed for the project. Notice the incremental way projects develop through the use of this methodology. Gradually, designers learn project requirements from the clients and their own expertise about project requirements. Then they research and present alternatives for client consideration; refine and finalize those initial results; and move on to the next phase of the project.

4. **Contracts Document Phase** After decisions about the project have been finalized, it is the designer's task to prepare documents ordering merchandise; to file for permits required for construction and installation of the finished project; and to request, obtain, and review bids from contractors. At the outset of the contracts document phase, the designer's tasks assume an administrative and supervisory nature. The extent of the designer's supervision of the project can become more apparent in the final stage of interior design project management.

5. **Contract Administration Phase** Once clients have approved final selections and chosen construction contractors, the final phase of

project management may begin. During this stage, designers may perform tasks such as tendering purchase orders to vendors and, where permitted, supervising work progress. This may be thought of as the installation phase of a project, although projects are by no means completed once installation has occurred. The contract administration phase usually concludes after all corrections and adjustments have been made and all outstanding payments for goods and services have been issued.

As you will learn in later chapters, there are a great many more details and issues to consider during each phase of interior design project management. This overview should highlight for you an important component of your work: As an interior designer you will likely provide an extensive range of services to your clients. What do you think is an important service interior designers should perform for both prospective clients and for themselves as they make early contact?

TROUBLESHOOTING STRATEGIES AT THE OUTSET

At first meetings with prospective clients, an important service may best be described as *critical listening* in an effort to gain and respond to useful information (James and Kratz 1995). Interior design is exciting to both designer and patron—so much so that it is easy for important project issues to be ignored or simply glossed over. Later, both designer and client may regret not having engaged in more meaningful dialogue before becoming immersed in a project. It is therefore important that designers learn to listen and then assess implications of what potential clients ask them to accomplish. **Active listening** may be defined as identifying and evaluating the implications of what is said by another. By actively listening, designers perform a great service for these prospects and for themselves. Through dialogue with the client, coupled with their own knowledge and insight, designers come to know how (or even if) they should be involved in a project.

Active listening is an important component of the practice of interior design. Some prospective clients may be new to the interior design process and may honestly not be aware of the time involved to complete even a small residential project. As a result, they may want a completed installation within a few months when it reasonably should take much more time. Nonresidential clients may want the designer to achieve the best results with an unrealistically small budget. In short, potential clients may not know what is required of a designer. By actively listening, and thus considering the implications of what clients want to be accomplished, designers can better serve their clients by educating them about what is *really* required. Active listening benefits designers as well. By considering what they will have to do in carrying out a project, designers educate themselves about the client and determine whether they will be able to successfully complete the client's project. Active listening requires practical experience as well as knowledge of professional practices. It also requires a designer to know how to ask meaningful questions of the client, even at the first meeting. Certainly experience can teach designers what important questions to ask. As you begin to learn about the interior design process, what are some questions to ask of prospective and actual clients that will engage your active listening skills to better serve both them and yourself?

First, acknowledge your excitement about meeting a prospective client and the possibility of gaining a new—perhaps your very first—project. To have reached this stage has involved a great deal of work on your part. As you will learn in subsequent chapters dealing with marketing and promotional activities, designers face a crowded marketplace for their services: There is a large number of interior designers from which consumers may choose. That you were able to interest a prospect in yourself, your work, not to mention your services, is an accomplishment.

What are some questions you should ask prospective clients? According to the American Society of Interior Designers Web site (www.asid.org/asid2/find/hire.asp), consumers who are interested in retaining the services of an interior designer tell prospective clients to expect a designer to ask the following questions. What inferences would a young designer make in beginning to actively listen to responses to the following questions?

1. *For whom is the space being designed?* It may seem obvious, but the implications of responses to this question may surprise you! Residential clients may simply say "for us" and offer no further elaboration. By considering the people for whom a project is ultimately intended, designers may assess whether they have the know-how to produce an appropriate space. Imagine if "us" meant a young couple, active in sports, or if "us" meant a baby boomer couple approaching retirement age: Each couple would present different physical situations or challenges that a designer should recognize from just knowing the in-

tended users of the space. With this information, designers should be able to address their clients' needs in their recommendations. Nonresidential projects may have many individual users; but step back a minute and consider the project itself. Who might likely inhabit or frequent such an establishment? What might they expect of a place of business they patronize, and, more important, what requirements are mandated for such a space? Designers focused primarily on residential space might want to assess whether they have the knowledge and experience to produce that kind of nonresidential space. By knowing who intends to use the space, designers who actively listen can discover the physical needs of the space as well as the personalities of those involved in the project.

2. *What activities will take place there?* Needless to say, a living room and a child's playroom have different design requirements, as would a restaurant in comparison to a large office space. What would an interior designer who actively listens conclude from responses to this question? Theoretically, understanding these implications gets to the core of what interior design is all about. To be more specific, however, think for a moment about all the details you have learned about specifying textiles and architectural finishes. Details about carpet grades and the abrasion resistance of surface textures (to give just a few examples) relate to their end use, that is, to their abilities to withstand activities to which they will be subjected. Responses to questions about activities that will take place in the project space should quickly bring to mind these issues. In addition, they should evoke your familiarity with the relevant design details, so that you know as soon as possible whether you can make the appropriate choices or need to research some more.

The implications of this question can pose further challenges for designers. Clients may intend to use a space for one purpose but make demands inconsistent with that use. This can happen, for example, when clients express a desire for light-colored carpeting in residential or nonresidential projects subject to heavy foot traffic. Even when correctly specifying the appropriate grade of carpet for installation, a designer should know and explain the main implication of using light-colored floor coverings in such situations: It may be difficult to keep the carpet looking clean. Using their education, project knowledge, and, as in this example, common sense, designers can explain to clients how the intended uses of a project space inform decisions that the designer makes.

3. *How long do you plan to occupy the space?* It may seem strange to ask this question; but in doing so, a designer should not think only in chronological terms. "Moving-up" residential clients interested in occupying a home only until they can afford a better one—perhaps for a few years at most—may not want to allocate a large budget for a design project. Other clients may feel that they have truly "come home" and, accordingly, wish to spend more on a designer's services. From the responses to this question, designers can determine how attached the client is to the project and, by implication, the client's flexibility about items such as budget and product quality. Clients indifferent to the amount of time they intend to stay in a residence may have less interest in spending more than was budgeted for upgraded products or high-quality workmanship. Again, it is the designer's task to listen to what is said, to make appropriate deductions from that information, and to suggest solutions and point out potential problems.

Nonresidential work is frequently installed in leased space for a predetermined time. A client may tell the designer that the space is available for use for only a certain number of years. Again, gaining a sense of the duration of use is important but so is the designer's awareness that a client tied to a lease of any appreciable length of time should be educated about the need for a budget permitting the appropriate product and workmanship specifications.

4. *What is your time frame?* Clients, especially those new to the interior design process, may not have a realistic idea about how long it takes for a project to come together. To them, a designer's work may seem to require very little time. It is critically important that you hear more than a designated time frame when seeking a response to this question. Instead, a designer who actively listens should understand whether the client has a reasonable, realistic understanding of how long a project will take to complete. Here, experience becomes useful when gauging a project's time frame. You will come to know approximately how long it takes to complete similar installations based on past projects. You can also learn to estimate time frames by consulting with other designers about their projects and how long it took to complete them. Remember that no matter how excited you may be about taking on a project, you must first listen to clients' expectations about project completion dates and then inform them about how plausible their proposed time frames are for their project.

5. *What is your budget?* Interior designers have been known to walk away from a proposed project after hearing the response to this question. Those designers are undoubtedly familiar with lawsuits that have arisen when designers have agreed to complete a project with a budget inadequate to accommodate the amount or quality of work necessary. When actively listening, a designer should hear more than a dollar amount or even a range of dollars. As in the time-frame inquiry, the designer should hear whether the client has a reasonable understanding of the many expenses interior design projects incur. Experienced designers therefore will not take on work budgeted for less than an amount the designer believes is plausible. Whether you adopt this approach you should listen very carefully to the client's suggested budget and then educate the client about the plausibility of completing the project (or any project) given those financial constraints. No matter how much you may feel the need to do a project or to work with a particular client, failing to ask beforehand for budget information or not informing the client about difficulties imposed by an inadequate budget sets the stage for serious problems later on.

6. *Are you relocating or remodeling?* The response to this question may give the designer some idea of how committed the client is to the project. Clients who want to fix up a residence for subsequent resale likely do not wish to spend a large amount of money on items or work they believe will not dramatically enhance sale proceeds. However, a full-scale remodeling of a residence in which the client wishes to remain may mean a larger budget with which to work.

7. *What image do you want to project?* The response to this question may help you determine whether you and a potential client share the same creative and aesthetic vision for the project. It may also help you to determine whether, if chosen for the project, you could work with the client to create a final product that both achieves the client's goals and serves as a useful addition to your own portfolio. As an interior designer, you likely have preferences for particular styles and objects as well as the final impression you would like your work to convey. Clients who indicate that they do not want the same results may be better assisted by another designer.

8. *What is the approximate square footage to be designed (for commercial projects)?* Many nonresidential projects are budgeted according to the amount of square footage involved. Although details of that practice

will be explained in later chapters, it is important for you to know now that responses to this question give contract interior designers or design firms an early idea of the budget for a proposed project. As noted, it is important that designers learn to listen for the implications found in the answer to even the most straightforward questions. This section has sought to make you aware of the need to do more than simply hear—rather, to understand through use of critical listening skills what services you will be required to perform in your work.

APPLYING PROFESSIONAL PRACTICE SKILLS IN YOUR WORK

The work of any professional includes knowing how to resolve problems. Often, young professionals find this to be an especially difficult task because they lack experience in recognizing situations that may be problematic. This section of each chapter is devoted to exploring how you, as a young interior designer, may recognize how particular problems may develop in your practice. With the ability to recognize troublesome situations comes the ability to apply your knowledge of professional practices to resolve them.

This chapter has provided an overview of the many non-design-related disciplines that interior designers must call upon as practitioners. Although application of many of these skills may seem obvious, are you aware of how subtle professional practice issues may arise in your day-to-day work? Just knowing terms and concepts abstractly will be of little benefit to you otherwise. Experience, also known as hard knocks, will teach you over time where professional practice skills should have been better applied; but there must be a way to help you now to understand the professional practice skills that apply in various aspects of your work.

While there may never be a typical interior design job, any more than there is a typical interior designer, all designers take similar steps to complete projects and conduct business operations. There may be exceptional examples, of course, requiring additional or unusual tasks; but carrying out even the most outlandish residential or technically advanced commercial project requires following the same pattern of identifiable steps from project to project. Is there a simple way to begin the process of learning which professional practice skills relate to particular aspects of your work?

You are undoubtedly familiar with templates of the kind found some-where on your drafting board. You use them to consistently produce the same results such as a circle of a particular size. The following overview of the sequential processes a designer completes during a project is similar to that template. In this text, the tasks designers routinely perform are illustrated by practice issues that, like the circle, consistently appear—usually. Comments on the practice issue are designed to help you recall that issue for later use in chapter projects and to set the stage for further text discussion. After reading each step, can you foresee what concerns might apply?

1. Designer is introduced to a potential client and discusses ideas for a project.

   Practice Issue to Recognize

   Informal Marketing and *Personal Selling Skills* made this meeting and interaction possible. Marketing activities may take many forms. Some of the more informal ones include networking at social events and obtaining referrals. Making the most effective use of even casual meetings can help you build rapport with prospective clients. Learning about their interests and recording them for future reference is one professional practice process that may help you turn these prospects into full-fledged clients. Prospective clients are also getting to know you at this time. Effective personal selling skills can be very helpful in obtaining clients.

2. Designer responds to formal written request to present concept proposals for a contract project.

   Practice Issue to Recognize

   Marketing Nonresidential interior design work is characterized by formal processes and interactions with many different people. Detailed written proposals for interior design work are usually prepared for review and comparison with other proposals. These proposals are as much marketing devices as the glossy ads and personal contacts acquired through social networking.

3. Designer learns confidential, sensitive information while gathering project information from a client. That information could greatly benefit the designer if he or she uses it for personal advantage.

   Practice Issue to Recognize

   Ethics Whether to act on information learned from a client or about a client should call to mind the issue of ethical conduct. Most professions impose some standards of ethical obligations on their practitioners. Interior design does as well through ethical codes adopted by governmental entities charged with supervising the profession and by voluntary groups such as the American Society of Interior Designers (ASID).

4. Designer and client sign agreement to work together.

Practice Issue to Recognize

Law The presence of agreements of any kind should signal to you that law relating to contracts is the issue for you to consider. Contracts are agreements that are legally enforceable through court actions in the event that one of the parties does not fulfill promised obligations.

5. Designer meets with client and presents final project proposal.

Practice Issue to Recognize

Project Management Skills Project should signal to you the issue of project management, particularly an aspect of it referred to as the **scope-of-service** analysis. Before beginning a project, the scope of services a designer is to perform must be detailed in writing. This detailed list usually is prepared as a result of negotiations between the designer and client. A major concern is to draft the scope of services in such a way that both designer and client know what is expected.

6. Designer meets with staff to review office budget and to interview candidates for new office receptionist position.

Practice Issue to Recognize

Business Accounting and Management Profitability is the business goal sought in any occupation. Correctly maintaining records of financial transactions, income, and expenses for later interpretation is a practices-related process important for those businesses, such as interior design, that require the expenditure of fairly substantial sums to operate. Management decisions in business must not only be made with the idea of maintaining profitability but also be sensitive to employment laws.

7. Designer and client discuss project budget and project schedule.

Practice Issue to Recognize

Project Management Project management issues are concerned with making efficient allocations of available resources. A key practice issue for interior designers is to determine whether these allocations have been accomplished in a way that satisfies client expectations for the project as well as the designer's goal of earning a reasonable profit.

8. Designer and client discuss ways in which the designer will be paid for services.

    Practice Issue to Recognize

    Charging Methods There are many different methods for determining a design fee. The key issue is whether the method agreed upon by designer and client adequately considers the nature of the work the designer will perform. Will the designer be required to purchase large quantities of merchandise for the project or need to devote a large amount of time to some aspect of the project? Different tasks make different demands on the designer. Careful preparation of the scope-of-services analysis will help the designer to determine the most appropriate charging method.

9. Designer specifies and pays for custom-designed furniture in trade showroom.

    Practice Issue to Recognize

    Law and Working with Trade Sources Here the designer has entered into an agreement with the trade source. Agreements should call to mind issues related to contracts and contract law. With respect to transactions involving the sale of goods, however, a particular set of laws takes precedent. These laws are based on what is called the Uniform Commercial Code and have been adopted by almost all states. When faced with practice issues related to the sale of goods, you must first consider whether these specialized forms of contract law apply. In addition to laws relating to the sale of goods, vendor relationships also affect interior design work. A designer's previous history of payment as well as individual showroom policies related to purchasing are all issues to consider when obtaining project merchandise from trade sources.

10. Designer considers leaving present work situation and going solo.

    Practice Issue to Recognize

    Career Development The time arrives when a designer perceives the need to seek out a new career direction. That may mean operating a solo or small group practice. Information about the operation of small businesses and related concerns is necessary to balance career aspirations with practical concerns such as earning a living.

This overview of the application of professional practices is, of course, just that: a general outline of what are, even for seasoned designers, complex tasks and decisions. Of course, there are exceptions, and many practice issues will likely require assistance from other professionals such as lawyers and accountants. However, as you are presented with steps or objectives throughout the text, think about what key professional practices issues are raised for you to resolve. In so doing you will learn how and why professional practice skills apply to the work that you do.

REFERENCES

Alderman, Robert L. 1997. *How to Prosper as an Interior Designer: A Business and Legal Guide*. New York: John Wiley & Sons.

American Bar Association. 2000. *The American Bar Association Legal Guide for Small Business: Everything a Small-Business Person Must Know, from Start-up to Employment Laws to Financing*. 1st ed. New York: Crown Publishing Group.

Bellman, Geoffrey M. 2001. *Getting Things Done When You Are Not in Charge*. 2nd ed. San Francisco: Berrett-Koehler.

Brint, Steven. 1994. *In an Age of Experts: The Changing Role of Professionals in Politics and Public Life*. Princeton: Princeton University Press.

Coleman, Cindy, ed. 2002. *Interior Design: Handbook of Professional Practice*. New York: McGraw-Hill.

Crawford, Tad, and Eva Doman Bruck. 2001. *Business and Legal Forms for Interior Designers*. New York: Watson-Guptill.

Goleman, Daniel, ed. *Business: The Ultimate Resource*. 2002. New York: Perseus Publishing.

Holland, J. Kent, Jr. 2003. *Construction Law and Risk Management: Case Notes and Articles*. Virginia: Ardent Publications.

James, Art; and Dennis Kratz. 1995. *Effective Listening Skills*. New York: McGraw-Hill.

Johnson, Spenser. 1998. *Who Moved My Cheese?: An Amazing Way to Deal with Change in Your Work and in Your Life*. New York: Putnam.

Knackstedt, Mary. 2002. *The Interior Design Business Handbook*. New York: John Wiley & Sons.

Mann, William J. 1999. *Wisecracker: The Life and Times of William Haines, Hollywood's First Gay Star*. New York: Penguin Putnam.

McGrath, Rita Gunter, and Ian MacMillan. 2000. *The Entrepreneurial Mindset*. Massachusetts: Harvard Business School Press.

NCIDQ. *Analysis of the Interior Design Profession*. 1998. Washington, D.C.: National Council of Interior Design Qualification.

Norman, Jan. 1999. *What No One ever Tells You About Starting Your Own Business: Practical Start-up Advice from 101 Successful Entrepreneurs*. Denver: Upstart Publishing Company.

Piotrowski, Christine. 2004. *Becoming an Interior Designer*. New York: John Wiley & Sons.

Pinchot, Gifford. 1985. *Intrepreneuring: Why You Don't Have to Leave the Corporation to Become an Entrepreneur*. New York: Harper & Row.

Root, Hal, and Steve Koenig. 2002. *Small Business Start-up Guide: A Surefire Blueprint to Successfully Launch Your Own Business*. 3rd ed. New York: Sourcebooks, Inc.

Siegel, Harry, and Alan Siegel. 1982. *A Guide to Business Practices and Principles for Interior Designers*. New rev. ed. New York: Watson-Guptill.

Stearns, David. 2001. *Opportunities in Interior Design Careers*. Rev. ed. New York: McGraw-Hill.

STRATEGIES-IN-ACTION PROJECTS

As you may have noticed, three special projects conclude each chapter. What are these projects all about? First, to provide some context, the NCIDQ definition of interior design lists experience as a basic qualification for a professional designer. As important as it is, experience is, nonetheless, difficult to obtain. After all, while you have been in school learning design skills as part of your education—another basic qualification for a designer—likely has been a challenge to gain much experience. In fact, you might not even know what to gain experience in! Certainly, experience in applying your growing professional practices skills within the context of residential and nonresidential contract work is a necessity, but you will be more than simply an interior designer once you begin your working life. You learned in this chapter that you will also be an entrepreneur, one who assumes the responsibilities of operating a business. In short, you will become a designer-businessperson, who needs to take commercial risks to succeed professionally. But entrepreneurial skills apply only to those who want to open their own interior design firms, right?

Certainly, learning how to run a business is necessary for those who intend to start their own interior design ventures. However, even if your goal is to obtain employment with a design firm or work with another designer or design-related business, don't forget that you will likely be an employee of an entrepreneur. How well that person manages or group of people manage the business will affect your professional and financial well-being. How will you recognize the impact of your employer's actions if you have not experienced or understood how business concepts are applied?

This text, unfortunately, cannot transport you to a real-world working environment, but it can and will attempt to simulate some of the experiences you might have in such an environment by means of each chapter's Strategies-in-Action Projects. Your first experience will be to complete a business plan in the Strategic Plan project. After learning necessary business terms and concepts in this chapter, you will have the opportunity to apply what you know by drafting a section of what will become a full-scale plan for your interior design business. At the conclusion of chapter 13, you will have developed your own plan for your ideal or dream interior design business. Remember, however, that you will be an entrepreneur, too. Knowing what you now wish to achieve one day, how are you going to make that ideal job a reality? First, you will need to take stock of what skills you now have; to do that you will complete a current résumé in chapter 14. The final step in beginning your transition from student to design entrepreneur is to develop a plan of action. In chapter 15 you will do just that, using your completed business plan as a goal and your résumé as a guide to the knowledge and experience you need to acquire to turn an ideal into an accomplishment.

Preparing a business plan allows you to consider firsthand the issues an entrepreneur faces. It may be many years before you feel ready to tackle a challenge such as starting your own business. However, you are probably very concerned about how you will handle early projects, especially those of substantial size. Is there any way to encounter professional practice skills as they might be applied throughout the life of a specific project? In the Residential Interior Design Project Simulation, you are introduced to a young interior designer working at her first job right out of school. Although not the designer's dream job, by any estimation, it does give her an opportunity to work on a project that could, unquestionably, launch her career. But there is a problem: The designer is unsure of many things—not least of which is her concern about how to apply the professional practices she learned in the classroom to real-world situations. The diary in which the designer has recorded her observations and concerns is available for you to read. You may be asked to complete various practices-related tasks for the designer or to answer questions she has posed. This will help you prepare to handle the same situations as those of your new friend.

Your third project—a Contract Interior Design Case Study—takes you away from residential interior design into the world of nonresidential, or contract, interior design. The name is derived, it is believed, from the fact that contractors, or construction professionals, are involved in carrying out the designer's concepts. These projects take a slightly different form but for a reason. Known as case studies, the projects are written to resemble the special reports used by businesspeople to analyze factual or hypothetical situations. From these studies, decision makers learn to identify problems that occur during the course of their professional activities. They then consider alternative ways to resolve these issues before reaching a conclusion they believe they could defend. How will you learn to solve gray-area questions, where the answers are unclear? The highly competitive, business like focus of contract interior design affords an appropriate setting for applying the more advanced professional practice skills. Thought provoking, sometimes difficult, but, it is hoped, always interesting and engaging, the three projects that conclude each chapter develop text topics that are relevant to you, your work, and ultimately to your career.

STRATEGIC PLANNING PROJECT:
INTRODUCTION AND BRAINSTORMING

What ideal interior design business or work situation could you create to attract interesting clients and projects? That dream may seem a long way off, but it's never too early to start planning your future in the interior design industry. You might think of this business-plan project as your first step toward finding your niche in interior design. Even as a student and especially as a young professional, the more clear the idea you have about how you wish to establish yourself in the world of interior design, the better you will be able to realize and explain your goals to others.

Without question, you want to accomplish a great many things; but to do so, it is common sense for you to start with a plan of some kind. An easy way to get started in the planning process is to imagine that you must describe, even justify, the existence of your ideal business to others. How do you go about doing that?

One method businesspeople rely on to make such presentations is to prepare a written description of their future enterprise in a form known as a business plan. These plans can be quite lengthy since they contain detailed information about the purpose of the new business and the expected expenses and income of that new business. Business plans also provide a description of the preferred location for the entity, and they offer marketing strategies such as a detailed analysis of the target market. Some plans also include management information about the new company and a description of any special laws or rules governing the business's operation. These plans are usually required by banks or business investors before they will advance sums of money or open lines of credit to the business. As a blueprint for a new business, these plans are both creative—contemplating something different from other existing businesses—and practical—detailing what will be required to be successful.

Undoubtedly you have thought about the kind of interior design business you ultimately wish to have or be a part of. This is the first of many projects in this text related to preparing a business plan. By the time you finish your practices course, you will have formulated an entire business plan for your ideal business.

Business plans begin with an idea—an objective—for a new venture. Where do these ideas come from? If you have not already done so, consider the ASID careers list; then decide what your particular interior design enterprise will be. With that idea in mind, you can then complete your own SWOT analysis using a worksheet to reveal the issues you will personally face in making that ideal business a reality. Then prepare a final statement detailing your business and those issues.

Here is how to get started: Look at yourself and your abilities. What are your strengths and weaknesses? Are you a people person, but do you lack business experience? If so, then you have identified two of the four components of the SWOT analysis and applied them to yourself. What opportunities do you see that you might pursue in the world of interior design? Are there positions in the industry you can become especially qualified to fill? Think about segments of the interior design industry that are most appealing to you. For example, there are a great many residential interior designers, but how many of those would be able to work with clients to make a private residence accessible to disabled or elderly residents? Sustainable design is a growing area of interest among designers and consumers. Do you see an ability to work as a design specialist in that area? This section will be more relevant and accurate if you think about several opportunities, not just one that you can find in a particular geographical area. So, related to carrying out the opportunities aspect of your analysis will be to think about exactly where you believe or know these opportunities to exist. After all, the unfilled needs of interior design consumers in one area may be the overworked design market in another. Finally, what threats will you have to overcome to capitalize on the opportunities you have identified? Are there too many well-established interior designers who are doing something similar to what you think is an underutilized opportunity? After you have had some time to think about the SWOT analysis as it applies to you, it should be easy work to make several entries for each of the four elements. Form 1.1, a brainstorming activity, should help you organize your thoughts.

Since 1974, the NCIDQ has established and monitored competency standards for the interior design profession. One way in which they do so is by promulgating, or making known publicly, those actions and characteristics that define the practice of interior design. As you review the definition in Box 1.1 and as you study for the NCIDQ accreditation exam, notice how closely the topics you encountered during your interior design education relate to this definition. Is it a coincidence?

RESIDENTIAL INTERIOR DESIGN PROJECT SIMULATION

How might you handle the first few meetings with prospective clients? Designers spend a great deal of time with prospects discussing ideas and projects in the hopes of gaining business. In this gray area of a project, where prospects are more than just names and faces but are not yet obligated to you—nor you to them for your services—what might you do to prepare? You are both still learning about one another and the project. How can you quickly and easily organize the information you obtain from prospects to effectively prepare your project proposal and later draft related business documents? (See question number 2 with related forms featured at the end of the chapter.) This early stage of an interior design project occurs before there is any agreement for services. Once a formal contract exists, the programming phase of project management begins. These early discussions may be best thought of as the pre-programming or project development phase (see Box 1.2).

Lee, a young designer, has agreed to share with you the experience of obtaining an exciting project. Read the diary entry to get a feel for what it is like out in the real world. Then, answer the questions that follow. In the remaining chapters, you will see how the project progresses, and you can advise Lee by answering questions that conclude each episode of the simulation.

PLANNING YOUR FUTURE IN INTERIOR DESIGN: BRAINSTORMING ACTIVITY

CAREER OBJECTIVE

Describe your ideal interior design business—one you would like to run or one in which you would like to participate.

_____

_____

_____

What would you like for your career to contribute to the practice of interior design?

_____

_____

_____

If you would like a career as an interior design educator, describe what kind of position you would seek and what your area of academic interest would be.

_____

_____

_____

What other goals do you have for your interior design career?

_____

_____

_____

PERSONAL ASSESSMENT

Think about where you are now in terms of your education and work experience. Then answer the following SWOT-analysis questions.

1. What is the greatest <u>strength</u> that will enable you to reach the career goal you described above?

_____

_____

_____

2. What is the greatest <u>weakness</u> that might prohibit you from attaining that career goal?

_____

_____

_____

(continued)

FORM 1.1. (continued)

3. What external <u>opportunities</u> exist for attaining that career goal? (For example, do you believe there is a great demand for the type of interior design business you wish to establish or desire to work in?)

_____

_____

_____

4. What external <u>threats</u> exist that might prohibit you from attaining the career goal you identified?

_____

_____

_____

Lee's Diary

I'm so excited I can hardly write! I've been just barely getting by financially working at a new store called Imagination Unlimited that specializes in furniture and accessories for children. It's been O.K. as a first full-time job. We earn commissions from the sales we make, and the owner said we should go after full-fledged residential interior design jobs of any kind, as long as the merchandise we specified for the project is sold through the store, at retail prices. But it's August! Who's going to sell anything, much less get a great project to work on when everyone's away on vacation? Well, guess what? Today I got a chance to be that person.

Now about the paperwork: This is a new business, and the owner wants to try to document everything, such as phone calls and anything we send out by fax or mail. It's been a lot of work to keep up with the calls in the phone log (see Form 1.2). The owner wants me to do it so that we can follow up with prospects. I've enclosed blank forms so that I'll have them for use. But take a look! I have to complete a job log (Form 1.3) and a time sheet or record (Form 1.4). Well, I hope the event of today will lead to lots of information to record on the forms.

A couple came in to return a baby gift for credit, and when I recommended some items they might want in exchange, we struck up a conversation. They seem to like my taste so much that they want to get together tomorrow and hear my ideas for turning an entire floor of their large, new home into a space for their children. Here are my notes about them and the project (also see Forms 1.5 and 1.6).

OFFICE TELEPHONE-CALL LOG

Date _____   Time _____   Received by _____

Subject of call   _____
                    _____
                    _____

Follow-up: Y/N, Explain   _____
                            _____

Date _____   Time _____   Received by _____

Subject of call   _____
                    _____
                    _____

Follow-up: Y/N, Explain   _____
                            _____

Date _____   Time _____   Received by _____

Subject of call   _____
                    _____
                    _____

Follow-up: Y/N, Explain   _____
                            _____

Date _____   Time _____   Received by _____

Subject of call   _____
                    _____
                    _____

Follow-up: Y/N, Explain   _____
                            _____

Date _____   Time _____   Received by _____

Subject of call   _____
                    _____
                    _____

Follow-up: Y/N, Explain   _____
                            _____

Date _____   Time _____   Received by _____

Subject of call   _____
                    _____
                    _____

Follow-up: Y/N, Explain   _____
                            _____

JOB LOG

Start Date	End Date	Job Name		Assigned Job No.

General System for Job Numbering

FORM 1.4. PROJECT TIME RECORD

PROJECT TIME RECORD

Client _____ Job number/ID _____
                                         Staff _____
Project address or reference _____

DATE	Specific Activity Performed Project Task Conducted	TIME Hrs./	Min.

Total Time Spent on the Following Activities:

Client meetings/Calls _____ Project technical (Rendering/CAD) _____
Project research/Design _____ Project management _____
Site-visit time _____ Project-related other (Travel/Installation) _____
Meeting with others _____

CLIENT INFORMATION WORKSHEET

This document records basic client information

Initial Contact Date _____
Referred by _____
Consultation Date _____

File No. _____

Contact Information

Client Names _____

_____

Subject Property Address _____

_____ Phone _____

Special Access Instructions (directions) _____

_____

Client Address (if different) or Client Place of Business _____

_____

_____ Phone _____

Other Contact Information

Cell phone # 1 _____   Cell phone # 2 _____

Fax _____

E-mail # 1 _____

E-mail # 2 _____

Project Information

Subject Areas

_____

_____

_____

_____

_____

_____

_____

Design Objectives

_____

_____

_____

_____

_____

_____

_____

_____

_____

Client Preferences/Dislikes

_____

_____

_____

_____

(continued)

Client Information Worksheet, page 2

Special Considerations

Children _____
_____
_____

Pets/Animals _____
_____

Health Concerns _____
_____

Social _____
_____

Other _____
_____

Desired Completion/Installation Date _____

Financial Information

Project Budget _____

Bank Information _____ **Bank Contact** _____
_____

Project Bank Account # _____

Client Credit Check _____ **Project Credit Account #** _____

Deposit Amount _____ **Other Fees**
Received _____

Appointments/Phone Log

_____
_____
_____
_____
_____
_____
_____

Notes and Comments

_____
_____
_____
_____
_____
_____
_____
_____
_____
_____
_____
_____
_____
_____
_____
_____
_____

Lee's Notes

Names: Bob and Carole Abernathy, both 41 years old. Just moved into a colossal home after spending 6 months looking for their dream house.

Four children—want each of the 3 older ones to have their own bedrooms near one another.

Sam, age 10, active in school sports

Darcy, age 8, active in school sports

Nicole, age 6, likes quiet activities such as painting and drawing in her room

New baby, Karen—want a nursery near the other children. Should be able to be converted into regular kid's bedroom when she's outgrown the crib.

Au pair, Elizabeth—almost my age and from England, cares for kids.

Couple wants all the bedrooms to open onto a common area that would serve as a playroom. Playroom to be multifunctional with facilities for toy and game storage as well as area for the preparation of the children's meals. Stressed that playroom and kitchen area must be child-friendly and safe. Of course! Au pair's room to be on the same floor and near the children's rooms, especially nursery and playroom.

House is ten-thousand square feet, three-level structure. 2015 Staffordshire Drive (exclusive street with homes overlooking Lake Austin and the city lights). Because of mountainous terrain and the way the house was situated on the lot, the entry level of the house is actually second floor. That level contains the house's formal living spaces; master suite and other "adult" rooms are on the level above. Children's space is entire lower level—almost 2000 square feet—accessed by staircase from entry level above.

During the initial visit the next evening, Lee takes many haphazard notes on a phone message pad as they talk on site in the space intended to be the new children's area. It is immediately obvious that the space will require substantial modification to conform to the couple's wishes, since it is currently comprised of five little bedrooms opening into a dark hall. The children now occupy this area but are unhappy with the small, dark rooms and that there is no place indoors to play together or have friends over. Lee notes "light issues," and, although the couple did not mention it, she notices a set of glass doors at the end of the hall, opening directly onto a deck with a large, unprotected swimming pool. The designer also takes some initial measurements of the space and records them on the back of a page.

As an afterthought, Bob Abernathy asks whether it would be possible to install a sophisticated phone-intercom system so that the family might

PROJECT RESEARCH NOTES

This document describes project research you may be required to undertake before making a formal presentation to the client. Frequently, clients ask for something—an object, a surface finish, or even an "effect"—with which you are perhaps less familiar or unaccustomed to using. Here is where you may record and research those requests.

Project File No. _____

Project Client Name _____

Subject Property Address _____
_____
_____

Project Requirement _____
_____
_____
_____

Available Resources _____

Contact _____

Project Requirement _____
_____
_____

Available Resources _____

Contact _____

Project Requirement _____
_____
_____

Available Resources _____

Contact _____

Project Requirement _____
_____
_____

Available Resources _____

Contact _____

communicate more easily throughout the entire house. He mentions a system made by the Fonocasa Company he saw in a friend's house and asks about it. Lee is not familiar with that particular company or system but agrees to look into it.

Questions

1. Here's where your early knowledge of professional practice skills can be useful. What specific questions would you advise Lee to ask these potential new clients at this early stage? Can you think on your own of any others the young designer could ask about the project that the couple might not have thought of? What plausible inferences might be drawn from the couple's responses to each of these questions?
2. Use Forms 1.5 and 1.6 to help Lee organize the notes from the initial meeting and the first visit to the Abernathy's house. As completely as possible, fill in information and observations about the potential client and the project. Keep your form for use in subsequent chapters.

CONTRACT INTERIOR DESIGN CASE STUDY: THE CASE OF THE GORGEOUS GYM

Practicing interior designers rely on case studies to keep apprised of design industry concerns. It is easy to become engrossed in the situations they present and wonder how you might solve the problem or problems they identify if you were involved in a similar situation. This chapter's case study asks you to address a simple professional practice problem that may arise in residential as well as contract interior design. However, because of the more formal ways in which contract work is carried out and information conveyed, it is logical to study the issue in the setting of a commercial project.

The problem concerns the difficulty of explaining to clients what activities a designer will engage in to carry out the various phases of a project. Often, even clients who are otherwise sophisticated about business matters have no knowledge of how and why designers work the way they do, especially how they organize projects. You will present your solution to this common problem as a draft of a letter written on behalf of the design team described in the case study.

Case Background

Fitness had always been a way of life for Joe Peak. He had excelled in varsity sports throughout high school and college and had won several important body-building competitions as a young man. Personable and friendly, Joe experienced little trouble attracting clients to the small store-front gym he opened in Palm Beach, Florida, when he was in his late twenties. By age thirty-five, however, Joe was tired of his "rinky-dink" facility and was ready to open a showplace, luxury gym. Joe envisioned a colorful, light-filled temple to fitness, evocative of the Miami Beach Art Deco style he loved. His ideal gym would contain a stylish reception area just inside the front door, where he and other trainers would greet their clients. Joe's wife, Christi, who had been injured in a skiing accident, would serve as the receptionist for the gym and would have an open office space in the reception area with a beautifully designed desk and a computer loaded with state-of-the-art software for managing the business. Joe had not yet consulted with her about what her physical needs were for access and mobility in the space. Of course, Joe had to have a sound system worthy of a large auditorium to make the place truly to his liking. He was keen to have one particular type of sound system, although it was designed to be installed only in theaters.

To obtain funds necessary to finance this venture, Joe approached a wealthy friend, Sam Jacobs, who agreed to invest in a new gym. They planned for it to be located conveniently for the extremely affluent residents they imagined would be the target market. After several months of Joe and Christi's fruitless scouring of the local real estate market for a suitable location, Sam approached them with an interesting idea: Why not place the gym in one of Sam's office buildings. A successful real estate developer, Sam had built an office complex comprised of ten two-story buildings, nestled around a small park, just a few minutes by expressway from the desired neighborhood. One building had never leased after being fully finished as "Class A" office space. This building had the unique feature of facing west, with a commanding view of the Palm Beach skyline. It was, however, extremely hot in the afternoon as the Florida sun beat relentlessly against the glass "skin" of the building. Prospective tenants gasped at the costs required to cool the building and then found other properties to lease. As a result, the building remained vacant for some time and required some measure of repair to its plumbing, electrical, and HVAC systems from lack of use. After much consideration, the Peaks and

TRANSMITTAL COVER LETTER

COMPANY NAME
Address
City
Phone No.
Fax No.

Date _____

Number of pages _____

To _____ From _____

_____ _____

_____ _____

Job No./ Reference No. _____ Client _____

Project location _____

Please do the following:

Add to project file _____ Keep for your information (as requested) _____

Review and return _____ Comment _____

Distribute to the following Other action required _____

_____

The following is enclosed or transmitted:

_____
_____
_____
_____
_____
_____
_____

Transmitted via

Fax (total pages including this one) _____ Courier _____ UPS _____

USPS _____ Delivery confirm _____ By hand _____ Interoffice _____

Forwarding co. _____ Other _____

Notes/Comments/Instructions

_____
_____
_____
_____
_____
_____
_____
_____
_____

Sam agreed that the space could become a gym—somehow. Joe was concerned about the air-conditioning issue. He also worried that the office space would not be large enough, or the floors strong enough, to accommodate the extensive amount of premium fitness equipment he already owned.

As plans for the formation of "Peak Fitness" came together, Sam and Joe are considering hiring a large, Los Angeles–based design firm, Vargas Associates, where you are an associate designer, to carry out the project. Although your firm has not worked in Florida, and no one on staff is familiar with local building codes or area contractors and suppliers, your firm was a logical choice to carry out the project because of the many public recreational facilities in its portfolio. You have seen pictures of the chosen site, with its many awkwardly arranged offices waiting to be transformed into a light-filled gym. The clients also want to add a climbing wall to facilities offered by the gym, but they are unaware whether the floors and walls could support such a feature.

Questions

You have been assigned the task of contacting Joseph and Christine Peak, with a copy to Sam Jacobs, describing the steps your firm will take during various phases of the project. Using what you know of both the facts of this case and project management, complete Form 1.7. Include questions that the prospective client will have to answer before your firm can complete the pre-programming phase of the project.

CHAPTER TWO

BECOMING A PROFESSIONAL

"My hope and my belief is that universal recognition of interior design as a profession is inevitable and imminent."

PHYLLIS MOORE, FASID

WHY THIS CHAPTER IS IMPORTANT TO YOU

The professional endeavor known as interior design is of surprisingly recent origin. Perhaps because of its youth, it continues to evolve as designers' contributions become more widely recognized and valued by society. Although a review of interior design's developmental past can be fascinating, the preparations for its future serve as the centerpiece of this chapter; for it is in the future that you, your work, and ultimately your career will flourish. How can we plan for both the future of your career and the evolution of the interior design profession? This chapter is important because it will teach you about the conditions that first gave rise to the practice of interior design and identify elements that remain relevant to it today. This information will enable you to form your own strategies for working within the current, multifaceted context of interior design to shape the future you will share with the profession.

PROFESSIONAL PRACTICES PORTFOLIO

After completing this chapter, you should be able to answer the questions that follow. Include your responses in your professional practices portfolio.

1. What elements contributed to the rise of interior design as a profession?

2. In what ways is the practice of interior design currently controlled by the individual United States and Canadian provinces?

3. What is advocacy, and how may it be applied to influence the future of interior design?

4. Distinguish between *practice* and *title* laws as they pertain to interior design.

5. What are several reasons that designers should engage in early project documentation practices, and how may they do so?

INTRODUCTION TO YOUR
DEVELOPMENT AS A PROFESSIONAL

Past, present, and future, the profession of interior design is fascinating to study. As late as 1900, the services of *interior decorators* were mostly a privilege available only to those with the social position and sufficient wealth to access and afford them (Massey 2001). That early exclusivity is a far cry from the amount of interior design–related activities and merchandise, especially those intended for residential use, available now to consumers of virtually all class levels. Even design activities related to commercial interiors have evolved from their earlier, more decorative origins; they are now considered important in achieving workplace satisfaction, worker efficiency, and strategic business goals. The challenge today for people interested in becoming interior designers in both residential and commercial contexts is learning how to process various amounts of information about the practice of interior design to understand how they may contribute to the profession.

This chapter discusses the factors that contribute to major milestones in the development of the interior design profession. It then examines the various educational and accreditation pathways that now provide entry into the profession and explores the basic ways in which current practitioners may influence its future evolution. It seems obvious that clients will expect someone claiming to be a professional in any endeavor, including interior design, to perform professional services in a professional manner. Developing methods to record prospective and actual clients' preferences is one simple way for designers to carry out their work for clients that at the same time will be beneficial to the growth and development of their business.

This chapter focuses on four objectives related to developing a useful set of professional development skills. Although the particular procedures and processes required to meet those objectives are important, they are not the only factors to consider as you review this chapter. Ultimately, the past, present, and future development of the interior design profession are integrated to form a whole. Interior designers who recognize the ways in which the different facets of their profession converge are well on their way to becoming the professionals they aspire to be.

OBJECTIVES TO CONSIDER

Chapter 1 established a context for defining the professional practices of interior designers by identifying the disciplines that influence those practices. Chapter 1 also provided an overview of the distinct phases in which designers classify the tasks required to complete projects, thus introducing you to the systematic procedures by which designers impart a sense of context to their activities. Now that you are more aware of the subject of your study as well as the ways in which designers organize their work, think for a moment about the role you play in interior design. In what context will you and your work develop? Among its objectives, this chapter aims to provide you with an understanding of the past and present state of interior design that will enable you to find your own future niche in the profession.

The first objective is to establish a historical context for the interior design profession. Its development as a formal vocation involves a highly colorful account of the creative triumphs and travails of individuals described as "imaginative, magnetic amateurs high on the social scale" (Siegel and Siegel 1982). Whereas anecdotes about the introduction around 1900 of Elsie de Wolfe's "revitalize(ed)" interiors, devoid of Victorian "jumble" (Massey 2001), are interesting and perhaps inspiring, it is important to consider the surrounding social factors that influenced the origins of the profession in the first place and that, arguably, still affect it to this day. Certainly, an era in which indoor plumbing and telephones were obscure rarities can seem very removed from the realities of today. However, certain factors common to society then and now continue to shape the interior design profession and bode strongly for influencing its future.

This chapter will identify these forces and their influence on the development of interior design.

The current organization of the interior design profession is characterized by diversity. This is reflected even in the names by which nonprofessionals refer to practitioners, the various educational pathways available to students interested in participating in the profession, and the different ways in which some jurisdictions—for example, the different states—provide for professional recognition of designers.

In an effort to explore the diversity of the interior design profession, this chapter will discuss how the *interior decorator* and the professional *interior designer* can be accommodated within the design community through appropriate demarcation of their respective roles and duties.

There are many ways in which you can pursue an interior design education. This chapter will detail the current administration of interior design education and certification through the examination process. You will also learn to distinguish between the meanings of such terms as *title* and *practice* as well as between *registered* and *certified* as they relate to the legal recognition of interior design professionals in jurisdictions that have enacted laws related to the regulation of design practitioners.

It is interior design's future as a viable, evolving profession that holds the most promise for practitioners. Learning ways to influence that future involves initially identifying trends gleaned from the broad range of disciplines that interior designers now consult. But it also means learning how practitioners can shape not only their own professional future but also that of the entire profession. You may already be aware of some of these methods, including participation in associations such as the American Society of Interior Designers (ASID) and the International Interior Design Association (IIDA). There are, however, specific techniques practitioners may use to advance their professional points of view in an effort to educate and influence decision makers and the public at large. In this chapter, you will learn about these important skills and apply one of them in a Strategic Planning Project.

Paperwork is probably an anathema to interior designers more interested in working on stimulating projects than in taking notes and opening files. Nonetheless, practitioners in both residential and nonresidential interior design should consider finding—and using—a simple method to document prospective projects and the concurrent needs of individuals who may seek only an initial consultation. Performing administrative tasks serves a variety of purposes, which becomes more obvious as prospects are identified as clients and projects formally enter the programming phase. Even if a designer is not retained to work on a project for which he or she performed early documentation tasks, those early efforts should still provide insights that may be used in other aspects of the business. Can you think of how that might be true?

PROCEDURES AND PRACTICES RELATED TO YOUR PROFESSIONAL DEVELOPMENT

The challenges in discussing the historic evolution of the interior design profession as a sequential account of events and individuals are twofold. Interior design students are usually fascinated by the more illustrious and influential among the early practitioners, who are already well-known to them. In fact, it is likely that a majority of students by the time they reach professional practices classes have had to do research on these individuals and their influences. Moreover, step-by-step accounts of their lives and work usually overshadow analysis of the significance of their innovations. Instead, identifying the societal factors that give rise to the organized practice of interior design is more useful in providing a framework in which to analyze the progression of interior design as a profession and to anticipate its future as well.

DEVELOPMENT OF THE PROFESSION: A HISTORICAL AND CULTURAL OVERVIEW

The arrangement of articles and use of ornamentation, either symbolic or decorative, in personal dwellings are practices centuries old, as is the interior organization of structures intended to accommodate large-scale public use (Pile 2000). While early examples of these practices seem far removed from today's highly sophisticated practices, think for a moment about what it was that made possible the prehistoric rendering of animals on cave walls in France and England as well as the building of ancient Greek and Roman structures. Did these examples of early design come about for much the same reasons that modern interior designers specify wall coverings that meet fire safety standards and plan commercial spaces that will foster the productivity, safety, and overall welfare of those who work in them?

As people become more knowledgeable about the world around them and learn how to apply that knowledge to enhance their interactions with that world, they may be said to have learned how to apply technology. Early examples of technology—which for centuries comprised mostly hand tools powered by manual labor—and of its application include the early cave drawings made of primitive, colored clays and the hewn ancient structures erected entirely by hand. From those earliest times until about the last 150 years, the technology used in building and furnishing physical structures was constrained in an important respect so as to prevent its wide-scale application.

During this period, the individual architects and craftspersons who are today remembered had learned to refine available technology and, in combination with an equally refined aesthetic sense, to produce items and structures still valued for their sophistication. A good example of these skills are found in the decorative products and structures produced in Western Europe during the eighteenth century. Versailles, the royal court of Louis XIV, is an epitome of available technology and skilled labor had been able to produce for centuries; and the objects found in the Sun King's court had been the provenance of royalty and of the extremely wealthy for as long. As advanced as the technology was for the time, it still required painstaking manual labor to animate it and give shape to its beautiful forms. It would take gigantic advances to make the products of technology readily available to a larger population and thus transform the once exclusive into the readily attainable.

Sociologists—or those who study human society and social interactions—credit the Industrial Revolution and the process of industrialization with transforming societies of the nineteenth and early twentieth centuries from cultures that depend on agriculture and handmade products to cultures that are based on manufacturing and related industries (Kendall 2003). The technological advances of mass production, in which items could be produced quickly and in large amounts, brought about a society in which something like the interior design profession could develop. No longer did one or a few artisans produce a single product in its entirety. Instead, a large labor force could be trained to carry out individual tasks that together would produce many examples of an item and often made with greater uniformity and precision than those made by their artisan predecessors. The making of textile products was one domain of manufacturing where the effects of technology were earliest felt (Schoeser 2003). Cloth became neither time-consuming to personally produce nor expensive to purchase once the complex elements of its pro-

57

duction were influenced by advances in spinning, dyeing, and weaving technology. In its ability to manufacture items that were previously costly of time and labor to produce, such as furniture and household goods, the technological advances of the Industrial Revolution may be considered as providing the material context for the development of the interior design profession. The effects of technology, however, were even farther reaching, for with the greater use of technology appeared other factors that contributed to the development of interior design.

With the industrialization that took place between 1760 and 1850 arose a phenomenon sociologists refer to as urbanization, which occurred when increasing numbers of people began to live in cities rather than in rural areas (Kendall 2003). This trend to move away from rural life was a response to the effects of industrialization, as more and better-paying jobs became available in factories situated in or near the cities. Perhaps most relevant for the interior design profession was the increase in numbers of people who became city-dwelling consumers instead of the rural-based producers they had once been (Kendall 2003). Urbanization and in particular technology-based industrialization are considered to have set in motion the origins of enterprises such as the modern-day fashion industry (Diamond 2002). With respect to the development of interior design, however, an additional factor was needed to provide a platform from which its practice as a profession could spring.

The rapid and wide-sweeping changes occurring in society through the effects of industrialization and urbanization also brought about new perceptions of the roles of men and women in that expansive society. In the United States, many of these changes in perception were borne out by action. Typically, in Victorian America, especially among its middle class, women were expected to manage the family home and assume responsibility for it (Massey 2001). Toward the end of the nineteenth century, their growing dissatisfaction with limits on their ability to participate in society other than through opportunities afforded by home, family, and church life gave women an impetus to find new outlets for their interests and talents. These interests, however, were still bound by the social constraints of the time. While "the idea of earning had entered into the minds of women" by about 1877 (Massey 2001), the means by which they could pursue that interest was still limited to pursuits deemed acceptable by society. One such pursuit involved furnishing and embellishing of the home.

An early advocate for the development of "**interior decoration**," as it was known, was Candice Wheeler (1827–1923), who was responsible for establishing, in 1877, the New York Society of Decorative Art, an organization intended to serve as an educational resource for women and as a marketplace for their handicrafts (Massey 2001). Wheeler was also responsible around 1883 for the founding of Associated Artists, a multifaceted firm responsible for services now recognized as interior design as well as the design of decorative products. Wheeler was also an early writer on the topic of interior design, publishing around 1895 articles about the suitability of interior decoration as a career for women as well as a book on decorating principles in 1903. The novelist Edith Wharton is credited with being influential in focusing attention on interior decoration with the publication, in 1897, of *The Decoration of Houses* with the New York architect Ogden Codman, Jr. Around 1904, there was sufficient interest in the subject of decorating to warrant offering classes in the subject at the New York School of Applied and Fine Arts (now known as Parson's School of Design). Thus the technology of the Industrial Revolution, the demographic effects of urbanization, and the interest among women for greater participation in society coalesced in the early twentieth century to give rise to what is now the profession of interior design. These forces next needed a catalyst in the form of a charismatic personality to bring them together. Elsie de Wolfe (1865–1950) is traditionally cited as being the "first" interior decorator, with her seminal project, in 1905, of New York's Colony Club considered the first to be carried out by someone other than an architect or antique dealer (Massey 2001). She is also considered responsible for authoring the first how-to book on interior decoration, *The House in Good Taste*, published in 1913 and, like Wharton's earlier book, still influential and widely available today.

This survey of early developments in the interior design profession has emphasized the importance of a variety of social factors. But economic and social-welfare considerations also influenced the development of interior design as a professional occupation. For example, publication in 1903 of *The Jungle* by Upton Sinclair prompted outrage at the working conditions and sanitation practices then prevalent in the American meatpacking industry. This outcry was instrumental in the establishment of the federal agencies responsible for protecting workers and the public against the kinds of horrific conditions Sinclair depicted. The issues of worker and workplace safety again came to the public's attention in 1911 in response to the Triangle Shirtwaist Factory fire in New York City, in which more than 100 young women perished. While it would take some time before issues of consumer protection and worker safety would come to the attention of interior design professionals, these early events set in motion laws and practices that greatly affected interior designers and their practices.

After World War I, America entered a time of economic and social expansion. Women had gained the right to vote and the United States enjoyed a period of prosperity. While much of that prosperity would later prove to have rested on dubious business and investment practices—mostly those of a speculative nature—the affluence it generated permitted new design practitioners to flourish with many fewer constraints than those faced by their predecessors. One notable practitioner was Dorothy Draper (1889–1969), who is credited with being among the first to concentrate her design practice on commercial interiors. The affluence of the times contributed to interior design in other ways. With greater discretionary income, household consumers began to seek information about how they might better enjoy their homes. For that information, they increasingly looked to department stores and magazines. Examples of good taste, of the modern style, were often themes of store displays or magazine features, which provided an early means of instruction that lay people could adapt on their own. Perhaps more important, these sources continued to whet the appetites of consumers for the items they portrayed and for the services of designers. In the late 1920s, design practitioners were becoming increasingly interested in their status as professionals and seeking more formal ways of organizing. To that end, (Piotrowski 2002) notes the rise of decorator clubs in various locations throughout the United States. Clearly, there was an interest among consumers for interior design–related goods and services, thanks to factors such as magazines and department stores, even the lavish movie theaters and motion-picture productions of the time. Equally clear was an interest among practitioners to be considered design professionals. The economic events of the next decade would provide an impetus for that recognition.

The economic depression that began in 1929 persisted in many parts of the country throughout the next decade. Its devastating effects on consumers and on life in general during that period have been well chronicled. Perhaps less obvious is their inspiration for founding the modern interior design profession. In 1931, at a time considered by some to be the nadir of the Great Depression, businesses providing many different kinds of goods, including furniture, were faced with the prospect of going out of business. As part of a national trade show to promote American-made furniture, held in 1931 in Grand Rapids, Michigan, a conference was planned to give voice to those practitioners seeking to establish an organization that would represent their interests as design professionals. From that conference came the founding of the American Institute of Interior Decorators, which in 1936 became the American Institute of Decorators

(AID). These early beginnings set the stage for the later development of the interior design profession. It would take the advent of new technologies and manufacturing techniques, as well as economic change, for the modern interior design profession to emerge as the force it has become.

The post–World War II era—from 1945 through much of the 1950s—was, for the most part, another era of economic expansion in the United States. Many forms of technology developed during the 1940s were soon adapted to consumer use, with both residential and commercial applications. Urbanization was still a potent force in society; only now workers, including former members of the military services, were drawn to cities to participate in educational activities and to work in offices. Magazines, stores, and television (a new medium) also stimulated the desire for new items for the home and workplace. "Going to work" was a recognized and accepted fact of life for millions, and the state of the workplace became an important concern for design practitioners.

Designers and Decorators

Whether a design practitioner should be referred to as a *designer* rather than a *decorator* has been an issue for decades. As the demands of technology as well as the building, health, and safety codes of the 1950s and 1960s required greater expertise to apply, the work of practitioners who were educated and experienced in resolving these issues seemed less like the activities of the earlier imaginative practitioners. Design practitioners started to embrace the new behavioral and psychological research and to incorporate it into their work; and the role of furniture placement and surface embellishment to comply with standards of good taste seemed far removed from the contribution of social research to projects. The distinction between the designer, trained in building and safety codes as well as psychology, and the decorator, concerned with furniture arrangement and the use of surface finishes and effects, continues to this day. According to commentator Phyllis Moore, FASID, "we must, as a profession, find a way to draw a more clear distinction between the designer and the decorator and to promote the message that there is room in the marketplace for both."

The Development of Professional Organizations

Since 1936, AID had served the interests of the design community; however, in 1957 some of its members formed a separate group referred to as the National Society for Interior Designers. In 1975 the two merged to form what is now known as the American Society of Interior Designers (ASID). The 1950s saw the first attempt, in 1951, at statewide regulation of the interior design profession in California. Although not successful at that time, it was the first of such attempts. Not until 1982 did the first state, Alabama, adopt such regulation.

The 1960s saw many changes in the professional development of interior design. Education was increasingly seen as important, and in 1963, the Foundation for Interior Design Education and Research (FIDER) was founded, assuming responsibility for reviewing and accrediting interior design educational programs. Although initially responsible for accrediting both undergraduate and graduate programs, it now focuses on the former.

The 1970s marked the advent, specifically in 1974, of the National Council for Interior Design Qualification (NCIDQ). Among other tasks, it is responsible for the preparation and administration of a qualifying examination now used as the basic method of determining minimum competencies in interior design skills and knowledge. The 1970s also saw a greater interest in the issue of consumer safety and its regulation. An awareness of the importance of safety, both in the workplace and in products available to consumers, was a social trend of the early 1900s. This early trend gained momentum during the 1970s, reflected in court decisions and jury awards for damages in increasingly large amounts. The issue of legal liability, or fault, is still a concern of interior designers and other professionals. Subsequent chapters will discuss ways in which interior designers can structure their business activities to reflect these concerns. From its early beginnings in response to industrialization and urbanization, the practice of interior design has developed by reflecting and responding to social concerns.

This historical and cultural overview of the interior design profession provides a context for understanding the emergence of the profession's current system of education and accreditation. Students will need to navigate within this system to become professionals. What issues can you expect to address along that path?

ADMINISTRATION OF INTERIOR DESIGN PROFESSIONAL CREDENTIALS

Essentially, courses of interior design study may be classified as *degreed* or *certificate* programs. Graduation from a four-year educational institution with a bachelor's degree in interior design is a clear-cut example of a degreed course of study. There are also two- and three-year programs found principally at local community colleges and specialized art and design schools. Programs offered at these institutions usually award associate degrees in interior design upon successful completion. Certificate programs, however, offer instruction in various interior design subjects, but with little emphasis on other educational material.

FIDER ACCREDITED PROGRAMS

After deciding which program is most appealing and appropriate for career goals, students choosing degreed plans should next assess whether a chosen program has received accreditation from **FIDER**. Since 1970, this organization has sought "(to lead) the interior design profession to excellence by setting standards and accrediting academic programs" (see FIDER Web site, www.fider.org/ 2003). FIDER further notes on its Web site that it "sets standards for postsecondary interior design education, evaluates college and university interior design programs (and) publishes a list of accredited programs that meet the standards." Institutions seeking FIDER accreditation voluntarily submit their interior design curriculum, or course of study, for extensive review by organization auditors. Central to FIDER's determination of professional-level accreditation is whether the institution's program offers at least 30 semester credit hours of instruction in disciplines other than interior design—for example, liberal arts, humanities, social science, or science. FIDER leaves requirements for specific courses and course sequencing to the discretion of the individual institution. Currently, FIDER offers no accreditation other than *professional level*. Four-year bachelor's degree programs that meet FIDER standards are accorded this designation as are those two- and three-year programs that meet the instructional standard of 30 hours in other disciplines. Many interior design programs are available that do not offer FIDER professional-level accreditation, or have pending accreditation. What are the benefits associated with choosing a FIDER-accredited program?

As a result of its own research and the involvement of interior design educators and professional associations, FIDER derived what it styles as a common body of knowledge required for the professional practice of interior design. According to the FIDER Web site, this lengthy skill set includes, among other topics, the importance of understanding "the application of laws, building codes, regulations and standards that affect design solutions in order to protect the health, safety and welfare of the public." It also includes knowledge of "the methods and practices of the business of interior design; and an appreciation of a code of ethics." Requiring professional practices classes of all its member institutions is one example of FIDER's efforts to ensure uniformity of instruction in all FIDER-accredited interior design programs. By undertaking study in such a program, students are assured that the education they receive is in accordance with recognized and authoritative standards within the interior design profession.

THE NCIDQ EXAMINATION

As you approach the end of your formal interior design studies, you will undoubtedly come across another, the **NCIDQ**. Refer to the short definition of an interior designer in chapter 1. This organization is responsible for promulgating that definition and other industry-related standards, the most important concerning individual professional certification.

The mission of NCIDQ is to "aid and assist the general public by establishing and administering an examination to determine which practitioners of interior design shall be certified as competent to practice in the field of interior design" (NCIDQ 2003). Further activities include maintaining a list of individuals who successfully completed the exam, as well as assisting in the reciprocity process by which an interior design practitioner educated and experienced in one state may practice in another without losing professional status. NCIDQ is gatekeeper to many industry organizations since successfully passing the NCIDQ exam is "a prerequisite for professional registration in those American states and Canadian provinces that have enacted licensing or certification statutes to protect the health, safety and welfare of the public (see Box 2.1). The NCIDQ examination must also be passed by every interior designer applying for professional membership." Passage of this important exam is also a prerequisite for *professional* entry into other organizations such as ASID and the IIDA among others. Ultimately, the council "seeks the acceptance of the NCIDQ examination as a universal standard by which to measure the competence of interior designers to practice as professionals."

NCIDQ is a not-for-profit organization incorporated in 1974 and located in Washington, D.C. Its incorporation documents provide that only state

BOX 2.1. NCIDQ EXAM ELIGIBILITY REQUIREMENTS

The exam eligibility requirements include interior design education and actual full-time interior design experience. They are as follows:

- Four to five years of interior design education plus two years of full-time work experience in interior design; or
- Three years of interior design education plus three years of full-time work experience in interior design; or
- Two years of interior design education plus four years of full-time work experience in interior design

Criteria for eligibility are counted up to the time of application submission, not up to the following examination period. The educational requirements are evaluated as follows:

- Five years: at least 150 semester credits (of which 90 or more are interior design–related); 225 quarter credits (of which 135 or more are interior design–related)
- Four years: at least 120 semester credits (of which 60 or more are interior design–related); 180 quarter credits (of which 90 or more are interior design–related)
- Three years: at least 60 semester credits or 90 quarter credits of interior design–related course work.
- Two years: at least 40 semester credits or 60 quarter credits of interior design related course work.

Education is evaluated on a review of college or university transcript(s) and, when necessary, copies of course descriptions from the college or university catalog in force at the beginning of course work.

The experience requirement is evaluated as follows:

In reviewing applications, full-time employment is defined as not fewer than 35 hours per week. It is recommended that employment be under the supervision of a full-time interior design practitioner who is either NCIDQ certified, licensed as an architect, or recognized by a state or provincial regulatory agency as an interior designer.

If you reside in and/or intend to become licensed in a regulated state or province, you must contact the appropriate state or provincial agency before completing the NCIDQ application to verify the state's or province's requirements for licensure.

Adapted from www.ncidq.org/examreq.htm.

and provincial regulatory agencies, not individual interior design practitioners, may be members of the council, as is true also of other interior design professional associations. Nonetheless, individuals usually apply directly to the council's administration first to determine exam preparedness and then for exam admission. Texas is a notable exception to this procedure, since exam candidates first apply to the Board of Architectural Examiners—the agency responsible for supervising interior design registration in that state—to determine their eligibility for exams. One research task you should undertake is to learn whether you must first apply to an agency in your state of preference or directly to NCIDQ prior to taking the exam.

The minimum educational requirement for exam eligibility is two years of academic instruction. You will note that NCIDQ does not require that study to take place at a FIDER-accredited, or any other kind of, educational institution. However, some states that have enacted registration laws for interior designers already require, or will soon require, applicants to have completed their course of study in FIDER-accredited programs. You should check if there are FIDER requirements in the registration or licensing rules of any state where you are interested in establishing your practice.

In evaluating educational achievement, NCIDQ requires the two-year minimum course of study to include at least 40 semester credits or 60 quarter credits of interior design–related course work. Remember, this is the baseline educational standard for exam eligibility. Three-, four-, and five-year educational achievement may also be considered. Educational programs are evaluated on the basis of whether the course of study comprises 60 semester credits (or 90 quarter credits) for three years; 120 semester credits, of which 60 or more must be interior design–related (or 180 quarter credits, with 90 or more being interior design–related) for four years; and 150 semester credits, with 90 or more hours related to interior design (or 225 quarter credits, with 135 or more interior design–related) for five years of study. While these standards of evaluation permit exam eligibility without regard to a particular course of study, they do pinpoint the number of educational hours devoted to interior design that must be successfully credited for exam eligibility. Students enrolled in college or university interior design programs will likely meet the educational requirements simply by completing their studies leading to associate and bachelor degrees. Interior designers working in the field who have not undertaken a formal course of instruction may not be eligible to sit for the NCIDQ exam since they cannot fulfill the two-year minimal educational requirement. As a result, these practitioners may not be eligible for professional-level membership in organizations such as ASID.

Education is one criterion for NCIDQ exam eligibility. Work experience is another. NCIDQ has also set forth full-time work requirements in detail. Quite simply, remember the number *six* and you will have in mind the combined education and work experience required for exam eligibility. With two years of education, for example, NCIDQ requires at least four years of full-time work experience; with three and four years of education, the full-time work requirement is three and two years, respectively. To be considered full-time work experience, it should comprise not less than 35 hours a week of interior design–related work activity. The council recommends, but does not require, work to be supervised by a NCIDQ-certified interior designer, a licensed architect, or an interior designer recognized by a state or provincial regulatory board. NCIDQ requires course transcripts and letters of recommendation to complete the application for exam eligibility.

Twice a year, usually in March and October, candidates found eligible by NCIDQ are seated for the two-day-long examination. Passing this exam is the last requirement—after confirmation of education and full-time work experience—for NCIDQ certification. The council estimates that, over the course of its administration, approximately 13,000 candidates, or 75 percent of those attempting the exam, have successfully completed all sections of the exam on either their first or successive attempts. The council does permit retesting of sections unsuccessfully attempted and, unless a state rule provides to the contrary, imposes no time limit for passing all sections of the exam.

The exam is comprised of three sections. The first section is titled "Principles and Practices of Interior Design" and contains 150 multiple-choice questions to be answered in three and one-half hours. The second section of the exam, titled "Contract Development and Administration," contains 125 multiple-choice questions for completion in three hours. Sections I and II are conducted on the first day of exam administration. The council offers for purchase an examination guide that includes sample questions taken from all sections of the exam.

The final section of the exam is the *practicum*, a design-scenario portion in which candidates are asked to present a solution to a design problem. This section is presented on the second day of the exam and is administered in two parts over a total of seven hours. Section III asks examinees to respond to a design scenario in which they have to plan a multi-use facility. In addition to the examination guide containing one sample practicum, NCIDQ also makes available for purchase additional design scenarios with critiqued solutions. The design scenarios currently available for review deal with planning a doctor's combined home and office space and the joint retail and production facilities of a winery.

The list of topics that may be found on the NCIDQ exam could be quite lengthy. However, recall the idea of scope-of-services woven throughout this text. With that concept in mind—in which even the most complex tasks may be broken into their smaller, more general components for analysis—you may more easily understand the subject areas tested on the exam and reasons for their inclusion. The council commissioned an extensive study, "Analysis of the Interior Design Profession," which lists six general *performance areas* encompassing tasks interior designers carry out in their work: project organization, programming, schematics, design development, contract documents, and contract administration. In examination literature, the council refers to these areas as *domains*. The council's study further identifies five components of each domain: health and safety concerns, public welfare, function concerns, business law and ethical issues, and design synthesis. Linking the five components to the six domains in grid-like fashion identifies 30 possible testing areas. Refer to chapter 10, "Managing Your Client's Project," in which details of the processes involved in performing NCIDQ-classified tasks are described.

Based on their study and input from testing authorities, NCIDQ allocated *domain* questions and their components for the three sections of the exam. The council determined that Section I, "Principles and Practices of Interior Design" should include questions covering the performance areas of project organization, programming, schematics, and design development together with their components for a total of 20 areas from which testing subjects might be drawn. Section II, "Contract Development and Administration," asks questions related to those 10 subject areas. Finally, Section III, "Schematics and Design Development," or the practicum portion, focuses on the integration of all 30 domain and characteristic nuances, particularly those related to the domains of schematics, design development, and contract documents. Before a project may be completed, it must be defined. By narrowing the list of all possible test subjects down to 30 components, you not only have a good idea of the subjects you will likely face on that exam, but also you have a study resource for determining what preparatory steps you require to complete your *exam proj-*

ect. Approximately 14 weeks after taking the NCIDQ exam, candidates receive their results in the mail. Once they have passed this exam, successful candidates may present their names and credentials (along with a fee) for formal registration to the appropriate regulatory agency in their state.

STATE CERTIFICATION LAWS

As of publication, there are 24 United States jurisdictions with laws permitting accomplished individuals to use the title *interior designer* in their professional undertakings after registration. Eight Canadian provinces similarly have passed laws allowing for post-registration use of the *interior designer* title. Of particular interest are the laws relating to interior design in the states of Alabama, Florida, Louisiana, and Nevada, and Washington, D.C. and Puerto Rico. These jurisdictions have passed very detailed laws, referred to as practice laws, defining the tasks practitioners may or may not perform. Furthermore, laws in these jurisdictions provide for the voiding of contracts entered into by unlicensed practitioners as well as the levying of penalties. These laws are comparable to laws regulating other professionals, such as attorneys, accountants, and physicians.

Sixteen of the remaining states have passed what are referred to as *title* laws, which do not require formal licensing as do states with practice laws. Under title acts, individual practitioners do not have to obtain licenses to engage in interior design activities. Title acts also do not constrain individuals from providing interior design services. As the name suggests, these kinds of laws regulate who may hold themselves out as being registered interior designers unless they have met minimum standards of education, experience, and examination set by that state. As of the date of this text, title act states include Arkansas, Connecticut, Georgia, Illinois, Kentucky, Maine, Maryland, Minnesota, Missouri, New Jersey, New Mexico, New York, Tennessee, Texas, Virginia, and Wisconsin.

Two states, California and Colorado, have slightly different laws, referred to as *self-certification* and *permitting*, respectively. The self-certification model for interior designers followed by California acknowledges that California has established an independent certifying board that is not run by the state. That body permits the use of NCIDQ exam results for certification and requires an additional examination of candidates on knowl-

TABLE 2.1
Summary of Interior Design Laws and Registrations (2004)

State	Type of Law	Title Registered
Alabama	Title/Practice	Interior Designer or Registered Interior Designer
Arkansas	Title	Registered Interior Designer
California	Self-certification	Certified Interior Designer
Colorado	Permitting Statute	No state registration as of 2004
Connecticut	Title	Interior Designer
Florida	Title/Practice	Interior Designer
Georgia	Title	Registered Interior Designer
Illinois	Title	Interior Designer or Registered Interior Designer
Kentucky	Title	Certified Interior Designer
Louisiana	Title/Practice	Registered Interior Designer
Maine	Title	Certified Interior Designer
Maryland	Title	Certified Interior Designer
Minnesota	Title	Certified Interior Designer
Missouri	Title	Registered Commercial Interior Designer
New Mexico	Title	Interior Designer
New Jersey	Title	Certified Interior Designer
New York	Title	Certified Interior Designer
Nevada	Title/Practice	Registered Interior Designer
Puerto Rico	Title/Practice	Interior Designer/Interior Decorator
Tennessee	Title	Registered Interior Designer
Texas	Title	Interior Designer
Virginia	Title	Certified Interior Designer
Washington, D.C.	Title/Practice	Interior Designer
Wisconsin	Title	Wisconsin Registered Interior Designer

edge of state codes. Colorado's *permitting* statute states that interior designers who have met education, experience, and examination standards set by the state are permitted to prepare interior design documents for filing and obtaining building permits. Table 2.1 provides a summary of state interior design laws.

ADVOCATING FOR THE FUTURE

So far, this chapter has emphasized issues affecting the past and present of interior design. What about the future of the profession? This book recognizes membership in professional organizations, such as ASID, and the use of advocacy skills as two ways in which practitioners may influence the future of interior design. Box 2.2 provides details about ASID membership eligibility.

According to information provided by ASID, the organization has a membership of 34,500 and "establishes a common identity for professionals and businesses in the field of interior design." The association

BOX 2.2. ASID MEMBERSHIP ELIGIBILITY

Professional membership is available to those who meet the organization's rigorous acceptance standards. To use the ASID appellation after their name, they must have met the following education, experience, and examination requirements:

- Have a combination of accredited design education and/or full-time work experience;

- Pass the two-day NCIDQ examination. Professional membership in ARIDO (Canada) or CODDI (Puerto Rico) is transferable to ASID upon proof of said membership.

Allied membership is available to those who practice interior design but have not yet completed the requirements for ASID professional membership. Applicants must fulfill any one of the following requirements:

- Four- or five-year bachelor's degree with major in interior design or architecture
- Two- or three-year degree or certificate in interior design, or
- A minimum of six years of full-time work in interior design or architecture

Allied members may note that membership status following their name. Successful completion of the NCIDQ exam entitles practitioner members to advance to professional membership.

Allied membership (education) requires active engagement as department chair or full-time instructor in a post-secondary program of interior design education at any university or accredited school of interior design that requires completion of 45 semester credit hours in interior design–related courses.

Affiliate membership is a category for individuals engaged in related design activities and for members of the press. Applicants for affiliate membership cannot participate in the practice of interior design or decorating.

Industry partner memberships are available to interior design industry manufacturers and their representatives, related trade associations, and market centers. Industry partners provide opportunities for interaction between interior designers and the interior furnishings industry that supplies services and manufactured products.

Student membership is available to students enrolled in an interior design program where an ASID student chapter exists, or independent student membership is available to students in interior design programs in an area not served by an ASID student chapter. Advancement to allied membership is available to student members who have graduated and are eligible for allied member status.

Adapted from www.asid.org/ASID2/about/memberinfo.asp.

notes that it has 48 chapters throughout the United States and more than 450 international members. As you will recall from the historical overview of the interior design profession presented earlier in this chapter, ASID was formed in 1975 through the combination of two earlier interior design organizations, the American Institute of Decorators (AID) and the National Society of Interior Designers (NSID).

Advocacy is defined as the process of supporting a cause, a belief, or a particular course of action. The various laws related to the interior design profession came about as a result of advocacy actions. These actions involved providing information, research, and proposed legislation that state lawmakers could use to propose new licensing laws. The case study that concludes this chapter considers a common example of advocacy and its use.

PROJECT DOCUMENTATION SKILLS

Another objective of this chapter is to develop project documentation skills, which are important even in early stages of getting to know a prospective client. Sometimes referred to as project development activities (Piotrowski 2004), these tasks note the preferences and project goals of prospective clients.

At an early stage of the project, usually before designer and prospect enter into a formal contract for the designer's services, it is important for the designer to engage in gathering information about the proposed project and the client. As you may recall from chapter 1, formal gathering of information regarding project details usually takes place during the programming phase, after designer and client agree to work together. Prior to that phase, designers may be in contact with prospective clients several times. During the course of these encounters, the designer may use forms of the kind included in this chapter (see Forms 2.1, 2.2, 2.3) to record basic information about the project, such as the prospective client's goals for the project and any current possessions that might be used (see Form 2.1). Performing these documentation activities helps in two ways. First, designers gain some idea of the kind and extent of services they may be called upon to perform. For example, they can determine the extent to which they will be responsible for design services such as space planning, for which one method of charging the client might be appropriate; and to procure merchandise, for which another method of charging for services

FORM 2.1. EXISTING CONDITIONS ANALYSIS: INVENTORY AND PROJECT SITE

EXISTING CONDITIONS ANALYSIS: INVENTORY AND PROJECT SITE

Item	Item
Location	Location
Condition	Condition
To do	To do
Item	Item
Location	Location
Condition	Condition
To do	To do
Item	Item
Location	Location
Condition	Condition
To do	To do
Item	Item
Location	Location
Condition	Condition
To do	To do

NOTES

(continued)

Existing conditions analysis: project site

Existing floor plan available _____ Source _____

Analysis of existing conditions _____

_____

_____

_____

_____

_____

_____

_____

_____

_____

_____

_____

_____

_____

_____

_____

_____

_____

_____

_____

_____

_____

_____

_____

_____

_____

_____

_____

_____

_____

Sketch

might be indicated. Later chapters will explore the relationship between the tasks designers perform—their scope of services—and methods for structuring their fee arrangements with clients. On the basis of this early project documentation, residential interior designers usually present to the client prospect a proposal for their design services.

In the area of nonresidential, or contract, interior design, the process is somewhat different. Usually prospective clients circulate what is called a Request for Proposal, or RFP. These requests spell out the demands of a particular project, including activities the client will expect the designer to perform. Interested design firms then respond to these requests in the form of a written proposal that specifies how they will carry out project requirements.

Of course, not every proposal in either realm of interior design is accepted. While responding to RFPs or residential clients and recording information takes time, doing so provides designers with insight into the issues and trends that are important in the marketplace. This information enables designers to develop a sense of what factors are critical in determining acceptance of their proposals.

PROBLEM-SOLVING STRATEGIES
FOR PROFESSIONAL DEVELOPMENT

Do you believe that your learning is finished once your formal education is complete? In fact, interior design professionals are always learning. Interior design is always changing, both in professional direction and in the concepts it adapts. This section focuses on ways to solve common problems that may arise after you leave school and as you develop professionally. Accordingly, it addresses three basic tasks interior designers should consider to keep abreast of changes in the interior design profession:

1. Consider taking the NCIDQ exam even if your jurisdiction does not require it.

    The exam promulgated and administered by the NCIDQ has become the accepted norm for entry into the profession. Even if the aspect of interior design in which you plan to or actually practice does not require it, one day it may.

2. Consider receiving ancillary certifications such as a general-contractor license.

Some states such as California make clear the division between interior design work and construction supervision work (which many clients assume designers provide as part of their services) by requiring a general-contractor license.

3. Keep current with education trends and proposed legislation affecting designers.

Even if you have no desire or time to actively participate in advocacy activities, make an effort to keep current with issues and proposed changes that affect you as a businessperson and an interior designer.

REFERENCES

Abercrombie, Stanley. 2003. *A Century of Interior Design: The Design, The Designers, The Products and The Profession: 1900–2000*. New York: Rizzoli.

American Society of Interior Designers (ASID). 2004. *The Interior Design Profession: Facts & Figures*. Web site information, www.asid.org/. 2003–4.

Coleman, Cindy, ed. 2002. *Interior Design: Handbook of Professional Practice*. New York: McGraw-Hill.

Diamond, Jay, and Ellen Diamond. 2002. *The World of Fashion*. 3rd ed. New York: Fairchild Books.

Foundation for Interior Design Education and Research (FIDER). 1993. *FIDER Fact Kit*. Michigan: FIDER.

Gombrich, E. H. 1995. *The Story of Art*. Rev. ed. London and New York: Phaidon Press.

Grey, Susan, ed. 2003. *Designers on Designers: 24 Essays on Influential Interiors*. New York: McGraw-Hill.

Hampton, Mark. 1992. *Legendary Decorators of the Twentieth Century*. New York: Doubleday.

Interior Design Educators Council (IDEC), Web site information, www.idec.com. 2003–4.

Interior Designers of Canada. Web site information, www.interiordesign-Canada.org. 2003–4.

Jansson, Bruce S. 2002. *Becoming an Effective Policy Advocate*. New York: Wadsworth.

Kendall, Diana. 2003. *Sociology in Our Times*. 4th ed. New York: Thompson Learning.

Knackstedt, Mary V. 2002. *The Interior Design Business Handbook*. 3rd ed. New York: John Wiley & Sons.

Massey, Anne. 2001. *Interior Design of the Twentieth Century*. London: Thames & Hudson.

Moore, Phyllis, FASID. 2004. *Interior Design Legislation: Achievements and Challenges*. Cited in *American Society of Interior Designers*. 2004. *The Interior Design Profession: Facts & Figures*, 2004, ASID publication, p. 18.

National Council for Interior Design Qualification (NCIDQ). Web site information, www.ncidq.org. 2003–4. *Analysis of the Interior Design Profession*.

Pile, John. 2000. *History of Interior Design*. New York: John Wiley & Sons.

Piotrowski, Christine. 2004. *Becoming an Interior Designer, A Guide to Careers in Design*. New York: John Wiley & Sons.

——. 2002. *Professional Practice for Interior Designer*, 3rd ed. New York: John Wiley & Sons.

Pressman, Andy. 1997. *Professional Practice 101: A Compendium of Business and Management Strategies in Architecture*. New York: John Wiley & Sons

Schoeser, Mary. 2003. *A World of Textiles: A Concise History*. London: Thames & Hudson.

Sen, Rinku, and Kim Klein, eds. 2003. *Stir It Up (Chardon Press Series): Lessons in Community Organizing and Advocacy*. New York: John Wiley & Sons.

Siegel, Harry, and Alan Siegel. 1982. *A Guide to Business Practices and Principles for Interior Designers*. New rev. ed. New York: Watson-Guptill.

Sowell, Teresa, ASID, IFMA. 2004. *The Value of Associations to the Interior Design Profession*. Cited in American Society of Interior Designers. 2004. *The Interior Design Profession: Facts & Figures*, 2004, ASID publication.

Stein, Leon. 1962. *The Triangle Fire*. New York: Lippincott.

Thompson, Jo Anne Asher, ed. 1992. *ASID Practice Manual*. New York: Watson-Guptill.

Woodhead, Lindy. 2003. *War Paint: Madame Helena Rubinstein & Miss Elizabeth Arden, Their Lives, Their Times, Their Rivalry*. New York: John Wiley & Sons.

STRATEGIES-IN-ACTION PROJECTS

STRATEGIC PLANNING PROJECT: UNDERSTANDING LICENSING REQUIREMENTS

Many decision makers who evaluate business plans have little knowledge of industries other than their own. As a result, they may not be aware of the specific licensing and regulatory environment controlling the practice of interior design should they be approached by an entrepreneur-designer. In this installment of the business-plan project, you will explain the licensing requirements imposed on interior designers by the state in which you want to practice, or a foreign country if you choose to practice in a country other than the United States. As you know, the purpose of a business plan is to provide a detailed, complete explanation of the characteristics of a proposed business. Your job in this section is to make those who will decide on your proposal aware of these rules. If you would like to practice in a state that does not as yet have any regulating laws, explain the current status of licensing laws in that state as detailed in many interior design resources such as the ASID Web site (ASID 2004). You will notice that these rules generally specify the education and work experience required before an individual may use the title *interior designer*. Increasingly, however, passage of the NCIDQ examination is also required before such terms as *registered, certified, interior designer* may be used. Does your chosen state have such requirements? May individuals apply for the NCIDQ exam directly? Or must they apply through a state regulatory agency first? If so, which agency?

Your explanation of the licensing requirements of your chosen state should specify for those who read your business plan what particular laws govern the interior design profession in that state. Other professionals, such as architects, physicians, accountants, and attorneys, have long had what are described as practice-based laws defining in great detail the educational requirements for their professions. Obtaining passing scores on lengthy exams has also been a condition for obtaining licenses in these professions, as is becoming increasing true for interior designers.

Interior design is increasingly trending toward *practice* laws very much like those of other professions. Nevertheless, other regulatory laws, known as *title* laws, allow individuals to practice under the title *interior designer*, once they have established their education and experience to the satisfaction of certain credentialing bodies. What licensing trends do you note in your chosen state? Your professional status as an interior designer hinges on successfully completing your chosen state's licensing requirements either now or in the future, and therefore, this is an important topic to address in your business plan.

RESIDENTIAL INTERIOR DESIGN PROJECT SIMULATION

In the simulation project in chapter 1, a young interior designer named Lee was approached by the Abernathy family about proposing a design concept for an exciting space in the home they share with four young children. That simulation was designed to explore the relationship between an interior designer and potential client as they meet each other and initiate project discussions. As in chapter 1, this chapter has emphasized that documenting information about prospective clients is important—even if the designer is not sure whether he or she will be retained for his or her services. Simple note taking on forms such as the Client Preference Survey (Form 2.2) is one easy way to accomplish this task. The information the designer records will, of course, become useful should the designer get the job; but even in the gray area of uncertainty, it does provide the designer with a basis for building rapport with the prospective client as well as knowledge on which to base follow-up marketing efforts. Even if designers are not retained, collecting client information can serve as a way for them to gauge what interests prospects in the marketplace.

This project presents several client-focused documents and provides insight into how to complete and maintain them. Far from just being paperwork, completing the documents and forms described here can build a foundation for subsequent phases in the relationship between designer and client. Read the following diary excerpt to learn more about these important tasks.

Lee's Diary

What a presentation! I met with the Abernathy family yesterday afternoon at their house, all 10,000 square feet of it, and 2,000 square feet just for the kids! They seemed to love my plans for the space. The couple said they would soon let me know what they had decided, and they asked whether $50,000 would be enough to devote to the project and whether it be done in six months. I'm not sure. I told them I would get back to them on that issue. I was so excited about this maybe-project until I got back to the studio. Long story made short— the store owner went nuts!

CLIENT PREFERENCE SURVEY

Style preferences

1. _____   Area _____

2. _____   Area _____

3. _____   Area _____

4. _____   Area _____

5. _____   Area _____

Color preferences

1. _____   Area _____

2. _____   Area _____

3. _____   Area _____

4. _____   Area _____

5. _____   Area _____

Fabric preferences

1. _____   Area _____

2. _____   Area _____

3. _____   Area _____

4. _____   Area _____

5. _____   Area _____

Wallpaper/print preferences

1. _____   Area _____

2. _____   Area _____

3. _____   Area _____

4. _____   Area _____

5. _____   Area _____

Notes _____

_____

_____

(continued)

Floor-covering preferences

1. _____   Area _____

2. _____   Area _____

3. _____   Area _____

4. _____   Area _____

5. _____   Area _____

Lighting preferences

1. _____   Area _____

2. _____   Area _____

3. _____   Area _____

4. _____   Area _____

5. _____   Area _____

Lighting schematics

Accessories preferences

1. _____   Area _____

2. _____   Area _____

3. _____   Area _____

4. _____   Area _____

5. _____   Area _____

It all started as I was telling her about how I planned to give each kid a room, and a room for the au pair—a room and a kitchenette—just by suggesting the addition of three non-load-bearing walls and changing several door adjacencies. I even told her about the play area I came up with for the space: Right in the middle of the common room I proposed a big tree-house-inspired "playscape," complete with step-up platform and a tree trunk reaching up to the ceiling right in the center of the room. I should have known something was wrong by the way the owner of the studio was looking at me.

First, the owner asked to see how I was documenting the project. What project? They haven't hired me, I told her. What was the point of opening a file before then? Then she asked, "Have you really ascertained what they want, or just made a lot of proposals they will expect you to fulfill regardless of how much time and effort it is going to cost you and the shop?"

I guess I must have looked really stupid or something because she then said, "I know I'm going to regret asking but have you at least documented anything?" We both just stared at each other—no one told me about any of this.

As she left the room, she told me to figure something out fast before I got in over my head and the company got in trouble. Anyway, I'm stumped. I don't know what to do! After all, they aren't even clients yet. Help!

Questions

1. Although great ideas demonstrated with a "WOW!" concept presentation are important toward obtaining a project, so, too, is preparing initial documents for internal use by the designer. What might the first of such documents (see Form 2.3) be?

   . . . No word on the Abernathy project today, but I've been busy at the shop with other things—including filling out forms about them, their children, and their interests!

2. Using the information found in this chapter's installment of the Abernathy "almost" project, complete Forms 2.1, 2.2, and 2.3 as completely as possible. Alternatively, interview a couple you know with children to find out their interests and record them on Forms 2.2 and 2.3.

CONTRACT INTERIOR DESIGN CASE STUDY: THE CASE OF THE VOCAL VOCATION

Advocacy is the process of showing support for a particular cause or proposal. In a typical scenario, members of professional organizations identify a concern important to that group, develop a stance or position, and

CLIENT INFORMATION SHEET

Date completed _____

Client _____

Project dates   Begin _____   End _____

Subject property address _____

Phone # 1 _____

Other contact information _____   Phone # 2 _____

Client requests

_____
_____
_____
_____
_____
_____
_____
_____
_____
_____
_____
_____
_____
_____
_____
_____
_____
_____
_____
_____
_____
_____
_____
_____
_____
_____
_____

Estimated project budget   _____
Bank/credit card information _____
_____

then do research to find out why their approach should be accepted or, in some cases, adopted into law. In the course of their research, they also develop arguments to counter opposing views. Depending on the goals of the group, they may then present their position and supporting arguments to lawmakers or to the general public. In the former instance, legislators introduce the group's concern to the political process in an effort to get it adopted into law. In the latter, the group may present their results to the general public in an effort to shape opinion or perceptions.

One result of advocacy in the interior design profession has been the passage of interior design legislation. As you are aware, there are at present 24 states with laws regulating who may engage in interior design work. Those laws, whether they are title or practice acts, came about through the advocacy process. Associations of interior designers, seeking statewide professional recognition, approached their lawmakers with proposals and arguments for these laws. Advocacy efforts continue today as groups in other states seek to influence the evolution of the interior design profession.

As important as advocacy is in the legislative arena, it is also an important way in which professional groups may educate the general public about their points of view. In this case study you will learn how to develop an advocacy-related instrument known as a position statement. As the name suggests, this is a written statement expressing the particular stance of a group on an issue that group deems important.

For purposes of this case study, you are a new member of a professional interior design association's advocacy committee. This group represents the interests of contract interior designers in expressing their particular concerns. Your task is to help draft the group's position statement on a topic of interest to the group, notably the importance of using sustainable elements in interior spaces planned for public use. For this task, you should first read the position statement on the following page drafted and passed by the Interior Design Education Council in March 2002. Then write a draft of a position statement you will share with others on your committee on the importance of using sustainable elements in the interior design of public spaces. In your proposed position statement, be sure to do the following:

1. Make sure the title of the statement informs the reader about the subject of that statement.
2. Define the term *sustainable* in such a way that readers outside the interior design profession, such as legislators or the general public, understand what the term means.

3. Define exactly the kinds of interior spaces that are the focus of your group's interests. For example, does your group intend to advocate for the use of sustainable elements in all nonresidential interiors, only in those owned or controlled by governmental entities, or only in those spaces developed by academic institutions?

4. Make clear who is responsible for implementing and advancing your position. Interior designers can do much to educate clients about the need for sustainability, but what could interior designers ask of other stakeholders in order to bring about the position they advance? *Stakeholders* may be thought of as those who have an interest in a project or undertaking. What responsibilities would you assign stakeholders in nonresidential interior design projects to see that your group's position is advanced?

5. Define your group's stance as precisely as possible. Position statements are frequently cited as defining what a particular group "stands for," so clarity in expressing its point of view is essential.

6. What other issues besides sustainability currently confront nonresidential interior designers? Have you considered issues such as product-sourcing or professional ethics? These topics could also be investigated and position statements drafted.

IDEC Position Statement

Position Statement of the Interior Design Educators Council Regarding Legal Regulation of Interior Design (March 2002) Developed by the Task Force for Legislative Concerns

The Interior Design Educators Council (IDEC) supports the legal regulation of the interior design profession. Professional interior designers combine critical and creative thinking, communication, and technology for the purposes of improving quality of life, increasing productivity, and protecting the health, safety, and welfare of the public in residential, commercial, and institutional interiors. The members of IDEC are responsible for the education of future interior design professionals and for research that builds the body of knowledge necessary for the design of interior environments. Interior design programs are qualified by known standards of academic achievement that converge with practical experience to prepare interior designers for professional examination. In jurisdictions where the profession is not regulated, a standard of practice also is not regulated and the public is at risk. Thus, legal regulation of interior design is important to the profession, the public, and the public welfare.

CHAPTER THREE

WORKING ETHICALLY

Designers who consider themselves service providers rather than advocates for ethical principles will lose out to competitors who take leadership positions in guiding clients to choose the right ethical solutions.

BEVERLY RUSSELL

WHY THIS CHAPTER IS IMPORTANT TO YOU

This chapter brings a more introspective approach to your study of the professional practices of interior design. Publicity surrounding corporate misdeeds has only emphasized the importance of ethical principles and behavior of business dealings. As you read this chapter, think of the many incidents of unethical business practices reported in the media. If ethics are so important, why do these problems arise? What business practices are likely to lead to ethical controversies? What motivates businesspeople to act unethically? What are "ethics," anyway? This chapter identifies and examines ethics and ethical behavior to reach a practical understanding of their meaning and application in the practice of interior design. The four chapters that make up part two move away from topics related to entering the interior design profession; instead they focus on four areas of business knowledge critical to the designer who is an entrepreneur or an employee. As you consider those topics in subsequent contexts, look back at the discussion of ethics found in this chapter. What ethical considerations do you need to bring to your work to inform your business decisions? This chapter will help you determine that for yourself.

PROFESSIONAL PRACTICES PORTFOLIO

After completing this chapter, your professional practices portfolio should include responses to the following questions:

1. Define the role ethics play in business decision-making processes.
2. Do professions have any incentives to enforce among their practitioners' ethics-related goals?
3. Name several influential writers on ethics. What are their contributions to modern ethical codes and rules?
4. In which areas of business does ethical decision making occur?
5. How does *goodwill* relate to the perceptions consumers have about businesses?
6. What is proprietary information, as distinguished from proprietary interests?
7. Explain the differences in meaning between *shall* and *may* as the terms are used in ethical codes.
8. What is a *privileged communication* as understood by the legal community? Does it apply to interior designers and their clients?
9. What does the concept of *standing* entail, and how does it relate to a complainant in an ethical-code dispute?
10. What are some penalties imposed for failure to adhere to codes of ethics and professional standards of conduct? How does the disciplinary process relate to enforcement of ethical codes and rules among interior designers. What actions may be brought against a designer who is not a member of a professional trade group?

INTRODUCTION TO
PROFESSIONAL PRACTICES: WHAT ARE ETHICS?

Ethical behavior is increasingly expected of businesspeople, especially those presenting themselves as professionals. Many groups responsible for regulating occupations, including those overseeing the practice of interior design, impose ethical standards on practitioner conduct by adopting *ethical codes*. These ethical codes are examples of professional practice standards. The state licensing and registration boards overseeing the practice of interior design in certain states, along with ASID and IIDA, are examples of state and industry groups that place ethical obligations on their members. The ethical requirements are detailed in writing, and members of these professional organizations agree to abide by them as a condition of membership and to obtain and keep licenses or registration/certification.

Despite these rules, ethics remain an elusive concept to explain, much less apply. Definitions of ethics may be written and the conduct of businesspeople analyzed to determine what constitutes ethical behavior; much discussion may focus on ways to *learn* ethics. Yet, despite these efforts, can ethical concepts really be taught and applied consistently in business situations? In many cases, ethically sensitive decisions go contrary to an organization's goal of gaining competitive advantage over other companies in their pursuit of customers and greater profitability. Competition of this kind is one of the hallmarks of a free-enterprise system in which businesses vie with each other to gain customers or clients, a process that may result in benefits for consumers. For example, competition may bring to consumers a greater selection of goods and services at more favorable prices. However, competition may result in harmful business practices in cases where business decision makers pursue greater profits rather than the welfare of those involved with the company. Examples in which the actions of individuals in large corporations have financially injured others through questionable business practices are still very much in the news and the subject of media coverage. Do these large-scale debacles—or scandals, as they have been termed—have any significance for the practice of interior design?

The repercussions of these large-scale occurrences of unethical business conduct are not as isolated as they might seem, and they have affected virtually every profession. A belief in the perceived lack of ethics in business is widespread enough that of 1,100 U.S. college students, not yet in the business community, surveyed in 2002 by Students in Free Enterprise (SIFE), 84 percent responded that the United States currently faces a "business-ethics crisis." Furthermore, many professions are undertaking a thorough self-examination of the role of ethics in their industries as a result of incidents such as those involving Enron and Global Crossing, to mention two prominent examples. Why might professionals—especially those in industries not involved in any scandal—be willing to undergo such self-imposed scrutiny?

You have already learned about the characteristics defining professions. Sociologists have identified additional features, including the autonomy professional workers enjoy (Friedson 1986; Larson 1977). Professionals often make their own decisions, sometimes based on information available only to them. In exchange for these freedoms, workers in professions, at least implicitly, agree to govern themselves as a way of protecting others with whom they interact (Ritzer 1993). This self-governance manifests itself in the creation of codes of ethics or other rules of professional conduct that all members of that profession voluntarily agree to follow. Failure to follow these guidelines usually results in loss of professional status.

Interior designers are no different in these respects from most other professionals. Most of the organizations regulating the interior design profession have adopted a code of ethics for their members to follow. Those who are found to have violated these rules lose their acknowledged status as interior design professionals. With the increasing interest and emphasis on the application of ethics in business practices, interior design practitioners can expect greater scrutiny from their supervising bodies, from clients, and from members of the general public (Long 2000). How might your own business practices as an interior designer look when viewed under such scrutiny? This chapter cannot teach ethics. Nothing can do that. However, this chapter can explain what the codes attempt to accomplish. How you address these concerns indicates how you will define yourself as an interior design professional. Solving the problem of the real and perceived lack of ethics in business simply begins with you.

"What exactly are **ethics?**" Many dictionary definitions of the term describe it as "a set of moral principles or values." However, this general statement may create more questions than answers for those seeking a definition of the term or an understanding of what it means to behave ethically. Because the concepts of *moral principles* and *values* have so many connotations, philosophers have explored the contours of ethics for centuries. In their writings, they have usually concentrated on considering the factors that determine whether the actions of individuals are *ethical*, *moral*, *good*, or *bad*. In ancient Greece, for example, the philosopher Plato (427 BC–347 BC) initiated inquiries of this nature by exploring value-related concepts such as justice and its meanings in *The Republic*. Over time, the study of ethics by philosophers developed along several distinct lines. One of the most influential has been termed *utilitarianism*, a school of thought that stresses goal actions performed to maximize happiness—what was known as the common good—for the greatest number of people while minimizing the harm to that group. Nineteenth-century philosophers

Jeremy Bentham (1748–1832) and John Stuart Mill (1806–1873) are considered the seminal proponents of utilitarian thought. Contrary to this belief was the view espoused by philosophers such as Immanuel Kant (1724–1804). Referred to as the deontological or nonconsequentialist approach, this school of thought held that ethical conduct was based on duty, what was known as the *moral imperative* and carried out under the guidance of a highly rational set of rules. Kant particularly stressed the idea that ethical conduct involved a sense of what he termed *respect* toward others. Kant argued that this concept of respect was more important in promoting ethical behavior than Bentham's idea of satisfying the common good. This respect, he further reasoned, should govern an individual's conduct toward others. Other people were to be treated not as the means by which individuals could achieve their own goals, but as ends in themselves who are worthy of respect.

Vestiges of these philosophers' thoughts have provided theoretical bases for drafting many modern laws and codes of ethics. In particular, you will note that codes of ethics like those produced by ASID and other interior design–related governing bodies speak in terms of *responsibilities* owed to others in the same vein as Kant's philosophy. These responsibilities impose a duty on those who agree to follow the codes. They also provide rules to guide design practitioners to protect groups that are defined by proponents of utilitarianism. The ASID Code of Ethics and Professional Conduct defines those to whom a responsibility is owed as being *the public, clients, other interior designers and colleagues, the employer* (where the designer works as an employee), and, finally, responsibilities owed *to the profession*. Although ethics may be a difficult subject to fully define, various governing bodies regulating the interior design profession can and have set basic standards of ethical conduct expected of practitioners and further defines those to whom ethical duties are owed.

OBJECTIVES TO CONSIDER

How and when do questions of ethics arise in the operation of business? What specific situations arising in an interior designer's daily working life call for application of ethical concepts? Recent writers in general business ethics have detailed four aspects of working life in which ethical problems can arise (Trevino and Nelson 1999). As a businessperson, a practicing interior designer will have to deal with these issues. They include:

- Making business decisions related to obtaining and retaining human resources
- Managing real and apparent conflicts of interest
- Maintaining customer confidence
- Using company resources

Although managing the operation of design businesses and those who work in them will be discussed more fully in chapter 6, "Managing Your Business," it is important to note here that general management and human resources have been identified as domains that require ethical evaluation and decision making. The hiring, advancing, and terminating of employees are common examples in the business world of such human-resource issues. You may already be familiar with the negative implications of these issues in those instances where actions taken by individuals on behalf of companies exclude the contributions of others based on their race, gender, ethnic origin, or religious beliefs. These types of discriminatory decisions are unethical and also proscribed—that is, made illegal—by state and federal laws.

This area of concern has been expanded in recent years by increasing interest in the status of workers who produce goods for consumption. This human-resource issue involves workers who are compelled against their will, and with little or no compensation, to produce items frequently intended for export to be used in other countries. Knowledge of the conditions surrounding the working environment of laborers who produce goods may be particularly lacking or sketchy where items are manufactured in foreign countries. However, even when actual knowledge of harmful working practices and conditions is lacking, should an ethically conscious interior designer be responsible for inquiring of their trade sources about such issues? Section 2.6 of the ASID code of ethics reads: "Members shall not assist or abet *improper* or illegal *conduct of anyone* in connection with a project [emphasis added.]" Does this section of the code address the matter? What issues should trigger ethical inquiries regarding the status of workers on the part of the designer?

Business decisions involving the use of company resources also call for businesspeople to make ethical evaluations. Theft by employees is one situation in which unethical decision making results in the misallocation of company assets. However, this context may also examine whether business decision makers seek to prevent or ignore the actual or perceived occurrence of what is referred to as *conflicts of interest*. A **conflict of interest** may be simply defined as an undisclosed form of favoritism.

Decisions that reflect conflicts of interest usually do not or only superficially consider the merits of the candidates under consideration (Trevino and Nelson 1999). Examples of such conflicts of interest may be quite familiar to you from media reports. **Kickback** schemes—in which monies are paid after receiving some form of favorable treatment—or outright **bribes**, in which direct payments are made to ensure favors—are clear conflicts of interest that are ethically and legally prohibited. Other examples of conflicts of interest include actions such as awarding contracts for work on the basis of personal relationships or paying undisclosed commissions or fees to encourage patronage of a business. Imagine a trade showroom offering designers financial incentives to place large orders, particularly when those incentives are not disclosed to that designer's clients—and you get an idea of an overt form of this type of conflict. Should designers accept such arrangements, they would have personal and financial reasons to specify products at odds with their clients' interest in obtaining the most appropriate goods for their projects.

Many businesses have strict policies to prevent the occurrence of overt forms of conflicting business practices. For example, they may require and enforce competitive bidding for work among contractors. These policies have another purpose as well. Companies and individuals running businesses of any size rely on the goodwill generated by their operation to attract customers and employees as well as other tradespeople. The appearance of a conflict of interest can hamper good feelings about patronizing, working for, or doing business with a company. Whether conflicts of interest actually exist, ethical decision making seeks to prevent their actual and perceived occurrence.

Conflicts of interest may also take more subtle forms. Imagine all the information you will come to know about a client and a client's business as an interior designer. But using the knowledge you gain on the job for purposes other than completing your client's project raises issues of conflicts of interest. Essentially, your own interest in using the information you learned on the job may interfere with the ownership or proprietary—that is, property—rights of those individuals or businesses from which you obtained this knowledge. This issue is usually termed misuse of **proprietary information**. Businesses control more than just their physical property; they control the know-how necessary to produce the goods or services with which the business is identified. Think of the expertise required to produce complex computer software programs. Knowledge of this kind is an example of that company's proprietary information. But how can something as intangible as knowledge be misused?

It is not uncommon for a designer to work on multiple projects at once. To work on, say, two or more residences or commercial projects at a time, and perhaps even in the same location, probably would not cause a conflict of interest. Yet, as a practical matter, how easy do you think it might be to inadvertently use or disclose knowledge about one client to another? Not only can misuse of proprietary information give you an unfair advantage over others who do not have this information, but it may also give your clients an unfair advantage over their competitors.

Misuse of proprietary information may also occur in cases where interior designers take information they obtained while employed with another designer or design firm and act on that information once they leave. Marketing, billing, client, and trade-source knowledge are types of information that would give competing firms a business advantage over the firm a designer is leaving. To prevent the use of such information, the policy of many companies is to require departing workers to agree in writing not to disclose this critical business information. Again, as a practical matter, how easy might it be to use or disseminate such information?

Customer confidence is another area that calls for ethical evaluation and decision making. Inducing customers to purchase goods or services based on a company's claims that are later found to be false or misleading is one clear example of unethical—and illegal—conduct directly related to customer confidence. More complicated examples of ethical misconduct include the business practices of companies—especially large corporations—in which stockholders and employees are victimized by elaborate financial schemes that deprive them of monetary or other benefits. Unethical actions also include business decisions that are found to adversely affect the environment through excessive pollution. Questionable labor practices in which workers are exploited by company actions are yet another example.

PROCEDURES AND PROCESSES IN PROFESSIONAL ETHICS

The following areas of day-to-day business practices call for the application of ethics to complex and competing goals. Businesspeople need not work unprofitably, but they should not work irresponsibly. By applying ethical guidelines, they can balance both of these concerns. Many times an ethical decision may not be as profitable as an unethical decision. However, there are costs—both financial and professional—for failing to operate according to ethical guidelines in business. The consequences of unethical decision making affect those who are directly involved. But they also create negative perceptions that have repercussions throughout particular industries and, if substantial enough, throughout the larger business world.

INTERPRETING CODES OF ETHICS

Nuances affect interpretation, whether you are specifying color choices for a design or closely reading the language of ethical codes. As you read different codes of ethics, your understanding of their meaning will be enhanced if you can make some important distinctions based on their language. What, for example, are the differences in meaning between *shall* and *may* in state codes of ethics and the ASID code of ethics and professional conduct? How can you read these codes for greater understanding?

For example, of the 28 provisions of the most recent ASID code, 23 employ the term *shall* or, alternatively, *shall not* in their statements. Use of the term *shall* is generally interpreted as imposing an affirmative obligation upon another to act in a certain way or to perform a specific task. Likewise, *shall not* is generally construed as imposing an affirmative obligation *not* to act in a certain way. Terms such as *must* also carry the same meaning as *shall*.

The meanings of these terms differ from the common understanding of the term *may*, as you are probably aware. Whereas language using the term *shall* imposes requirements, *may* simply permits action of some sort. Two of the twenty-eight provisions in the ASID code allow a member designer to "offer professional services to a client for any form of legal compensation" and to render second opinions to clients and serve as an expert witness in dispute-resolution proceedings; since the provision does not require a designer to fulfill these duties, a designer may decline to engage in these activities: Design services are not mandatory.

Finally, one provision of the ASID code states that "members *should* respect the confidentiality of sensitive information obtained in the course of their professional activities." Use of this term imparts a more subtle meaning to that provision and bears further explanation. Were the term *may* substituted for *should*, the provision would read as permissive in nature. With such language in place, a professional member could be free to disclose to whomever any sensitive client information without fear of censure. Surely, a client is entitled to more protection than that.

Alternatively, were the term *shall* employed, the designer would be required to *always* respect confidential information, even if it so means incurring some penalty. To put this provision into context, you should be aware that communications between clients and professionals such as clergy, lawyers, and physicians are considered privileged in legal actions and not subject to disclosure except in very few instances. Interior designers enjoy no such form of privileged communication with their clients. In other words, revelation of information a designer learns from a client may be compelled by a court of law. A designer obligated by code language to prevent such disclosure would likely subject the designer to legal contempt penalties. As a result, a designer *should* keep confidential information confidential, *unless* a court of law requires otherwise. Should clients tell you something confidentially, it might be a good idea to remind them of this constraint.

Understanding code language is important with regard to membership in professional organizations. It is also relevant to understanding the rules of professional conduct that many states have in place regarding the formal practice of interior design. Membership in professional organizations such as ASID is optional. Designers may join such groups if they wish. Should designers want to obtain formal certification or registered status in a particular state, then they must comply with the provisions that jurisdiction has enacted. Many of those provisions include codes of conduct using language very similar to that found in the codes discussed here. Understanding how to interpret that subtle use of language is therefore a *must* for the designer.

ENFORCEMENT OF ETHICAL CODES

Considering the importance of ethics in the conduct of business, how are ethical provisions enforced? Are penalties incurred for failure to comply with these requirements? As you might imagine, a professional found to have violated ethical provisions may face fairly severe penalties. However, recall the concept of proprietary information. An interior designer who has obtained state certification or is a member of a professional design group possesses something similar to proprietary information. In this case, a designer is said to have a proprietary interest in the license, certification, or trade-group affiliation. Designers' memberships in these groups is their "property," in other words. Because of this interest, a state license, certification, or organizational membership cannot be taken away from the designer simply on the basis of a complaint. To assess the merit of the complaint and protect the practitioner's proprietary interests, important procedural steps are taken by the appropriate authority. These steps make up the process by which ethical codes are enforced.

Enforcement of ethical codes begins with determining whether the practitioner against whom an action is brought is a member of a professional board. The first issue involves the membership status of the designer against whom the complaint is brought. In order to invoke the enforcement powers of either a state board responsible for supervising the interior design profession or an industry group such as ASID, the designer must hold a license or certification from that state or be a member of the industry group. Lacking these qualifications, the only recourse against a designer to satisfy an ethical complaint would be through formal civil law proceedings such as a civil lawsuit.

Another threshold issue concerns the status of bringing a client ethics charge against a designer. This person or group of people is usually referred to in legal proceedings as the **plaintiff** or plaintiffs; in administrative, nonlegal actions they are known as the **complainant** or complainants. Courts of law require a person bringing legal action to show what is referred to as **standing**. This requirement is usually met by the person proving he or she was harmed or suffered damage in some form from actions caused by the plaintiff. In all likelihood, it would only be persons so injured who would bring such claims either before a state board or a trade group. However, reread the ASID code. Little is said about exactly who may bring a complaint, and the same is true of many state codes. Usually, the regulatory body that oversees the ethics hearing makes a formal determination on whether this requirement has been satisfied.

After these initial concerns have been addressed, a formal written statement defining the problem is made by the complainant. This document is made available for the designer's response and sets out in detail the circumstances giving rise to the complainant's concerns. A designer's response to the original complaint may satisfactorily resolve the matter for the complainant. If not, the matter continues with the complaint being forwarded to an ethics committee for review. If that committee determines that an ethics code has been violated, the process continues with a formal review by a committee of the state board or a national trade group formed to render decisions on these and related complaints. These types of committees are usually referred to as **judicial committees**, although they are not courts of law.

The judicial committee holds a formal hearing in which both the designer and the person bringing the action have an opportunity to present their respective versions of the issue. Because resolution of the matter could result in the deprivation of a designer's proprietary right to practice or use a professional affiliation, lawyers representing both sides may be present at these formal hearings. After the presentation of evidence through the form of oral testimony and written documents, the disciplinary committee then makes a final determination on the controversy by determining whether an ethics violation occurred and, if so, what degree of punitive, or punishing, action is indicated. If the judicial committee does not find an ethical violation, they may simply dismiss the complainant's action altogether. However, if an ethical violation is found, it may result in censure of the designer and even revocation of state certification and group membership. The names of designers against whom such penalties are invoked are published in disciplinary action sections of state professional journals and in industry periodicals such as ASID's magazine, *ICON*.

PROBLEM-SOLVING STRATEGIES

The study of ethics and concern about ethical violations have developed over many centuries, but it remains very much a contemporary matter. With this chapter's introduction, you have gained some understanding of the nature of ethical concepts and how they emerge in daily business. You also are aware that ethics are enforced not only by voluntary professional organizations, but also by the professional licensing and accreditation boards of those states that oversee the profession. Both these groups as well as the general public will expect designers to practice according to ethical guidelines. And in the course of your work, you will frequently be called upon to make ethically based decisions.

MAKING A PLACE FOR ETHICS IN PRACTICE

The challenge now is to find a way in which to incorporate ethics as standard operating procedure into your practice. Fundamentally, of course, business decision makers need to believe in the importance of ethics and their application. No set of rules or codes can effectively instill beliefs that are not shared among decision makers. The need to recognize standards of ethics within an organization is primary. But what if no such need is perceived or is ignored in favor of the aggressive pursuit of profits? Increasingly, the actions of all sorts of professionals are scrutinized and challenged by consumers and industry-specific trade groups. To ignore ethical constraints can thus become a liability affecting an organization's future and the professional status of those involved in it.

CODES OF ETHICS AND MISSION STATEMENTS

In light of the growing concern about ethical business practices, many organizations seek to integrate these concepts by implementing and enforcing their own ethical codes. These codes can guide the actions of those involved in the operation of the enterprise by clearly establishing what ethical standards the organization has agreed to pursue and maintain. Many business plans include values statements, or **mission statements**, which offer similar insight into the ethical fiber of an organization. As you might suspect after reviewing the ASID code of ethics, codes may be substantially more detailed. However, both codes and mission or values statements emerge from a unified effort throughout an organization to promulgate ethical standards. Input from organizational stakeholders, such as employees and leaders, concerning the goals and content of such codes set in motion the process of integrating ethics into the organization. These early efforts are then usually refined into preliminary codes and then finalized before adoption. Once the codes are implemented, formal review procedures have been put in place to evaluate questionable conduct and make corrective recommendations.

Process aside, what do such codes contain? Business writers usually note that these codes should reflect the company's *values* and *traditions and unwritten rules*. As a practical matter, draft versions of such codes should also be checked for industry and legal compliance before final companywide adoption. Imagine, for example, a large interior design firm, whose principles and employees were subject to the ASID code of ethics, that chose to adopt ethical standards condoning actions not permitted by the ASID code or chose to condone actions of an illegal nature. In such a case, how effective or even persuasive would the company code really be? As you contemplate this chapter's first project, ask yourself to define the ethical principles that guide you and that you believe should be incorporated into your business code of ethics (see Form 3.1). Even small businesses can adopt procedures similar to those used by large organizations to instill ethical values into daily practice.

UNDERSTANDING THE ASID CODE OF ETHICS: SOME PRACTICAL EXAMPLES

How well do you believe you understand ethical principles? Refer to the ASID code of ethics (see Box 3.1 on page 110) to help you find out. Each of the following mini-studies profiles a specific action on the part of an interior designer that may violate the ASID code. After reading the facts of these occurrences, determine first what, if any, prohibited action occurred; then locate and name the relevant section of the ethical code you believe was violated. Assume that all designers are professional members of the group and therefore subject to the provisions of the code.

1. *Jonathan S.* This interior designer frequently selected paintings and other works of art for use in his projects from an art gallery in the city where he was located. The gallery owner would take the designer out for expensive meals several times a year to express her gratitude. One of the designer's clients, having observed the two having lunch, now seeks your opinion as to whether these free meals might be grounds for an ethics complaint against the designer. "Of course, he's going to choose objects from that particular dealer after all that schmoozing!" the client has told you.

2. *Audrey W.* This interior designer received a remarkable commission to fully plan and furnish the multi-floor office space occupied by a prestigious law firm in downtown Chicago. To make the already substantial budget go even further, the designer ordered low-quality, cheaply–plated brass desk lamps that somewhat resembled the custom-made solid brass models shown in the project presentation. "No one, and I mean no one, can tell the difference just by looking at them. By doing this, we now have more money in the budget for something else. This is supposed to be a high-class project after all!" she told her team. Soon after final installation of the project, one of these lamps shorted out, igniting its shade and setting fire to the contents of an office, causing extensive damage. The law firm seeks your opinion about what ethical grounds it might have to pursue disciplinary action against the designer.

FORM 3.1. MISSION STATEMENT WORKSHEET

MISSION STATEMENT WORKSHEET

How might your own personal mission statement read?

_____
_____
_____
_____
_____
_____
_____
_____
_____
_____
_____
_____
_____

Using your personal mission statement as a guide, define the mission statement of your own interior design business, or draft a suggested mission statement for the business in which you would like to participate. If you choose interior design education, what might you, as a faculty member, include in a mission statement for the interior design department?

_____
_____
_____
_____
_____
_____
_____
_____
_____
_____
_____
_____
_____

3. *Sidney B.* As a prominent interior designer in the Hancock Park section of Los Angeles, California, this designer usually has several large-scale residential projects under way at the same time. He frequently spends money given to him by one client toward completing another client's project. None of the designer's clients are aware of this practice, although they do complain about the length of time products take to arrive. They also do not understand why the designer can never answer their questions about the status of orders. "My method of paying for items and billing clients usually just works itself out. I wait for money to come in from clients, then figure out which projects need attention at the time," he has been heard to say to them. Nonetheless, one of his clients, tired of waiting for a rug that never arrived, asks your opinion about the conduct of this designer.

4. *Laura G.* Tired of the constant phone calls from clients asking about the status of their projects, this designer instituted call-blocking on her telephone line. The client has not been able to reach the designer for several weeks either by phone or mail. The designer's home phone number was not listed with directory assistance. "I'll call her back when I know more myself," the designer has told her assistant. The client has asked your opinion about the designer's ethics based on these actions.

5. *Gail S.* Having purchased two étagères with her clients' funds, the designer determined that using both pieces would crowd usable floor space in the clients' den. So she retained one set of shelves for use in her own home. The clients were aware that the designer had ordered two of these items, but they were not aware that the designer had taken the other one for her own use. "Oh, the clients always understand these little things. After all, we are such good friends; besides it's part of my fee to take a piece now and then," the designer said to one of her staff. After the clients received the final bill and noticed the discrepancy, they have asked you whether the actions of this designer are "all right."

6. *Henry F.* This designer competed with another designer to obtain the same lucrative project. Unfortunately for Henry F., the other designer was selected. At a party, Henry F. told the clients who did not give him the job that he was "surprised" they chose the other designer. "I'd make sure you check every bill he sends you," he continued. "After all, you know he went broke last year and has to pay off all his debts somehow." It is true that Henry F.'s rival did file for bankruptcy protection, although not many people were aware of it. The client mentioned this conversation to Henry F.'s rival, but chose to ignore the comments. The rival interior designer asks you to comment on the ethics of Henry F.'s actions.

7. *Diane D.* This noted authority on commercial interior-space planning was shocked to learn that a contract project she was "sure" she would get was awarded to a design team she felt had little experience with offices. "You should have seen their last project," she told the client who hadn't offered her the job. "It was a disaster! Doors banging into each other, incorrect furniture and textile choices for a working environment. If I were you, I'd rethink your decision. Those guys don't know what they are talking about!" To prove her point, the designer showed photographs of the other team's work. "Do you really want your office to look that that?" she asked. The

client ultimately decided not to work with the original choice, then chose to hire this designer based on her representations. The team that was originally selected now asks you to consider whether the actions of Diane D. violated any ethical codes.

8. *George K.* This experienced contract interior designer, over the course of his twenty-year career, had dealings with most of the contractors in the city where he worked. One contractor in particular was known by the designer to *skim*, or take a portion of client money from project funds for personal use. The designer chose to do nothing. "No one will know," he said. No one, in fact, ever learned whether the designer ever knew about the contractor's actions. Are there any ethical grounds for a complaint against the designer?

How about if in exchange for receiving a "cut" of the client's money that had been skimmed by the contractor, this designer would frequently modify client billing records to "clarify" billing discrepancies. "No one will know," he said. An accountant for one of the designer's clients did, however, discover the designer's actions. The client now wants to know whether there are any ethical grounds for filing a complaint against the designer.

9. *Roy G.* Because this designer's drafting and rendering skills are mediocre, he would frequently hire college architecture or interior design students with superior skills to execute work for him. He would then affix his own name and seal and present this work to clients as his own; and he would use this work for his own projects. Unfortunately, in one such drawing a student failed to include several important plumbing details that were not incorporated into the finished project. Correcting these deficiencies resulted in delay of the project installation. The plumbing contractor pointed out the omission to the client, who then asked the designer for an explanation. The designer could not give an adequately answer since he had barely looked at the finished drawing some time ago. The client asks you whether there might be any grounds for an ethical complaint against the designer.

10. *Angela W.* This residential interior designer did not think she had enough time to write out in elaborate detail all the tasks she had been hired to perform for a client, so she wrote only "living-room interior design consultation and realization" in the letter of agreement describing her scope of services for the project. The client understood the scope of services to mean that the designer was being

paid to work on both the home's living room and entry area, since the two were not physically separated and were visually interrelated as well. The designer insisted that she was hired to work only on the living room interior design, and she refused to do any work related to the home's entry area unless the client paid her an additional fee. "After all," she told the client, "the living room is all that I agreed to do." The client has come to you to determine what, if any, ethical grounds might exist for filing a complaint against this designer.

This same residential interior designer did not think she had time to specify in detail all the expenses related to the project, and so she did not include in the project budget sales-tax estimates for the goods she ordered. Since the designer had not told the client she would have to charge sales tax in accordance with state law, and the client was not aware that sales taxes were imposed in this situation, the client was surprised to receive an additional invoice from the designer for many thousands of dollars in sales tax that the designer claimed was owed. The client refused to pay the sales tax. Angela refused to deliver the furniture to the client. The furniture then languished in a warehouse where it was damaged and rendered useless. The client asks you to determine if there are ethical grounds for filing a complaint against this designer.

11. *John G.* As a fully accredited interior designer and owner of The Antique Hutch, this designer frequently runs advertisements in which he describes the salespeople in his shop as experienced "interior designers." None of his sales staff received formal design training. A customer of the shop engaged the services of a sales clerk, believing him to be a designer, and was dissatisfied with the outcome of the project. In your opinion, based on your knowledge of the ASID code of ethics, is there any justification for the client to file an ethics complaint—and if so, against whom, John G. or the sales clerk?

12. *Ann L.* Although recently out of school and having completed few design projects of any kind, this designer nonetheless accepted a commission to complete the interior of a 10,000-square-foot mansion. Although the designer felt swamped and was at times unsure of her ability to handle the project, it was completed. "How do you ever learn to handle a project and client relationships without just diving right in," the designer tells you. The clients, however, were unhappy that the project took as long to complete as it did and that it cost

more than they initially had thought it would. They accepted the final results, but they have asked you to look into whether they might have grounds to file an ethics-based complaint against the designer.

This designer also accepted a commission to complete the interior of her client's private jet plane. Neither the designer nor the client ever discussed her qualifications for undertaking such a project. The clients loved her design concept and considered that alone as their reason to hire her. The designer spent a great deal of time attempting to learn the many rules and regulations related to aircraft interior design. The finished jet, however, did not receive authorization from the appropriate authorities to fly until after her numerous mistakes were corrected. The clients were upset with the designer for the delays and considerable additional expenses caused by the many denials of authorization. They have asked you to look into whether they might have grounds to file an ethics-based complaint against the designer.

13. *Michael L.* This much sought-after Boston, Massachusetts, interior designer was commissioned to complete the interiors of a 25-room luxury hotel and restaurant in Provincetown, Massachusetts. The project involved both renovation work to an old house and a newly constructed addition for the restaurant. The clients, affluent Bostonians, were away on a trip when this designer made an executive decision and ordered all new, custom-milled windows for installation. Originally, he had specified only refurbishment of the original windows; but in the midst of the project, the contractor pointed out the window glazing was "just a mess" and would cost almost as much to fix as to replace. The new windows cost many thousands of dollars more than was originally budgeted for all the windows in the new facility. "I only do quality work. After all, I have my reputation on the line with every project," the designer told the clients when they returned. The clients have asked you to advise them on the ethics of this designer's actions.

14. *Christopher Q.* This designer sought to leave the prestigious firm with which he had been associated for nearly ten years. The design director of that firm refused to allow the designer to take any drawings or renderings from the premises on the day his resignation letter was received. "They all belong to the firm, not to you," he was told by the director. This designer has come to you for an evalua-

tion of the situation and for advice about the ethical grounds on which the firm could make such a decision.

15. *Adrian H.* This designer and his team were responsible for the execution of the interiors of the corporate headquarters of a large financial firm. The company president told the designer many details about his and other directors' questionable business practices. The designer swore to keep these details to himself. At the president's trial related to these practices, the designer was called to testify about what he knew about the alleged misconduct. The designer refused to testify, claiming that to do so would violate the designer's obligation of client confidentiality. Were the designer's actions ethically proper? Are there any limits imposed on confidentiality rules?

REFERENCES

Brass, Daniel; Kenneth Butterfield; and Bruce Skaggs. 1998. *Relationships and Unethical Behavior: A Social Network Perspective.* Academy of Management Review.

Copleston, Frederick C. 1994. *A History of Philosophy: Modern Philosophy from the French Enlightenment to Kant. Vol. 6.* New York: Doubleday & Company.

Freidson, Eliot. 1986. *Professional Powers.* Chicago: The University of Chicago Press.

Larson, Magli S. 1977. *The Rise of Professionalism: A Sociological Perspective.* Berkeley: University of California Press.

Long, Deborah. 2000. *Ethics and the Design Profession*, Continuing Education Monograph Series, National Council for Interior Design Qualification: Washington, D.C.

Ritzer, George. 1993. *The McDonaldization of Society: An Investigation into the Changing Character of Contemporary Social Life.* California: Pine Forge Press.

Mills, John Stuart. 1987. *Utilitarianism*, ed. George Sher. Rev. ed. London: Hackett Publishing Company.

Stock, Gregory. 1991. *The Book of Questions: Business Politics and Ethics.* London: Thomas Allen & Sons, Limited.

Students In Free Enterprise (SIFE). 2002. *Back to School: Business Ethics is Focus on College Campuses.* Missouri.

Trevino, Linda K., and Katherine A. Nelson. 1999. *Managing Business Ethics.* 2nd ed. New York: John Wiley & Sons.

STRATEGIES-IN-ACTION PROJECTS

STRATEGIC PLANNING PROJECT: THE MISSION/VISION STATEMENT

In chapter 2, you began the process of drafting a business plan for your ideal interior design business. There you formally set out the *objectives* of your enterprise and described the business formation you determined would be most appropriate. Where might you find a statement that describes the values informing the actions of those involved in running a business? What ideals do these businesspeople wish to advance? Business decision makers are also interested in this more philosophical aspect of your ideal enterprise and will refer to that section of your business plan setting out its mission statement.

It is not easy to arrive at a formal definition of a mission statement because mission statements differ greatly from organization to organization in their levels of detail and content. Usually, these statements broadly describe the goals of a business and how members of that organization define successful completion of those goals, and present a general plan the organization will follow to strategically achieve these goals. Some entities also perceive the need to include a vision statement in their business plans along with the mission statement. The vision statement serves as a means of articulating the point of view shared by members of the organization regarding their work. A simple way to distinguish between the two statements is to note that mission statements express organizational goals, while vision statements detail values held by the organization's members. Inclusion of both these statements is optional. Those organizations seeking to enunciate the values shared by leaders and other business personnel include both statements.

How might a mission statement read for *Imagination Unlimited*, the interior design firm and retail store where Lee, our designer friend, works?

Imagination Unlimited Mission Statement

Being a child should be exciting and enriching and fun. Imagination Unlimited seeks to realize those goals in every interior environment by creating environments with innovation and integrity so that we may continue our work with the children of those who first shared their own childhood with us.

As you can see from this portion of their business plan, Imagination Unlimited defines its basic business function of interior design by its reference to "interior environments." The mission of the business is informed by its belief that childhood should be "exciting and enriching and fun." The guiding values of "innovation and integrity" have been linked in the statement with the company's strategic plan of serving the children of those who first experienced their design work while they themselves were children.

Whichever approach you prefer—either a single mission statement or a mission statement combined with a values statement—think about the qualities you most want your ideal business to represent to consumers. Many times, business writers refer to excellence in a particular area or the ethical manner in which they strive to carry out their business goals. There are many descriptions from which to choose, but which ones best reflect your vision for your enterprise? The Imagination Unlimited owner chose the values of "innovation and integrity" to convey not only the role creativity would play in motivating the business, but also the company's trustworthiness, which the term *integrity* would convey to its clients. What will be the catchwords for your ideal interior design business? After you think about the ideals you most wish to represent in your business, draft a mission statement, or both a mission and value statement, and share it with your class or group for comment. If it would help in your task, write a personal mission statement for yourself, defining in any form you think applicable those values and beliefs that will guide you in your professional and interpersonal relationships. Then, adapting those same concepts, begin to draft a mission statement for your ideal business. Defining what a business seeks to accomplish and the values underlying its endeavors are important steps in strategically planning for the future of any business, including yours.

RESIDENTIAL INTERIOR DESIGN PROJECT SIMULATION

While waiting for word on whether she had the Abernathy project, Lee receives a phone call from the prospective client. Read what transpired; with your knowledge of ethics and using the ASID code of ethics as your guide, answer the questions following Lee's diary entries.

Lee's Diary

OK. A strange thing happened today at the store, and I'm still really not too sure what to make of it all. Mr. Abernathy called me from his cellphone (I could tell he was with a lot of people from all the noise). Of course, I was about to pop. I thought he was going to let me know whether I got the project or not—but no!

So he asked me a couple of weird questions. First, he tells me how much both he and his wife just love my idea about the big tree house in the middle of the playroom and how they really appreciate me leaving all my sketches with them so that they can look them over.

Then, he just point-blank asks me, "Now what was the name of the contractor you said specializes in doing these one-of-a-kind special projects?" See, I made a point in the presentation of not mentioning any trade source names, but on the phone I just blurted out, "Rob Ellis with Southern Contractors on West Avenue," without thinking. Ellis is the only contractor in town who knows how to make movie-set-quality constructions like a tree house that would really look like a tree house and be safe for kids, too. He and his company built the big Texas chuck wagon in our shop. "Oh, thanks—I was just wondering. I've been showing your ideas to someone and couldn't remember," Mr. Abernathy said, really cool, like.

Then he asks me another zinger. Here goes: "You are familiar with projects like this, aren't you?" Very pointedly, I thought. Well, what am I supposed to say? I need the job! Of course, I am familiar with the project. . . . I did it . . . but this is my first "real" project (other than Mom's living room). Did he mean had I done a huge project like this before? So I said, "Why, yes, of course, I am!" I mean I am familiar with it, right? He said something like he "thought so," and that they would "get back to me soon." Click, he just hung up on me.

I cannot believe how dumb I was! Now, they can just call the only guy and the only company in town and have the biggest part of my idea done and not have to pay me! Maybe they won't if they think I can handle the job. At least I didn't blow that part. I have some experience as an interior designer by now. I never thought they would just show my ideas around, either.

Of course, the owner of Imagination Unlimited blew up again at me! When she got back to the shop, I told her all about my conversation with Mr. Abernathy, and she just stopped me and asked: "What do you mean you did not get them to sign a nondisclosure agreement, one where you both agree not to tell others about the project?" Then she said: "Well, if you don't mind having your work being handed out free . . ." So, on that note, I'll "talk" to you soon!

Questions

Can you identify the issues raised by Mr. Abernathy's call and Lee's response to his questions? Here are a few to get you started.

1. Based on the facts you know about the children's-room project, what are some concerns Lee should have about Mr. Abernathy?
2. What obligation, if any, does Lee have to Mr. Abernathy or herself as both consider whether to participate in this project?
3. Does Lee have any obligation to the owners of Imagination Unlimited before taking on this job? What is the role of Imagination Unlimited likely to be in the Abernathy project?
4. How might designers balance the risk of working on an unfamiliar project, in which they may have little previous experience, with their ethical obligations regarding professional "experience"? Could a member justify taking on an unfamiliar project under the ASID code of ethics, section 5.2.: "Members shall seek to continually upgrade their professional knowledge and competency with respect to the interior design profession." After all, won't taking on an unfamiliar project have the ultimate effect of "upgrading" a designer's professional competency? Or do you think that section of the code refers to something else?
5. Finally, before Lee begins to conceptualize the Abernathy project and prepare for her presentation, what obligations does she have to these potential clients, even before she has been hired? How and in what form might these obligations be satisfied?
6. Could obligations of any sort, including ethical ones, be satisfied legally by simply obtaining consent from prospective clients?

CONTRACT INTERIOR DESIGN CASE STUDY:
THE CASE OF THE TALKING TAMALE
(SEE BOX 3.1: ASID CODE OF ETHICS, SECTION 3.5)

This case study asks you to identify and interpret some of the subtle ways in which designers are faced with ethical obligations whether they are aware of them.

After five years of successful operation, the Dallas, Texas, restaurant Bocadito, owned and operated by Chef Carlos Portillo, was ready for a second location. Chef Portillo was known for his unique food, especially his tiny, crispy tamales, the recipe for which was known only to Portillo and a few staff. Customers speculated that this signature dish of the restaurant was comprised of pork and a savory blend of various olives, but no one knew for sure. The demand for the tamales was one reason Portillo was able to expand, and he approached interior designer Harley Horn to

(continued on page 113)

BOX 3.1. ASID CODE OF ETHICS AND PROFESSIONAL CONDUCT

- PREAMBLE
- RESPONSIBILITY TO THE PUBLIC
- RESPONSIBILITY TO THE CLIENT
- RESPONSIBILITY TO OTHER INTERIOR DESIGNERS AND COLLEAGUES
- RESPONSIBILITY TO THE PROFESSION
- RESPONSIBILITY TO THE EMPLOYER
- ENFORCEMENT

1.0 PREAMBLE

Members of the American Society of Interior Designers are required to conduct their professional practice in a manner that will inspire the respect of clients, suppliers of goods and services to the profession, and fellow professional designers, as well as the general public. It is the individual responsibility of every member of the Society to uphold this Code and the Bylaws of the Society.

2.0 RESPONSIBILITY TO THE PUBLIC

2.1 Members shall comply with all existing laws, regulations and codes governing business procedures and the practice of interior design as established by the state or other jurisdiction in which they practice.

2.2 Members shall not seal or sign drawings, specifications, or other interior design documents except where the member or the member's firm has prepared, supervised or professionally reviewed and approved such documents, as allowed by relevant state law.

2.3 Members shall at all times consider the health, safety and welfare of the public in spaces they design. Members agree, whenever possible, to notify property managers, landlords, and/or public officials of conditions within a built environment that endanger the health, safety and/or welfare of occupants.

2.4 Members shall not engage in any form of false or misleading advertising or promotional activities and shall not imply through advertising or other means that staff members or employees of their firm are qualified interior designers unless such be the fact.

2.5 Members shall neither offer, nor make any payments or gifts to any public official, nor take any other action, with the intent of unduly influencing the official's judgement in connection with an existing or prospective project in which the members are interested.

2.6 Members shall not assist or abet improper or illegal conduct of anyone in connection with a project.

(continued)

BOX 3.1. (continued)

3.0 RESPONSIBILITY TO THE CLIENT

3.1 Members' contracts with a client shall clearly set forth the scope and nature of the project involved, the services to be performed and the method of compensation for those services.

3.2 Members may offer professional services to a client for any form of legal compensation.

3.3 Members shall not undertake any professional responsibility unless they are, by training and experience, competent to adequately perform the work required.

3.4 Members shall fully disclose to a client all compensation which the Member shall receive in connection with the project and shall not accept any form of undisclosed compensation from any person or firm with whom the member deals in connection with the project.

3.5 Members shall not divulge any confidential information about the client or the client's project, or utilize photographs or specifications of the project, without the express permission of the client, with an exception for those specifications or drawings over which the designer retains proprietary rights.

3.6 Members shall be candid and truthful in all their professional communications.

3.7 Members shall act with fiscal responsibility in the best interest of their clients and shall maintain sound business relationships with suppliers, industry and trades to ensure the best service possible to the public.

4.0 RESPONSIBILITY TO OTHER INTERIOR DESIGNERS AND COLLEAGUES

4.1 Members shall not interfere with the performance of another interior designer's contractual or professional relationship with a client.

4.2 Members shall not initiate, or participate in, any discussion or activity which might result in an unjust injury to another interior designer's reputation or business relationships.

4.3 Members may, when requested and it does not present a conflict of interest, render a second opinion to a client, or serve as an expert witness in a judicial or arbitration proceeding.

4.4 Members shall not endorse the application for ASID membership and/or certification, registration or licensing of an individual known to be unqualified with respect to education, training, experience or character, nor shall a Member knowingly misrepresent the experience, professional expertise or moral character of that individual.

(continued)

BOX 3.1. (continued)

4.5 Members shall only take credit for work that has actually been created by that Member or the Member's firm, and under the Member's supervision.

4.6 Members should respect the confidentiality of sensitive information obtained in the course of their professional activities.

5.0 RESPONSIBILITY TO THE PROFESSION

5.1 Members agree to maintain standards of professional and personal conduct that will reflect in a responsible manner on the Society and the profession.

5.2 Members shall seek to continually upgrade their professional knowledge and competency with respect to the interior design profession.

5.3 Members agree, whenever possible, to encourage and contribute to the sharing of knowledge and information between interior designers and other allied professional disciplines, industry and the public.

6.0 RESPONSIBILITY TO THE EMPLOYER

6.1 Members leaving an employer's service shall not take drawings, designs, data, reports, notes, client lists, or other materials relating to work performed in the employer's service except with permission of the employer.

6.2 A member shall not unreasonably withhold permission from departing employees to take copies of material relating to their work while an employee of the member's firm, which are not proprietary and confidential in nature.

6.3 Members shall not divulge any confidential information obtained during the course of their employment about the client or the client's project or utilize photographs or specifications of the project, without the express permission of both client and employer.

7.0 ENFORCEMENT

7.1 The Society shall follow standard procedures for the enforcement of this Code as approved by the Society's Board of Directors.

7.2 Members having a reasonable belief, based upon substantial information, that another member has acted in violation of this Code, shall report such information in accordance with accepted procedures.

7.3 Any deviation from this Code, or any action taken by a Member which is detrimental to the Society and the profession as a whole shall be deemed unprofessional conduct subject to discipline by the Society's Board of Directors.

Adapted from: www.asid.org/design_basics/professional_credentials/code_of_ethics.asp

plan the interior spaces for the restaurant's new place in North Dallas. Mr. Horn, a registered Texas interior designer and a member in good standing of the local ASID chapter, had previously designed many hospitality projects. Mr. Horn accepted this new offer although he had another restaurant commission, already under way, planned for the same shopping center as Portillo's.

Because of his work load, Horn hired an unlicensed designer to complete office paperwork. The assistant, Liz Watkins, inadvertently failed to draft a nondisclosure agreement for Horn's trade sources to sign and failed to attach any confidentiality notices to many of Horn's project documents, particularly those depicting custom-designed furnishings. For the Portillo project, Horn had commissioned an East Texas ironsmith to produce an unusual dining chair composed of tooled leather suspended within an iron frame. The chair was both easy to make and inexpensive to produce in mass quantities. Seeing no confidentiality notice on Horn's drawing, the ironsmith assumed it would be all right to reproduce the chair and sell versions of it himself.

One afternoon, while Horn and Portillo discussed details in the kitchen of the original restaurant, the chef offered Horn a taste of what he was preparing. At first, Horn thought it was a large black olive, but after he ate it he realized that it was something else entirely.

"It's great, but what is it?" he asked Portillo.

"Dates, you know, the fruit, but dried and marinated in vinegar," he told the surprised designer. Nothing more was said about the tasty but unusual snack Horn had sampled after they returned to their previous conversation. Soon, Portillo's new restaurant opened and was an instant hit. Unfortunately, its success meant Chef Portillo had even less time to spend with his family and friends. One night, he told Harley Horn he was tired of working all the time and wanted to retire.

"Now, don't tell this to a soul, but I have bought some land near Abilene, Texas, and I am going to retire there at the end of the year," he said to the designer. The local newspaper out there wrote it up on the front page in an article saying I bought an old farm and was going retire shortly."

"I won't tell anyone. You have my word on that!" Horn said.

As successful as Portillo's new restaurant was, the same could not be said for the other project Horn had designed. It had attracted few diners, its appeal lost due to its close proximity to Portillo's.

"We are being trounced by that Bocadito place," spat the owner, who knew Chef Portillo was also Horn's client.

"I wouldn't worry about that," said Horn. "He's going to retire at the end of the year."

"If we last that long!" the owner replied. "I need something—some new, fun dishes that people will like almost as much as Portillo's tamales.

"You know, I had the craziest snack a while back," Horn told the owner. "I can't remember where, but these things looked like olives, but they were dates soaked in something, I think it was some kind of vinegar. Boy, were they great! Sweet, but tangy, too! That would be a good little thing you could whip up to nibble on, right?"

"Hum, could be . . . ," the restaurant owner thought. Over the next few minutes, the interior designer and restaurant owner thought about how to prepare a dish incorporating the mixture into meat pies similar to those Portillo offered. The owner of the competing restaurant then added the new dish he had conceived with Horn's help to the menu, and it became very popular with diners.

Chef Portillo, meanwhile, retired as planned, but Harley Horn's business, however, faced several problems. It came to Horn's attention that the East Texas ironsmith was selling copies of the chair designed for the Bocadito project. Furious, Horn went to his office files and discovered that Liz Watkins had failed to obtain signatures on the nondisclosure agreements before sending working drawings to his craftspeople, and that she also failed to affix confidentiality and other notices.

After firing her, he began discussions with his attorney to bring legal action against the East Texas ironsmith. He also began the process of filling out a formal complaint against Watkins with his local chapter of ASID. Before she left Horn's employment, Watkins took several out-of-date furniture catalogs from the shelves of Horn's library as well as some discarded restaurant floor plans he had thrown in the office trash can, all without asking for or receiving Horn's permission. An example of a blank Library Log is featured in Form 3.2. This log should be used to track vendor catalog lists, periodicals, and swatch books.

Questions

1. Does it matter that there were no notices of any kind on Horn's chair design? Should the artisan be free, in this instance, to assume the designs were available for his use?
2. How successful do you predict Horn's formal complaint against Liz Watkins to the appropriate ASID disciplinary body will prove to be?

FORM 3.2. LIBRARY LOG

LIBRARY LOG

Vendor catalogs list	(Subject matter)	Annual dates

Periodicals		Dates included

Swatch books	(Subject matter)	Annual dates

3. How would you characterize the nature of Chef Portillo's recipes and ingredients in his dishes? How and where did Horn learn the "secret recipe," or did he learn anything?

4. Was it a conflict of interest for Horn to agree to work on Portillo's project when he already had another restaurant project under way in the same location?

5. Does the fact that many people apparently already knew of Chef Portillo's retirement make his request for Horn's confidentiality any less meaningful?

6. Describe Liz Watkins's taking both the catalog and the floor plans in terms of any violation of rules of ethical conduct.

7. Since the owner of the competing restaurant did not ask about Chef Portillo and his restaurant, he did not cause Harley Horn to violate any confidence the designer might have had with the other chef, right?

8. Assuming that Horn is not successful in obtaining professional sanctions against Liz Watkins, are there other means by which he might be compensated for her oversight?

9. How successful would Liz Watkins's claim, be—made before the appropriate ASID judges—that Horn should be sanctioned for his failure to review all documents that went out under his name and seal? Could Chef Portillo, the client for whom the chairs were designed in the first place, successfully make the same claim?

10. What actions might Chef Portillo bring against Horn regarding Horn's statements about Portillo's retirement and the content of Portillo's tamales? How are those two statements different? What actions might the appropriate ASID disciplinary body take against Harley Horn on its own to assure that its members do not breach client confidentiality?

YOU AND
YOUR BUSINESS

Part One of this text gave you a sense of the factors that influence you and your work as an interior designer. With that in mind, you are now ready to explore some of the disciplines upon which you will rely if you open your own interior design business. What do you think having a business will involve for you? Whether you have your own business or you choose to work for someone else you will need to possess some knowledge and skills. Part Two focuses on describing four domains of business knowledge relevant to the practice of interior design. These include an overview of the legal issues with which an interior designer should be familiar; managerial and financial accounting practices pertaining to the operation of an interior design business; design-office management; and the challenges involved in marketing interior design services.

What is unique about this text's discussion of these topics, however, is their application to the specific tasks interior designers carry out in their work. By way of example, chapter 4, "Understanding Law and Your Business," identifies the steps you will take in the process of completing a design project and then defines the important legal issues related to those tasks of which you should be aware. Similarly, chapter 5, "Planning Your Business Finances," defines financial objectives that are important for interior designers to consider as well as the financial concepts underlying those objectives. chapter 6, "Managing Your Business," discusses specific management objectives important to interior designers whether they own and manage their own design businesses or are employed by others. Promotional or marketing skills are critical for making others. Chapter 7, "Promoting Your Work," seeks to enable you to combine this important business function with your own creative point of view.

CHAPTER FOUR

UNDERSTANDING LAW AND YOUR BUSINESS

While most designers do not set out to break the law, uncertainty about legal issues may be their undoing.

CINDY COLEMAN

WHY THIS CHAPTER IS IMPORTANT TO YOU

Part Two of this text explores the influence that business disciplines, such as law, finance, management, and marketing, have on interior designers. Chapter 4 considers how and why various laws affect the activities of interior designers when they are participating in a business and working with clients. This chapter examines the actions designers perform when working in both capacities before considering the legal impact of those actions. From the student's perspective, this chapter is important because it clarifies the legal context of interior design work. It is not intended to scare you into believing that your actions as a designer might result in legal problems. Rather, this chapter seeks to provide a background of information that will enable you to conceive an informed strategy for preventing or minimizing law-related problems.

PROFESSIONAL PRACTICES PORTFOLIO

On completing this chapter, you should be able to answer the questions that follow. Include your responses in the professional practices portfolio you have created.

1. Describe some of the limitations imposed on interior designers by various laws that seek to regulate their practices.
2. What are the ways in which businesses may be formed to meet certain objectives of their organizers?
3. What are some of the objectives business organizers typically have with respect to ventures they start?
4. As agents of their clients, what legal obligations are traditionally assigned to interior designers and others when they act on behalf of clients?
5. What are the elements considered legally necessary to form a valid, enforceable contract?
6. Describe some of the specific laws of which a designer should be aware relating to the planning of interior spaces for accessible, safe use.
7. Define the legal terms *tort* and *negligence*.
8. How have individual states extended protection to consumers in ways other than through *common law*?
9. What body of laws specifically covers topics such as the sale of goods and the conduct of merchants?
10. Describe some basic legal concepts that should be familiar to an interior designer.

INTRODUCTION TO LAW AND YOUR BUSINESS

The purpose of this chapter is to survey those laws and legal concepts likely to be encountered by interior designers. But how might one begin this challenging and possibly even confusing study? As you may have observed, many different laws appear to control modern life, including activities related to interior design. To understand the pervasiveness of law, recall from earlier chapters the number of states that have enacted laws setting out requirements for the lawful practice of interior design in those areas. Because of the extensive influence laws exert on business activities, it is necessary to focus this discussion on those legal issues most likely encountered by designers as they operate businesses and work with clients. How can you identify those legal concepts and issues important to you as an interior designer?

Designers describe the specific tasks they will perform to complete their projects by drafting what is referred to as a scope-of-service analysis. Of course, designers also perform other tasks not usually included in a scope-of-services analysis, such as activities related to the general organization and operation of their businesses. However, articulating the various tasks performed by a designer in the course of participating in a business and working with clients provides entry into the legal context of interior design practice. A scope-of-services approach that recognizes both professional practices and legal issues will thus form the basis of this chapter's objectives.

OBJECTIVES TO CONSIDER

The activities of interior designers may be broken down into the following series of discrete tasks:

- Practice interior design within legally prescribed bounds
- Participate in a business entity
- Work on behalf of clients
- Enter into legally enforceable agreements
- Plan accessible spaces for safe, lawful use
- Specify appropriate fixtures, furnishings, and equipment for use
- Purchase products for resale to clients
- Understand common legal concepts related to business

Using this approach, you can see how a daunting number of legal concepts may be narrowed appreciably. Might other laws and concepts apply to you and your business? Certainly, designers with specialized, unique practices or with businesses in countries other than the United States may have additional or entirely different legal concerns; however, for most design practitioners, the tasks and associated laws identified and explored here are most likely relevant. After defining this list of basic activities in which a designer engages, you need to consider the legal concepts and terminology related to those tasks.

This discussion of the impact of different laws on interior designers is intended to help you to understand and achieve the objectives listed here.

In terms of the tasks identified in the scope-of-services list, consider the first of these activities. How do you think laws have defined the practice of interior design?

DEFINING THE PRACTICE OF
INTERIOR DESIGN FROM A LEGAL PERSPECTIVE

At present, 24 states have promulgated laws related to interior design. Previous discussion in this text focused mostly on legal requirements for entry into the profession. Those laws, however, also define the kinds of activities in which interior designers may and may not engage. Such descriptions of interior design activities are ways in which laws prescribe the professional limits within which interior designers must work. The remaining states, which have no laws specifically related to the practice of interior design, do, however, have laws related to the practice of architecture and can also prescribe qualifications for those who supervise construction projects. Whether a specific state has considered the professional activities of interior designers or, instead, defined the practice of architecture and construction supervision, states have imposed some form of legally prescribed limit on the practice of interior design. What are some of these limits, and why should a designer be aware of them?

To begin, many of the state laws related to interior design track the definition of interior design promulgated by NCIDQ by including in their definitions the organization's stated intent of "protecting the health, safety, and welfare of the public." Furthermore, the interior design laws of several states, such as Arkansas and Illinois, note, as does NCIDQ, that an interior designer is one who is "qualified by education, experience, and examination." Many of these laws then specify those activities in which an interior designer may engage, again in language drawn from the NCIDQ model. For example, the laws of Connecticut specifically mention that interior designers perform "services relative to interior spaces, including: programming (and) design analysis." Other state laws—Michigan's, for example—note that interior design includes specifying "finishes, systems, furniture, furnishings, fixtures, equipment." For purposes of this discussion, it is important to focus on the legal language that establishes limits on the activities of designers.

Paramount among these legal constraints is the prohibition against interior designers engaging in the practice of architecture by making specifications concerning load-bearing interior construction systems and components. One state, Louisiana, clarifies the activities specifically excluded from interior design in that state as follows:

> Interior design specifically excludes the design or the responsibility for architectural and engineering work except for specification of fixtures and their location within interior spaces. Interior design also specifically excludes construction of structural, mechanical, plumbing, heating, air-conditioning, ventilation, electrical or vertical transportation systems, fire-rated vertical shafts in multistory structures, fire-related protection of structural elements, smoke evacuation, and compartmentalization, emergency sprinkler systems, and emergency alarm systems.

Many state laws even prohibit interior designers from working on other details. Some states, notably California, also allow designers to prepare only plans of a nonseismic nature, essentially prohibiting designers from specifying engineering-related work. Other states, such as Florida, specifically prohibit interior designers from engaging in engineering work. Once you have identified a state or jurisdiction in which you wish to practice, your next step is to determine whether any specific prohibitions exist regarding the practice of interior design and to understand those limits.

This knowledge is important to you for several reasons. Perhaps the most important is that by practicing outside legal limits, designers can incur severe penalties such as possible incarceration or loss of license to practice, as would be the case in states such as New York, Illinois, and California. In addition, designers can incur financial loss in the form of penalties. Courts of law also do not permit interior designers to receive any financial compensation from a client when they were not legally permitted to do the work that they performed. In short, failure to understand the scope of permissible professional activities can seriously endanger a designer's career. While this principle may seem obvious—after all, you have received much instruction in other courses about what constitutes structural or engineering tasks—it can embroil designers in other less apparent ways, especially when it comes to supervising the very projects designers conceive.

Some states, such as California, permit only those licensed in that state as general contractors to supervise or inspect the progress of construction.

Interior designers in such cases must also be licensed general contractors to engage in project supervision and related activities. As a practical matter, designers can avoid this issue by requiring their clients to engage the services of a general contractor, but doing so requires that designers know beforehand whether they are legally permitted to supervise project construction. Many clients are not aware of such provisions, and designers who also do not know the laws risk loss of compensation and imposition of legal penalties. Performing prohibited activities may invite legal sanctions against the designer by state regulatory agencies as well as civil law actions brought by the designer's clients. Knowing how relevant laws define the tasks that constitute an interior designer's professional activities is a necessity, given the legal system's regulation of interior designers and their businesses.

Whether they have an ownership interest in an interior design business, or are employed by others who own such a business, design practitioners play a role in business entities. What are these business entities, and why is their organization so important? Interior designers practice their professions in many different settings. Some choose to work in home-centered studios, while others select large firms. And there are many other work environments that fall somewhere between these extremes, such as midsize retail stores. What is important to realize is that there is some identifiable thing that serves as the base of operation for designers, regardless of its physical location or size. That nebulous base of operation is referred to by legal professionals as a **business entity**. What, besides the services or products these entities provide, differentiates them? And why might that be of interest to you?

From a legal perspective, business entities are *not* distinguished from each other neither by the services or goods they provide nor by their physical size or location. Instead, these commercial beings are differentiated by the ways in which they are organized and the business-related goals that can be met by those different organizational forms. The names of these types of formations—and your knowledge—give you an idea of how they satisfy various business objectives. A *sole proprietorship* sounds very much like a business operated by one person who likely desires ease of operation. A *corporation*, as you know, can be a large business involving many people; it is itself a legal entity, separate and apart from the individuals who operate it. In order to make informed decisions about which of these entities might be appropriate choices for a business you might start or manage, consider the not-so-obvious details and consequences of each form of business organization.

SOLE PROPRIETORSHIPS AND PARTNERSHIPS

Many aspiring businesspeople barely have enough money to get their new ventures off the ground, much less to devote to complicated agreements that require a lawyer or accountant's expensive assistance. In addition, they may also wish to keep their organizational structure as simple as possible so that they may concentrate their efforts on carrying out their work instead of managing business operations. In order to satisfy these objectives, some businesspeople frequently begin operation without legal formalities or documentation at all. Individual entrepreneurs who follow this course of action are said to operate in a **sole proprietorship**. Two or more individuals who prefer this same type of operation are usually considered to operate in the form of a **general partnership**.

The low cost and simplicity of these business formations also include the ease with which these entities may be managed. Sole proprietorships, since they are run by one person, may operate in any commercially acceptable and viable manner the owner chooses. General partnerships also may operate as fluidly, provided the general partners all agree on the actions. These businesses may cease their operation easily as well: sole proprietors may simply close their businesses when they wish, with no further action required. Likewise, a general partnership may *dissolve* when one of the partners decides to leave. Logically, sole proprietorships come to an end with the death of their owners, as do partnerships when one of the partners dies. Interestingly, successful solo entrepreneurs may find that they can sell the business they created to other interested parties. A general partner's interest in a partnership may also be sold or transferred, either to other members of the group or to a new partner, provided all other partners agree to this change. Little paperwork evidencing their existence or operational details are required of both of these forms of business; usually only those business licenses and permits applicable to the area in which the business is located are legally necessary for operation. Sole proprietors and general partners do have the obligation of maintaining accurate, extensive financial documentation of their business activities for tax-reporting purposes. The sample tax form, titled "Schedule C," required of sole proprietors, shows that even the simplest business form requires that time and energy be devoted to its financial maintenance. Finally, general partners who seek to work together and share financial responsibilities should have some form of written agreement describing their business relationship to each other in order to minimize possible misunderstandings.

Special Considerations for Partnerships

Assume you and a friend want to start an interior design business together. As you talk about it, you both realize that neither one of you really knows what has to be done to start and run that business. It seems logical to write down the details you both agree to, but which ones? What is important for would-be partners to consider?

One of the easiest ways to make business decisions is to ask, "What happens if something goes wrong?" Keeping that question in mind, you and your friend learn that certain laws apply if you, as business partners, end up in a dispute. With the exception of Louisiana, every state has in its books laws usually called Uniform Partnerships Acts (or some recognizable variation). These laws are applied to resolve problems that arise when partners have business disagreements. This is true unless the partners have thought about, and written down beforehand, details governing their partnership. Although neither one of you can foresee problems or disagreements, neither wants to have to rely on partnership arrangements with which you are not familiar. Based on this, you and your friend continue to think about what you both consider important about your would-be business.

You both know the new partnership should have a name, so you come up with a name that you think is appropriate. Your friend reminds you that money is tight, but it might be possible to come up with enough for his or her share of the business. "How much should that be?" your friend asks. The second question you and your friend address is how much each of you will contribute financially to your new business. If he or she contributes more than you, your friend should own a little more of the business. You and your partner agree to this and also agree that because of this slightly larger contribution, your partner will be entitled to a slightly greater percentage of the business's profits. After completing your discussion, you and your partner shake hands over the terms of your arrangement, and both of you sign copies of a written agreement in which you both spell out important terms such as the full name of your partnership; the amount of money each of you will contribute to the partnership; the way in which you both will share the many expenses; what percentage of profits each of you will be entitled to; how you will make decisions affecting the business; and the management duties each of you will have. You both want the possibility of admitting new members to your design partnership, so you agree on a procedure for doing so. Finally, neither one of you can know what the future will hold—you may move, your partner may get married, any number of different possibilities could occur—so you both discuss these issues in your agreement and write down what should be done in the event any of those possibilities occur. By taking care of these tasks, you and your friend will have addressed many of the concerns facing people who work in partnerships; but other concerns remain.

Sole Proprietor and Partnership Concerns

Both sole proprietors and partners have responsibilities to those with whom they come in contact while operating their businesses. These responsibilities are quite numerous. In fact, both sole proprietorships and partnerships carry with them considerable risk in the form of individual liability. The most important aspect of this liability is the personal accountability of sole proprietors and general partners for any and all financial and legal difficulties that occur while running their respective businesses. For example, suppose one of the trade sources from which you purchase light fixtures is run by a sole proprietor. Due to poor business decisions, the store owner accrues considerable debt but little profit from the business. In the event the lamp store closes, those to whom the proprietor owes money would look to both the sole proprietor's assets found in the store and the owner's personal property, such as checking and savings accounts, to satisfy these debts. Should a store patron be injured while using a lamp found to have been negligently assembled by that sole proprietor, the customer could seek monetary damages from the personal assets of the owner. General partners face the same kinds of liability that do sole proprietors through a legally imposed arrangement known as **joint and severable liability**. This means that general partners assume legal responsibility for the consequences of their actions that are determined to have harmed others as both partners and individual entities. Should your partner cause another to be injured, or accrue considerable debt with creditors of the business, you would face responsibility for paying all of those claims if your partner could not.

Based on these examples, you should have some idea about the differences between sole proprietorships and partnerships. A brief list of the advantages and disadvantages of each may be of further assistance.

A sole proprietorship is composed of one person who chooses to simply start a business after obtaining the licenses or permits required in order for them to carry out their occupations. Advantages of this form of operation are fairly obvious.

- Sole proprietorships are easy to start and manage.
- Sole proprietors keep all the profits that remain after paying expenses and taxes.
- Sole proprietors report those profits as the personal earnings they are. Accordingly, they are taxed only once at the individual sole proprietor's effective tax rate. Deductions for business expenses can, therefore, lower the taxes the sole proprietor pays.

On the other hand, with these advantages come some fairly serious drawbacks to sole proprietorships.

- Sole proprietors are personally liable for the full amount of any and all debts, taxes, and legal judgments brought against or accruing to the business. Insurance payments add to the expenses sole proprietors incur.
- Sole proprietors are self employed, a status requiring them to file specific income-tax forms detailing their business's finances. Thus, the sole proprietor needs to keep accurate financial records while attending to the business. Self-employed individuals are also required to pay self-employment taxes and are not eligible for unemployment benefits.
- Sole proprietors must multitask well. Not only must they know how to attract new business while carrying out existing work, but they also must maintain operational aspects of the business, which include paying income taxes quarterly and maintaining financial records and their office facilities—all at the same time.
- Because the sole proprietor *is* the business, it usually ends with the death of the sole proprietor unless he or she is able to convey it to another person or business entity before death. Doing so may or may not be realistically possible.

General partnerships have some of the same benefits as sole proprietorships.

- General partnerships are fairly simple ventures to start. Although written agreements between the partners are prudent, they are not required.
- Provided all the general partners agree, management and control of the business can be easily accomplished.

◆ The profits earned by partnerships are taxed at the individual tax rates of the general partners.

The disadvantages of general partnerships include the following:

◆ General partners are personally liable for the full amount of any and all debts, taxes, and legal judgments brought against or accruing to the partnership. Even if one partner was not responsible for or involved in the activity causing the debt, expense, or injury, he or she would still be legally and financially responsible for it.
◆ Should the assets of the partnership be insufficient to satisfy partnership obligations, those who seek financial satisfaction may look to the partners' personal assets.
◆ General partnerships dissolve, or cease to exist, at the death or incapacity of one of the members. This could create problems if that partner's assets are closely tied to the business.
◆ The success of general partnerships relies on how well members agree regarding business decisions and on their mutual trust of one another. Lack of agreement and trust can destroy what was an otherwise successful business venture.

Table 4.1, "Types of Business Organization," highlights the distinctions between sole proprietorships and general partnerships.

Specialized Forms of Partnership: Limited Partnerships and Joint Ventures

There are two kinds of specialized business formations that relate to partnerships that may be important to designers. These are limited partnerships and joint ventures; each offers a way of organizing business in a way that minimizes some disadvantages caused by forming a general partnership.

Under **limited-partnership** laws found in most states, an entrepreneur may obtain financial backing from others without forming a general partnership. These backers are usually referred to as **limited partners**, while the entrepreneur is usually called the **general partner**. Unlike a general partnership, limited partners may contribute funds to the business without making management decisions. In fact, the laws related to

TABLE 4.1

Types of Business Organization

Business Objectives	Sole Proprietorship	General Partnership	Joint Venture	Limited Partnerships	Corporation	"S" Corporations	Limited Liability Company	Professional Corporation
Conserving time/money when starting business	Little to no expenditures legally required	Little to no expenditures legally required	Usually involves effort and cost to form	Formal agreement and filings with state required	("C" Corporations) Expenditures required to establish correctly	Expenditures required to establish correctly	Expenditures required to establish correctly	Expenditures required to establish correctly
Keeping business form simple, easy to understand	No formalities required to maintain business once started	No formalities required Written partnership agreement recommended	May be complex depending on agreement	General partner(s) manage business Limited partner(s) provide financial backing to venture	Formalities of corporate operation must be followed Many different Federal, state requirements to follow	Fomalities of corporate operation must be followed Many different federal and state requirements to follow	Formalities of corporate operation must be followed Many different Federal, state requirements to follow Must use initials L.L.P.	Option limited to state licensed professionals Must identify PC form in name
Flexibility in starting, ending, or adding members to the business	Extremely flexible may begin, end, change at any time	May begin, end, change by agreement of partners	Relationship contractual in nature, not a separate legal entity	Limited flexibility formal requirements for role of partners	Limited flexibility, Shareholders may change management through voting	Limited flexibility Shareholders may change mangement through voting	"Managers" control business operation; "Members" similar to general partners, investors	Limited flexibility, Shareholders must be licensed by state to practice particular profession
Protecting assets of those involved in the business	No protection of business or owner's assets	No protection of business or owners' assets	Depends on business formation of parties; making up venture; other agreements	General partner(s): Personal assets may be reached Limited partner(s): only to extent of investment	Central reason for choosing: assets only at stake to extent of contribution in corporation, no personal assets at stake	Central reason for choosing: assets only at stake to extent of contribution in corporation, no personal assets at stake	"Members" personal assets protected from exposure	Personal assets of shareholders protected

Limiting legal responsibility of those involved in the business	Unlimited personal liability of business owner	Unlimited personal liability of business owner	Depends on business formation of parties; making up venture; other agreements	General partner(s): personal liability Limited partner(s): only to extent of investment	Officers and directors only, no stockholder liability	Officers and directors only, no stockholder liability	"Managers" fully liable "Members" no personal liability	Officers and directors only, no stockholder liability
Limiting effects of taxes	Earnings taxed at rate of owner Subject to self-employment tax	Earnings taxed at rate of owner Subject to self-employment tax	Depends on business formation of parties; making up venture; other agreements	Both General and Limited Partners taxed at individual rates	Double taxation: Corporation pays taxes on profits and stockholders pay taxes on dividends paid to them	Distinction from "C" Corporations: Taxed as if a partnership with profits taxed at officer's and shareholder's rates	Managers/members may elect taxation as either a corporation or a partnership	Double taxation: Corporation pays taxes on profits, and stockholders pay taxes on dividends paid to them
Preserving business over long periods of time	Business ends at death of owner unless conveyed previously	Partnership ends at death or incapacity of a partner unless remaining partners agree to continue partnership	Joint venture time- or project-specific; longevity of business not intended	General Partner's death will end unless interest conveyed and new partner agreed upon Limited Partners may convey interests to successors	Potentially indefinite; a legally recognized entity	Potentially indefinite; a legally recognized entity	Unclear: each state may provide differently	Potentially indefinite; a legally recognized entity

forming limited partnerships usually prohibit any management input from limited partners. Why might an investor be interested in providing money to an entrepreneur if that investor will not be allowed to participate in business decisions? One reason involves, as you might suspect, financial return: A limited partner is allowed to share in profits earned by the limited partnership. Another reason an investor might be interested in contributing financial resources as a limited partner relates to liability for partnership obligations. As you remember, partners in a general partnership are each liable for obligations accrued in the course of the general partnership's operation. A limited partnership is distinctly different in this regard: A limited partner has responsibility for the partnership's obligations only for the amount of money the limited partner has contributed to the business. Limited partners do not, therefore, have the virtually unlimited exposure to risk that they would in a general partnership. While such an arrangement is advantageous for the limited partner, the general partner, or partners, are each liable for partnership obligations as if they were in a regular general partnership—that is, unlimited personal exposure for all obligations of the partnership.

The rules that govern the formation and management of limited partnerships are usually quite detailed about the role limited partners might have in the operation of the business entity. Usually, these rules declare that a court of law may determine even minor amounts of management and specific activities may result in the limited partnership being considered a general partnership, and, accordingly, impose higher degrees of liability on the parties involved in the partnership. Similarly, a limited partnership may dissolve when a limited partner leaves, either through withdrawal from the continued financial backing of the business or the death of the limited partner. In general, the death of the general partner or partners dissolves the limited partnership.

As you can see, this type of business organization is fairly complex and requires that an entrepreneur allocate resources for legal advice regarding its correct formation according to applicable state laws and its operational details. This chapter will later explore another form of business organization that is similar to a limited partnership, but satisfies an important objective lacking in a limited partnership. To get you thinking about what that objective might be, ask yourself whether it would be important to you to be able to obtain financial backing for your business as well as to have it continue indefinitely. For many entrepreneurs, the longevity of a business they founded is an important objective.

Qualified longevity may best describe a **joint venture**, as it exists for only as long as its members initially agreed it would continue, or as long as a specific project takes to complete. A joint venture is formed when two or more individuals or business entities enter into a binding agreement, a contract, under the terms of which these members consent to share financial and other obligations necessary to complete their undertakings. After accomplishing that objective or after members agree otherwise, the joint venture ends. This type of business organization requires an allocation of resources for legal assistance to create the joint venture contract between the parties that seek to form it, which would mean another operational expense. That contract may provide specific guidance on how the parties intend to assume financial and other responsibilities, such as allocation of the venture's expenses, profits, and losses. However, most laws that relate to these relationships declare that each member of a joint venture may be sued individually—although not the joint venture itself, since it is a contractual relationship and not a separate business form. The idea of joint and severable liability applies to joint ventures as it does to general partnerships: Each member separately and all members together are responsible for joint venture obligations. In other words, the actions of one member of the venture could result in all the members being legally responsible for something they did not directly cause (see Table 4.1).

The allocation of tax liability usually follows that of partnerships, with each member being taxed as if in a general partnership. This means that each member would be taxed according to his or her taxpayer status. The joint venture relationship offers groups of diverse talents and resources the ability to realize projects difficult for individual members to accomplish successfully on their own. Real estate joint ventures in which a landowner, an architect, and a builder come together to complete a development project is one very common example of a joint venture relationship. Interior designers interested in product development may also consider joining forces with a manufacturer in such a relationship in order to jointly share expertise. As a vehicle for joining entrepreneurs, joint ventures offer opportunities to bring about projects that might not otherwise be possible. However, they do require expert advice regarding their correct structure; and there is a possibility of a fairly large amount of tax and liability exposure for its members. By now, you may get the idea that businesspeople frequently wish to limit their exposure to risk of various kinds. What are some ways in which business laws permit them to do so?

CORPORATIONS AND THE CORPORATE
FORM OF BUSINESS ORGANIZATION

Corporations are often perceived as only being large businesses. However, a corporation may also be as small and familiar as the local dry-cleaning establishment you patronize. A corporation's defining characteristic is not its size, but rather its separation from those involved in its operation. In other words, a **corporation** is a legal *being* or entity in its own right. You will recall that founders of sole proprietorships and partnerships are closely identified with the businesses they operate. The same is not true for those involved in corporations. Once established, a corporation may carry on even after the death of its founders. Knowing that corporations are an altogether different form of business organization, what business objective that results from the corporation's separation from those who operate it do you think might be most attractive to businesspeople?

Business organizers are usually attracted to the corporate form of organization for their ventures because it allows them to limit their personal financial responsibility for the business. This means that those who start corporations and those who are stockholders are generally not responsible for paying money to run the corporation or to satisfy legal claims that a law court determines the corporation must pay. The founders and stockholders are responsible for paying only the amount of money they have invested in the corporation. For their investments, stockholders— also called shareholders—receive dividend income, or a portion of the corporation's profits, based on the percentage of the corporation they own.

Before describing the corporate form of business organization in detail, it is necessary to explain how these businesses are formed. Of all the methods available to businesspeople, the corporate form requires the greatest allocation of time, money, and specialized expertise to originate. However, failure to properly form and run a corporation risks jeopardizing the benefits that make corporations attractive types of business organization.

All states have laws related to the formation of corporations in their books. These laws vary in many respects. In some states, it may be more or less advantageous to organize in the corporate form; however, these states usually prescribe the same general requirements for corporate organization. Those who wish to use the corporate form to organize their business venture must first prepare and then file a document called the

articles of incorporation. Usually, the assistance of an attorney is required in order to prepare this and other documents, such as an offering of shares of stock, related to the formation of a corporation. Once completed and duly signed by the officers and directors of the new corporation, the articles are filed for review with a state governmental officer charged with overseeing corporations. This is usually the secretary of state or similar state official.

Working in the corporate form thus has many advantages, although a corporation can be quite complicated to start and can require an extensive allocation of resources. Is there any other form of business organization that can accomplish some of the same goals as a corporation—notably protection of its investors' personal assets from financial claims—but with fewer organizational tasks? To address that concern, some states have adopted laws that permit what are referred to as **limited liability companies (LLC)**. In essence, this form of business organization is a blend of partnerships and corporations. What this means for businesspeople who select this way to form a new venture is the organizers enjoy both protection of their personal assets from claims (as with corporations) while possibly having to observe fewer organizational and operational formalities (as would be the case in partnerships). It should be noted that laws for organizing in the LLC form continue to develop and, depending on the state where the new venture is located, may impose extensive registration requirements. Table 4.1 summarizes the various types of business organization and the ways each type relates to important business goals.

The laws of every state provide very specific rules to follow to correctly organize most commercial ventures according to that state's individual terms. These laws also require entrepreneurs to file detailed documents about their businesses with state officials in some instances. In addition to these very detailed organizational laws, both federal and state tax laws relate to businesses are extremely detailed and often change. Failure to comply with tax laws may incur serious economic penalties to businesses and its operators. In order to navigate these strict requirements and to assess possible legal and financial impacts on businesses, attorneys and accountants advise entrepreneurs about which of approximately eight different options for business organization is an appropriate choice. All entrepreneurs should consult these professionals about organizational options best suited to their objectives, even when those objectives may not be very complicated.

INTERIOR DESIGNERS AND THE LAW OF AGENCY

It seems obvious to state that interior designers work for clients. But how might that relationship be formally defined in legal terms, and what importance does such a definition hold for practitioners? Precedents found in written legal opinions handed down over time by the courts have identified a business relationship referred to as **agency**. This relationship occurs when an agreement exists between two parties, historically referred to as *master* and *servant*, and now usually styled **principal** and **agent**. The essence of agency agreements declares that the latter will represent the interests of the former in a business relationship. Design practitioners enter into agency relationships with clients when they agree to perform interior design services and related activities, such as rendering professional services or purchasing merchandise.

Agency relationships specify duties each party owes to the other. Agents are traditionally considered to owe their principal duties such as the following:

◆ Using reasonable diligence and skills in the performance of their activities
◆ Working obediently for the principals and their interests
◆ Informing the principal of all matters related to the agency relationship
◆ Expressing loyalty to the principals and their interests

Similarly, principals have been found to owe their agents duties such as the following:

◆ Providing reasonable compensation for the services of the agent
◆ Repaying expenditures the agent incurred during the course of the agency relationship
◆ Indemnifying, or providing financial compensation, to anyone injured as a result of the agent's action while the agent acted within the scope of the agency relationship

As you can see, once an agency relationship is found to exist, each party in that relationship owes certain duties to the other. In the event that a court of law finds one party to have failed to satisfy its respective duty or duties to the other, the court may award the injured party monetary damages.

LEGALLY ENFORCEABLE AGREEMENTS

The fourth objective of this chapter is to explore what comprises a legally enforceable agreement and to consider how designers enter into them. Controversies can develop over whether the elements compromising contracts have been met and can, therefore, be enforced by courts of law. The general body of law known, not surprisingly, as **contract law**, or the **common law of contracts**, governs legal determinations of this kind. Before describing what constitutes a contract and how it applies to an interior designer's business dealings, we should consider several preliminary topics.

The first relates to the use of the word **agreement**. To say that an agreement exists in business dealings is to say that there is, in fact, a contract, or that a contractual relationship exists. For this reason, businesspeople are, or should be, careful to distinguish between negotiations or initial talks (where terms of what may become an agreement are still subject to discussion and determination) and the resulting contractually binding agreement itself. The reason for making this distinction is found in the idea of **mutual assent**.

Mutual assent between two parties is one of the requirements necessary to establish a contract. One element that courts consider in contract disputes is whether mutual assent, or *mutuality*, exists. It is generally considered to be present when there is a consensual intent to be bound by terms of an agreement. A court may determine that there was, in fact, no such intent present and that, accordingly, this requirement was not satisfied. Similarly, a court may find mutual assent lacking when the facts indicate that any one of several problems existed. It makes sense that this requirement is likely not satisfied where one of the parties entered into the agreement because of **undue influence** or **duress**. The exercise of some influence over a party to a contract that is powerful enough to supersede the exercise of that individual's own free will is said to be the exercise of undue influence. The use of actual threats, usually involving the imposition of some harm, to induce someone to enter into a contractual relationship characterizes duress, as opposed to undue influence.

For businesspeople, mistake and fraudulent misrepresentation refer to more relevant ways by which mutual assent may be found lacking. **Mistake** in this regard is usually found by a court when it appears one of the parties to the agreement misunderstood the terms of what the contract called for them to do. Agreeing to a bad deal—for example, paying too much for something later determined to be of little value—is not what usually constitutes a mistake in legal thinking. Rather, a mistake is likely found where parties to a contract entered into that agreement reasonably believing they were required to do something other than what was actually required. Finally, in cases where one party deliberately misrepresents facts about contract terms to the extent of being outright dishonest, courts will usually find lack of mutual assent based on **fraudulent misrepresentation**. As you can see, the idea of mutual assent, or agreement between interested stakeholders, is the essence of a contract.

It is also necessary to distinguish between what is meant by the terms contract and contract documents. For those who like logic puzzles, the distinction may be summarized by noting that a contract may be a contract document, but a contract document may not be a contract! Puzzles aside, a brief explanation should help. A **contract** is an agreement made enforceable through legal action because certain requirements have been met. A contract document—or **contract documents**, as they are frequently called by architects, interior designers, and contractors—consists of *all* the many individual agreements among the designer, client, and other professionals involved in the project as well as the drawings, plans, specification sheets, and schematic representations used to bring a project to fruition. Only if those many documents contain the elements necessary to establish legally enforceable agreements—for example between the designer and client—does it become a contract. A contract document may just be a collection of drawings, notes, and invoices. Businesspeople frequently use the term the contract document to refer to the written form of the agreement itself. Clients are frequently savvy businesspeople but may be confused by terminology used in a particular way that is unfamiliar to them. It's your job to prevent misunderstandings or confusion from occurring. Further discussion of contract documents as understood by interior designers is found in chapter 11, "Defining the Client Relationship," where you will apply the basic knowledge of contractual agreements you learned here in order to prepare these project documents and explain them to clients.

Contracts form the backbone of many commercial relationships: They are involved in agreements for the provision of services and for the purchase of merchandise or goods. This discussion of agreements will detail only the former activity: the provision of services. The law of agreements relating to the sale of goods is *entirely* different and is discussed in a later section of this chapter. Once you have gained experience in dealing with business agreements, this distinction will become second nature to you in your practice; but since it may be less obvious to you now, it deserves separate treatment.

ELEMENTS OF A CONTRACT

From your course work in historic furniture and architectural styles, you may recall the formal, orderly structure inherent in the English design sensibility of the seventeenth and eighteenth centuries. Those same traits may also be said to have permeated the legal sensibilities of the time. The practice of law was a profession well established in England by then, its practitioners relying on the orderly logic of inductive reasoning and the ornament of the written word to create what has become known as the common law of contracts. This **common law** was based on the legal principle of *stare decisis*, in which past decisions made by courts of law are looked to for *precedent*, or reasons for making decisions about similar issues occurring later. *Case law* is another term for this body of law. Agreements were frequently the subject of legal determinations made by the English courts, since the country's commercial activities were also greatly advanced during this time. From these early determinations, additional elements emerged concerning what constituted an agreement that the court would enforce.

The terms *offer*, *acceptance*, and *consideration* as requirements necessary for a valid contract appear to be straightforward enough on the surface. The reality is that each has a history of development during which these requirements have been interpreted, modified, and frequently reinterpreted first by the seminal English courts through the modern-day U.S. courts—to reach their current meaning.

An **offer** is said to exist when a court determines that there was an indicated intent on the part of the parties to enter into a binding agreement with each other in the first place. In addition to this initial intent, an offer is said to exist when a court further determines that the parties had indicated to each other what each was to do and, furthermore, had communicated this indication to each other.

To fully **accept** an offer (as opposed to have offered a counteroffer) is to have agreed to each and every term of the offer, making no change or imposing no condition upon it. This is frequently referred to as the *mirror image* rule: The acceptance must reflect exactly the same terms as the

139

offers or, if it changes *any* term, becomes a **counteroffer**. As with the offer, the agreement should be fully communicated to the one making the offer.

As simple as these first two contract elements may appear, courts today—centuries after their early development—are called upon to determine whether actions of the parties resulted in the formation of a contract. A **unilateral contract** is said to result when an offer is accepted through the *actions* of the other: The performance of the requested act serves as an acceptance of the offer. Alternatively, a **bilateral contract** is said to result where one party makes a promise (usually a promise to pay sums of money), and, as a result of that first promise, another party promises to do something (or not to do something the latter party has a legal right to do). The doing of the action and the promise to act in these examples are respective acceptances; but the fact that the act and the promise to act exist indicate satisfaction of the next element required of contracts—*consideration*.

The requirement of **consideration** is not exactly what you might think. Consideration, meaning acts of kindness, was not what early courts determined satisfactory or even necessary for this contract requirement. Early courts looked for consideration in the form of a "bargained for" exchange between the parties. This bargaining, the courts found, should result in one party (the person making the offer) receiving a *benefit*, while the other (the person accepting the offer) incurring a *detriment*, which means an obligation to do something. In unilateral and bilateral contracts, the person making the offer is said to have received the benefit of the act or promise to act of the other; however, the person doing the act or making the promise to act has incurred an obligation by accepting the offer.

How much consideration is enough to inspire actions or promises? The early courts did not look to the sum of money that was to be paid after performance of the requested act or the sum that induced the promise to act. In other words, they did not question the adequacy of consideration, only whether it was present. That quaint idea is now simply thought of as paying the price. Once a design fee, for example, is received, consideration is said to have passed, the offer is said to be accepted, and the contract (all other requirements being met) formed.

In addition to the three requirements of offer, acceptance, and consideration necessary for contract formation, there are several other requirements, notably that the parties must have contractual capacity, that is, be legally able to enter into contractual relationships. This requirement considers the status of the parties to the contract by looking at whether they are of legal age to enter into a contract or are of sound mind to do so. Youngsters and those who are unable to understand the nature of what they are undertaking are clear-cut examples of parties lacking in contractual capacity. A more difficult question arises in business dealings when someone who appears to have the authority to enter into contracts in fact does not have any such authority. Prudent businesspeople determine who is empowered to enter into contracts in order to avoid such problems. Finally, a contract must be formed for a legal purpose or it is considered by the courts to be *void ab initio*, or "from its very beginning." Contracts that require actions made illegal by criminal law or actions found to be counter to sound public policy usually fail to be enforced on these grounds.

THE STATUTE OF FRAUDS

Are contracts required to be in writing to be enforceable? The answer is an unequivocal maybe! For transactions involving many real estate activities, for the sale of goods over $500, for certain promises regarding offers to pay debts or to marry, or for agreements "not to be performed within one year of (their) making," writing is universally required. These requirements originated in passage by the English Parliament in 1677 of a doctrine known as the Statute of Frauds, an early attempt to protect consumers from dishonest practices arising from oral contracts. Vestiges of this doctrine were introduced into and still remain in American contract and commercial law. Occurrences other than those specified by the statute are said to be outside it and require no writing. What this means is that oral agreements may be enforceable agreements if contract terms can be established in court through the introduction of other evidence. A statement made by a designer—heard by witnesses—in which the designer offered their services to work on an individual's entire ten-thousand-square-foot house for only $10,000 might be enforceable against the designer if the person to whom that offer was made accepted it.

A related question to the writing requirement is whether a contract needs to be signed in order to be valid. From early times to present, courts have generally held that a signature is required for a contract to be valid. In particular, the party to be charged, usually clients, must make their mark or sign their name on the contract itself. Suppose you begin your interior design work without having your clients sign a contract indicating their agreement for you to do so. In such cases, you may face a lengthy and expensive court battle to receive any design fees you might have earned, should any client fail to recognize the existence of an agreement and refuse to pay those fees. Under such a circumstance, a court of law hearing the dispute would be the one to determine whether you would receive those fees and what amount, a process that might have been avoided altogether by following the formalities for forming a contract and obtaining the client's signature.

Validity is one concern; enforceability of terms in a contract is another concern. It is highly likely that some form of signed written contract between interior designer and client will exist. While these documents may be called *letters of agreements*, most businesspeople are well aware of the simple rule to get it in writing. In the excitement of gaining a new project and a new client, many professionals do write down some things. However, the next question is not whether a valid contract was formed, but whether enough details are spelled out to enable all terms of the valid contract to be enforced.

Major professional associations such as the ASID and IIDA provide standard form contracts, which will be explored further in relation to managing a client's project (chapter 10). However, a brief scan of these boilerplate contract forms indicates that for a contract to benefit from the court's ability to enforce all of its terms, that contract must, at the very least, contain a date, identify the parties to the contract, spell out the scope of services to be performed, state the amount and method of compensation, and be signed. Once the contract is signed, contract performance is usually initiated.

CONTRACT PERFORMANCE

The performance of agreed-upon terms usually signals the end, or **termination**, of a contract. Of course, the parties to the original agreement may agree to end their contractual obligations at any time; however, performance of contract terms is more prevalent in business settings. Determining the acceptability of the performance rendered under a contract involves an understanding of what is meant by the term *reasonable*. The use of objective standards permeates legal reasoning; after all, how could a judge or jury actually know what someone else might, subjectively, be thinking?

Performance may be of three kinds. One way in which performance may be rendered is referred to as **complete performance**. As the name implies, this kind of performance succeeds in satisfying each and every term agreed to in the contract. Perfect performance is easy to understand. Not quite perfect performance, however, raises the question whether that performance was reasonably and substantially similar to the kind agreed on in the contract. As a practical matter, **substantial completion** is found in cases where performance does not differ greatly from what would otherwise have been complete performance. Finally, **inferior performance** may be said to characterize those instances where a court determines that the performance rendered was much different in quality from what was initially bargained for by the contracting parties.

An interesting situation sometimes arises with respect to contract performance—for example, when no formal, written contract is in place between the parties because only an oral agreement exists. Realizing the absence of a contractual obligation, it is then not uncommon for one of the parties to stop performance and refuse to carry out further action on the grounds that no written, signed contract existed in the first place. An example involving the singer Cher is one such case where a contractor worked for some time on Cher's California residence but was not paid the final, substantial amount owed. The singer claimed the lack of a contract between them did not require her to do so. This example of performance without the presence of a contract presents several contract ideas particularly relevant to those, including interior designers, who render services to others.

Along with formal courts of law in England, a separate court system arose known as *courts of equity*. These courts sought to soften the sometimes harsh effects caused by judgments from the courts of law. Two early English doctrines developed by equity courts made their way to sunny Malibu through adoption into California law. These courts developed the legal theory of **promissory estoppel** (sometimes referred to simply as *estoppel*) and *unjust enrichment*. The idea behind estoppel is to preclude parties from claiming the absence of an existing contract as a reason to excuse their actions when they themselves acted as if there were a valid contract. Although lacking a signed contract, Cher did permit the contractor to complete large amounts of work on her property and even paid the contractor as work progressed. The California court found that on that basis the singer was *estopped* from claiming lack of a contract as a reason not to pay. Much of the reasoning behind promissory estoppel was based on the idea of preventing one person from receiving a disproportionate benefit, or **unjust enrichment**, at another's expense (Holland 2003).

BREACH OF CONTRACT

All businesspeople will face situations in which others with whom they have contracted do not perform what they had agreed to do. Related to this is the situation in which the performance that was rendered was unreasonably wrong, or not performed in accordance with standards imposed on similar professionals or tradespeople in the community. In these instances, a **breach of contract** is said to have occurred. Breaches of contract may vary little from what was initially agreed upon and are considered to be minor breaches of the contract. Although technically a breach, courts generally do not excuse the injured party from its contract performance—such as paying for the work done—on the basis that to do so would permit that party's unjust enrichment. In most cases involving a minor contract breach, one party usually is not required to pay or perform its obligation until the minor breach is "cured" by the other.

As you might suspect, there are also instances where a court determines that a breach was major enough—in the instance of inferior performance, for example—to discharge any further contractual obligations on the part of the party affected. Such instances are referred to as *material breaches*. Determinations of a material breach by a court usually allows the injured party to *rescind*, or cancel, the contract and seek *damages* from the other party.

CONTRACT DAMAGES

What happens when contracts go wrong? A valid contract had been formed; yet performance either did not occur or was materially different from what was agreed upon, causing a breach. What recourse or resolution is available to the harmed party? Contract damages are said to be appropriate in instances of contract breach; but how are those damages determined? Contract damages may take two forms: financial compensation for the economic losses the non-breaching party suffered; or court-ordered completion of the performance. An order of *specific performance*, in which the party that breaches the contract is compelled to carry out the actions upon initially agreed, is rarely imposed in the case of contracts for services, which would characterize contracts for interior design work. English courts of equity originated this form of relief, but applied it in only extreme or very unusual circumstances. A breached contract to sell land is one early example, still applicable today, where an award of specific performance might be possible. The rationale, then and now, is that an award of monetary damages should sufficiently compensate the party against whom the breach occurred. If money damages are the legally preferred method of remedying contract breaches, how are they determined?

Monetary damages may compensate the injured party for the actual amount of financial loss. These are known as **actual damages**. On the other hand, the court, if sufficiently shocked at the actions of the breaching party, may impose **punitive damages**, an amount additional to actual damages and sufficiently large enough to set an example for others to not act as the breaching party did. Other forms of economic damages exist as well, notably **nominal damages**, in which a court makes a token, relatively small award to the injured party, usually in cases where any form of compensatory damages would be speculative or conjectural.

This overview of contract law has covered many hundreds of years in legal thought and volumes of legal decisions interpreting contract issues. Although not inclusive of all nuances of this law, it should provide you with an understanding of the subject sufficient for understanding future discussions relating to design contracts.

PLANNING ACCESSIBLE SPACES FOR SAFETY

What should interior designers understand about the law related to planning accessible spaces for safe, lawful use? Two important considerations are the Americans with Disabilities Act, which applies nationwide, and local fire and safety codes. © The Americans with Disabilities Act. In 1992 Congress enacted the **Americans with Disabilities Act** (known by its initials ADA). This legislation sought, among other goals, to make public and some private buildings more accessible to all individuals regardless of their physical abilities. In other words, it sought to create barrier-free public environments that were as accessible to handicapped individuals as to the nonhandicapped. Title III of the act sets forth building or retrofitting requirements for those areas it describes as "places of public accommodation." This section of the act includes new construction requirements for public places built after its effective date and also includes what the act terms requirements for "readily achievable" modifications to preexisting places of public accommodation. This legislation has particular application to nonresidential interior designers, since the ADA does not apply in all but a few nonresidential spaces. Private residences, for example, are excluded from the purview of the law, as are those "commercial facilities" that although nonresidential in nature, are not open for access to the general public.

Provisions of the ADA are enforced by the U.S. Department of Justice; however, state and municipal governments throughout the United States have adopted the ADA regulations in their own codes or have made the ADA applicable through local passage of enabling laws. In general, an individual claiming a Title III violation must first file a complaint with the U.S. Department of Justice, which will then initiate an investigation and, if appropriate, attempt to negotiate an agreement with those against whom the complaint is brought. Should attempts to reach a settled agreement fail, then suit may be brought in federal court by the Department of Justice on behalf of the claimant to compel compliance with provisions of the law. As a practical matter, every effort should be made to comply with the provisions of the ADA, even in those instances where an exception might exist. In some instances, individual business owners have claimed that ADA-required modifications to their existing facilities are too costly and thus not—in the language of the ADA—"economically feasible." Even without suing establishments in federal court for their failure to comply with the ADA, there have been instances where disabled customers have protested outside places such as restaurants and bars to raise the public's awareness of the problem and seek the owners' compliance.

Building and Fire-Safety Codes

Municipalities pass various codes related to the safe occupancy of structures within their jurisdiction that should be of interest to interior designers. These codes are usually classified as building and fire-safety codes. Compliance with these codes is necessary in order to obtain a final certificate of occupancy or other authorization that the structure complies with code. Failure to conform to these codes carries with it penalties from heavy fines to closing the premises for public use. Professional competency requires designers to know and understand relevant building and fire-safety codes. They must also be aware of the legal consequences for failing to correctly apply their provisions.

The challenge for the interior designer is to keep abreast of changes in the requirements imposed by these local rules. Each city or town has its own codes describing the types of construction techniques and materials that may be used. Currently, local building codes may be based on any of several sets of codes that have been used throughout the United States. Existing codes are drawn from three sets of building codes: Uniform Building Code; Standard Building Code; and the Basic/ National Building Code. Recently, the International Building Code (IBC) has been promulgated with an eye toward achieving building-code uniformity. At present, this new model of code has not been adopted. Code manuals may be fairly easy to obtain from building sources and online. These codes apply to structures within the jurisdictional purview of the relevant municipality. For that reason, an interior designer's library should contain up-to-date codes that apply to the locations of their on-going projects.

SPECIFYING APPROPRIATE FIXTURES, FURNISHINGS, AND EQUIPMENT (FF&E)

One of the tasks designers seem to enjoy most is researching and specifying products for use in client projects. As interesting as this activity may be, what legal responsibilities does a designer have to clients regarding the products they choose to complete a project?

The concept of *tort law* is centuries old, originating in the common law of Great Britain. Tort law, today, is usually found in the laws of specific geographical areas that are under the control of a particular set of courts. These areas are known as jurisdictions. States are one example of an area of jurisdiction. Usually an individual or business brings a tort-law claim in the courts of the state in which the questioned action occurred. Those courts then decide the outcome of these cases by applying legal standards to the specific facts of that complaint and render an opinion as to which party should be responsible. *Juries*, or groups of citizens of that jurisdiction, sometimes are called to decide legal responsibility as well. Either a judge or a jury may determine responsibility and what damages, if any, should be awarded to the aggrieved party. Successful tort claims usually result in awards of money to the injured person or group. Often, special testimony in court from an *expert witness* may be used by either party to the dispute. An expert witness is usually an individual who has very specific, specialized knowledge or expertise relevant to understanding the matter in dispute. For example, an experienced interior designer might be called as an expert witness to explain some aspect of the profession in open court to strengthen one party's claim against the other. With that general knowledge of civil law procedures in mind, there are several areas in which state laws may affect interior designers.

PURCHASE PRODUCTS FOR RESALE TO CLIENTS

Many, but certainly not all, designers first purchase products, such as furniture and textiles, then resell those items to their clients. Chapter 12 explores details of this process, such as how designers may determine the final price they will charge for those items. However, as you survey in this chapter the various laws that may impact designers and their practices, you should be aware of laws that relate to agreements and transactions that involve the sale of goods. Known as the Uniform Commercial Code and adopted in some form in almost all states, this complex series of laws pertains to a variety of commercial transactions.

To begin learning about this set of laws consider first its general purpose and history as well as its very name. Under the common law of contracts, it would be possible for the courts in various states to interpret laws differently, a result that could lead to problems, especially in transactions involving businesses in several states. In such cases, confusion as to which law might govern the activities of those involved might occur. To prevent these occurrences and to generally facilitate commercial transactions, a group known as the National Conference of Commissioners on Uniform State Laws first drafted a set of laws in 1892 to establish *one* set of laws that states might then adopt to facilitate business transactions. A uniform set of laws containing provisions substantially the same in all the jurisdictions whose legislatures adopted that set of laws was the result. That set of laws, however, was then organized into a series of codes grouped by subject matter. Under the terminology used, one section of the code, Article Two, concerned commercial, or business activities related to the sale of tangible, physical objects, capable of being moved and conveyed, known as goods. Many interior designers work with goods and, as you might suspect, provisions of the Uniform Commercial Code can and do apply to that activity. This section will first describe how the code relates to the common law of contracts with which you are already familiar. The section will then describe some typical issues designers face involving code provisions.

As you progress in your knowledge about business concepts, such as contracts, it may help if you first ask about the subject matter of any contract. Think about whether the contract is for a service, such as your interior design services; or involves real property, such as a home; or involves a sale (a form of transfer of ownership of tangible items). In the first instances involving interior design services or real estate property, provisions and requirements you have learned as being part of the common law, or case law, of contracts will usually apply. Alternatively, if you determine the subject matter of a contract relates to the sale of tangible goods, provisions of the Uniform Commercial Code will usually apply. Despite this theoretical split in laws governing contracts, many of the provisions of the Uniform Commercial Code, especially those that describe how valid, enforceable contracts may be formed, are generally very similar. For example, under both contract common law and the Uniform Commercial Code, the three elements of offer, acceptance, and consideration are required in order for two or more parties to form an enforceable contract. However, one intention behind the passage of the Uniform Commercial Code was to facilitate commercial transactions. Might such common law concepts as the mirror image rule in which the terms of the acceptance must mirror or track the terms of the offer (or else be considered a counteroffer), hinder a sale of goods, especially when such things as the date the item is expected to be shipped or delivered is not known beforehand? In commercial sales, including those that involve goods that interior designers sell, a purchase order submitted by a buyer for goods (i.e., the offer), is commonly followed by an acknowledgment (i.e, the acceptance) sent to the buyer from the seller. Often, many but not all the terms found in the acknowledgement are the same as in the original order. However, some terms may not be the same or, as with the date for delivery issue noted above, may have been omitted entirely. Under the early established common law, had the subject matter of the contract been for a service, its provisions would likely not be enforced by a court of law. On the other hand, under the Uniform Commercial Code, a valid, enforceable contract may well be found to have been created by a court of law should the seller make "a definite and seasonable (i.e., timely)" acceptance of the terms of the original offer and neither the buyer nor the seller imposes any condition or further requirement on the other (UCC 2-207). In short, the code modifies the more stringent mirror requirement found in contract case law.

Typical sales contracts usually address such issues as the description of the goods being ordered, their price, the terms of delivery and payment, and, most important for Uniform Commercial Code purposes, the quantity of items that is the subject matter of the contract. In very general terms, inclusion or exclusion of all but one of these terms is not detrimental to the finding of an enforceable sale of tangible items; what is important is the intention of the parties involved. If it appears to a court that the parties to the contract for goods intended to enter into such a contract, then that intention alone would substantiate such a finding (UCC 2-204). Furthermore, the code provides what are referred to as *gap filler* provisions to address situations when terms of a contract, such as price, payment, and delivery terms are omitted.

There is one important exception to this rule found in the code. Again, in very broad terms, should a purported sales contract not contain a sufficient number of terms for a court to make a determination of the parties' intent to enter into an agreement of any kind, or if the quantity or amount of items involved is not clearly identifiable, then the presence of a contract is not likely to be found. With respect to the latter requirement, remember that a court of law hearing a sales contract dispute usually is called upon to assess a monetary award, referred to as damages, for a party found injured by the actions of the other. Without a quantity indicated, it might be impossible for the court to make such an award. In short, the lack of a stated quantity term in contracts involving the sale of goods should raise your awareness of a possible problem.

You will come to learn more about issues related to how sales concepts relate to such concepts as transfer of ownership in chapter 12. What, however, are some basic sales contract issues of which an interior designer should be aware? The first such issue identified here concerns whether contracts for the sale of goods are required to be in writing in order to for their provisions to be enforced. As you have seen already, some contracts must be in writing in order for them to be enforced by the courts. Under the terms of the Uniform Commercial Code, contracts for the sale of goods over the amount of $500 must be in writing to be enforced as well (UCC 2-201 (1)), although there are several exceptions to this rule.

Among these exceptions is one relating to oral communications between two parties, classified under code language as *merchants* (UCC 2-201). Might interior designers be considered merchants? Consider the following language: "'merchant' means a person who deals in goods of the kind or otherwise by his occupation—holds himself out as having knowledge or skill peculiar to the practices or goods involved in the transaction" (UCC 2-104). Consider further an oral agreement between a designer and a supplier who regularly provides merchandise to the designer. If a court finds both designer and supplier are merchants within the definition of the code, then an oral contract between the two might be further found valid in the event one of those parties sent the other a written confirmation of the agreement and the party receiving such a confirmation failed to object to those terms within ten days of its receipt (UCC 2-201(b)).

In general, instead of relying on exceptions of rules, the better course of action for interior designers is to make sure a written contract exists between both between the designer and the client as well as between the designer and any seller or vendor with whom they choose to supply goods. By doing so, designers usually then have the ability through the common law of contracts to initiate legal action to obtain payment from a client who refuses to pay for goods ordered on their behalf. Similarly, designers also have legal recourse through application of the Uniform Commercial Code against vendors who fail to provide specified goods ordered by the designer.

A common problem confronting designers concerns the actual receipt of goods for which the designer contracted. In many instances, the merchandise received is not the merchandise ordered. For example, one type of fabric received is not of the type ordered by the interior designer; perhaps the one received is of a different quality or has different characteristics. Such goods are considered under the code to be *nonconforming* with what was ordered. What should a designer do in such a case? The code provides buyers with a specific right to inspect goods that are delivered before accepting or rejecting them (UCC 2-513). Furthermore, in the event those goods are found to not be in compliance with what was agreed upon, the buyer may then reject all or any part of the nonconforming order received (UCC 2-601). To avoid having to pay for any nonconforming items, the designer must then notify the seller of the nonconformity and of their rejection of them. This overview has provided you with some of the differences between common law contract principles and provisions of the code as well as explored two common ways in which the Uniform Commercial Code can impact interior designers and their practices.

Tort laws that relate to the idea of *negligence* seek to address those instances where a legally described standard, known as a *duty*, was not met by one who had an obligation to fulfill such a requirement. In general, tort law imposes a duty on professionals, including interior designers, to act like other reasonable and prudent professionals in that same line of work. Imagine, if you will, a situation in which an interior designer disregarded basic principles of design such as those learned in school relating to space planning and color usage. As a result, the finished project was not merely unusable according to the client's specifications, but also not in reasonable conformity to any objective standards prevailing among other interior designers.

What actions brought by the client, or *plaintiff*, could a designer anticipate as a result of producing such work? Under the tort of negligence, an aggrieved client might assert that the designer, or *defendant*, first had a duty to that client to complete the project not so much according to the client's specifications, but, more specifically, according to the standard of care of a designer acting in a reasonable and prudent manner in that community, using practices and procedures common among other interior designers. In other words, if other designers would not have produced work of that kind, then for this designer to have done so would not be reasonable. The plaintiff would then usually assert—after establishing the existence of a duty to him or herself and the breach of contract or failure of the defendant designer to carry out that duty—that the failure to act in such a reasonable manner resulted in some type of *foreseeable harm* to him or herself. The breach of the duty owed to the client is, in legal terms, the **proximate cause** of the injury that was suffered. Plaintiffs might claim as harm that they incurred the actual, out-of-pocket expenses that they have spent on a project and, most likely, the estimated costs they would incur in order to be *made whole*, or in the same position they were prior to undertaking the designer's services. Usually, plaintiffs attempt to obtain other forms of damages for anguish, or mental distress, as a result of a designer's actions.

In those extreme instances where the actions of a professional were found by a court to have been grossly negligent, or so lacking in the use of any standard of care as to be considered shocking, a court may also decide that the defendant should pay *punitive damages*. Such damages might be awarded in cases where a defendant was found to have acted with practically no regard to a client's interests or even concern about completing the project in a reasonable manner. The policy behind these types of awards is to require payment of an amount in damages that sets an example and thus prevents future actions of this kind by other professionals.

It should be further noted that the concept of negligence does not arise merely because a client does not like a designer's final work product. The final results of a project may not be what the client expected, or hoped for, in which case the client and designer should attempt to find an acceptable resolution through additional negotiation. Standards of taste and beauty vary from person to person and thus are not easily defined even by a court of law. Rather, what courts usually consider in tort law would be whether the work actually carried out by the designer was done in a manner consistent with interior design industry standards as evidenced by the work standards of other designers in that area. Although the finished project, completed strictly in compliance with specifications, might be unacceptable to the particular taste of the client, that same project might not have been produced in a negligent manner if it was found to have been completed according to the professional standards prevailing among other interior designers in the community. Clients will look to a designer's specifications as a source to question the actions of a designer's work that is found unsatisfactory. Were, for example, the specifications appropriate for that type of project? Did the designer adequately inform the clients of any risks associated with those specifications? Did the designer comply with all applicable laws in carrying out the installation? Communication between designer and client is necessary to facilitate a project's successful completion. In the modern world of business, that communication now includes written documentation of virtually every aspect of a project, whether there is good news or bad news to report. Although it may be impossible to satisfy every whim of every client every time, the designer should make every effort to prevent misunderstandings about what exactly is being used and bought for the project and how exactly the client may be affected. A history of careful communication should be of assistance in documenting that the interior designer has conformed to the necessary standard of care.

A claim of negligence may be defended against in several ways. If, for example, a plaintiff knew about and agreed to take the risk involved in an action performed by the defendant, then a court might conclude that the plaintiff *assumed the risk* of the action. In such a finding, the plaintiff would be denied compensation for any injuries suffered. Many times, clients will not understand the practical implications of a design choice they insist be made. Paint and floor finishes that will not wear well, carpets intended for different levels of wear, a particular fixture that cost much more than the budget called for—are all common occurrences in the design world, where a designer may accommodate the client's wishes to satisfy that client. In such cases, however, designers would do well to document in writing that they informed their clients of the ramifications of the changes those clients insisted upon. Furthermore, designers should get their clients' written consent to any changes, noting that clients are aware of any risks associated with the change and expressly consent to the change. By doing so, designers take steps to effectively establish that their clients have assumed the risk of insisting that their own wishes be fulfilled.

Another defense to a claim that a designer acted negligently arises when defendants can prove that the plaintiffs were in some way negligent in their actions as well. This defense is known as **contributory negligence** and, in early law, resulted in a plaintiff receiving no damages if proven. This defense would have the effect of pitting designer against client to assert this claim. Assume an interior designer were sued on a negligence theory, and the plaintiff asserts that the designer's actions resulted in the delay of a project's completion and that such delays were the cause of damage to the client: For example, the client paid more to complete the project because of the designer's actions. To prevail on a contributory negligence defense, an interior designer would have to show that the clients themselves acted in some way that was negligent. Some examples of such negligence might be failure on the part of the client to review and approve work in a timely manner or make payment for that work. In early law, this defense—as with that of assumption of risk—if successful, resulted in complete exoneration of the defendant. Over time, however, most states have adopted **comparative fault** laws, which apportion percentages of fault as a means of calculating damages. Under these laws, the percentage of fault of each side would be determined, and damages, if any, awarded based on that determination.

In an effort to discourage negligence claims before they are brought, many businesspeople attempt to limit possible liability for perceived negligence by making oral or written statements claiming they take no, or only very limited, responsibility for their actions. Signs posted in parking garages stating that the garage owner is not responsible for damage to cars parked in that garage is a common example. Attempts to limit the liability of professionals, however, may take many sophisticated forms, such as written clauses to that effect in contracts. In general, attempts to limit possible damages accruing from the actions of a professional found to be negligent are not viewed favorably by courts, and the use of disclaimers and limits on liability may ultimately prove futile. Professionals are often seen as having better bargaining positions than their clients because of their education and experience, and thus more likely to offer agreements that are more favorable to themselves.

In addition to case-law negligence, there are other types of civil tort laws that arose with the idea of protecting the public. These more specific consumer protection laws came about within the last several decades through the passage of specific codes—groups of related laws—affecting those who make or sell merchandise or other consumer goods. Most states now have some form of consumer protection law designed to protect the general public by defining what standards must be followed when making or selling certain types of products or when making certain representations in the course of conducting business. A design professional should be aware of two of these laws, known in general as *product liability* laws and *deceptive trade practice* laws.

Product Liability Laws

At the urging of consumer action groups, state legislatures began passing these protectionist laws about 30 years ago. Instead of relying on the case law of negligence to help decide issues of liability, these governing bodies passed other civil laws, based on existing tort law, for determining when products and practices should be considered harmful to consumers. In addition to these statutes, many states adopted versions of the Uniform Commercial Code, which includes specific provisions that relate to warranties made about goods sold and applies in transactions to protect business merchants. Use of these laws is fairly widespread because of their relative ease of application compared to traditional tort law as well as the increased amounts of monetary damages these new laws provide. As a result, plaintiffs may now fairly easily receive monetary awards for amounts many times greater than previously available, and they can more easily recover their costs for having brought the action.

Product liability legislation seeks to protect consumers from those items that are deemed, according to the language in most statutes, to be defectively designed, manufactured, or marketed. Defectively designed products are considered to be inherently dangerous. Although, these products may well perform the task for which they were intended, some characteristic of the product makes it dangerous to use. Manufacturing defects occur when the item is made, while defects in marketing are considered to have occurred when the consumer is provided with improper instructions and warnings.

Product liability refers to the liability for damage of any party involved from the chain of manufacture to final selling of a product. Possible affected parties in this liability scheme include the maker of components used in the product, the entity assembling the product, and the wholesaler and store selling the product to the consumer. Interior designers, since they function as wholesalers selling the product as part of their services, would likely be included in a product liability action. If you break product liability laws it is considered to be a *strict liability* offense; finding a product to be defective triggers liability on the part of an individual or a company selling these products. As part of their product knowledge, designers should be aware of current legal news and technical information relating to the products they specify for use. The use of particular products should be avoided if any court, even one in a different jurisdiction, has determined under product liability law that a particular product is dangerous.

Licensing and product development can be one way in which a local interior designer may branch out to attract a wide, possibly international, audience. However, designers who take an active role in the creation and development of products should be aware that they and any manufacturer who employs them to design these items—or that designers employ to produce—may be liable for injuries sustained by a consumer, even if that consumer misuses the product in some way.

There is no effective way to completely design and produce a product that will never be linked to an injury. Rather, designers should make every effort to ensure that the products they specify are in accordance with the standards prevalent for all such products used in the industry. Their product knowledge should include awareness of the latest legal and technical developments in order to know which products to avoid. Furthermore, any contract between a manufacturer and designer should include language describing as completely as possible how the parties will defend themselves against any such lawsuit, knowing that both parties would likely be called as defendants in a product liability action. Interior designers who might be involved in product development should consult an attorney specifically about how their jurisdiction's product liability laws could be invoked.

Deceptive Trade Practices Laws

Is the item specified for use in a project a Hansen lamp? Do the textiles selected have the characteristics a designer claims? Is the chair really an antique or merely a good reproduction? The representations designers make, either orally or in writing, about a particular object or item they specify may be the deciding factor in clients' decisions to authorize an item's purchase or use. In the case of antiques, rare decorative objects, and works of art, the representations made about an object may be as alluring as an item itself. Preventing false or misleading statements made by any seller of goods, including but certainly not limited to art or antiques, is the intent behind **deceptive trade practices** legislation. Many states have adopted some form of these laws, which encompass a wide variety of business practices. In essence, these laws seek to prohibit the dissemination of statements that are found to be false concerning such matters as the quality or other characteristics of consumer goods offered or sold; false representations concerning the quality of a competitor's goods; or false reasons for sale prices. The determination that a businessperson has engaged in deceptive trade practices carries with it in many states large monetary damage penalties.

Common sense might conclude that there should be some liability on the part of a designer who intends to deceive clients by making false statements. However, what should happen in cases where a designer unwittingly passes on a source's representations of goods that later are proven by the client to have been false? Most designers, as a practice, specify items based on the representations of their sources. The designer in such a case may have clearly made a false statement without the intent to deceive. Many states now have in place statutes listing a set of proscribed representations, including representations that claim a product has certain qualities or characteristics it, in fact, does not have. In some instances, the designer's reliance on the source's representation may limit the designer's liability if such reliance was found to have been reasonable according to that jurisdiction's law. For example, the court may find it to have been reasonable for a designer to have relied on the written statements provided by the vendor, such as certificates of authenticity. This might occur when the designer had no reason to question the veracity of the representation made by the vendor that the designer then passed on. Designers should aim to work with vendors who have a reputation for making honest, well-founded representations; but there is no guarantee for preventing claims of this nature.

Puffing, or making enticing statements about goods, is a long-standing practice among those who sell products. As such, puffing is not illegal. However, legal counsel should be sought for guidance on cases where enticing language might become misleading, and thus become a a prohibited representation to a consumer. The interplay of puffing and deceptive trade practices is found in the following example. Suppose a designer claims that "this is the most luxurious and comfortable Baker sofa ever made!" when the sofa was actually stuffed with cheap sawdust and made by a company other than Baker. The terms *luxurious* and *comfortable* may reflect the designer's personal opinion, but are used to puff the sofa. However, the fact that the sofa was not actually made by the Baker company, as claimed by the designer, could give rise to a possible claim of deceptive trade practices.

UNDERSTANDING COMMON LEGAL CONCEPTS IN BUSINESS

Federal laws may seem far removed from the practice of interior design. However, such laws are applicable to and enforceable in all of the United States. Usually, compliance with federal laws is monitored and enforced by agencies that, like the federal laws, came about by congressional action. The Federal Trade Commission and the Internal Revenue Service are two of the many examples of overseeing and enforcement agencies known to businesspeople. In addition, federal laws may be fairly broad in their scope in the sense that they address policy concerns affecting the entire nation. It should be noted that under the U.S. system of government, individual states may pass laws similar or related to those passed by Congress; however, those laws usually more narrowly address particular concerns of the specific state that enacts them. Over a century ago, for example, the U.S. Congress became concerned about the practices of some large companies that were believed to have the effect of limiting or even excluding other companies from operating in areas throughout the United States. Lawmakers in the individual states then addressed the specific concerns of their own citizens by passing laws that sought to prevent exclusionary business practices in their own states.

The Sherman Antitrust Act

Several federal laws are important to interior designers. The **Sherman Antitrust Act** of 1890 and related pieces of legislation, such as the Clayton Act of 1914, sought to curb the exercise of excessive commercial power that large companies could exercise over smaller, less powerful business entities. Monopolies sought to exercise this control in two major ways—through what were called *agreements in restraint of trade* and price fixing. For more than 100 years, the Sherman Antitrust Act and the many laws stemming from it have been still remain present, as are the questionable business practices the Sherman Act attempted to prevent. These **antitrust laws**, as they are collectively known, are overseen at the federal level by the **Federal Trade Commission (FTC)**, a regulatory agency created in 1914 with the power to investigate and prosecute possible violation of these and other laws related to antitrust.

To understand the central tenets of the Sherman Act, suppose two or more companies agreed to operate only in certain geographic locations. In particular, these entities agreed not to operate in areas where any other parties to that same agreement operated. The reason, or intent, behind the companies' agreement was that they did not want to compete with each other for customers. With less competition from other businesses, those companies already established in a given area could reap enormous economic benefits. Early legislators, particularly Senator John Sherman, for whom the act is named, sought to prohibit what they saw as an alarming increase in these types of arrangements. Thus, the purpose behind passage of the Sherman Antitrust Act was to prevent these unfairly collusive, or hidden, ways in which companies could sometimes operate in an effort to make money. As a practical matter, however, this law also benefited consumers, for under these forms of collusion they had fewer choices of companies in their area with which they could do business.

One other concern of the Sherman Antitrust Act was prevention of a practice known as price fixing. At the time of the original act, some manufacturers were requiring to sell the goods they made at their set price, a *fixed* price, to every consumer who wished to buy that product. The wholesaler, or middleman, under this scheme, had no ability to change the price at which the item could be sold. The Sherman Antitrust Act prohibited this practice. As a result, merchants may now only suggest a retail price at which their goods may be sold by middlemen; an interior designer, or merchant, may ignore the manufacturer's suggestion when setting final retail prices.

Applying the Sherman Antitrust Act to the practice of interior design produces an interesting question for students and practitioners alike. Suppose a group of designers began talking among themselves about the fees and commissions they charged their respective clients, and, specifically, how there should be a standard, set percentage, or at least a minimum dollar amount, clients in that area should be charged for interior design services. Might such discussions give rise to a Sherman Antitrust Act complaint? Or at least lead an outside designer who is trying to establish a business in that area to infer an agreement in restraint of trade might be in effect among design practitioners who are seeking to keep others out? To answer this question, consider a recent example from the art world concerning the actions of two famous New York auction houses, Christie's and Sotheby's. In that case, it was claimed and proved in federal court that an agreement existed between the principle directors of the two auction houses to set nonnegotiable commission rates that potential clients of the firms would be charged. By agreeing that sellers of art objects would be subject to substantially the same, unalterable commission rates at either of the two auction houses, neither house, according to the scheme, would gain an advantage over the other; furthermore, other auction houses would have difficulty establishing a presence in the lucrative but fairly small world of fine-art auctioning. Even more than 100 years later, the Sherman Antitrust Act is still found to apply to modern business practices.

The Robinson-Patman Act

Another federal law that was based on the Sherman Antitrust Act is the **Robinson-Patman Act**, passed in 1936. Of importance to interior designers is a provision of that act that prohibits price discrimination practices among merchants. Simply put, a merchant, such as a manufacturer, must charge another merchant, such as a store or even an individual interior designer selling goods to the public, the same price for a specific item that they charge any other merchant for that same product. A manufacturer, in other words, cannot favor merchants and charge beneficial prices to one that would result in less favored merchants being disadvantaged. There is, however, an important exception to this rule concerning the business practices of a purchasing merchant. Where a purchasing merchant, or even an individual interior designer, has a documented history of buying or handling such a large quantity of the manufacturer's goods in the course of doing business that there exists an economic incentive to sell goods to the interior designer at a discount—passing the savings on, in other words—a violation of the Robinson-Patman Act might not be found. It should be noted that this law does not apply to sales between merchants and consumers. Merchants, such as stores or interior designers, may charge consumers who will personally use the items whatever they wish for the same goods. It is the consumer's choice to decide whether to pay the amount asked for or shop around for a better price available at another shop or through another designer.

It could be argued that almost all federal laws might in some way apply to any business, even the practice of interior design. The Sherman Antitrust Act and the Robinson-Patman Act are two antitrust laws of particular relevance to designers, the former especially applicable in light of recent discoveries about the collusive pricing practices of internationally known auction houses. There are, of course, other federal laws that might be applied to the interior design profession, and designers should make an effort to know the federal laws applicable to their specific areas of practice. A designer who specializes in sourcing products from other countries, for example, would do well to understand federal laws related to importation of goods into the United States. Importing of textiles from outside the United States is one application: Designers must be aware of the many federal laws that relate to tariffs and quotas placed on fiber goods or risk violation of those laws and the resulting penalties. Additionally, discussion in chapter 7 will focus on federal laws that relate to copyrights and the legal protection afforded intellectual property.

The Application of Civil Laws

Although interior designers may not face criminal-law issues in their practice, other laws, known generally as *civil laws*, may very well be applicable. Agency and contract laws are examples of civil laws that have been discussed earlier in this chapter. A basic distinction between civil and criminal law concerns who is involved in the various actions. Criminal laws are brought by a governmental body, while civil actions are brought by specific individuals or groups of individuals—for example, a company or other business enterprise. Since practicing interior designers work with these individuals or groups, they need to have a thorough understanding of several civil laws that may affect their practice.

Essentially, a designer is responsible for creating an interior design concept and bringing it to fruition according to the specifications of the client and under the terms agreed upon by both designer and client. Usually these specifications are (or certainly should be) spelled out in a contract or letter of agreement between the two. Moreover, these written agreements should also spell out what each party should do in the event the completed, or even unfinished, job fails to conform to what designer and client agreed; this was discussed with regard to the concept of contract *damages*. There are, however, other civil laws that might apply in instances where the work undertaken by a designer fails to conform to some standard deemed to be acceptable.

TROUBLESHOOTING STRATEGIES

It is important for you to keep abreast of legal developments arising from and affecting business practices. This can be done fairly easily by reading local newspapers and most major business periodicals, such as *The Wall Street Journal* regularly; or by checking various Internet news sites, such as CNN, or others that carry legal news and analyses of current business events and practices. Industry-specific resources—such as ASID publications—also routinely provide updates about legal developments affecting design professionals.

Just as no do-it-yourself book can substitute a trained interior designer's professional advice, neither can a single text substitute an attorney's counsel regarding legal matters. It can only make you aware of general legal issues and better prepare you for communicating with legal professionals. Creativity is your stock in trade, but so, too, is your professionalism. While only lawyers have the ability to keep up with the latest legal developments affecting the business community, design practitioners should be aware of the legal issues presented in this text as they strive to provide competent design services for their clients. Doing so not only enhances designers' professional abilities, but also better enables them to assist legal advisers should a controversy develop.

Interior designers must have a basic awareness of the legal constraints imposed on their industry by federal, state, and local governments as well as a knowledge of professional standards. Furthermore, designers should keep abreast of changes in the law and legal current events affecting other industries to foresee possible future problems facing the interior design profession. For example, with regard to recent successful lawsuits related to defective automobile tires, interior designers should be aware of possible liability for failure to recognize safety hazards not only in finished products specified for a project, but also for failure to identify possible hazards in components of those products. Do you know whether both the fabric *and* the upholstery filling in specified seating items meet fire-safety standards?

TORT LAW AND THE PRACTICE OF INTERIOR DESIGN

Tort law is similar to criminal law in the types of protection it offers. *Intentional torts*, for example, recognize that society should provide redress to those individuals, not government entities, who have personally suffered the effects of some type of offensive action that a defendant was found by that court to have consciously wanted to occur. Actions such as hitting another person, or making another person afraid of being hit, taking another's property, or writing and speaking false statements that ultimately were found to have injured another person's reputation are examples of intentional torts. Several of these types of torts occur frequently in business.

False statements, either written or spoken—which are found to have injured another person's reputation and as a result of which the plaintiff is found to have suffered some form of damage—form the basis of the intentional tort of *defamation*. This tort is further classified according to whether such statements were written (**libel**) or spoken (**slander**). Proving the falsity of such statements is one of the requirements a plaintiff to such an action must meet to succeed with a defamation lawsuit. This requirement is frequently referred to as the plaintiff's burden of proof and is a characteristic of defamation laws in the United States. That plaintiff must also prove such false statements resulted in some damage to their reputation. Usually, a plaintiff would need to show a loss of business as a result of the false statements. A defendant to such an action, on the other hand, will usually prevail if the judge or jury determines the defendant spoke the truth about the plaintiff. Proving all the necessary elements to prevail in a defamation action can be difficult for a plaintiff, especially establishing that the statement in question, and only that statement, adversely affected the plaintiff. Defamation laws are complex, and further counsel would be necessary if faced with such an issue; however, as a practical matter, all businesspeople, including interior designers, should be aware that their respective working environments are fairly small, and that much possibility exists for "word to spread." Clients love gossip as much as anyone else, especially if they sense tension between designers and wish to obtain favorable fees for design work. As a result, statements about other designers and their work should be kept to a minimum to prevent even a misunderstanding about what was said.

Another intentional-tort issue that may arise in a creative enterprise is *conversion*. For example, what redress is available to a fabric company when a loaned sample book is returned with a (usually very expensive) swatch missing? Conversion torts provide redress when a defendant exercises dominion and control over the property of another so as to deprive its owner of its use for some period of time, even permanently. In such a case, the defendant owes the plaintiff for that property's value. In this instance, the swatch snatcher might face tortuous liability for his or her actions. Many criminal codes provide laws of a similar nature, known as **criminal conversion laws**, so that governmental entities may bring these actions on behalf of individuals. Conversion is similar to a related tort known as **trespass to property**, or **trespass to chattel**, as it was referred to in common law; the difference between the torts concerns the extent to which the taking of property has occurred. Suppose, for example, that an interior designer damaged, but did not destroy, an object owned by the client in the course of a project. That damage might give rise to a trespass-to-property claim, since the designer's actions interfered with the owner's exclusive enjoyment of that object. Of course, if the designer were unfortunate enough to destroy the object, then a claim for conversion might ensue.

In addition to security concerns involved in the taking of photographs, what redress might a client have against an interior designer who mistakenly thought the client wouldn't mind and, without the client's permission, took and distributed photographs of a completed project? Tort law developed a cause of action for instances such as these in which individuals believe that their personal privacy has been invaded or infringed upon. Extending this theory of *invasion of privacy* to other areas of interior design, care should be taken to keep confidentiality and prevent the dissemination of all information relating to a client, even a potential client. In this context, confidentiality rules prohibit the introduction of information during a judicial controversy when that information is obtained from certain sources. For example, juries usually will not be permitted to hear testimony from a doctor, lawyer, priest, or spouses about what was said by or to a party to the dispute while under the care of that professional or member of the clergy or during the course of a marriage. Such conversations are deemed **privileged** under federal and state rules that concern the kinds of evidence that may be used in court. No such privilege, however, exists that prohibit the introduction of any conversation that occurred between interior designers and their clients, unless, of course, there is another applicable privilege. Nothing, short of a court order—usually referred to as a *subpoena*—requires designers to tell what was said between them and their clients while working on a project. However, in instances in which a husband-and-wife client divorces during the course of the project, there exists no privilege prohibiting testimony from the designer as part of the divorce proceedings. The designer may have no choice but to explain to the court how marital financial assets were spent, or risk being censured by the court.

Privileges concern the type of evidence used in courts of law; however, interior designers should be aware of several other torts, or civil wrongs, that may arise in the course of their practices. Two torts relating to land are also of concern to designers. *Trespass to land* occurs when an individual intentionally or negligently enters onto the property of another without the permission of the landowner or someone with a right to control that land. As a practical matter, a designer should obtain written permission from all necessary parties who control access to the premises to complete an installation. Failure to do so may result in at least an oral claim that the premises are private property, not to be trespassed upon, and denying further access. Permission from a client given to a designer to be in an apartment or office space may not persuade an attentive building superintendent or security guard that a designer or crew should be allowed beyond the building lobby. Inevitably, damage to property that occurs due to trespass—for example, broken windows or doors or trampled landscaping—may result in a lawsuit seeking compensation for those damages.

Project installations can be lengthy, inconvenient events for everyone. The noise, dust, bright lights, and larger numbers of people and cars in an area sometimes occasioned by project work may interfere with others' quiet enjoyment of their own nearby property. The tort of *nuisance* addresses the right on the part of landowners and land occupiers to not have that enjoyment infringed upon or the value of their property diminished because of others' actions. Successful plaintiffs may be awarded injunctions prohibiting or seriously curtailing further work (whether the project is completed or not) as well as money damages for any diminution in property value found to have occurred. Careful project planning is a necessity; and any restrictions on local or building-location work time and manner should be thoroughly understood and conveyed to all parties involved in the project to avoid any possible nuisance claims. Granted, plaintiffs in these instances must show they were damaged in some way by these actions, or prove that their property diminished in value as a result, both of which can be difficult to prove. Nevertheless, careful project planning is necessary to prevent as much as possible inconveniencing surrounding tenants to the extent that inconvenience rises to tort level.

STATE CRIMINAL LAWS AND THE INTERIOR DESIGN PROFESSION

Most people are familiar with the popular media's treatment of law and the legal process. Many television shows and films feature plots based on dramatized or fictionalized accounts of crime stories. While entertaining, these stories focus mostly on those legal interactions, usually referred to under the category of **criminal law**, where a state or other governmental body seeks to protect the interest of the public from the actions of those who are found to have acted with either an actual or inferred intent to harm others. Although mentioned here under state law for the sake of clarity, be aware, too, that the federal government can also pass criminal laws.

Individuals do not bring criminal actions against one another. In criminal law, an individual files a complaint with law enforcement officials, who then act on the basis of that complaint. Criminal laws are usually found in *codes*, which are compilations of laws grouped and defined according to some system of classification—type of offense, in the case of criminal codes. These, or related codes, also include punishment provisions for violations. Courts or juries apply the provisions of these criminal codes to specific allegations of fact about an individual or group—for example, the actions of a corporation—brought before them by a prosecutor seeking enforcement on behalf of the state. After both prosecution and the accused have an opportunity to be heard and questioned, a decision or verdict is reached and judgment rendered by the court. Theft-of-property crimes, such as robbery, burglary, embezzlement, and the many forms of criminal assault on persons are common examples of crimes, as are more complicated actions such as criminal fraud and conspiracy. Any professional, including an interior designer, who meets unknown members of the public on a daily basis, should learn how to maintain his or her personal safety as well as the safety of the premises where the designer does business.

Identity Theft

Crime is an unfortunate aspect of life made even more unfortunate and detrimental as it grows increasingly sophisticated with technology. In your professional practice, or in your own daily life, think of how often you leave information about yourself with persons about whom you know very little or nothing at all. In particular, think about what information could be gleaned about you just from someone having access to your Social Security number, credit-card numbers, and checking-account information. Because they purchase large numbers of items with credit cards and checks, designers should take special care to be aware of the possibility of *identity theft*. This crime is a concern of both state and federal law, although it is related to the old common-law crime of fraud, or intentionally using a false identity—yours—to deprive another of his or her property. The crime is made more pervasive then single acts of fraud by the power electronic technologies now have on virtually all aspects of life. Information about you can be transmitted around the world in seconds. Prevention of this crime may be difficult or impossible according to crime experts because many of its aspects, including the identity and location of perpetrators, are still the subject of worldwide criminal investigations. Regular and attentive review of credit-card charges, personal and business credit reports, and bank statements should at least assist in mitigating identity-theft damages should they occur.

Theft by Check

A criminal-law issue involving the use of bank checks should also be mentioned here. Many jurisdictions have passed law and actively enforce against an offense known as **theft by check**. This offense involves the passing of a bank draft, for which there are inadequate funds to satisfy the face amount of the check, with the intent to deprive another of property. In order to avoid possible prosecution on theft-by-check charges, businesspeople should make sure that there are adequate funds available in all of their checking accounts, so that no intent to steal using checks may be inferred by law-enforcement officials. Many banks offer overdraft protection with their checking-account plans, and such protections should be considered by active interior designers who purchase frequently using bank checks.

Security and Safety Issues

Many designers will not come in contact with criminal-law issues, particularly not of the kind depicted so dramatically in the media. In practice, therefore, a designer may need to view crime preventively. That is, designers should ask how best to protect themselves, their clients, and the client's possessions from crime during and after completion of a project. For nonresidential interior designers, security and safety requirements are probably more explicit in their responses to a potential client's request for project proposals (RFPs). These designers must consider security measures as part of their work in obtaining the commission. However, even residential interior designers should be attuned to security issues involved in their work. To that end, it may be necessary and professionally appropriate to employ the services of a security consultant to advise your residential clients, especially very affluent or prominent ones, about safety concerns. Your goal and professional obligation should be to create design solutions that are both aesthetically pleasing and security conscious. For example, if necessary, how can security gates and cameras be incorporated into a design plan in an acceptable manner and within set budget constraints?

The security concerns of clients are important for interior designers in a way that may not be readily apparent. Many clients are reluctant to allow photographs of the finished project for fear of attracting thieves or, at the very least, unwarranted attention from strangers. This concern can occur although the client's name may not be mentioned in the publication featuring the project. Although understandable, this prohibition deprives interior designers of perhaps the most valuable marketing tool for their services: visual representations of the work they are capable of producing. As a practical matter, therefore, negotiations on whether the final project may be photographed for promotional purposes should be addressed at the early stages of project planning. At a minimum, the designer should negotiate for a release from the client allowing the designer to show pictures of the completed project only to other potential and/or actual clients. Of course, a designer should make no representation, particularly as an inducement for photographic publication, that nothing will happen to the client or their property by allowing publication of photographs. Releases for photographs and related intellectual property concerns are further addressed in chapter 7.

Finally, as a risk-management measure, an interior designer should seek to work only with contractors who carry adequate indemnity insurance against losses attributed to the actions of their employees and of their subcontractors. Many such contractors use the term *bonded*, meaning *insured* to convey that they have such coverage; but designers should inquire further about what specifically those contractors are insured against before engaging their services.

WHERE DISPUTES CAN BE RESOLVED

The chief difference between criminal and civil law concerns the entity bringing the complaint to the court's attention. As noted, enforcement of criminal laws is usually sought by a governmental body or administrative organization given power to enforce laws. The Internal Revenue Service (IRS) is one example of the latter.

In contrast, most civil actions, including those of negligence or intentional torts, are brought by individuals or groups on their own behalf. Civil and criminal liability should not be thought of as mutually exclusive remedies, however. A plaintiff may bring a civil action against a defendant; and a governmental body, acting on behalf of the community in which the act occurred, may bring a criminal action arising from the same situation that formed the basis of the civil action. Thus, both civil and criminal liability may occur for the same proscribed act.

As the interior design profession develops, so, too, will administrative remedies of self-regulation. Design practitioners should be aware that, in addition to filing a possible civil and even criminal cause of action against them, a client who thinks that the work performed was substandard may also file a complaint against a designer to the attention of the interior design accrediting body. Practitioners should be aware that a plaintiff's successful legal claim may form the basis for revoking a professional license. Many times, complaints will result in an investigation of the named designer's practices and, later, a hearing among administrative decision makers that may result in professional censure.

It should also be noted that many aggrieved clients may also register a complaint against a designer with the local Better Business Bureau. By doing so, that a complaint will remain on file as a public record for others in the community to see. If deemed serious enough, such agencies may instigate their own investigations of alleged unfair business practices. Finally, any businessperson should not underestimate the power of a client's word-of-mouth recommendation or condemnation. The censure of an influential client can be devastating to the reputation of any businessperson, and may seriously hamper that professional's ability to develop further business in the community.

Laws frequently determine whether work in any endeavor—including creative work—is ultimately deemed acceptable or not. For example, an interior designer might be required to remove, or substantially rectify, what would have been an otherwise aesthetically and functionally acceptable installation because the completed project failed to conform to requirements dictated by certain laws, such as local building codes or city ordinances.

Interior design practitioners are gaining increasing stature as professionals. Many states now formally recognize the interior design profession and its practitioners through licensing and certification processes. Greater industry recognition by state governments will undoubtedly come to mean greater accountability to consumers for the actions of interior designers as well as greater educational supervision from state-controlled accreditation agencies. Whether your area of specialization is residential or commercial interior design, your clients will look to you to be up-to-date on laws that affect your industry. A greater understanding of laws related to the interior design profession undoubtedly will be required as a result of this expansion.

REFERENCES

Alderman, Richard M. 2000. *Texas Commercial and Consumer Law, Annotated.* Texas: Imprimatur Press.

American Bar Association. 2000. *The American Bar Association Legal Guide for Small Business: Everything a Small-Business Person Must Know, from Start-Up to Employment Laws to Financing.* New York: Crown Publishing Group.

Allison, John, and Robert Prentice. 2001. *Business Law: Text and Cases in the Legal Environment.* 3rd ed. New York: Thompson Learning.

Berger, C. Jaye. 1994. *Interior Design Law and Business Practices.* New York: John Wiley & Sons.

Coleman, Cindy, ed. 2002. *Interior Design Handbook of Professional Practice.* New York: Mc-Graw Hill.

Dewalt, Suzanne. 1999. *How to Start a Home-Based Interior Design Business.* 2nd ed. New York: Globe Pequot Press.

Garner, Bryan A. and Campbell, Henry, eds. 1999. *Black's Law Dictionary.* Missouri: West Publishing.

Goleman, Daniel, ed. 2002. *Business: The Ultimate Resource.* London: Persus Publishing.

Jentz, Gaylord A. et al. eds. 2000. *West's Business Law: Text and Cases—Legal, Ethical, Regulatory, International and E-Commerce Environment, 8th Printing.* Missouri: West Publishing.

Siegel, Harry, and Alan Siegel. 1982. *A Guide to Business Practices and Principles for Interior Designers.* New rev. ed. New York: Watson-Guptill.

STRATEGIES-IN-ACTION PROJECT:

STRATEGIC PLANNING PROJECT:
LEGAL ISSUES FOR YOUR FUTURE BUSINESS

Virtually all business activities are controlled by laws and the operation of the legal system, and interior design is no exception. In this portion of your business plan, you will devote several paragraphs to a description of the laws that you believe will have the greatest affect on your interior design business. Before you begin this project, review previous strategic planning projects in which you identified the focus and attributes of your venture. What are you going to do as a designer: concentrate on residential work or focus on product development? Each practice specialty has its own unique legal concerns. In this project, tell other business decision makers who are reviewing your plan what you believe those concerns to be.

To help you do so, consider the basic objectives of this chapter listed on page 121. Describe how your ideal interior design business will or will not be affected by the following:

- Practicing interior design within legally prescribed bounds
- Participating in an organized interior design business
- Working on behalf of clients
- Entering into legally-enforceable agreements
- Planning accessible spaces for safe, lawful use
- Specifying appropriate fixtures, furnishings, and equipment (FF&E) for use
- Purchasing products for resale to clients
- Having a basic understanding of common legal concepts

RESIDENTIAL INTERIOR DESIGN PROJECT SIMULATION

Our friend Lee has let us read about what's been going on in the Abernathy project. Here are two diary entries for you to consider.

Lee's Diary

*Guess what? There is this new group of designers in town called the Society of Furniture Arts and Sciences (SOFAS, no less)! I was invited to join because the owner of Imagination Unlimited has told everyone I got the big Abernathy project. This **SOFAS** group requires all its members to choose certain areas of town to work in and never, ever to compete directly against other members in their areas. If that weren't enough, we all have to agree to never charge a client less than a certain dollar amount. They say all this is necessary to keep* *the prestige level of designers high, but the president told me, confidentially, the organization is really trying to prevent "cheap" designers from getting started in town. "Stealing our clients right out from under us," she said. She keeps calling me, asking me to join the group. I keep putting her off. I'll think of something. It just sounds really prestigious, but also like a lot of hassle . . .*

I had a problem today. . . . a fabric order arrived at the store for the Abernathy project, and it was all wrong. I mean, what were they thinking? They didn't send me anything that I specified, so they sent something they thought was "close." I thought it was what I ordered, but the hang-tag indicated a different fiber content from what I specified, and, as a result, the stuff was too flimsy to use for upholstery; it would shred in days with all those kids jumping up and down on it. The delivery guy told me to just sign for it. Thank goodness I looked first and said, "No way." The owner of Imagination Unlimited said to just go ahead and sign for it and accept the order. I didn't want to take the stuff if it wasn't what I ordered. The invoice said something about the fabric being substituted satisfactorily completing my order, but it wasn't. I called the company rep, and he said he would see what could be done. But I couldn't use it, and the project may fall behind as I wait for the right fabric—the one I specified and the client agreed to!

Here is a list of Residential Interior Design Project Simulation questions that correspond to the project above.

- ◆ After reading about the purpose of SOFAS group, what concerns might you address to Lee about joining such a group?
- ◆ To what specific body of laws would you refer to substantiate the concerns you raised?
- ◆ What specific body of laws covers aspects relating to the sale of goods in almost all states?
- ◆ Was the young designer correct in her actions of checking the order of fabric when it was delivered to the store before she decided to accept it?
- ◆ Using the terms found in the body of laws you noted above, how would you describe the goods the designer received compared to those she specified and ordered?
- ◆ If you find the designer was correct in her actions with regard to the fabric she received, what steps would you advise she take next to prevent having to pay for something she did not order?

CONTRACT INTERIOR DESIGN CASE STUDY: THE CASE OF THE RELUCTANT SWIMMER

After years of complaints and dwindling membership, the board of directors of the Downtown YMCA approved funds to reinvigorate the facility, particularly its 40-year-old swimming pool area. To begin the process, they circulated an RFP, or Request for Proposals, to attract local interior designers. The design firm of Lauren Mitchell Ltd., under the direction of Ms. Mitchell, was soon chosen, based on her estimate of the amount of money required to execute interior plans for the new pool pavilion. Her estimates were astonishingly lower than those submitted by comparable design firms. However, her reputation in the community instilled confidence in her abilities, so much so that the chairman of the selection committee simply wrote "accepted" across the face of the firm's response and faxed it to her.

Thrilled with the new commission—although several details remained to be resolved, such as the full extent of Ms. Mitchell's participation—she began work on the project. Her initial plans envisioned first removing a series of louvered glass windows, usually left open, affording passers-by a view of the almost naked swimmers. Ms. Mitchell declared to the board in her design presentation that such windows were hideous and, in her professional opinion, that they served no purpose. To "break the visual monotony," as Ms. Mitchell termed it, caused by the installation of gray-colored decking material, she specified random placement of colorful glazed ceramic tiles across its surface. To coordinate the effect, she further suggested placement of a tile border in matching colors around the perimeter of the pool. A city building-code provision required multiple exits from the pool area; and, using her recollection of how she solved this problem when working on a project in another city, Ms. Mitchell placed two sets of doors right next to each other, at the far side of the deepest end of the pool. "This way," she said, "we 'meet code' and don't have to pay to have a separate door framed along the side walls."

On the day of city inspection, the final step before the club would be granted the permit necessary to operate the pool, a municipal inspector reviewing the facility took umbrage with Ms. Mitchell's recollection of the city's building code. Citing the explicit provision enacted by the town council related to public recreational facilities there, the inspector refused to grant the required permit until two doors—separate and apart from each other, one at one end of the pool, the other along the already completed wall—were installed. Ms. Mitchell had to use funds allocated for other amenities to remedy the faulty door construction.

Soon after the pool opened, other problems appeared. Lifeguards complained of constant headaches due to "the chlorine smell." An alarming number of pool users suffered painful falls while walking across the pool deck. One afternoon, a lifeguard fainted, presumably from the chemical fumes, and fell from her perch onto the pool deck below, suffering a severe concussion. The paramedics sent to assist her had great difficulty navigating themselves and their equipment along the sides of the pool and were suddenly drenched, as was their stretcher, by splashes of water.

Later that same afternoon, another troublesome event occurred. John Kerbey, a former professional cyclist—now, after a terrible accident, a paraplegic confined to a motorized wheelchair—was pitched into the water when the wheels of his chair spun against the wet ceramic tile decoratively framing the pool edge. Embarrassed, but little harmed, the athlete warned the club's managing director to watch out for those tiles. The director informed Kerbey that the pool area had been made compliant with the requirements of the ADA provisions for public swimming pools, at least according to representations made by the designer, Lauren Mitchell.

Alarmed about these events, the club director determined that the tiles were unsafe for pool areas populated by wet, barefoot swimmers. He ordered black rubber mats installed throughout the pool area and charged their expense to Ms. Mitchell. The director further arranged for an air-quality assessment to determine why the pool's noxious fumes did not subside. These tests quickly showed that chlorine gas evaporated from the pool's water and remained trapped in the unventilated area. The director found on his computer Ms. Mitchell's e-mail message to the effect that there was no reason to install windows or a special ventilation system in the new space. Her message, sent many months earlier, simply said: "The height of the ceiling should be sufficient for ventilation." When informed of the apparently dangerous choices she had made, Ms. Mitchell responded by letter pointedly noting that the board had approved each and every choice she had specified. Representatives of the club and Ms. Mitchell are considering what legal actions to take. In the meantime, Ms. Mitchell wonders whether it matters if she had never incorporated her business.

Questions

Attorneys frequently call upon other professionals to assist them with the preparation of legal actions. Known as expert witnesses, these advisers are knowledgeable about the professional standards deemed reasonable for practitioners in their line of work. Expert witnesses also have an understanding of law and its application to their profession. You are to act as such an expert witness and advise the club's attorney about the actions Ms. Mitchell took in carrying out the pool commission. Your first task will be to identify as many legal issues as you are able from the case study, then suggest which areas of law would apply in resolving them. What do you suspect the outcome might be if a judge or jury were to hear these issues in a legal proceeding? Based on your observations, state your opinion.

CHAPTER FIVE

PLANNING YOUR BUSINESS FINANCES

It has been our experience that interior designers make the worst possible candidates for the bookkeeping profession and certainly bookkeepers would probably make the worse kind of interior designer.

HARRY SIEGEL AND ALAN SIEGEL

WHY THIS CHAPTER IS IMPORTANT TO YOU

Chapter 4 provided you with an account of the many legal issues that arise in interior design businesses. Similarly, chapter 5 seeks to make the basic financial principles applicable to interior design businesses understandable and usable. This chapter is important to you because it identifies three processes that, together, form a system that enables you, as a practicing interior designer, to administer, measure, and evaluate financial information about your business—easily. Having this knowledge of basic financial principles is necessary for any professional. Although there are many computer programs that now assist businesspeople in these tasks, interpreting the data generated by such programs still requires that you understand financial terms and concepts of the kind found here. Specific financial concerns, especially those related to taxes, will most likely require consultation with financial professionals. Again, understanding the terms and concepts presented in this chapter will help you to form your own strategy for working with those whom you consult about financial matters. Of course, your foremost interest is producing meaningful interior design work. However, nothing prevents you from also being a sound financial manager.

PROFESSIONAL PRACTICES PORTFOLIO

After completing this chapter, you should be able to answer the questions that follow. Include your responses in your professional practices portfolio, which you can keep as a handbook of business strategies for later use.

1. What are some of the ways of administering the finances of a business?
2. What is involved in the financial planning process for a business?
3. What are *accounts payable* and *accounts receivable*?
4. What general area of business finances is concerned with measuring the financial position of a business?
5. What is a *transaction* in financial accounting terminology?
6. Define the following: *assets, liabilities, owner's equity, revenues,* and *expenses*.
7. Identify the three basic documents of financial accounting, and state the purposes of each?
8. What is managerial accounting, and what purpose does it serve in business?
9. What information do *ratios* provide about a business's finances? Give some examples of several different kinds.
10. What ways of obtaining financial resources for businesses are available to entrepreneurs?

INTRODUCTION TO BUSINESS FINANCES

Perhaps even the thought of business finance, much less studying its many details, seems less interesting to you than the study of other subjects.

Such feelings are understandable, since you may have limited exposure to finance-related subjects. You would be correct, too, to be concerned about the numerous details. There are so many details that they cannot all be included in this chapter. Yet, despite any lack of familiarity with the subject and its breadth, there are ways to make your study of business finances interesting and, moreover, relevant as you consider what is involved in operating an interior design business. This chapter explores the basic objectives of business finance by discussing three interrelated processes that, together, form a system for managing the financial matters that are necessary for the operation of interior design businesses.

ADMINISTRATION

Most discussions of financial concepts begin with lengthy definitions and other details. The approach of this chapter is to first ask you to think about the financial operations of most businesses. For example, most business owners and managers regularly establish and monitor methods for handling payments that the business owes or that is owed to the business. Methods of working with the available cash the business has acquired as well as ways of recording expenses and retaining receipts for payment are other important concerns. These are examples of activities that may be thought of as making up a process by which the business's finances are administered. Before the financial status of the business may be scrutinized and evaluated, there should be in place a specific process for generating and retaining the kinds of financial information required for those later tasks. Accordingly, this chapter describes what is involved in administering the finances of a business. Many large interior design firms or practice groups include staff members who are designated to carry out these tasks. Managers and business owners frequently call upon that group for information about financial matters, which are critical in making important decisions, such as whether to work with certain clients or extend credit to them. On the other hand, in many small shops, made up of only one or a few practitioners, designers themselves may be responsible for carrying out administrative tasks. These practitioners use the financial information obtained through administrative processes for largely the same purposes as their counterparts in larger firms. In both scenarios, interior designers rely on the financial information gleaned from routine administrative processes.

MEASUREMENT

After financial information is acquired and retained, it must be interpreted for use in ways that benefit a business and its ongoing operations. Understanding and recording the financial effects that result from operating a business—determining, for example, whether the business made or lost money—require a distinct process. The role of financial accounting principles and practices is to provide such a process. **Financial accounting** is generally described as the process of recording, organizing, and interpreting information related to financial transactions and performance. To carry out these functions, financial accounting relies on the use of three different documents, known collectively as **summary reports**. These reports are referred to individually as *balance sheets*, *income statements*, and *statements of cash flow*. How exactly these reports are constructed is discussed in many accounting texts. This chapter is concerned with their importance in measuring the financial performance of an interior design business.

EVALUATION

Financial information may be used for measuring the periodic performance of a business or as the basis for making more complicated business decisions. Interpreting financial information with the intent of using those results to make decisions or to evaluate different options is a process distinct from measurement. Managerial accounting principles and processes provide a method for business owners and managers to analyze and interpret current or prospective business activities. Businesses can evaluate financial performance using a form of fractions called *ratios*. Depending on the components of these ratios, they may be used to measure three different kinds of financial activity: the ability to pay obligations; the ability of the company to generate a profit or economic surplus from the operation of the business; and the ability to use the business's assets—that is, certain kinds of property that the business owns—effectively.

Interior design businesses, as you know by now, require a great deal of monetary resources to operate. Using financial management guidelines, for example, enables designers to fully understand the impact of expenditures on a business's ability to not only function but also to show a profit. Although financial processes of any kind may seem remote from what is involved in planning attractive, functional interior environments, the cost and labor-intensive nature of interior design work, combined with the very real-world need for any business to show an economic profit as quickly as practicable, make your study of financial topics highly relevant.

OBJECTIVES TO CONSIDER

From the introduction you should have identified the following three major objectives of this chapter:

◆ What is involved in administering the finances of a business?
◆ What are the methods of measuring the finances of a business?
◆ What questions about business finance does the evaluation process answer?

The details involved in meeting these objectives are explored in the following discussion.

WHAT IS INVOLVED IN ADMINISTERING THE FINANCES OF A BUSINESS?

Think of all the bills, receipts, and related items you receive in your personal life. Now, imagine the number of such items received by a small business. When you give further consideration to the vast number of such items a larger firm or practice receives, the need for an organized, systematic approach for administering the business's finances becomes apparent. What is really involved in the task of administering the finances of a business? What kinds of issues can interior designers expect to encounter, and, more important, what can they do to make the administrative process as easy and useful as possible?

In a sense, every business is different. Some interior design businesses are small enough that the owner is able to handle the administrative details almost as if the business were an extension of the owner's personal finances. No matter how informally some businesses may be managed, however, once any business gains a degree of size and complexity, it becomes necessary to identify ways of handling its financial activities. There are several issues of financial administration common to most businesses: establishing procedures for handling cash coming into and going out of a business; handling the expenses a business incurs from its operation; extending credit to clients; and keeping records of a business's financial activities for later measurement and evaluation purposes. Consider each of these activities.

1. Dealing with the cash flow of a business: Businesses of any kind require cash to pay for such things as inventory and operation expenses. While it may be difficult to determine exactly what specific amount of cash will be necessary, business owners and managers can estimate what typical expenses the business has incurred in the past and would, based on that historical information, be likely to incur in the future. Gathering this information may require extensive amounts of record keeping of expenses and revenue on a monthly basis. The importance of cash management for interior designers becomes apparent in those instances where designers have good months and bad months financially. Some designers choose to work in locations where their business varies according to time of year, gaining more business in certain seasons than in others. Also, many designers face similar variability as their businesses gain a following of clients. Regardless of the reasons for incurring financially strong and weak periods, designers must know how to accumulate then marshal cash reserves accordingly. As noted, record keeping of financial activities from previous periods is important as is monitoring current levels of sales and expenses.

2. Handling the expenses of the business. From an accounting perspective, such resources as cash described above are considered part of the assets of a business. However, there are obligations incurred by a business that must be satisfied in order for that business to remain in operation. These are typically referred to as liabilities and may be thought of as obligations or claims against the assets of a business before any profit can be determined. The key to recognizing one form of accounts payable is to look to see whether the business has received, but not yet paid, for goods or services. Other forms of accounts payable include promissory notes (a kind of debt) for which a business has received a financial loan that it must repay, but has not, or expenses it has incurred but not yet paid. Operating any business is an expensive undertaking, interior design being no exception.

Finding ways to monitor expenses, project their occurrence and plan for meeting those obligations in a timely manner is critical for the ultimate success of any business.

3. Another way in which business owners and managers administer the finances of their ventures is through the practice of extending credit to customers. This practice forms another asset of the business known as accounts receivable in which sums are owed the business by others. A common example of accounts receivable occurs when an interior design business extends credit to its clients by allowing them to pay outstanding balances over a period of time instead of all at once. Usually, design firms charge for this by imposing interest charges. This is a general overview of some of the ways in which business decision makers administer the financial operation of their ventures. Apart from these very basic decisions, what are more specific ways they may measure the effectiveness of the decisions they make?

WHAT ARE METHODS OF MEASURING THE FINANCES OF A BUSINESS?

Many creative people gravitate to careers in interior design precisely because numerical or quantitative skills are not usually emphasized. However, you are also in the process of becoming an entrepreneur willing to assume the risks inherent in running a business. How can you assess such risks? An old adage states that "sometimes you just have to put pencil to paper to figure out what to do." You put pencil to paper when realizing a design concept; here is how you can do much of the same kind of preparation in order to realize your goal of establishing, managing, or functioning in a profit-focused design business. Becoming familiar with the context in which you will use these accounting and financial management skills is the first step in that process.

Many people refer to money-related determinations as simply *accounting* when in fact there are two distinct divisions within the accounting profession, each making its unique contributions to quantitative business decision making. Financial accounting is perhaps the more commonly known and understood. Every time you determine the balance of your checking account, by matching deposits (revenues) with deducted payments (expenses) using the actual sums of money you have deposited in your account, you are engaging in a simple financial accounting process.

With that in mind, you know that financial accounting concerns the measurement (the balance you achieve as a result of the addition and subtraction of funds) and reporting (the entries you write down) of monetary resources available.

Financial accounting has two other characteristics. Financial accounting occurs periodically, that is, at predetermined times. Many people, for example, balance their checkbooks only at certain times during the month in order to ascertain whether any money remains in their bank account until they receive their next paycheck. Business owners and managers, on the other hand, may balance their company's accounts daily in order to maintain adequate funds for operation from one day to the next. In addition, while you may balance your checkbook only for your own information and use, many businesspeople employ financial accounting practices to provide necessary information to those outside their organizations. Financial accounting practices are thus usually used to generate information for review by external parties. For example, preparation of financial accounting documents is frequently done for review by prospective and current company stockholders and government taxing authorities. Others external to the company usually given access to financial accounting information include those extending credit or lending money to a business—a requirement you explore in some detail in this chapter's Strategic Planning Project—along with those either permitted by the company or otherwise required by law to have such information. Of course, accounting information may be used by those within the business for evaluative purposes such as determining the amount of cash available for business operations.

Every profession has its own, unique terms used to describe important concepts. Each entry, or **transaction** noted in your checkbook represents an account, or record of any increase (**credit**) or decrease (**debit**) affecting an overall balance. These transactions are usually recorded in chronological sequence as they occur in what is called a **journal**. Your checkbook is a type of journal.

Documents of financial accounting include the following:

- ◆ **Balance sheet** The purpose of the balance sheet is to indicate the financial balances—the relationship of credit to debit—for a company at a particular time.
- ◆ **Income statement** An income statement is intended to show the operating performance of a business for a specific year, as reflected by changes in the company's net income.

◆ **Statement of cash flows** This statement breaks down a company's monetary resources according to where it derives its income and how it uses its available cash.

WHAT QUESTIONS ABOUT BUSINESS FINANCE DOES THE EVALUATION PROCESS ANSWER?

Of the two areas of accounting discussed here, managerial accounting is likely less familiar to you. **Managerial accounting** focuses on processing quantitative, or numerical, information for use within a company to evaluate options available to the business and then make decisions based on these assessments. What this means, more simply, is that managerial accounting determines the financial picture of some aspect of a company's operation and then evaluates options for possible company action based on that information. Determining, for example, whether a company makes money, or is profitable from some activity it undertakes, is one important aspect of managerial accounting. With this information, owners and managers usually make decisions about actions the company should undertake, continue, discontinue, or modify in some way. The primary method of processing financial management information is through the use of mathematical formulas. Although detailed, these formulas, you may be relieved to learn, are based on ratios, or fractional percentages determined through division. More complicated managerial accounting formulas combine percentages with addition, subtraction, and multiplication, all processes with which you are familiar.

You may have already employed a form of managerial accounting in your personal life without recognizing it as such. Your analysis of whether to work while in school to pay tuition—less time to study now, but no costs later—or, alternatively, to take out a student loan—more time to study now, but higher costs later—is a process involving managerial accounting. One specific application of this kind of decision faced by businesses involves determining the percentage of obligations the company owes to others compared to the assets, or things of value, the company has available to pay those obligations. The **debt ratio** is a simple fraction in which the total amount of these debts is divided by all company assets. Very high debt ratios, indicating that a company owes much more money compared to what it has available to pay those debts—a situation referred to as being *highly leveraged*—ultimately may endanger a company's survival.

Financial and managerial accounting skills are important for prudent business decision making. In this chapter, financial and managerial accounting principles are explored within the context of operating an interior design business, namely those concerning the amount of project income, the timeliness of its receipt, and the payment of project expenses. This chapter focuses on methods of recording and interpreting these items as they relate to the overall operation of the design firm. Think for a moment about what financial information would be of interest to you as you operate or manage your own interior design business (see Form 5.1). Wouldn't you like to know the financial picture of your company at any given time? Think back to the reasons why you balance your checkbook and the role financial accounting plays in that process. Don't you want to find out how much money you have on hand and what your expenses are? Business operators desire the same kinds of information; methods of managerial accounting allow them to evaluate the financial position of a business and make decisions based on those determinations. These businesspeople use a process referred to as ratio analysis, in which mathematical formulas usually in the form of fractions are used to interpret financial information. There are three basic kinds of ratios used: effectiveness ratios, liquidity ratios, and profitability ratios.

◆ Effectiveness ratios measure how well the company uses its assets, including how quickly the company collects payment on its accounts receivable. There are several commonly identified effectiveness ratios used in businesses, including the A/R turnover and inventory turnover. To see how these work, consider the application of the first of these effectiveness ratios. A low accounts receivable ratio, for example, in which the number representing a business's net credit sales is divided by a denominator representing the business's average gross receivables, divided by 360 (for days in the year), means the business collects payments in a timely manner. A high number that results from this formula can, conversely, mean those to whom the business has extended credit typically wait long periods of time before paying, a result that can seriously affect the business's ability to pay other obligations as necessary. That ratio is as follows: A/R turnover (days) = net credit sales/(average gross receivables/360).

◆ Liquidity ratios measure the amount of money a company has on hand to pay its obligations as they become due for payment. Typical liquidity ratios include the current ratio in which a business's current assets, or the property and financial resources it owns, are divided by the

FINANCIAL INFORMATION WORKSHEET

1. **Target Market Location** _____

2. **Monthly Personal Expenses**

Student loans	_____	Utilities/phone	_____
Practice fees	_____	Car payment	_____
Home/apartment rent	_____	Car insurance	_____
Health insurance	_____	Credit cards	_____

Total Monthly Personal Expenses _____

3. **Beginning Business Expenses**

Initial Location Costs _____
(Include rental deposit, other fees related
to obtaining office/studio space)

Initial Utility Expenses in Target Market Location _____
(Include deposits for phone, electric, gas
required for office function)

Design Library Expenses _____
(Include an initial amount required for
trade magazine subscriptions, catalogs, swatches)

Creative Supplies _____
(Include beginning expenses for purchasing supplies
necessary for creative work, art supplies)

Office Supplies _____
(Include beginning expenses for supplies necessary
for conducting business, business cards, and others)

Computer Expenses _____
(Include beginning expenses for a new computer,
necessary design softwear, and Internet access)

Total Beginning Expenses _____

4. **Recurring Monthly Business Expense Estimates**

Monthly rent	_____	Monthly business credit card	_____
Estimated utilities	_____	Monthly business insurance	_____
Monthly phone	_____	Monthy supplies	_____
Monthly Internet/computer	_____		

**Total Estimated
Monthly Expenses** _____

(continued)

FORM 5.1 (continued)

Expense-Income Projections

1. Total Beginning Expenses _____

2. Total Monthly Personal Expenses _____

   Total Estimated Monthly Expenses _____

3. Total Expenses _____

   Based on your *Total Beginning Expenses* at how much of a variance (if any) will you operate if you have the following amounts available with which to begin your business?

Beginning

$1,500   Beginning Amount Projected _____   Variance _____   positive/negative

Beginning

$2,500   Beginning Amount Projected _____   Variance _____   positive/negative

Beginning

$3.000   Beginning Amount Projected _____   Variance _____   positive/negative

Beginning

$5,000   Beginning Amount Projected _____   Variance _____   positive/negative

Beginning

$8,000   Beginning Amount Projected _____   Variance _____   positive/negative

Beginning

$10,000   Beginning Amount Projected _____   Variance _____   positive/negative

How much money will it take for your *Total Beginning Expenses* to equal amounts available?

Beginning Break-Even Dollar Amount _____

business's current liabilities, or obligations such as debts. Other examples of liquidity ratios include the acid test ratio, in which, the sum of the following three elements are divided by the current liabilities of a business: cash equivalents + marketable securities (such as shares of stock) + net receivables (what is owed to a business by others)/current liabilities. If the effect of a business's current liabilities is to diminish the financial benefits of the other elements of the equation with a resulting low number from using the acid test, the business, it may be concluded, faces serious problems.

◆ Profitability ratios measure how well the company is able to generate profits from its activities. Perhaps, the most common example of a profitability ratio, one with which you may already be familiar, is that of gross margin. In that ratio, net income is divided by net sales. Net income is derived by subtracting all expenses from the total revenue earned by the business. Similarly, net sales are derived from the total of all sales less the costs to the business of generating those sales. Use of this ratio makes clear the extent to which the business is able to show a profit from that business's sales.

PROBLEM-SOLVING
STRATEGIES FOR FINANCIAL PLANNING

There is yet another hurdle to cross on the way to becoming a design professional: obtaining the financial resources to begin your enterprise. If you are still debating whether a solo or small interior design firm is for you, this financial hurdle may help you decide if or when you might be able to start your first business venture.

IDENTIFYING SOURCES OF FUNDING FOR
YOUR INTERIOR DESIGN BUSINESS

Essentially, there are two major sources of funding available to businesses. These may be classified as either public or private. As you might imagine, *public* sources are available to businesspeople and the business community at large. These include U.S. government–backed entities such as credit unions, traditional banks, and other lending institutions. The financial services offered by these sources are usually available to any businessperson or company meeting predetermined standards of acceptance. In contrast, *private* sources are financial resources that may be available to only one or a few people, based on friendships or family connections. Financing from these sources may range from outright gifts of money to loans with very lenient repayment terms, or other forms of financial advantage not made known, much less made available, to the general public. Each type of financing, whether public or private, should be considered with care before you enter into an agreement that obligates you as a new business owner to someone. Most of these sources will impose some sort of obligation for repayment or exert some expectation that must be met by you and the business entity you seek to establish.

Regardless of which form of funding you ultimately choose—public, private, or some combination of the two—most sources will require that you present something in writing that explains your plan for establishing and running your business. You are already familiar with the role of business plans in describing your enterprise to others. Even if a business plan is not specifically required, application forms may ask questions that elicit the same kind of information contained in such a plan. When you examine the information requirements for a Small Business Administration (SBA) loan (see page 191), you will notice its similarities to portions of a business plan.

Even private sources of funding may wish to see your business plan in writing; however, in these circumstances the plan may not have to be as exhaustive as plans submitted to public sources. In addition to asking exhaustive questions about your proposed business and your plans for running that business, public sources of financing will also ask many exhaustive questions about you. In particular, these lenders will look at your preexisting history of repaying obligations such as student loans, credit cards, mortgages, and other debt that appears on credit reports compiled by credit-reporting agencies.

Before you apply for a loan or seek financing, it is a good idea to check your credit rating through any of several sources readily found in print and Internet media. Your credit rating is one of several factors lenders consider when deciding whether to grant a loan in the first place and also whether to charge higher or lower interest rates on the sums you borrow. Usually, the better your credit rating—showing careful stewardship of existing credit obligations—the better the terms of any new loan, all other factors, such as income stability, remaining constant. Fair, Isaac and Company at www.myfico.com is an example of a credit-reporting agency. The FICO score is mentioned and used by many lenders in making credit determinations. Although other agencies report historical credit data, such as the number of late payments over time, Fair, Isaac has developed a proprietary mathematical score, or scale, which predicts how well or poorly individuals are estimated to control their debt obligations.

In addition to preparing a written business plan, a credit score is another consideration an interior design entrepreneur should take into account before seeking financing.

PUBLIC SOURCES OF BUSINESS FUNDING

Banks, credit unions, and savings-and-loan institutions are readily available sources for operational funds. Each of these entities offers loans to small-business entrepreneurs who can meet the guidelines imposed by the U.S. government and a particular bank's own lending policies. These guidelines include concerns such as the credit rating of a borrower and whether that borrower has any assets that can be offered to the lender as security for making the loan.

Loans from Banks and Other Financial Institutions

As part of the lending process, and in addition to the borrower's credit rating, virtually all public sources will require written documentation attesting to the nature of the business as well as the borrower's formal business plan. Some types of loans, known as **secured loans**, will also require the borrower to pledge some asset of value, such as equipment or real estate. This is considered security against which the lending institution may seek financial satisfaction in the event of the borrower's inability to repay the loan. Secured loans usually have lending terms and interest rates more favorable to the borrower than types of unsecured loans that require no pledge of assets.

In addition to considering credit scores and secured loans, designer entrepreneurs should also be aware of the financing options available at specialized lending institutions such as credit unions or cooperatives in which they may be eligible for participation. Many universities sponsor or are affiliated with credit unions that are available to their students. These institutions may offer better loan terms and rates to their members than might otherwise be found elsewhere in the community. Researching sources of funds for your design business includes seeking out all possible alternatives available in your community. It also means that you understand the obligations that an entrepreneur, as a loan recipient, has to the lending institution for repayment. You should understand the recourses that institutions will take to obtain satisfaction against debors who cannot repay loans under the terms of agreement; this is critical for successful borrowing.

SBA Loan Guarantees

Banks and other public lending institutions make loans directly to qualified borrowers. However, in those instances where, for example, a potential borrower has established a business with a viable cash flow but does not yet have a strong credit history to qualify for a conventional loan, certain government loan programs are available to guarantee a loan or assume at least part of the lending risk should a borrower default. These public sources of funds are not loans from the federal government in the traditional sense. In fact, a borrower would seek these types of guaranteed loans from a bank or other lending institution and not from the federal government or private individuals. Such programs provide the federal government's insurance to a lender to make a loan it otherwise could not make on reasonable business terms.

These loan-guarantee programs act as another, although indirect source of financing to entrepreneurs. An overview of these Small Business Association (SBA) loans states the following:

> To qualify for an SBA guaranty, a small business must meet the SBA's criteria, and the lender must certify that it could not provide funding on reasonable terms without an SBA guaranty. . . . The SBA can guarantee as much as 85 percent on loans of up to $150,000 and 75 percent on loans of more than $150,000. In most cases, the maximum guaranty is $1 million.

Note the language in this statement about certification from the lender that financing on any reasonable terms is unavailable. In other words, for a variety of reasons, the borrower may not be eligible to receive any loan from any lender according to federal banking and lending policies. Poor credit, for example, may be a reason for many lenders to decline the loan, except for the assurance of the SBA. However, the addition of language stating that a governmental assurance can be based on broad criteria may make it possibile for potential borrowers to obtain funding with the assistance of the SBA. Among these criteria for assurances is the following description of what the SBA looks for in a loan application:

Repayment ability from the cash flow of the business is a primary consideration in the SBA loan decision process but good character, management capability, collateral, and owner's equity contribution are also important considerations.

Finally, all but a few types of businesses may avail themselves of the SBA loan guarantee. The agency spells out what types of businesses are ineligible for its support. These include such enterprises as real estate speculation and pyramid schemes, "in which proceeds gained from the financial contribution of later investors in a business are used to pay 'profits' to earlier ones." Careful review of the type of business being conducted is necessary on the part of the entrepreneur and lender before making a formal application. Of note to interior designers is the prohibition against guaranteeing businesses that seek to use floor plan financing. Suppose a design entrepreneur sought to establish a retail store from which to operate an interior design business. The store, moreover, would carry a particular manufacturer's furniture that it obtained on credit from the maker. While retail stores may well be a permissible SBA-backed undertaking, a store in which merchandise is obtained by the store owner on credit from the manufacturer may not be eligible for an SBA-supported loan. Essentially, the store owner, under this type of agreement with the furniture manufacturer, does not own the furniture that serves as the principle asset backing the loan. In the event of the store owner's inability to pay, the furniture manufacturer may be found to have superior ownership rights to the furniture in the showroom, leaving the lender with no other recourse but to seek reimbursement from the SBA. Again, it is important to carefully review the type of entity that an entrepreneur is seeking to establish through the use of an SBA-backed loan before obtaining governmental assurance.

Credit Cards

Credit cards and the use of debt are now relatively commonplace in life and in business practice compared with their use as little as a generation ago. Some have argued that perhaps it is now too easy for people, whether they are starting businesses, to obtain credit; many who do so now do not understand how expensive and potentially detrimental these financing sources really are. Nevertheless, the use of debt is widespread, particularly among those who are starting new businesses, precisely because credit cards are so easy to obtain. An understanding and appreciation of the effects of credit card–debt on a new business is another requirement for the design entrepreneur. It is thus necessary to understand certain aspects of the operation of debt financing through credit cards.

Every source of money, except for an outright gift, will inevitably require repayment of borrowed money, usually with the addition of some type of finance charge, known as interest. Every businessperson should therefore be aware of two important issues. First, is the percentage of interest the lender will charge for the use of its funds. Many credit cards tout the cash advance feature of their cards, which enables cardholders to obtain cash readily through automated teller machines (ATMs). However, most cards charge a higher percentage of interest for cash obtained in this way. Using credit cards to obtain cash advances is a more expensive way for a consumer to obtain funds than by means of a bank loan, for example. Debt and credit-card calculators are readily available for businesspeople and can even be found on many Internet sites. Every businessperson, especially one who is working in an expense-laden industry such as interior design, should be aware of how much it will cost to obtain working funds.

Just as important as the cost of funding is awareness of the length of time before sources require repayment of borrowed money. Credit cards require payment of some or even the entire amount borrowed approximately within a month of incurring the debt. American Express is one commonly used credit card that requires full payment at the end of the billing cycle for individuals and business patrons. Other sources may permit longer repayment times. Unfortunately, it takes time to establish any business, particularly one in which projects are obtained through professional networking and personal referrals, as is true of interior design. What this may create for a designer is a *cash flow* problem: Few, if any, new funds are available from projects, while start-up expenses accumulate and payments to creditors are due. Applications of the cash-flow concept are discussed in chapter 6, but introduced here so that their importance can be understood from the outset. Many credit cards tout the low interest rates they apply to balances carried from one billing session to the next. Care should be taken not to fall into the introductory rate trap, in which low rates are charged for a period of time, only to be exchanged for higher rates later.

It should also be noted that paying merely the minimum payment may result in a long payment time until the entire balance of principle and interest are paid off. As a result, it may take as long as several decades for a cardholder to pay off a high balance just by paying those low minimum payments.

All cards seek repayment eventually. Unfortunately, these repayments may unhappily coincide with periods in which no revenue is earned and the business cash flow is compromised. As a practicing interior designer, beware of the temptation to "kite," which is revenue earmarked for use in one project is used instead to pay items such as debt incurred in another project. Recognizing such problems before they arise is necessary so that a new business does not soon become mired in debt.

As careful as a professional must be in using credit-card debt, the prudent use of credit cards may nevertheless become a type of asset for the business. Businesses may gain an increasingly favorable rating among the credit-reporting agencies that track credit-card use and payment history. A long practice of prudent credit-card use may result in issuers increasing the amounts of money that card users may borrow as well as in relatively lower interest rates applied to balances carried on those cards.

PRIVATE SOURCES OF BUSINESS FUNDING

Among the basic sources of funding available to get a business started, perhaps the simplest source is personal savings. Unfortunately, for young designers getting started right out of school, there may be little or no savings after years of education. At some point, however, a design practitioner should accumulate an amount in savings to do such things as sustain their personal and professional expenses or pay accumulated debt.

Personal Savings

By saving, through practices such as setting aside into an interest-bearing account a given amount of money from each project, or, as one recent author has suggested, cutting out only ten dollars a day of nonessential purchases (Chatzky 2004), designers can begin the process of building a financial cushion enabling them to sustain both themselves and their active practice. The balance of income and expenses may be skewed in favor of the latter at some time during the designer's career. For that reason, a savings plan should be initiated from the start. Budgeting for expenses as well as estimating living and professional costs incurred over a six- to nine-month period will help not only in understanding why savings are important, but also in understanding how much money is required for both daily living and work.

However, even experienced designers should approach using savings cautiously. For example, many practitioners have accumulated amounts in 401(k) or other retirement plans. Use of such funds may result in substantial income-tax penalties in the event withdrawals are made before a certain age or scheduled payment date. Any plan to use these types of funds should be made only after careful consideration and consultation with knowledgeable financial professionals.

Savings-account plans providing some payment of interest to the account holder are readily available at most banks and savings-and-loans. The percentage of interest paid to account holders should be researched to obtain the most advantageous rate. In addition, the frequency and number of withdrawals available to depositors using the plan should be ascertained by asking questions of the lender's account representatives and reading material related to the accounts. Many institutions have established savings plans that transfer certain amounts from a savings account into a checking account every month. The goal of your research should be to find the savings account that offers the most convenience, but charges the least for fees or penalties.

Gifts and Related Agreements

Gifts of money may be one source of funds that can be used to establish a design practice. A gift, in the true sense of the term, is one in which the recipient does nothing in order to receive it—there is no consideration in legal terms for the making of the gift. In addition, a true gift is given with the intent or expectation on the part of the givers that it not be repaid (Merriam-Webster 1996). Outright gifts of the nature described here are, indeed, very attractive financial resources. However, gifts of any kind, particularly those of cash from one individual to another, should be memorialized in writing. All that may be required is a simple written statement to the effect that the sums advanced are a gift made without expectation of repayment, and for which the recipient did nothing to occasion it being made. Such a statement will prevent any misunderstanding later concerning whether the money was actually a loan to the person to whom it was given and for which the donor expected to be repaid. This is a common misunderstanding surrounding gifts. In addition, such written statements can serve to counter possible claims that the money was stolen or obtained through coercion. Legal counsel should be sought to ensure that the language of the acknowledgment mirrors the jurisdiction's definition of what constitutes a gift.

195

Gifts made to a married person are usually considered to be the property of the individual recipient, not jointly held by the couple as an asset of the marriage in most states (Mennell and Boykoff 1988); however, any monetary gift given to a married person should be drafted with the help of an attorney to make clear the ownership rights of the sums advanced. The more specific a gift acknowledgment is, the less opportunity for later misunderstanding about the reasons for the gift's donation, purpose, and use.

The requirement of writing down the specific terms of a gift become necessary in the event of gifts of great value, either cash or property. In general, these large gifts may expose the recipient to income-tax liability. Any large gift should be made with the advice and counsel of relevant experts, such as an attorney and accountant or tax specialist. In general, an individual may give up to $10,000 annually to a recipient with no income-tax liability accruing to the recipient. However, the income-tax reporting requirements on these examples of largess are complex enough to warrant informed advice.

Monetary gifts may be of a more complex nature as well. This is particularly true in those instances in which the gift is made with the specific intent that either some or all of it is to be repaid, in which case the gift is really more of a favorable loan. Also, a more complex gift may be one in which the donor expects to have some measure of control, or say-so, in the operation of the business. It should be apparent that such gifts have substantial strings attached. In order to avoid any serious misunderstandings between the donor and recipient, a formal written agreement, possibly drafted by an attorney and notarized by a notary public who has confirmed the identities of all the parties to the transaction, should be executed—with the terms of the gift spelled out as clearly as possible. In some instances where the donor is willing to underwrite an enterprise in its entirety or to some substantial degree, a formal partnership agreement should be drafted by legal counsel. Recollections and handshake agreements are imperfect, especially when surrounded by conflict or controversy. Offers of gifts of working capital, especially in those instances where lenient repayment or donor-control of the enterprise is contemplated, should be very carefully thought out before agreeing to enter into them; and under no circumstances should these agreements be left to the unwritten understandings of the parties involved.

Gifts made to a recipient through a will or a trust arrangement are other more complex mechanisms for obtaining funds to establish a business.

These gifts involve legal and administrative steps bring them about. As a result, the administration of wills and trusts usually requires the assistance of an attorney and, perhaps, an accountant to ensure that all legal and tax requirements are met. There are costs, sometimes substantial, associated with seeking the assistance of these professionals. Nonetheless, ready availability of financial resources is necessary for the establishment of any business enterprise, interior design included.

Suppose a worst case scenario for your financial prospects when you leave school. You do not have a job or wish to be self-employed. Your savings are minimal after years of being in school; loans are difficult to come by for someone with little business experience; and gifts of the magnitude necessary to start your business are just a dream. What should you do? Remember the definition of entrepreneurs: describing them as those who organize, manage, and assume the risk of businesses. Your job is to first organize your business's finances. In an interview, one designer noted that she began her decades-old practice with little available cash. To generate business and to obtain funds for further growth, she placed a series of small ads in her local newspapers. In these ads, she offered to help prospective clients choose colors and furnishings for their apartments or starter homes. She also offered to work with her clients' existing furniture and within limited household budgets. On the basis of these first ads, she started and grew a business that, as she also noted, grew with her clients. From their first homes to their retirement homes, she completed projects for repeat clients that she had met as a result of these early ads. In short, these ads proved to be not only a source of working capital, but also an investment in her business's future. That's an example of an entrepreneur's strategic business planning!

SEEKING PROFESSIONAL ASSISTANCE IN YOUR PRACTICE

This section aims to discuss practical ways of enhancing professional practice skills as you carry out interior design work and related business activities. Think for a moment about being an interior designer. While you will be responsible for many, if not all of the conceptual and organizational tasks involved, you will also need assistance to perform a great many others. From what kinds of professionals might further assistance be necessary? The focus of this chapter's troubleshooting strategies has been to make you aware of important resources to assist you in your working life. Thus far the text has examined fundamentals of business organization and finance. In keeping with that trend, consider the business advisers you should seek out and some of the business issues with which they can assist.

The Role of Accountants

Practitioners in the accounting profession concentrate their work in two distinct areas. Financial accountants gather and interpret financial information according to guidelines known as *Generally Accepted Accounting Principles* (GAAP) as well as the appropriate federal and state tax laws. In the most general sense, financial accountants assist in periodically evaluating and reporting the financial status of a business or person. Those who have completed formal educational requirements and passed state professional exams are known as **Certified Public Accountants** or **CPAs**. Practitioners in the other area of accounting specialization, managerial accounting, have also met rigorous education and examination standards and are known as **Certified Managerial Accountants**, or **CMAs**. These professionals use mathematical equations, usually based on fractions or ratios, to evaluate the financial performance of a business. In this chapter, you learned the application of basic financial accounting concepts and record keeping and will describe common financial-management ratios. Later discussions will help you to communicate with accounting professionals and to understand how you may best interact with them. When you consider engaging the services of an accountant, do some research and ask for referrals to accountants who have worked well with other interior designers. Not all accountants understand how interior designers work; find one with whom you can easily communicate and who can explain accounting procedures and practices to you in a meaningful way. At this early stage of your education in strategic professional practices, you should be aware of the important role financial accountants can play in your work. Following are several critical questions to ask a financial accountant if you are not seeking to start your own design business:

- What kinds of documentation should I seek from my employer for tax purposes?
- As far as taxes are concerned, what difference does it make if I am an independent contractor rather than an employee?
- How should I prepare personal records for income-tax purposes?

- What do I need to do now so that I can own my own interior design practice or retail store or, for that matter, retire from work?
- Is it economically feasible to open my own interior design practice?

If your plans involve immediately starting your own interior design business—or your ultimate plan is to open your own business after working for others to gain experience—then you will definitely need an accountant's assistance to answer the following questions:

- Are my plans for a new interior design business financially feasible, or should they be modified in some way?
- What kinds of financial records will I need to keep as a business owner, and how do I do so?
- How much cash should I accumulate in order to sustain my business for the first year?
- How should the business be best structured for income-tax purposes?
- Can I afford to hire other full-time designers, or should I hire free-lancers as needed; and, if feasible, should the latter be classified as employees or independent contractors?

These are, of course, only a few of the questions that you might address to a financial accountant. Regardless of your ultimate career intentions, or even if you have a knack for numbers as well as design, the assistance of a financial accounting professional is critical if you want unbiased opinions about matters such as a business's financial status at a specific date and its exposure to the imposition of taxes by governmental authorities.

The Role of Attorneys

Attorneys provide advice and counsel about the applicability and effect of laws on a wide variety of activities. These professionals have pursued educations in law after college and then passed state-sponsored licensing exams before being permitted to practice law—especially the ways in which sale, use and income taxes affect design businesses, their owners, and their employees. During the course of their education and experience, attorneys—like interior designers—develop areas of specialized knowledge. When you consider engaging an attorney, the assistance of an attorney who understands construction and design-build issues and other concerns related to interior design work will likely serve your purpose better than someone who is unfamiliar with these topics. Be sure to do research and ask other designers to refer you to attorneys who have worked successfully with interior designers and their businesses.

From the standpoint of interior designers who participate in design businesses they do not own, the assistance of an attorney may not seem necessary until problems arise. But, in fact, a critical legal response to the following questions might better prepare an employed designer for working life.

- What are the legal limits on the activities in which an interior designer can engage in this state?
- How is the business for which I work organized—sole proprietorship or corporation—and how does that affect employees?
- What do the provisions of the firm's standard form design contract mean?
- How can the firm for which I work help employees when legal issues arise in the course of work?
- Who owns the design documents I prepare—the firm or me?

Be aware that the assistance of a legal professional should strongly be considered when opening your own interior design business. In that event, an attorney can answer a great many questions, including the following:

- What are the legal limits on activities in which an interior designer can engage in this state?
- Which form of business organization is best under the circumstances for my business as planned?
- What kinds of documentation are necessary to establish the indicated business entity, and what has to be done to keep those documents up to date?
- What provisions should my firm's contract for design services contain, and why?
- What are ways to limit me and my firm's exposure to lawsuits, and are insurance policies enough?

These are only a few of the questions to ask an attorney when you are starting a new business. Accountants and attorneys are professionals who can assist you with your business needs. Will you need others to assist you in completing project installations? Later you will learn troubleshooting strategies that you can use in assembling a team of construction and design-trade resources to assist you in executing those installations.

REFERENCES

Chatzky, Jean. 2004. *Pay It Down Today: From Debt to Wealth on $10 Dollars A Day*. New York: Portfolio Press.

Fields, Edward. 2002. *Essentials of Finance and Accounting for Non-Financial Managers*. New York: AMACOM (American Management Association).

Fridson, Martin S. and Fernando Alvarez. 2002. *Financial Statement Analysis: A Practitioner's Guide*. 3rd ed. New York: John Wiley & Sons.

Kieso, Donald E. et al. 2003. *Intermediate Accounting*. 11th ed. New York: John Wiley & Sons.

Knackstedt, Mary V. 2002. *The Interior Design Business Handbook: A Complete Guide to Profitability*. 3rd ed. New York: John Wiley & Sons.

Loonin, Deanne et al. 2002. *Money Troubles: Legal Strategies to Cope with Your Debts*. 8th ed. California: Nolo.

McGuiness, Bill. 2000. *Cash Rules: Learn and Manage the 7 Cash Flow Drivers for Your Company's Success*. New York: Kiplinger Books.

Mennell, Robert L. and Thomas M. Boykoff. 1988. *Community Property, Nutshell Series*. Missouri: West Publishing Group.

Mose, Arlene K. and Gary Downs. 1997. *Day-to-Day Business Accounting*. New Jersey: Prentice-Hall.

Mulford, Charles W., and Eugene E. Comiskey. 2002. *The Financial Numbers Game: Detecting Creative Accounting Practices*. New York: John Wiley & Sons.

Pinson, Linda. 2000. *Keeping the Books: Basic Recordkeeping and Accounting for the Successful Business*. 5th ed. New York: Dearborn Financial Publishing (Kaplan).

Schilit, Howard M. 2002. *Financial Shenanigans*. 2nd ed. New York: McGraw-Hill.

Siegel, Harry, and Alan Siegel. 1982. *A Guide to Business Principles and Practices for Interior Designers*. New rev. ed. New York: Whitney Library of Design.

Siegel, Joel G., and Jae K. Shim. 2000. *Accounting Handbook*. 3rd ed. New York: Barron's.

White, Gerald I. et al. 2001. *The Analysis and Use of Financial Statements*. 3rd ed. New York: John Wiley & Sons.

Wood, Linda Picard, ed. 1996. *Merriam-Webster Dictionary of Law*. New York: Merriam-Webster Inc.

STRATEGIES-IN-ACTION PROJECTS

STRATEGIC PLANNING PROJECT: IDENTIFYING SOURCES OF FUNDING

Business plans are usually written for the purpose of obtaining the financial resources needed to begin operation of a new commercial venture. In this section of your strategic business plan, identify three sources of funding realistically available for getting your ideal interior design business started. Draft a two- to three-paragraph statement in which you list some advantages and disadvantages of each source.

RESIDENTIAL INTERIOR DESIGN PROJECT SIMULATION

The Abernathy project has been an ongoing challenge for Lee. Read about Lee's current problem and consider how you might be able to assist her.

Lee's Diary

Keeping up with Mrs. A. has been really difficult! She talks and goes a mile a minute, even when shopping for new furniture for the children's rooms! But, I must say, we got a lot done during the day we were at the Dallas Market. It was exciting registering in the lobby. Although I had registered in the state as an interior designer, I could have gotten in just by showing my pocket identification card with my name and state registration number. However, the owner of Imagination Unlimited wanted to register the store as a retail store with the Mart, so we had to go through the whole registration process, which involved showing the following things. As you can see this was a lengthy process!

- *Copy of state sales and use tax permit with appropriate SIC codes*
- *Voided business check*
- *Personalized imprinted business card (valid for owner only)*
- *Picture of storefront with signage or $10,000 wholesale invoices within last 12 months. Must show purchases in quantity.*
- *To add additional buyers, provide bank cancelled payroll check with earnings and deductions or personalized corporate credit card.*
- *Photo ID (one per buyer)—must be 18 years or older*

And one of the following:

- *Business advertisement*
- *Signed quarterly states sales tax return and copy of payment check*
- *Copy of deed/lease (*mandatory for antique/craft mall—must provide lease agreement with copy of itemized sales form one quarter).*
- *Business phone listing with directory assistance.)*

And that was just the start of what turned out to be a long day!

Before we left the store, the owner told me to write down all my expenses for that trip, so we could bill them to the client, who is supposed to reimburse me for these expenses (see Form 5.2). I have so much left to do, though. . . . Maybe I'll get around to it soon!

Questions

1. As you begin this project, can you think of reasons why the admissions policies for the Dallas Market Center (which mirrors those of other centers) are so strict?

2. Using Form 5.2, Project Expense Report: Travel and Miscellaneous, note the following expenses and calculate the total for presentation to the client:
   - Round trip of 345 miles total. Note that certain tax rules permit Lee to receive $0.30 for every mile as depreciation expenses on the automobile in addition to the $40.00 for gasoline expenses.
   - Lunch purchased by the designer for her own consumption at the Mart, without the client, for $12.75.
   - Rental at the Mart of $20.00 for use of a cart to transport items while there.
   - Porter's fee and tip of $45.00 for assisting the designer and client with loading a floor sample they were able to purchase and take with them.

This exercise is important to you for two reasons. First, it is critical to keep records of the time and expenses required to complete projects to receive the maximum compensation to which you are entitled. This important recordkeeping is often overlooked, as here, in the rush to finish other tasks. Second, by making expense recordkeeping part of your overall financial billing strategy, you can learn to distinguish expenses that

PROJECT EXPENSE REPORT: TRAVEL AND MISCELLANEOUS

Staff _____   Date _____

Type of Expense	Amount	

Reconciliation	Total	
	Reimbursement	
	Advanced Amounts	
	Amounts Owing	
	Final Reimbursement	

are truly necessary for completing a project from those that drain ready cash from your business.

CONTRACT INTERIOR DESIGN CASE STUDY: THE CASE OF THE ILLIQUID LOCATION

Nightclub impresario and Manhattan socialite Toni Adams was most definitely the "it" girl of New York nightlife. Her first nightclub, Hut 101, had been the whispered secret of the city's fashionable nocturnal denizens when it first opened. After newspapers and magazines reported several scandalous incidents there that involved well-known celebrities, hopeful tourists from all over the world began to appear nightly, each vying for passage across the club's perpetually unyielding velvet entrance rope. Recognizing that a dash of scandal and a splash of fashion stirred together with a lot of attitude made a successful blend for a highly profitable nightclub business, Toni continued operating Hut 101 long after its original habitués had deleted its phone number from their cellphone's direct-dial memory.

As the lease came up for renewal on the space housing Hut 101, Toni decided that instead of keeping the club open, she would move on, and, taking what were rumored to be the substantial profits she earned from the operation of that club, start a new club even more exclusive than Hut 101 ever was. Toni did not disappoint in that regard and soon signed a lease on an underground space that, decades ago, had been part of the New York subway system. Long abandoned for any use other than storage, the space, beneath coats of dust and grime, still retained its original 1920s-era black-and-white tile work, among other vintage features. The new club was to be named Tube, and even as Toni approached you and your firm for interior design services related to this new project, there was buzz about it among New York's social set. "In other words," said Toni at your initial meeting, before entering into any contract with you for your firm's services, "I need your services and snappy! I have people waiting to get in already, and the club isn't even open yet!"

The space in question required extensive cleaning, which Toni stated in your first meeting she would contract for herself. In addition, the complex sound and lighting systems needed to give the club ambience would be handled by her people and would not be the responsibility of your firm. However, what you and your firm would be responsible for appeared from your first talks with Toni to be substantial, but potentially highly profitable. Mostly, the project would involve conducting detailed programming studies about how the former subway storage space could be made into a usable and, moreover, safe space destined for daily public use. Based on that research, you and your firm would also be responsible for completing extensive space plans, noting ways that the unusual space might be safely and attractively used for the variety of activities occurring in a nightclub. These studies would, by necessity, require completion of detailed design plans documenting your intent for the project. As for purchases of the vintage-inspired fixtures, furnishings, and equipment requested by Toni, you have a supplier with whom you have worked on numerous other projects who can provide them less expensively than almost any other source. As a business decision intended to attract Toni as a client, you propose to provide these items on a lump sum basis, with one set fee covering all their costs.

During the course of your conversations with Toni, your business manager sends a message asking you to read an article that appeared in the "Saturday Styles" section of the local paper featuring your soon-to-be client. The article begins with a full color photograph of Toni, grinning behind the wheel of an expensive Italian sports car. Further descriptions of Toni's lifestyle included accounts of her exquisitely appointed homes in New York City, Miami, and the South of France. Finally, the article notes that she is on a first-name basis with all the major jewelers and fashion boutiques along New York's Madison Avenue. Your business manager ended her message to you by asking: "Does she have any money left over for us?"

As you prepare a preliminary budget for the Tube project, which you will present at your next meeting with Toni and her entourage of business advisers, you propose the following:

You estimate the budget for a project of the kind proposed here to be $7,250,000, which will cover your services as well as purchases for the project. You will specify the labor of the project's contractors as part of your fees for design services but, according to firm policy, Toni will contract for and pay for that work herself.

You will need to collect a retainer of 10 percent—or $725,000—of the total estimated project budget at the time the contract is signed. This will ensure that products are ordered in a timely fashion according to the project's expedited timetable and that initial work will begin on programming project requirements.

You propose a schedule of payments as follows:

- 45 percent of the total due as the schematic-design phase begins
- 45 percent of the total due as the contract-documentation phase begins
- 10 percent of the total due as the contract-administration phase begins

Questions

1. Considering Toni's penchant for luxurious living and the expense of the Tube project, what steps might you take to determine whether it would be advisable to pursue this project?

2. Which activity do you believe might be the most profitable one for interior designers: providing clients with detailed services such as project research and drafting contract documents or purchasing and then reselling to clients design products such as furniture? What factors do you think influence that determination? Charging for your interior design services is further detailed later in the book; but it is important that you think about the financial effects of business decisions in the context of this chapter, which discusses how to handle income and expenses generated from your services (see Form 5.1).

3. Using the working capital formula, determine whether Toni has an adequate amount of working capital for undertaking this project, by subtracting the amount of her current liabilities from the amount of her current assets. What does her asset position appear to be? Although Toni may not appear to have a sound financial base for the Tube project, what mitigating circumstances might a designer consider for taking on the project anyway? Would Toni's popularity with the press influence your decision to work with her? Should it? As you think about these questions, evaluate, as you will do in actual practice, what potential there might be for gaining subsequent business from taking on an initial commission on which you might lose money because of the client's shaky finances. How comfortable are you about making financial choices such as these (see Form 5.3)?

Form 5.4 provides you with an approachable method for evaluating different aspects of a business's financial performance. Assume Toni was an interior designer running a store instead of a nightclub. In that case, financial issues related to the store's sales might be of interest to her for her to determine whether the store generates adequate income for it to remain open. Similarly, issues related to Toni's

FORM 5.3. VARIANCE ANALYSIS WORKSHEET

VARIANCE ANALYSIS WORKSHEET

What is the implication of having negative variances, below your break-even amount, as you begin your business?

Based on your *Total Monthly Expenses,* at how much of a variance (if any) will you operate if the following amounts are available as income from your business?

Monthly	$1,500	Monthly Amount Projected _____	Variance _____	positive/negative
Monthly	$2,500	Monthly Amount Projected _____	Variance _____	positive/negative
Monthly	$3,000	Monthly Amount Projected _____	Variance _____	positive/negative
Monthly	$5,000	Monthly Amount Projected _____	Variance _____	positive/negative
Monthly	$8,000	Monthly Amount Projected _____	Variance _____	positive/negative
Monthly	$10,000	Monthly Amount Projected _____	Variance _____	positive/negative

How much money will it take for your *Total Monthly Expenses* to equal amounts available?

Monthly Break-Even Dollar Amount _____

ability to collect amounts due her from those to whom she has extended credit would also be of interest to her. Whether you work for yourself or for others, measuring the financial performance of the business with which you are associated is an important part of the management process.

4. After some extensive research about Toni's past business dealings reported in back issues of the financial section of local newspapers as well as your accountant's estimate of Toni's assets available for financing the Tube project, you determine the following:

Toni's personal and business liabilities, which are difficult to separate, appear to hover around $11,325,000. Taking into account income such as that derived from a small inheritance she received and whatever profits she earned from operating Hut, Toni appears to have available $5 million for use on this project. She also has lines of credit open at several banks, totaling almost $20 million. Using the quick ratio, determine Toni's liquidity. Does she have an adequate working-capital ratio for undertaking this project (see Form 5.4)?

MAKING FINANCIAL MANAGEMENT DECISIONS

Objective 1: What you need to know to quickly understand the finanacial status of the business

Terms you need to know:

Current Assets

Curent Liabilities

Mathematics you need to determine the financial status of the business

Current Ratio	$\dfrac{\text{Current Assets}}{\text{Current Liabilities}}$	**Quick Ratio**	$\dfrac{\text{Current Assets–Inventory}}{\text{Current Liabilities}}$
Debt Ratio	$\dfrac{\text{Total Debts}}{\text{Total Assets}}$	**Working Capital**	Current Assets–Current Liabilities

---

Objective 2: What you need to know to determine the status of a particular financial decision

Terms you need to know:

Total Assets	**Owner's Equity**
Net Income	**EBIT**

Mathematics you need to determine the status of a particular financial decision

Return on Total Assests (ROA)	$\dfrac{\text{Net Income}}{\text{Total Assets}}$
Return on Equity (ROE)	$\dfrac{\text{Net Income}}{\text{Owner's Equity}}$
Return on Investment	$\dfrac{\text{EBIT – Total Liabilities}}{\text{Total Assets}}$
Net Profit	$\dfrac{\text{EBIT}}{\text{Net Sales}}$

Objective 3: What you need to know to determine how well your sales and collections are doing

Mathematics you need to determine your sales and collections

Profit Margin on Sales	$\dfrac{\text{Net Income}}{\text{Total Sales}}$
Inventory Turnover	$\dfrac{\text{Cost of Goods Sold}}{\text{Average Inventory}}$
Average Collection Period	$\text{Accounts Receivables} \times \dfrac{360}{\text{Total Sales}}$

CHAPTER SIX

MANAGING YOUR BUSINESS

What's needed is more thoughtfulness . . .

a sense of community in the organization

HENRY MINTZBERG

WHY THIS CHAPTER IS IMPORTANT TO YOU

Whether you work on your own as an interior designer or are employed by an interior design firm, you will call upon your knowledge of the topics discussed in this chapter to assist you in making business decisions. Perhaps the subject of management will be among the most important since at some point in your working life you may be personally responsible for managing the operations of a business, supervising workers, or having your own activities supervised by managers. Therefore, this chapter is important because it will make you aware of the various roles managers perform; the critical distinctions between managing businesses and workers; the kinds of issues that affect management decisions; the ways in which management policies are presented; and issues relating to the management of teams. These topics apply to the daily operation of interior design businesses, allowing you to develop your own thoughtful strategies for nurturing a sense of community in any business in which you participate.

PROFESSIONAL PRACTICES PORTFOLIO

After completing this chapter, you should be able to answer the questions that follow. Include your responses in your professional practices portfolio.

1. Define management, and describe the working environment and functions of managers.
2. What are some of the noted functions performed by managers?
3. What is personnel management, and what are some of its functions?
4. What are some stages of development in business entities?
5. Describe some issues related to business and personnel management that occur during each of these phases.
6. What are *staff* and *line* positions?
7. Describe the roles each of the following plays in interior design organizations:
   ◆ Design assistant
   ◆ Designer
   ◆ Project designer
   ◆ Design director
8. How do managers formally present company policies and procedures?
9. How do laws impact the management of businesses and personnel?
10. What are some components of employee handbooks?
11. What are the functions of job descriptions and employee evaluations?
12. What are some issues that designers should be aware of when working in teams?

INTRODUCTION TO MANAGEMENT: PRACTICES FOR INTERIOR DESIGNERS

As you begin this chapter, think about an interior design project you might be called upon to complete. That project will require you to plan and monitor many activities; and to do so, you will have to assume responsibility for running the entire project, which involves coordinating the actions of others. In short, your management of that project will be similar to the ways in which business managers influence the operation of their businesses. This familiar scenario emphasizes your awareness of the activities performed by those holding management positions. Just as designers coordinate the complete design of interior spaces, managers plan, implement, and oversee activities related to the functioning of their businesses. This often includes directing the actions of individuals involved in the business. What skills do you think may be required of those who wish to manage interior design businesses and the workers in those businesses? There is much to be explored on the topic of management, including different philosophies of management, or the federal and state laws relating to management practices. How might an interior design student, on the verge of becoming a practitioner, learn about these topics without becoming lost in their numerous details?

That understanding begins by establishing a helpful context in which business management issues arise. Recall the discussion of business formation in chapter 4. There you learned that entrepreneurs may choose from among several different ways to initially organize their businesses, some of which are sole proprietorships, partnerships, corporations, or limited liability companies (LLC), among others. As you begin this chapter you might inquire whether these different types of business organization affect how businesses are managed. After all, different ways to organize and structure a business indicate precisely those business activities in which entrepreneurs may and may not participate. How do management activities relate to the operation of the business?

As discussed in this chapter, management activities involve relationships internal to the business—for example, the roles traditionally carried out by *staff* and *line* workers, terms you will come to know more about shortly. The business types analyzed in chapter 4 refer to relationships external to the business, for example, to those who extend credit to the business or those who are in various ways harmed by the business. Laws unrelated to business formation, such as federal and state laws regulating employment practices, are some of the more important controls the legal system places on internal business operations. An overview of the influence of these laws on management practices is found in this chapter.

Internal management practices may be considered in two very general categories: those practices seeking to advance the goals of the business itself and those related to workers in the business. This chapter refers to the former practices in terms of *business management* and to the latter in terms of *personnel management*. The chapter's objectives are to explore fundamental concepts of both types so that you can recognize and utilize them when you participate in interior design business.

OBJECTIVES TO CONSIDER

If you had wanted to be a manager, it is likely you would have concentrated on a corporate managerial career rather than a career in interior design. But it is also true that management activities affect virtually all professionals in some way. Since they work alone, sole proprietors must engage in management activities for their businesses to prosper, even if doing so affects only themselves. In larger, more complex businesses, management practices are necessary to ensure the businesses' survival. This chapter identifies five basic questions you may have about management. When you conclude this chapter, you should be able to answer them.

◆ What functional roles do managers play?
◆ What are some of the different ways in which businesses and workers may be managed?
◆ What are some of the ways management decisions may be influenced?
◆ Where are management policies and procedures presented?
◆ How are teams managed?

UNDERSTANDING THE FUNCTIONS OF MANAGEMENT

"To direct or carry on business affairs" is the basic way in which Webster's dictionary describes the function of **management**. From your own experiences working with, or even as, a manager, you know that a great deal is required when directing or carrying on affairs related to a business. In fact, a list of the specific activities in which managers engage in any business setting, including the practice of interior design, would likely be quite lengthy. Many interior designers who operate their own businesses, or have controlling interests in a firm—as might a principle in a large design practice—are responsible for performing a wide variety of tasks ranging from the seemingly routine job of paying the bills to the more influential function of instructing employees about company policies. Managers also perform tasks that are critical to business growth such as identifying and approaching potential new clients or formulating strategic plans for the future. Because of its seemingly all-encompassing nature and its ready application to most business practices, the scope of management and the work of managers have fascinated business writers. Many of these writers offer new theories about management practices, but one influential study conducted approximately 30 years ago is noteworthy today for having defined the working life of managers and delineated the roles managers play in business (Mintzberg 1973). That study is particularly instructive because it not only provides a useful context in which to discuss management, but also because its findings are applicable to the practices of interior design businesses.

The environments in which managers operate require that they perform a great deal of work, often under tremendous time pressures (Mintzberg 1973). This finding underscores a major challenge faced by all professionals, including interior designers: how to accomplish their managerial duties and still be able to perform the work for which they were educated and trained. By now, you have a detailed understanding of the many activities that make up interior design work. Imagine combining those activities with managerial tasks, and you will have a better idea of how and why those in management positions in any line of work, including interior design, constantly face a time crunch.

Mintzberg's study also found that managers perform highly diverse activities, characterized by traits such as variety, brevity, and fragmentation. In other words, a typical manager may perform many small tasks that fall across a spectrum of duties. Think of the previous example of a manager paying the business's bills, then working to develop new clients for the business. Even in an interior design business, it would not be uncommon for a manager to engage in a variety of very different tasks within a particular day.

According to Mintzberg (1973) managers prefer to handle issues related to the business that are current, specific, and nonroutine. Current issues require attention and resolution immediately or at least in the near future. Vague or undefined issues are difficult to both ascertain and resolve since they may not come to the fore as full-blown problems and will likely encroach on the manager's performance of more immediately demanding tasks. No one, including a manager, likes routine, repetitive tasks. Managers, according to this study, prefer to delegate repetitive tasks to others and to focus on those issues requiring a response to specific facts or problems that need to be solved. Think again of the managerial tasks that have been mentioned. Although paying company bills is a routine task, interior designers in small firms may have no one but themselves to whom they can delegate that responsibility; at the same time, they need to attend to a range of more demanding professional duties.

Mintzberg's study of the working life of managers also found that managers act within a web of internal and external contacts. Think back to the examples given of management activities, which include such tasks as instructing employees (internal contacts) and seeking new clients for the business (external contacts). Studies such as Mintzberg's provide additional depth and meaning to basic definitions of managment as well as a context in which to discuss the roles of managers in business.

How might the functional roles of managers be described? We are not interested so much in an exact listing of every task a manager performs as if it were a template of general kinds of activities. Applying the same business theorist's approach, managers can be said to perform three basic types of roles when carrying out their work: interpersonal, informational, and decisional (Mintzberg 1973). Consider how each of these three roles may be performed by managers who work in interior design businesses.

- *Interpersonal* This managerial role encompasses three basic components: representing the business to those outside the business; acting as a leader who seeks to motivate and unify people working within the organization in order to carry out the goals of the business; and working with other managers. Refer back to the brief discussion of specific activities performed by managers. You will note activities such as meeting with potential clients (*figurehead* representation of the business to outsiders) and instructing employees about business policies (promoting a unified effort to carry out those policies). Working to define strategic business goals usually requires the ability to work with other managers in all but the smallest of organizations, that activity relates to work with other managers (*maintaining lateral contacts*, as Mintzberg formally defined that activity).

- *Informational* The informational role is perhaps the most visible and therefore most recognized role performed by managers. Consider the activity of instructing employees about company policies. That is a traditional role performed by managers, described in Mintzberg's study as the role of disseminator. One way in which managers hand down company policies is through verbal and written communications. This chapter discusses the latter in more detail, particularly in relation to preparing handbooks explaining company policies for employee reference and use. In addition to communicating company policies, managers also monitor the activities of employees under their supervision as part of their informational roles. Finally, managers act as spokespersons for the business, imparting information to others outside the business.

- *Decisional* Of course, managers have to make decisions about many issues. Planning the strategic course of the business is very much a decisional activity, as are activities such as formulating budgets that allocate the resources of the business to different activities and handling unique or difficult problems (Mintzberg 1973). It should be noted that decision making requires identifying goals, evaluating information, and then planning activities that will satisfy those goals. In this context, you are carrying out the decisional role of a manager in completing the Strategic Planning Project found at the end of each chapter.

The roles managers perform, the working environments in which managers operate, and even the purposes of management vary greatly according to the particular business being managed. A very small interior design business, for example, requires that a designer perform all of the managerial roles discussed here as well as the professional duties of an interior designer. In a larger interior design business, or an interior design practice group that is part of large architecture firm, an interior designer may perform only a few management roles, depending on the internally determined division of work duties among managers. Although it is possible to compartmentalize particular management roles, in many instances all of them affect the nature of working life for managers and those whom they supervise. If you have given some thought to owning and operating your own interior design business, you should have an understanding of management basics as well as the general conditions under which managers work to determine whether, or to what extent, you wish to assume such responsibilities in addition to those required of interior design professionals.

MANAGING WORKERS

After defining management and management roles, it seems logical to focus on the workers whom managers manage. First it is important to recognize that management tasks focused on coordinating the activities of workers is frequently referred to as **personnel management**, to distinguish it from other management activities.

A discussion of personnel management requires a distinction between two different kinds of workers found in business: employees and independent contractors. An **employee** has been defined as "a person who works in the service of another person under an express or implied contract of hire, under which the employer has the right to control the details of work performance" (Allison and Prentice 2001). Employees are entitled to benefits offered by the company as well as unemployment and worker's compensation insurance should employment end or on-the-job injury occur. On the other hand, the person hiring an **independent contractor** has control only over the independent contractor's finished product. Employers may either accept or reject the final results produced and may or may not pay the workers for their labor; but they cannot direct the *means* and *methods* by which they were produced. Independent contractors receive no company benefits, nor are they entitled to unemployment and worker's-compensation benefits. Another difference between employees and independent contractors concerns whether an employer must withhold portions of earnings, known as deductions, for federal and state income-tax purposes as well as deductions for Social Security and Medicare. These deductions are required for employees but not for independent contractors. Independent contractors are responsible for paying self-employment taxes on their earnings.

How is the employment relationship defined from a legal perspective? Would it surprise you that under most circumstances an employer can terminate a working relationship with an employee without giving prior notice to the worker or a reason for termination? Under what is referred to as the employment-at-will doctrine, which is recognized in most states, this can and does occur. Likewise, according to this doctrine, an employee may simply quit a job with no prior notice or reason given to the employer. There are, of course, limits on the application of the employment-at-will doctrine; for example, an employer may not terminate the worker for discriminatory reasons or out of retaliation for the worker's actions. Nevertheless, the employment-at-will doctrine is the prevailing viewpoint defining the relationship between employers and employees.

THE ORGANIZATION CHART

Within an organization, there are further distinctions made between workers, particularly employees. These workers hold positions referred to as either *staff* or *line*. You have likely seen organization charts for many businesses; in many respects they resemble a genealogical family tree, since they often show tree-like structures bearing the titles of positions within the organization. In interior design businesses, these positions are usually listed, in descending order, design director, project designer, designer, and design assistant. Different firms may use other titles for these positions, such as designer 1. Regardless of title, however, the position of these workers on the organization chart results in their being referred to as **line positions**. This distinction relates to the belief that holding a line position could result in moving up the line to positions higher on the chart with greater responsibilities, prestige, and, of course, pay. In a typical scenario, a design assistant, after gaining an initial measure of experience and the confidence of management decision makers, might ascend to the position of designer. The line is also important in the organizational structure because it establishes what is called the **chain of command**, or lines of authority within an organization.

THE STRUCTURE OF INTERIOR DESIGN BUSINESSES

Within most interior design firms of any size, or within interior design departments of architectural firms, the first-line position is usually that of design assistant. This is most often an entry-level position held by recent graduates of design programs with little experience outside the classroom. Once these designers gain experience handling projects that are relatively small in scope and have earned some amounts of revenue, they may progress to the position of designer. Sometimes this next position may be called staff designer, who work under the direct supervision of others. Nevertheless, the position is not a staff position since it is both on the organization chart and requires the independent exercise of professional judgment that workers need in order to carry out tasks—characteristics uncommon among true staff positions.

Positions found on a business's organization chart pertain to those held by workers who carry out the principal function of a business, be it accounting, law, or interior design. People holding these positions do not rely on other line members to assist and support them in the conduct of their individual tasks; they rely on what are referred to as **staff members**. An administrative assistant is one type of staff member found in most businesses, while a drafter of design drawings and CAD specialists are examples of staff members particular to architectural and interior design firms.

Rising from the position of designer to that of project manager is the next step design professionals may take in their organization. Project managers not only have extensive experience carrying out their own complex and financially important projects, but also a demonstrated ability to supervise others effectively. These positions frequently call upon the worker to oversee the work of many designers as well as support staff and also to assume some marketing activities. Interior design professionals with extensive project experience, often gained as a result of years of practice, and who have demonstrated abilities to oversee others and attract remunerative clients may be eligible to ascend to principal in firms.

Firm **principals** may include entrepreneurs who initially founded the firms at which they work, or workers who rose to this high level from other positions within the organization. Usually, principals are primarily responsible for their firms' creative direction and for interacting with clients, especially important clients. Principals are also responsible for forming strategic plans concerning major firm activities, such as the nature of future projects and methods for charging clients for services. These individuals may sometimes be referred to as partners, although the organization itself may not legally be a partnership (see chapter 4), perhaps having been formed as a corporation or limited liability company. The way in which the business was formally established will control management decisions.

COMMUNICATING INFORMATION AND EVALUATING WORKERS

Organizational structure is important for several reasons. Hierarchical in nature, it also suggests an established route by which information is conveyed throughout a business of any size. In small businesses, the chain of command—the pathway that members of the organization recognize and follow when communicating business information to each other may be quite truncated: a junior-level worker may be able to relay information directly to a firm principal, as can a principal to the worker. In more highly structured organizations, upper-management workers communicate through those in intermediate, or middle-management positions, to convey policies and instruction. Entry-level workers, under a formal chain-of-command structure, would report only to those directly above them in the organizational scheme—for example, assistant designers might direct questions to designers who oversee their work. In this way, the organizational structure within a business influences how communication of managerial information will flow.

An important activity in which managers engage is evaluating worker performance. Determining the degree to which a worker understands and adheres to established companywide communication procedures is often a consideration in these evaluations. In some businesses, chain-of-command and organization structure play a large role in determining how managers will conduct these evaluations. Chain-of-command and organizational structure are important when companies utilize what is referred to as **360-degree feedback**, in which colleagues situated in the organizational scheme above, below, and on the same level as a worker (as well as the workers themselves) prepare written statements describing their perceptions of the quality of work produced by that individual and their working relationship with that worker. This inclusive approach is gaining acceptance in large organizations, particularly those that utilize many layers of management. Its implementation depends on whether there is sufficient organizational structure in place to generate enough relevant information from which to draw conclusions about a worker's performance. Because this approach is expensive and time-consuming, it is less likely to be used to evaluate the performance of staff workers or of line workers who hold entry-level or low-level positions, although the institutional policy varies in this regard.

FACTORS INFLUENCING MANAGEMENT DECISIONS

Managing businesses and personnel are not activities that exist in a vacuum; rather they are influenced by factors both internal and external to the business itself. As you complete your education, you have undoubtedly thought about your future employment in interior design; perhaps you have had conversations about job market. In doing so, you have identified one of the external components that influences management decisions: the economic conditions prevalent in the marketplace, both national and local.

THE EFFECT OF THE ECONOMY

National and local economic conditions profoundly influence management decisions, especially those related to hiring new workers. Individual sole proprietors—in essence their own managers—make decisions based on these conditions as well. Economic health determines the availability of new jobs as well as the longevity of those in existence. In good times, as in the late 1990s and early 2000, national and most local economies expanded, so that individuals and businesses had greater monetary resources at their disposal. That availability of capital, for example, provided the financial impetus for the commission of new interior design projects, both residential and commercial. Managers therefore had more reasons to hire designers and create new design-related positions: There was a greater demand for the services of designers. As a result, those seeking employment in established firms and practice groups, or working in individually owned businesses, faced fairly good prospects for obtaining work.

Unfortunately, economic conditions changed and the demand for designers decreased, so that managers had to react by reducing, sometimes drastically, their existing staff. Employment figures for designers dropped considerably during the period ranging from 2001 to early 2004. Currently design jobs are slowly being added in the workplace. Employment of designers in sectors such as government work has grown in the interim, with increased demand for design services in governmental and military projects. Managers in these areas have responded by posting more government-sponsored jobs for interior design services; however, the extent to which managers in other sectors recognize the incremental advances in the economy and respond by hiring new workers remains to be determined.

Both businesses and workers are affected by economic conditions, whether good or bad. As you have seen, in expanding economies, management decision makers scramble to fill positions in order to meet the demands of many new projects. The challenge for managers then becomes determining the extent to which these added workers can be retained when economies contract. As you plan your career in interior design, ask yourself how you would enjoy the responsibility for making sometimes difficult management decisions that stem from changing economic conditions, as many business decision makers are required to do.

THE INFLUENCE OF FEDERAL AND STATE EMPLOYMENT LEGISLATION

Another important external factor that influences managers and the business decisions they make concerns personnel management, specifically the federal and state laws that relate to employment practices. A detailed survey of this topic could fill entire volumes and still remain incomplete. For the purpose of your study of personnel management, an overview of these laws along with a thumbnail description of their major provisions as they apply to interior design businesses should serve as an effective introduction. The formal titles of the major federal laws affecting employment practices are as follows:

- Civil Rights Act of 1964, Title VII (sometimes referred to as *Title VII*)
- Age Discrimination in Employment Act of 1967 (amended in 1990)
- Equal Employment Opportunity Act of 1972 (EEO)
- Civil Rights Act of 1991

The combined effect of these major pieces of employment-related federal legislation is that employers, especially those in businesses that have 15 or more employees, cannot discriminate on the basis of race, color, gender, age, marital status, or national origin in hiring and employment practices. Business managers responsible for personnel decisions must not only be aware of the provisions of these laws, but also must incorporate these provisions in internal business documents, such as employment applications, to ensure that potential hirees know that the revelation of prohibited information is not required. Terms found in employment handbooks must also be crafted by managers to reflect provisions of these and other laws. In this context, personnel managers are also tasked with organizing employment practices, such as the conduct of employee evaluations and terminations, in equally compliant ways.

Other federal laws related specifically to employee pay and benefits have also influenced the actions of business managers. Prominent among them are the following:

- Equal Pay Act of 1963
- Family and Medical Leave Act of 1993 (FMLA)

According to provisions of the Equal Pay Act, employers must pay all employees holding the same or similar jobs and having the same kind of work experience the same starting salary. Provisions of FMLA require that employers of 50 or more employees (who must have been with that business for at least one year on a full-time basis) provide those workers with up to 12 weeks of leave in order to care for a parent, spouse, or child. In addition to these and other federal laws related to employment practices, most states have enacted specific legislation applying to businesses in their jurisdictions. Managers are, of course, responsible for knowing the provisions of state laws and incorporating them into organizational practices as well.

Internal Factors Affecting Business Decisions

Management decisions are also influenced by conditions internal to their businesses. Two particularly influential internal factors involve understanding the developmental stage of a business's life and the kinds of services a business offers. It is important to note that these internal considerations do not exist apart from the external factors affecting management decisions. Managers need to be aware of the interplay of all these factors when making business decisions.

Developmental Stages of a Business

Businesses, like the people who work in them and the products they sell, transition through different phases throughout their lives. Whether referring to an infant or an introductory phase, you may notice a parallel development in the lives of people, products, and businesses. Characteristics of these different phases affect management decisions. These stages of business development may be defined as early, middle, and late.

In the early stages of a business—for example, when it first opens—managers may be called upon to make relatively few personnel decisions. Small firms in particular may have only a few or no workers other than the owner. In many instances, an owner and initial group of workers share similar beliefs about a company's purpose and direction, so formal management practices are of less concern. Instead, decisions made during an early stage are likely to focus on getting the business off the ground. Doing that may require that the owner and workers collectively decide to forego many benefits, or even regular salaries, to make adequate resources available to the business.

The middle stage of business life may be thought of as having two distinct phases: increasing growth and maturity, the latter sometimes referred to as a business's *peak*. As the terms *growth* and *maturity* suggest, management activities increase as the business becomes a viable entity and the need arises for greater internal structure to organize the business. In addition, management activities are increasingly required in order to assure compliance with laws regulating business and employment practices. Perhaps because of the services the firm offers or the economic conditions present at the time, or some combination of these factors, once the services of a nascent business become recognized, managers have an incentive as well as a financial ability to add employees to meet the demand for services and to focus on strategies reinforcing a business's position in the marketplace. In short, with the success of a business and its resulting growth, management activities traditionally increase to handle this development.

The second phase in the middle stage of a business's development is its maturity, or peak. Management practices during this phase are directed toward identifying new areas for firm growth as well as finding ways to organize its increasingly complex structure. By this time, a business's founders may have been joined by others who may not share the same beliefs that held the original core group together. In addition, the need for workers at this stage becomes more specialized and compartmentalized. Managers are responsible for finding ways to integrate the different beliefs into existing business practices along with identifying, hiring, and retaining workers who satisfy organizational needs.

The final stage of business development is referred to as the late, or decline, stage. Management decisions during this phase may focus less on retaining new workers than on finding ways to accommodate a business in what by then would be a substantially different marketplace for its services than was present at its beginning. Winding up a business's activities in preparation for the retirement of its owners may be one focus of management, as might locating a buyer for the business's assets. Merging the business into another entity may also be an activity for managers of especially large firms or practice groups.

It is important for interior designers seeking employment to assess the stage of a business before applying to work there. Young businesses may offer the excitement and freedom of less structure, but may also be riskier choices than work at a more seasoned firm with an established clientele and procedures. On the other hand, by choosing an established firm in which to work, a designer may be subject to more management supervision, especially with regard to business-development concerns. Many larger firms and practice groups place specific requirements on assistant designers seeking to become owners in a firm to attract profitable work. In their later stages of development, firms may offer much in the way of name recognition and prestige; but they may also have long entrenched practices and values that are not conducive to new or different points of view. Determining the stage of a business within its developmental life cycle can provide important clues about the working conditions, management practices, and opportunities to be found there.

Services Offered by a Business

Another important internal factor influencing management decisions involves the services provided by firms. Chapter 7 of this text, focused on marketing interior design services considers how a design firm identifies and promotes the specific "niche" it seeks to occupy. Before such marketing and promotional decisions can be made, however, business managers must focus on the exact services firms provide and the extent to which the consumer marketplace recognizes the need for those services. Knowing their businesses' services enables managers to formulate strategic plans for the businesses.

Strategic plans identify business goals and define ways to meet them. Strategic plans may include determining what areas of practice on which to concentrate or on which to put less emphasis. For example, many commercially trained interior designers, working in a crowded marketplace for office design, may choose not to work in that practice area but rather to apply their skills to designing health-care facilities. Even within the field of office design, designers tired of simply "warehousing" workers may combine extensive research in corporate culture with their design skills in order to offer services that more creatively mesh a company's identity with the physical environment in which that company's employees work. These new directions for applying interior design services are often the results of strategic planning in which designers realize how their services can be differentiated from those of others in their field. Once management decisions are made about the new direction of services, they can be followed by personnel decisions relating to the new business goals.

UNDERSTANDING
MANAGEMENT POLICIES AND PROCEDURES

Earlier in the chapter you learned that among the key roles performed by managers is their activity as an informational source, disseminating knowledge about the company and its operations to workers. On a daily basis, much of that information is likely conveyed in an informal manner, orally, or in the form of e-mail messages. Businesses, especially those in later stages of their development, usually require consistency in the language and interpretation of management policies. To that end, managers are tasked with assembling and disseminating employee handbooks. Often published in the form of a spiral-bound notebook, these handbooks are intended to provide participants in a business, whether employees or managers, with a comprehensive source of information about company policies and procedures. As noted, one rationale for disseminating this information is to maintain consistency of policy; these handbooks are also a convenient source of company policy since they are usually made available to every worker through personnel managers.

As you might suspect, these books provide detailed information about the conduct of practices adopted for use by the business. That information, and much more, may be found in various sections of the handbook. Typically, these books contain sections defining employment and business practices such as the following:

1. How the business is organized
2. The employment procedures followed by the company
3. How pay and benefits are determined by the company
4. Daily operations of the business
5. Termination procedures followed by the company when employees leave the organization

Most businesses provide their employees with handbooks and frequently require employees to acknowledge having received one. Think for a moment about the discussion of contracts in chapter 4. In particular, do you recall the stages in forming a contract: offer, acceptance, and consideration? Referring to these characteristics, many employees have argued that once they signed off on receiving a company's employee handbook, a type of contract known as an *implied contract* was formed between them and the company. The terms of this implied contract are those found in the employee handbook. In general, courts of law have recognized that claim as valid; and courts have further agreed with employees in related claims that companies breached those contracts by, as is usually the case, terminating the services of employees without following the terms and conditions specified in the company's handbook. Managers of businesses need to be aware of the possible effects of distributing employee handbooks and should seek assistance from legal professionals to assess those effects.

MANAGING TEAMS

Just as management practices do not exist in a vacuum, interior designers do not work in isolation. An increasing challenge for managers in interior design businesses is to find ways of managing the groups of professionals who collaborate in carrying out projects. The project manager is frequently responsible for coordinating the actions of these project teams. Because project managers must collaborate with, even motivate, other skilled professionals, their work requires a uniquely diversified set of skills. This section first identifies the professionals with whom project managers interact, and then defines some advanced management skills necessary for project managers.

Perhaps the most important of the advanced management skills required of project managers is the ability to foster a sense of collaboration among a project's constituents (Coleman 2002, 704). However, no amount of team building can ignore the fact that the project manager needs strong technical skills in order to convey the project's design intent and the means for bringing that intent to fruition. Project management and organizational skills, as well as interpersonal ones, are also necessary to integrate the various project components to successfully satisfy budget, schedule, and end-use requirements.

REFERENCES

Alderman, Robert L. 1997. *How to Prosper As an Interior Designer*. New York: John Wiley & Sons.

Allison, John and Robert Prentice. 2001. *Business Law: Text and Cases in the Legal Environment*. 3rd custom ed. New York: Thompson Learning.

Berger, C. Jaye. 1994. *Interior Design Law and Business Practices*. New York: John Wiley & Sons.

Coleman, Cindy, ed. 2002. *Interior Design: Handbook of Professional Practice*. New York: McGraw-Hill.

Knackstedt, Mary V. 2002. *The Interior Design Business Handbook*. 3rd ed. New York: John Wiley & Sons.

Mintzberg, Henry. 1973. *The Nature of Managerial Work*. New York: Harper & Row.

Siegel, Harry, and Alan Siegel. 1982. *A Guide to Business Practices and Principles for Interior Designers*. New rev. ed. New York: Watson-Guptill.

STRATEGIES-IN-ACTION PROJECTS

STRATEGIC PLANNING PROJECT:
IS MANAGEMENT FOR YOU?

In this section of your plan for your ideal interior design business, focus your attention on the specific position you wish to fill in the organization you want to establish. For example, do you wish to assume the full range of management and design responsibilities as design directors commonly do? Or do you wish to organize your own job in your ideal interior design business in such a way that others will assume management and administrative tasks and leave you to concentrate primarily on design activities? As you begin this project, think first about the balance you wish to strike between carrying out management and design-related activities. Some design professionals wish to focus their attention only on detailed activities such as product development, having little interest in business management and personnel supervision. Such professionals, especially those who started their own businesses, hire others to take care of managerial matters. However, many designers enjoy the management process since it allows them to mentor the development of other designers. At the opposite end of the spectrum are designers who have assumed many managerial responsibilities, retaining only those creative and design-focused projects that promise very high design commissions or much publicity. They have chosen this approach because often their very large firms require concentrated attention from senior members to address its many management issues. Which of these scenarios might be the right one for you?

Questions

To complete this project, recall the following segments of most job descriptions:

1. *Responsibilities* Spell out the exact responsibilities, related to both management and design-oriented tasks, that you wish to assume in your ideal interior design business. List approximately eight to ten functions that you consider important.
2. *Skills* Describe the kinds of skills you will need to acquire to carry out the responsibilities you have described. This portion of the business-plan project is intended to get you thinking about the extent to

which you want to assume the management activities required to operate a business and supervise the professional activities of others. Does it seem less important or interesting for you to perform management activities or somehow challenging and exciting? Make sure your viewpoint on this issue is apparent in the job description you draft for this project.

3. *Title* How would you describe the position you wish to hold? As you complete this project, devise a title that you think is appropriate for this position, and list it above your description of responsibilities and skills.

RESIDENTIAL INTERIOR DESIGN PROJECT SIMULATION

You received a letter in the mail from Lee, the young interior designer. The Abernathy project is taking a great deal of time, so the letter is only a brief account of what is transpiring. Lee and the family are making further refinements on some of the products selected for use in the project. But Lee has also sent you an application for employment at a local design studio (Form 6.1). The studio is actively recruiting for design assistants right out of school who are interested in ground floor, entry-level positions. In an attached note, Lee wrote:

I knew you would be interested in this position, so take a look at this application, and fill it in. Since you've never done one of these before, notice all the details you have to know about yourself. Even the number of references you need. It's a lot, that's for sure, but take the time to really think about who those references might be, and write down all the other jobs you've had before and what exactly you did. Really let the reader know about all the great stuff you can do: space planning, drafting, product specifications, and ordering—everything! Better get used to it—this it what it's like on the "other side." Also, be sure to read the stuff at the end of the application, and discuss it with someone in class. Employers assume you know what it all means, so make sure you do!

This assignment introduces you to the first of the management documents—job descriptions, employee handbooks, and employee evaluations—discussed in this chapter. Management responsibilities include establishing procedures for devising, implementing, and retaining the variety of documents necessary for business operation. Are the activities of interest to you?

APPLICATION FOR EMPLOYMENT

COMPANY NAME
Address
City, State, Zip Code

Date: _____

PLEASE READ: We are an Equal Opportunity Employer and consider all applicants soley on the basis of individual qualification without regard to age, ancestry, color, marital status, medical condition, national origin, physical handicap, religious beliefs or creeds, gender, or sexual orientation.

Applicant Information

Name _____
       Last   First   Middle Initial

Address _____
       Street   Apt.   City   Zip Code

E-mail Address: _____ Phone: ( ) _____

Social security number: _____ Can you submit written proof of legal ability to work in the United States?   YES/NO

Were you previously employed by this organization?   YES/NO
List any relatives or acquaintances who work or have previously worked for this organization:
_____

Position for which you are applying: _____
How did you hear about this position?: _____
When would you be able to begin work, if hired?: _____
Have you ever been convicted of a crime which would have a substantial relationship to the function and responsibilities of the position to which you are applying?   YES/NO
If YES, please explain: _____
_____ Date of conviction: _____

Education
High School
                           _____
                           Name and Address   Major/Area of Study
Graduate: YES/NO   Diploma/Degree Obtained: _____

College
                           _____
                           Name and Address   Major/Area of Study
Graduate: YES/NO   Diploma/Degree Obtained: _____

Other Education
                           _____
                           Name and Address   Major/Area of Study
Graduate: YES/NO   Diploma/Degree Obtained: _____

(continued)

Page ____ of ____

Describe any internships or specialized education you believe would be of benefit to the position for which you have appied: _____

_____
_____
_____

Employment: Please describe your employment from current, or most recent to earliest

Are you employed now?:   YES/NO

ONE	From:	To:

Name of Company/Employer: _____

Address: _____

Phone: _____   Supervisor/Contact: _____

Job title and description of duties performed:

_____
_____
_____

Beginning annual salary: _____   Ending annual salary: _____

Reasons for leaving this position: _____

May we contact this employer for reference?   YES/NO

TWO	From:	To:

Name of Company/Employer: _____

Address: _____

Phone: _____   Supervisor/Contact: _____

Job title and description of duties performed:

_____
_____
_____

Beginning annual salary: _____   Ending annual salary: _____

Reasons for leaving this position: _____

May we contact this employer for reference?   YES/NO

THREE	From:	To:

Name of Company/Employer: _____

Address: _____

Phone: _____   Supervisor/Contact: _____

Job title and description of duties performed:

_____
_____
_____

Beginning annual salary: _____   Ending annual salary: _____

Reasons for leaving this position: _____

May we contact this employer for reference?   YES/NO

(continued)

Page ____ of ____

FOUR	From:	To:

Name of Company/Employer: _____

Address: _____

Phone: _____ Supervisor/Contact: _____

Job title and description of duties performed:

_____

_____

_____

Beginning annual salary: _____   Ending annual salary: _____

Reasons for leaving this position: _____

May we contact this employer for reference?   YES/NO

Skills: Please describe any technical skills or abilities you believe would enable you to successfully perform the duties and responsibilities of the position to which you are applying: _____

_____

_____

_____

Please note any other proficiences you have relevant to your ability to perform the duties and responsibilities of the position to which you are applying: _____

_____

_____

_____

Activities/Honors/Awards/Professional memberships:

Please describe any of these you believe would enable you to successfully perform the duties and responsibilities of the position to which you are applying. This may include any offices or positions held. Please omit reference to any of these that may indicate age, ancestry, color, marital status, medical condition, national origin, physical handicap, or religious beliefs or creeds, gender, sexual orientation.

_____

_____

_____

References:

1. Name of Reference: _____

   Address: _____

   Phone: _____   E-mail address: _____

   How long have you known this reference?: _____

   In what capacity or context do you know this reference?: _____

2. Name of Reference: _____

   Address: _____

   Phone: _____   E-mail address: _____

   How long have you known this reference?: _____

   In what capacity or context do you know this reference?: _____

(continued)

FORM 6.1 (continued)

Page ____of ____

3. Name of Reference: _____
   Address: _____
   Phone: _____   E-mail address: _____
   How long have you known this reference?: _____
   In what capacity or context do you know this reference?: _____

Acknowledgments and Declarations by Applicant:

I acknowledge all facts and information provided in this application are true and complete.

I understand and acknowledge any false statement or omission in this application shall be sufficient cause for this company to refuse to hire me or, if employed, dismiss me.

I understand and consent to the use of any and all information given in this application to determine whether or not I will be retained for employment by this company in the position to which I have applied.

I understand and acknowledge this company, and I may terminate my employment at any time, either with or without prior notice of any kind.

I understand and acknowledge that this Application for Employment is in no way a contract or agreement for my employment.

Applicant's signature

_____
Date of application

CONTRACT INTERIOR DESIGN CASE STUDY: THE CASE OF THE AMPLE AMPHORA

After you read the following case study, respond to questions about how you might resolve the issues presented here.

The place to shop for fashionable San Franciscans and visitors to that city is charming Maiden Lane, across the street from Union Square. At the turn of the twentieth century, the street had a reputation for being dangerous. Now, the only peril to be had is to the bank accounts of shoppers who peruse its expensive offerings. Most of the buildings housing the stores had been fashionably transformed except for the subject property, located away from the square toward the corner of Kearny Street. With boarded doors and windows, the 1930s Art Deco–style building seemed simply forgotten on the otherwise bustling street.

Although eschewed by the chic mavens of Maiden Lane, the building was nevertheless quite popular among legions of itinerate inhabitants who had made it their home. For a period of just a few years, the building had become a veritable city unto itself, populated on an ever-changing basis with homeless inhabitants from all over the world. During the time they were on the premises, each staked out his or her own space, using patches of decades-old plaster and original wrought-iron railing, along with other vintage, irreplaceable found objects. Although electricity and water had long since been discontinued, these inhabitants had found ingenious ways to "borrow" electricity and water from neighboring buildings. This gerry-mandering was, of course, treacherous and completely noncompliant with city utility code. If the building were ever to be renovated, the damage done by its "tenants" would have to be corrected by cadres of specialized contractors and fabricators. These workers would all have to be retained and supervised by someone skillful enough to not only identify, but also specify, and supervise the kind of work they would have to perform. With boarded-up windows and an obscured entrance, few passersby could be aware of what was happening inside the old structure.

Certainly, the real estate acquisitions committee of the French cosmetics and perfume company Beautemonde was not aware of the building's many inhabitants. They were, however, aware of their company's need to have a commanding presence in such a prestigious shopping district. The company sought the space as a site for a branch of their popular cosmetics store Amphora, named after the vessels ancient Greeks used to hold unguents and salves. This store was intended by Beautemonde to be among the first of many new stores in the United States and would feature the exciting design elements for which the company stores were known throughout Europe and Asia.

One idea for the San Francisco store was the use of vending machines to sell its wares. With this concept, all customers had to do was slide credit cards across an electronic strip, then retrieve their selected products, already fashionably wrapped, from an opening in the machine after completing their purchase. This idea came about after the company ascertained that many customers already knew the products they wished to buy on entering the store and disliked having to wait in line at cash registers. Of course, the machines slated for use in the store were not the kind of metal boxes that usually dispense cheap snacks and sodas. These were custom-designed structures built to resemble a dressing table, complete with mirrors and built-in seating. The machines were extremely expensive to make and install. In fact, they required the person responsible for planning their installation to know a great deal about the construction standards relevant to installing complicated machines and technical devices, since an incorrectly designed procedure could ruin the machines. Because the machines had been designed in France, they also required someone to modify their specs so that the units could be built to conform to code standards found in the United States.

The French company also wanted each store location to be instantly recognizable and visually consistent with the others. Accordingly, the interiors of Amphora stores throughout the world all contained 20-foot-tall replicas of their namesake amphora. These huge items, which weighed approximately two tons, often had to be hoisted into place by cranes through the ceiling after much of the structural and finish work had already been completed. Since narrow Maiden Lane was closed off to automobile traffic, the only way such an item might be installed on-site would be to have it set in place by helicopter. The store planners noted that doing so might be an impediment; but they acknowledged that a project manager could be found who would know how to plan the installation, coordinate the necessary permits with the city, and schedule installation times when few passersby were present.

From Paris, Beautemonde optioned the purchase of the building, relying only on representations made by the real estate agency responsible for selling the property. Under such an arrangement, the French company could choose, after conducting its own inspections of the premises, not to purchase the space. No sooner had notice appeared in a local newspaper that the company was considering purchase of the building than an unforeseen avalanche of publicity appeared.

To begin with, city officials in charge of issuing the permits publicly refused to consider future plans for renovating the building until its groups of inhabitants were evicted. Furthermore, city property taxes on the building had not been paid for that year. Someone would have to pay those substantial sums before the city would act further. In short, before any progress could be made in renovating the building, including the issuing of necessary permits, these issues would have to be resolved.

But that was just the beginning. An art historian in neighboring Berkeley, California, alerted a local historical-preservation group to the fact that the Maiden Lane structure was one of the last remaining examples of pure California Art Deco in existence. The façade's swirling, stylized palm-tree motifs formed on etched glass blocks, the expert argued, should not be altered in any way, and especially not accompanied by a glitzy store sign. Members of this group of dedicated preservation-conscious citizens began to appear daily bearing signs reading, "Damsel in Distress: Save the Maiden Lane Building."

The problems, however, intensified. According to state law, homeless individuals are entitled to receive notice of a pending eviction and to be allowed an opportunity for city officials to hear of their housing needs. Once the city paper reported on the option to purchase the building, advocates for these individuals appeared at the site, also bearing signs reading "Hear Us Out! Don't Throw Us Out!" The issues raised by both groups—the preservationists and advocates for the homeless—were soon scheduled for public hearings in which group members and project representatives from Beautemonde would have an opportunity to comment on the proposed new use to which the building would be put.

On the day executives from Beautemonde appeared at the site, both legions of opponents were out in full force. All points of entry to the structure bore official city notices proclaiming the building in arrears on its taxes and threatening imminent governmental action. On top of those notices were numerous citations from city utility companies listing violations of electrical codes found by inspectors and demanding payment of fines.

Questions

An internal memo has alerted you that Beautemonde wishes to complete the purchase of the building. One of your many tasks as a corporate design director of Beautemonde is to write a job description for the position of project manager on the Maiden Lane project. This position should be filled by the individual possessing the unique combination of skills necessary to make the store a reality under the complex conditions described here.

For the purpose of this case study, draft only the responsibilities portion of the job description, using the facts of this case study as your guide to the kinds of skills any newly appointed project manager would need to have. From your reading of this chapter, you know that such wide-ranging qualifications will include technical, organizational, and interpersonal skills (Coleman 2002). What are some *specific* skills that should be included in this job description? Demonstrate that your understanding of the project manager's role encompasses the widest range of conceptual, management, and interpersonal abilities as well as detailed technical skills and knowledge.

CHAPTER SEVEN

MARKETING AND PROMOTING YOUR BUSINESS

The successful firm will be one that can articulate

why it is better—what sets it apart.

LISBETH QUEBE, FSMPS

WHY THIS CHAPTER IS IMPORTANT TO YOU

Marketing and promotional activities are similar to interior design projects in that all three require design practitioners to know how to apply basic concepts through organized processes in order to achieve acknowledged results. This chapter is important because your studies will make you familiar with the marketing concepts required to identify and plan ways to make public the services you and your business offer. Additionally, you will be familiar with several promotional activities, including personal selling techniques that are commonly used to meet planned marketing objectives.

Marketing and promotional tasks should not jeopardize your other business activities. As you approach this chapter, think of how you might balance the need to use current resources, such as available amounts of time and money, to advance the professional interests of the firm and attract future business opportunities. Chapter 7 is intended to help you devise your own strategies for striking a balance between the marketing and other concerns of your interior design business. This chapter concludes the overview of general business knowledge and skills required of design entrepreneurs. The following parts of the text focus on the specific business skills necessary for interior designers to interact professionally—and, moreover, profitably—with their clients.

PROFESSIONAL PRACTICES PORTFOLIO

On completing this chapter, you should be able to answer the following questions. Include your responses in a professional practices portfolio that you create and keep as a handbook of business strategies for your later use.

1. Define marketing as described in this chapter, and draft a short statement on what you believe marketing activities should seek to accomplish.
2. Define promotion and what it seeks to accomplish.
3. Distinguish between types of promotional methods.
4. Define selling and the process related to its use.
5. What are the ways in which the marketing process is organized?
6. How might you define marketing plans and their components?
7. What role do marketing budgets play in the marketing process?
8. What is contact management, and what does it seek to do?
9. What is a *prospect* in sales terminology?
10. What does it mean to *qualify* a prospect?

INTRODUCTION TO MARKETING
AND PROMOTING YOUR BUSINESS

As you look around your classroom, perhaps you notice that you and many other students are wearing those ubiquitous pants called blue jeans. These garments look highly alike to many. Yet, isn't there something different about each pair? Although jeans are fundamentally the same kind of product, it is likely you can distinguish a unique image, be it "classic" or "designer," among the different pairs. Even the names on the labels of these jeans may evoke a particular image and suggest a particular group of consumers to whom they are intended to appeal. The differences you perceive among such very similar products are the result of successful marketing and promotion.

To distinguish yourself, your business, and your work from other interior designers, you will have to engage in marketing and promotional activities much like those that influenced your choice of jeans to wear. Of course, there is one obvious distinction: As an interior designer, you are interested in attracting clients to your services, not to a particular product you make or sell. To be sure, interior designers, particularly those with residential practices, can and do sell products in the course of implementing their projects; however, this is merely an integral part of what they provide to clients—their services. This chapter acknowledges the importance of marketing and promotional activities related to the presentation of products, or tangible goods, for consumer acceptance. However, its focus is on how interior designers may plan for and promote recognition of that intangible thing known as their services. Before considering the nuances that distinguish services from products, think for a moment about terms such as *marketing* and *promotion* and even *advertisement* and *personal selling*. What do you think these terms—sometimes used mistakenly—really mean, and how do they relate to the business of interior design? The following chapter objectives define these and related terms that designers should understand as they go about their business activities. This chapter will then explore the procedures and practices commonly used by design professionals to make their services known.

OBJECTIVES TO CONSIDER

This chapter identifies three major objectives to guide you in understanding marketing and promotional activities and how to apply them.

1. Defining marketing and its basic concepts within the context of interior design
2. Distinguishing promotion from marketing as well as recognizing promotional concepts and how they may be used in interior design
3. Describing selling and sales skills as they relate to interior design services

Keep these objectives in mind to help you explore this intriguing area of professional practices.

DEFINING MARKETING WITHIN
THE CONTEXT OF INTERIOR DESIGN

As a subject of study and an important business activity, the concept of marketing has many different interpretations. Academics and writers have honed definitions based on their own theories and experiences; however, one industry group, the American Marketing Association (AMA) has defined **marketing** as "the process of planning and executing the conception, pricing, promotion, and distribution of ideas, goods, and services to create exchanges that satisfy individual and organizational goals" (Bennett 1995). Considering each part of this comprehensive definition should give you a better idea of what marketing means and what is involved in the process to which it refers.

THE MARKETING ANALYSIS

At first, you will note the definition defines marketing as "the process of planning and executing." As with most business activities, marketing activities require you to carry out concerted efforts. These efforts usually begin with a process referred to as a **marketing analysis**. This first step seeks to identify, for later use, the particular services a designer or design firm provides. It also identifies the specific group of consumers—individuals, groups of individuals, or business entities—to whom the services of that designer or design firm might appeal. In addition, marketing analyses include a survey of services offered by other design professionals working in the same business community. To be meaningful, a marketing analysis should examine each of these components in detail, so that the interior designer and design firm can have a better understanding of themselves as well as the market for their services. Marketing analyses form the basis for subsequent **marketing plans** that define specific goals and the means by which the designer or design firm intends to achieve them. Marketing plans typically include things such as budget information and scheduling related to the implementation of the plan. Because these are both important aspects of marketing your interior design business, you should be more aware of what these components are and what function they serve. A marketing budget shows how a business proposes to allocate its financial resources to make known the services offered. Marketing activities in the form of simple print advertisements in newspapers or magazines, other printed materials such as brochures handed to potential clients, or even business cards are all business expenses. During the budgeting process, the decision makers of the design business first determine what kinds of media they wish to use to promote that business then learn costs associated for doing so. For example, principles operating a new interior design business might wish to run a series of print advertisements in a local area homes magazine for a successive series of months as well as have brochures available that show examples of work the firm is capable of producing. Determining the costs for producing these items, then ascertaining whether the firm can afford some or all of these costs without jeopardizing other business activities, is one simple way a firm may budget for marketing expenses.

The timing of marketing efforts is also important if they are to be successful. Advertisements run during times when many people are looking for homes and interested in interior design are likely to be more effective than advertisements run when events such as holidays or non-vacation times occur. Thus, determining a schedule for when things such as publication of advertisements will occur is an important consideration when planning marketing activities.

Niche Marketing

Defining market analysis in terms of "the particular services a designer or firm desires and is able to provide," "the specific group of consumers to whom the services . . . might appeal," and "competition" should suggest to you one of its important goals: to make the services provided by a designer or design firm appear unique and attractive to those most likely interested in them. This concept of identifying specific services and their potential users is referred to by many different names. Perhaps you have heard the terms *market segmentation* or *market differentiation*, which are frequently used by marketing professionals. Other ways to refer to the process include *niche marketing* or *positioning*. Whether in a small or large practice with either a residential or commercial focus, interior designers can benefit from detailed marketing analyses that seek to identify these niches.

For example, contract interior design increasingly requires practitioners in that area to understand and know how to apply building, health, and safety codes as they plan environments made increasingly complex by these demands. A market analysis prepared for an individual or groups working in this field would first seek to establish the kind of commercial work for which these practitioners are best suited—by interest, education, and experience—to pursue. Commercial designers with interests and abilities in programming and designing retail spaces would likely not have an interest in, or be suitable candidates for, work in the area of health-care interior design. Quite aside from that obvious example, marketing analyses that pinpoint precise niches in the broad areas of commercial retail or health-care design suitable for a particular designer or group of designers can be informative. Individual practitioners may develop specific areas of practice over time, which they enjoy and from which they can profit financially. Larger practices may engage the services of outside marketing experts to survey firm members. By doing so, decision makers in those practices learn about the interests and abilities available in-house, and with that knowledge identify a service niche or niches for the firm.

Marketing analyses benefit residential interior designers as well as their commercial colleagues. Would a residential practitioner, for example, interested and experienced in producing environments informed by mid-century American styles be a likely candidate for an English Victorian-era restoration project? Probably not—and, again, a marketing analysis for such practitioners would likely consist of a fairly straightforward "yes" or "no." Individual practitioners may simply stay away from projects that are not of interest to them with no further thought of conducting a marketing analysis. Think for a moment, however, about a residential design firm with practitioners who have many different interests and specializations. A formal marketing analysis might identify specific areas of residential work that firm could pursue. In short, an important function of a marketing analysis in any specialty or niche is to identify what the firm wants to do and is capable of doing.

The Target Market

Another important function of a marketing analysis is to identify those individuals and groups to whom specific design services might be appealing. This group is frequently referred to as a **target market** for the individual or firm. Given the multifaceted nature of consumers, target-marketing efforts may identify more than one specific group to which designers' work may appeal. Before discussing some of the complexities involved in conducting a target-market analysis, consider how it can assist designers.

Commercial interior designers frequently obtain work by responding to requests for proposals (RFPs) issued by businesses in need of specific design work. For example, a large retail company interested in establishing a series of stores in different shopping malls may seek input from prospective project designers. The decision to respond to such formal inquiries, itself a lengthy and detailed process, may depend on whether a design firm has identified, through a target-market analysis, that particular retailer (or at least others very much like it) as a possible client for the firm's services. Among residential interior designers, target-marketing efforts can be equally instructive. Designers with specialized knowledge of how to incorporate fine art into interior environments, for example, may use simple target-marketing techniques, such as identifying members of their community known to have an interest in such services and the financial means to afford them. Having such information available, the designer can plan how best to approach or respond to potentially interested clients.

The process of conducting target-market analyses is highly detailed. There is no single factor that alone identifies a target market. In fact, many factors come into play in determining the group or groups to which specific interior design services might appeal. Some of the more commonly used factors in target-market analyses include the following:

◆ Demographic data based on interpretations of information on population age and income
◆ The geographic location of possible clients
◆ Psychographic profiles of the lifestyles of different consumers and the products and services these groups would likely use

These target-marketing factors can serve as the basis for focused efforts by designers to identify potential clients. Particularly in large firms with appropriate financial resources, designers often seek assistance from marketing survey firms that specialize in conducting demographic, psychographic, and other forms of consumer research to identify potential clients, their traits, interests, and geographic locations.

Another important aspect of a marketing analysis involves assessing services offered by competitors. Your colleagues in the design community, especially those with similar professional specialties, are also your competitors for clients. This fact makes differentiation of the services you or your business offer all the more important, for potential clients often do not perceive or understand the unique subtleties that characterize your practice. Promotional techniques, such as advertisement, may use marketing information to position your services in such a way that they and you are identifiably distinct. This is one way designers may attract clients in a crowded marketplace.

SERVICES VERSUS PRODUCTS

Looking back at the formal definition of marketing, it is important to next consider the reference to the "pricing, promotion, and distribution (of goods, ideas, and services)." What does this part of the definition mean, and how do you think it might apply to interior design businesses?

Intangibility

Services, including those related to interior design, are *intangible* (Berkowitz 2000). In other words, you cannot touch them as you can touch your jeans; yet you are aware of them. Some marketing experts consider services to be invisible, but nonetheless capable of being marketed to consumers (Beckwith 1997). In order to better promote your services to potential consumers, think about several ways in which services differ from products. One central difference has already been noted: Services are intangible; they cannot be held, touched, or seen before a purchasing decision is made (Berkowitz et al. 2000). Think for a minute about the implications of this characteristic. Prior to purchasing your jeans, for example, you have the opportunity to evaluate whether a particular pair satisfies any number of needs and wishes: Do they fit well? Are they cool? However, prior to purchasing a service such as a haircut, you do not have that same opportunity to evaluate whether the stylist's efforts will be satisfactory. Prior to hiring you for your services, your clients are in the same position as you are with respect to your hairstylist. How can you focus your marketing efforts to address the intangibility of services? Ultimately, after purchasing your jeans and even your haircut, you receive a benefit—some value asset, good, or advantage from having done so. With respect to marketing efforts for your services, explaining or demonstrating the benefits to clients from the use of your services enables those prospects to evaluate your product or services. With your increasing experience and professional recognition, the benefit to your clients may simply be your agreeing to work on their project!

Inseparability

In addition to their intangibility, services are also considered to be inseparable (Berkowitz et al. 2000). Within a marketing context, *inseparability* means that the consumer cannot separate the provider of a service from the service itself (Murray 1991). Your hairstylist, for example, is the force animating the scissors used to cut your hair in a particular way that will result in the style you desire. Similarly, you as the designer and the interior design services you provide are inseparable. Who else but you can conceptualize interior design plans in the exact way that you can? The concept of inseparability presents interesting challenges in marketing interior design services. Keep in mind that many established interior designers enjoy a high degree of name recognition in their communities. In fact, linking their name to a project may be a telegraphic way of describing their distinctive style and even their clientele. For example, the late San Francisco–based interior designer Michael Taylor became known for originating the "California Look" about 40 years ago; the style became popular among socialites and celebrities throughout the United States. Many clients seek out the services of famous or locally well-known designers not only on the basis of talent, but also because those designers and their cachet are inseparable from the services they provide.

For young designers, however, the concept of inseparability presents challenges different from those experienced by well-known designers. If, as a provider of interior design services, you are inextricably linked to those services, how might you use marketing techniques to link your name to your services so as to attract attention? "Marketing outrageously" (Spoelstra 2001) or "being remarkable" (Godin 2003) are some of the catchy phrases used by recent marketing writers to suggest that providers of goods and services offer "something phenomenal, or flat-out unbelievable" (Godin 2003) to attract consumers. The premise behind this viewpoint is simply that customers and clients have become bored with and accustomed to traditional means of marketing (Levinson 1999). In this chapter, you will learn about a variety of promotional and selling methods. Think about how you might creatively use them to differentiate yourself and your services from other designers.

Inventory

Inventory is a third characteristic of the marketing of services. Inventory is frequently considered in terms of items held for sale to others by a merchant (Lovelock and Wright 2001). Since services primarily utilize the time and expertise of the individual providing the service, in theory, at least, inventory costs should be much lower for service providers; but are they? From the knowledge you have about the practice of interior design, how do you think inventory issues affect designers? Think about the concept of "time and expertise."

The store selling your jeans likely does compute the costs involved in offering those jeans to customers. Quite simply, the store must spend certain sums to obtain a particular style of jeans and hold them until they are eventually sold. These sums are known as the store's *carrying costs* for those jeans. Now, imagine that you have your own interior design studio; only you and your services are the "product." Do your services have a carrying cost associated with them, as do the jeans? While you may not be able to quantify to the exact penny the personal costs necessary for making you available to work, intuitively you know that each day you do not work will "cost" you. How will you pay your fixed-cost expenses, discussed in chapter 5, if you do not have the required income? The costs associated with your services are known as **idle production capacity** and may be thought of as your carrying costs for services. As a side note, this idea of determining your labor costs becomes especially important when determining the rate at which you will charge clients, an issue further discussed in chapter 9. It is important for you to realize that the costs of whatever salary you might earn as an interior designer (even if you pay it to yourself) and the costs of equipment you need to carry out your work make up your carrying costs for working, even if you do not have any physical inventory offered for sale. Of course, if you offer merchandise for sale, then those inventory costs should be added to your production capacity.

Inconsistency

Another characteristic that differentiates services from products is their *inconsistency*, or variability in the way that services are rendered each time they are performed. With perhaps only minor exceptions, one pair of jeans is very much like another of the same style made by a manufacturer. On the other hand, no service provider ever provides exactly the same service in the same way each time they work. As you know, different circumstances and the desires of different clients will cause you to carry out your interior design work in different ways. Each project site, for example, has different features. Some clients want to play an active role in the design process, while others are less interested in doing so. In short, you will perform your services inconsistently, according to differing demands. For many potential clients the idea of inconsistency presents several concerns. Clients want creative, unique solutions to their design concerns. No client ever wants to feel processed or, even worse, to have a finished project look exactly like someone else's. The marketing challenge for interior designers is to convince clients that the inherent inconsistency of interior design work does not mean that you are unqualified to handle their projects. Therefore, interior designers may promote their services by stressing their experience and professional qualifications for carrying out particular types of projects. The goal of this approach is to minimize client concerns about a designer's ability, while acknowledging the variety of ways in which a designer must work. Services are differentiated from products by their characteristics of intangibility, inseparability, inventory needs, and inconsistency—all of which offer challenges to those who market interior design services. Subsequent discussion will detail how to incorporate these differences into a viable marketing plan.

EXCHANGE

The idea of *exchange*, as expressed in the AMA definition of marketing, refers to a mutual giving of something of value or the reciprocal importance of the parties involved. For example, in response to your marketing efforts—either print advertisements or *word of mouth* (WOM) personal referrals—clients can seek out and compensate you for the services you have offered to provide. The AMA's definition of marketing also refers to "planning" and satisfaction of "goals," topics developed throughout this chapter and the entire text. Before beginning a discussion of marketing and its related processes, it is important to distinguish among various commonly used marketing terms.

PROMOTIONAL PRACTICES IN SERVICE MARKETING

As you recall, promotional activities are practices that seek to achieve the objectives identified in marketing plans. People often confuse the promotional activities by which businesses make themselves and their products and services known to their markets with the broader concept of marketing. Getting the word out may be thought of as the purpose underlying the use of promotional activities. These activities can be as simple as eye-catching business cards that convey a sense of the designer's specialized practice area or as familiar as advertisements. Some promotional activities can be more detailed and difficult, such as distributing press releases and those promotional activities related to the Internet. Four broad categories of promotion used by interior designers are advertising, sales promotion, publicity, and personal selling.

ADVERTISING AND SALES PROMOTION

Advertising is a term often misused as a synonym for *marketing*; yet the two are decidedly different in what they seek to accomplish. **Advertising** is the paid transmission of a marketing message to arouse a desire in potential clients to buy the goods or services offered by the advertiser or to produce a favorable image of the advertiser on the part of those exposed to the message. Advertising may thus be considered one of the techniques marketers use in an overall plan designed to facilitate exchanges of goods and services. Broadcast advertising includes television, Internet, and radio. Of the various print media, interior designers typically favor newspapers and magazines, particularly "shelter" magazines with established bases of readers who are potential clients interested in seeing examples of interior designers' work.

Sales promotion is another marketing-related term that needs to be further defined since it, too, is sometimes confused with the broader concept of marketing. Promotional activities such as special incentives or token gifts given to clients are examples of ways interior designers may attempt to establish their identity and call attention to the goods and services that they offer.

PERSONAL SELLING

In everyday language, many people use the term *marketing* to mean what is better referred to as *selling*. Think of marketing representatives who call on the telephone or talk to you on campus. Are their activities as broadly focused as the AMA definition for marketing suggests, or are they trying to entice you to purchase something immediately? Selling is a crucial part of any business's overall marketing efforts as it is usually the first and sometimes only contact a business will have with potential customers or clients. Thus, sales or **selling** frequently involves a mostly spoken presentation given one-on-one or in small, controlled groups in which the attributes of goods or services are presented for purchase consideration (Baldridge 1999). In your favorite apparel store, has an employee ever spent time asking what you were looking for in a pair of jeans and then shown you new styles of jeans with those features? Now suppose you are in the salesperson's position—only this time you are selling your interior design services. What would you say to potential clients when you are face-to-face with them? Which of your attributes would you emphasize for those prospects' consideration? Whether the goal is to encourage the purchase of jeans or interior design services, selling is an important business skill for an entrepreneur to develop. Techniques associated with personal selling are described in greater detail later in this chapter, and you can address questions about personal selling skills in the Residential Interior Design Project Simulation.

Personal selling plays an important role in the overall marketing efforts of any kind of product or service. It involves your identifying specific consumers' needs, then personally telling consumers why your services should be chosen to address those needs. The sales process concludes with what is called a **close**, during which the salesperson making the *pitch* asks for the prospect's business. As simple as that may seem, the idea of selling anything—much less services—is difficult for many people, even established professionals. In part, the difficulty stems from the risks involved in selling. These risks include rejection and failure to make the sale. Understandably, most people have a fairly low tolerance for these risks and wish to avoid them. After all, it is only human to desire the acceptance and approval of others. No one wants to be thought of as pushy or trying to manipulate people to buy something through trickery. Yet, among the promotional methods available to designers, personal selling is arguably the most important because it is perhaps the most commonplace and least expensive. Before examining details of the selling process, think for a minute about what it is you may not like about the idea of selling. By doing so, maybe you can understand how you may best harness this technique and turn it to your advantage.

First of all, is selling really necessary for a designer? Creative professionals view the product of their work very differently from consumers of design products and services. Consumers may desire design solutions that meet their immediate needs and require nothing more. Design professionals, on the other hand, have studied the process of design from different perspectives and tend to view their design solutions as representing or being inspired by those studies. For some design professionals, the results of their creative training should need no explanation, much less touting for the purpose of obtaining work. However, the merits of a design solution, while obvious to a trained professional, may not be apparent at all to nondesigners. After all, these consumers lack the same training and experience as designers. A brilliant idea may remain forever on the drawing board if your clients cannot understand how that idea meets their needs. Personal selling skills are perhaps the best way to make the client aware of the merits of a designer's solution. To be sure, most clients are extremely sophisticated consumers of professional services. However, selling skills on the part of the designer help to ensure that clients interpret correctly the ideas behind a designer's work.

Anyone with a telephone or who has ever bought a house or car has likely been subjected to an unpleasant, intrusive selling experience. As a result, many professionals think that personal selling is not a desirable way in which to promote their services. This belief may also stem from the centuries-old practice of forbidding some professionals from actively engaging in certain promotional activities such as advertising. But think for a moment about the many interior designers seeking work. If you don't promote yourself or your business, isn't it likely that other designers who do promote their services will capture your share of the market?

PUBLICITY

In contrast with advertisement, which can be extremely expensive to produce and get to the public, a distinctive aspect of **publicity** as a promotional tool is that there is usually no cost for getting the message before the market. The *content* of the message may involve considerable expense, but the dissemination of the news is free. For example, a design firm may host a lecture at its studio for the public or for the local chapter of ASID. A catered reception for the speaker could be costly, but making the intended audience aware of the lecture could be accomplished at no expense by issuing a **press release.** This is a prepared, written statement, usually intended to announce an upcoming event, an individual or group's significant accomplishment, or another circumstance of potential interest to media sources. These sources can be influential editors and writers, who may find the information contained in the release relevant and interesting to their readers. Obtaining a major design commission is another example of news that may merit an interior design professional's use of a press release. Usually, an interior designer or a public relations professional hired for the purpose of writing and placing a press release will have media contacts, such as editors and journalists whom they know personally or have worked with previously. In the event that you have no prior history working with a contact, it is a good idea to call that source and introduce yourself and explain the significance of the press release prior to sending or electronically transmitting it. Otherwise, your efforts may be wasted or rendered irrelevant should the release be published too late for its message to be effective. Finally, always call after you have submitted a press release, even if you know your contact well. In this way, you will have an opportunity to clear up any possible confusion or answer any questions that your contact might have about the subject of your press release. Press releases are one way for interior designers to build relationships with journalists and others interested in making their work known. As you begin plans to promote your interior design business, you will find that the sources listed below are very helpful.

REFERENCES

Aaker, David A. et al. 2000. *Marketing Research*. 7th ed. New York: John Wiley & Sons.

Ali, Moi. 2001. *Effective Public Relations*. DK publishing, Inc.

Baldridge, Joy. 1999. *Fast Forward MBA in Selling: Becoming a Self-Motivated Profit Center and Prosper*. New York: John Wiley & Sons.

Beckwith, Harry. 1997. *Selling the Invisible: A Field Guide to Modern Marketing*. New York: Warner Books.

Bennett, Peter D., ed. 1995. *AMA Dictionary of Marketing Terms, 2nd ed.* Chicago, Ill: NTC Publishing Group.

Berkowitz, Eric N. et al. 2000. *Marketing*. 6th ed. New York: Irwin McGraw-Hill.

Buzan, Tony, and Richard Israel. 2000. *Sales Genius: A Master Class in Successful Selling*. Brookfield, VT: Gower.

Day, George S. 1999. *The Market-Driven Organization*. New York: The Free Press.

——. 1999. *The Market-Driven Strategy*. New York: The Free Press.

Duncan. Todd M. 2002. *High-Trust Selling*. New York: Thomas Nelson.

Fox, Jeffrey J. 2000. *How to Become a Rainmaker: The Rules for Getting and Keeping Customers and Clients*. Concord, NH: Hyperion Press.

Gitomer, Jeffrey, and Ron Zemke. 1999. *Knock Your Socks Off Selling*. New York: AMACOM.

Gladwell, Malcolm. 2000. *The Tipping Point: How Little Things Can Make a Big Difference*. New York: Little, Brown & Company.

Godin, Seth. 2003. *Purple Cow: Transform Your Business by Being Remarkable*. New York: Penguin.

Heiman, Stephen E. et al. 1998. *The New Strategic Selling: The Unique Sales System Proven Successful by the World's Best Companies*. New York: Warner Books.

Heymann, H. G. and Robert Bloom. 1990. *Opportunity Cost in Finance and Accounting*. Westport, CT: Greenwood Publishing.

Kendall, Dick. 1995. *Nobody Told Me I'd Have to Sell: How to Sell Your Services and Skills Even If You Are Not in Sales*. New York: Carol Publishing.

Knackstedt, Mary V. and Laura J. Haney. 1992. *Marketing and Selling Design Services: The Designer-Client Relationship*. New York: John Wiley & Sons.

Levinson, Jay Conrad. 1999. *Mastering Guerilla Marketing: 100 Profit-Producing Insights That You Can Take to the Bank*. New York: Houghton-Miflin Company.

Lloyd, Steven. 2000. *Selling from the Heart: In the New Millennium, Selling is Everyone's Job*. Arlington, Tex.: Sterling & Pope Publishers.

Locke, Christopher. 2001. *Gonzo Marketing: Winning Through Worst Practices*. Cambridge, Mass.: Perseus Publishing.

Loeffler, Robert H. 1994. *A Guide to Preparing Cost-Effective Press Releases*. Haworth Press.

Lovelock, Christopher H., and Lauren Wright. 2001. *Principles of Service Marketing and Management*. 2nd ed. New York: Pearson Education.

McKenna, Regis. 1997. *Real Time: Preparing for the Age of the Never Satisfied Customer*. Boston, Mass.: Harvard Business School Press.

———. 2002. *Total Access*. Boston, Mass.: Harvard Business School Press.

McQuarrie, Edward F. 1996. *The Marketing Research Toolbox: A Concise Guide for Beginners*. Thousand Oaks, Calif.: Sage Publications.

Murray, Keith B. 1991. A Test of Services Marketing Theory: Consumer Information Acquisition Activities. *Journal of Marketing* vol.: 10–12.

Quebe, Lisbeth. FSMPS. 2002. "Marketing: Position and Identity". In *Interior Design: Handbook of Professional Practice*, ed. Cindy Coleman. New York: McGraw-Hill.

Rackham, Neil. 1988. *SPIN Selling*. New York: McGraw-Hill.

———. 1996. *The SPIN Selling Fieldbook: Practical Tools, Methods, Exercises and Resources*. New York: Irwin McGraw-Hill.

Rosen, Emanuel. 2002. *Anatomy of Buzz: How to Create Word-of-Mouth Marketing*. New York: Doubleday & Company.

Sandhusen, Richard L. 2000. *Marketing*. New York: Barron's Educational Series.

Spoelstra, Jon. 2001. *Marketing Outrageously*. Austin, Tex.: Bard Press.

Stanley, Thomas J. 1997. *Networking With the Affluent*. New York: McGraw-Hill.

Templeton, Tim. 2003. *The Referral of a Lifetime: The Networking System That Produces Bottom-Line Results Every Day!* San Francisco, Calif.: Berrett-Koehler Publishers.

Tracy, Brian. 1994. *Advanced Selling Strategies*. New York: Simon & Schuster Audio.

——. 2002. *Be a Sales Superstar: 21 Great Ways to Sell More, Faster, Easier in Tough Markets*. San Francisco, Calif.: Berrett-Koehler Publishers.

STRATEGIES-IN-ACTION PROJECTS

STRATEGIC PLANNING PROJECT
THE BUSINESS CARD "MINI" PROJECT

By now you have devoted a great deal of thought and energy into planning your ideal interior design business. You likely have a mental picture of what you would like it to be. This chapter has examined how designers may use marketing to plan ways of communicating their services to potential clients. It also discussed some promotional methods available to professionals to carry out those plans. Think for a moment about one of the most common methods individuals use to market their services—a printed business card. While there are more complex forms of technology and more far-reaching advertising campaigns available, something as simple as a business card can send a powerful marketing message. In this project, which in its first section deviates from the task of drafting sections of a business plan, you will design a business card for your ideal interior design business.

As part of the design activity, you have free reign to use any combination of typefaces, photographic images, colors, printing methods, even textures of paper that you choose. From a creative perspective there are no limits, except for time and availability of resources. However, remember the finished business card must carry out an important marketing message to its recipients: It must convey, in a space that is typically only $3^{1}/_{2}$ by 2 inches in its final form, the following information:

- Who you are
- How an interested party may contact you
- The physical address of your business or place of employment
- The essence of your ideal business.

Is it enough to say you are an interior designer, without giving readers some sense of your area of specialty or your conceptual style or point of view? Think back to the mission statement you drafted in chapter 3. Does that give you any idea of what you might want—through words, images, and other forms—to convey through your business card? This project is one way for you to see how business concepts, such as promotional practices, can be an integral part of a creative design process.

Creativity, however, cannot come at the expense of sound, profit-focused business methods. Marketing activities and promotional methods are expensive, in terms of time and monetary resources, to initially produce and sustain. Even producing a business card utilizes these resources. In the second portion of this project, you will return to creating a plan for your ideal interior design business by drafting a short initial promotional budget.

Questions

Once you have completed your business card, determine the following:

1. Given a budget of only $250 determine how much it would cost to have an initial print run of 1,000 $3^{1}/_{2}$-by-2-inch cards, as you have specified. Remember, the more elaborate the card—for example, those that fold or have cut-out sections—the more expensive it will be.
2. Determine how much it would cost to run a copy of the card in a local telephone or other directory for about one year. How much of your initial $250 would you have left?
3. Finally, think about the time and effort you spent in carrying out this project. Then consider the many other tasks that design professionals must perform. Can you see how even simple marketing and promotional activities, not to mention more complicated procedures

such as business development, speaking, and writing, are expensive in terms of time and money? In the last section of your initial promotional budget, describe how you will be able to balance the reality of performing the design work for which you have been retained with the challenge of actively seeking new work through marketing plans and promotional activities.

Business cards are admittedly marketing and promotional activities of a fairly small scale; but they are significant for design professionals, many of whom enter their specially designed and produced cards in international competitions, such as those found in graphic-design magazines. Business cards are visual representations of you and your business. As you conclude this project, share with others the components you have chosen for your ideal interior design business card. In the process, make clear how those components implement the marketing message you wish to convey.

RESIDENTIAL INTERIOR DESIGN PROJECT SIMULATION

Lee, the young interior designer, has been busy with the all-encompassing Abernathy project. Despite various problems, Lee has managed to keep the project moving along to the satisfaction of her clients. In fact, Lee and the clients have gotten to know each other quite well, so much so that the couple has invited the designer to an informal get-together they are hosting in the finished portion of their spectacular home. Lee wishes to share with you her diary entries written both before and after the party, so that you may suggest how she could make the best use of this occasion to overcome her understandable stage fright and possibly meet prospective clients.

Lee's Diary

OK, I've been so busy working on the Abernathy children's space I have neglected you some. Lots of work bringing the pieces together, I can tell you that! Guess what's up: I got invited to a party! I was on-site today when Mrs. Abernathy told me that she and Mr. A. were having a few people over this weekend, two days away, for "a casual get-together," as she called it. She asked if maybe I could stop by to meet some of their friends and explain what was going on downstairs in the children's room. I remember her saying, "Lee, you should circulate and articulate. Tell people about yourself and all the wonderful things you do in your work." Can you believe that? That afternoon, I ran over to the print shop and had some new business cards made on better stock than the cheap-o ones the store provided for us. That way I'll have enough "good" cards to take with me.

Another thing: Mrs. A. said I should be able to tell people at the party about my creative point of view. "You know," she said, "describe your inspiration, the feelings your work evokes, even how you blend the client's wishes with your own design knowledge—so they know what you're all about." I didn't have the heart to tell her that I have never really thought about how to describe myself and my work. I just "am," and I thought my work would speak for itself! I mean, shouldn't most people understand what my design intent is just by looking at my drawings and the finished project? I pulled out the rendering I did for the children's rooms and, with the Abernathys' permission, I'll put it up so that people at the party can see what I planned the finished space to look like. I'm going to have to think a little bit about what I'm going to tell people. I'm a little scared, actually. What if they don't like who I am and what I do? Yikes!

Question

1. After reading about the upcoming event at the Abernathy home and Lee's uncertainty about how to make the most of this opportunity for personal promotion, maybe you can think of a way to help her. With the aid of the Professional Image Development Worksheet (see Form 7.1), see if you can put together a statement that Lee could make at the party. Then, do the same for yourself. What would you say to people who might be interested in your services? The personal description for Lee and you should use language that may be understood clearly, even by those not involved in the practice of interior design. Having completed these tasks, read Lee's diary entry about what transpired at the party. You may need to help Lee develop her personal selling skills.

Lee's Diary

Diary—when I think "casual party," I think of the pizza parties we have in the dorm. Well, that's not Mrs. Abernathy's idea of casual. A catered affair with a valet service to park cars, since the Abernathys had invited so many people

FORM 7.1. PROFESSIONAL IMAGE DEVELOPMENT WORKSHEET

PROFESSIONAL IMAGE DEVELOPMENT WORKSHEET

Step 1

"I am inspired by . . ."

Brainstorm about your many sources of inspiration
then decide which sources most inform your work.

Step 2

"The feelings I seek to evoke in my work are . . ."

How do you want clients and others who approach your
work to feel? To what senses do you wish to appeal?

Step 3

"My goals for my projects are to . . ."

What do you seek to accomplish in your design work?

Step 4

Your responses to these statements has perhaps given you an idea of how
to explain your creative focus.

"I am inspired by _____ to evoke a sense of _____

In my work. With each project I try to _____."

last Saturday is what's casual to her, and I was overwhelmed! I'm glad I took
extra business cards and had practiced how I was going to describe myself
and my work. Everyone wanted tours of the new children's area, and they
wanted to hear what I had to say!

All right. . . . I met three couples at the party. All of them seemed interested in me and what I focus on in my work! Maybe they'll contact me.

First, I met a retired couple, Frank and Carolyn Johnson. They listened to
me describe plans for the children's space but didn't ask a lot of questions.
They said they have five grandchildren and had talked about doing something for their playroom before. They had never heard of Imagination Unlimited and didn't seem too sure where it was after I gave them my business
card with the store name and location on it. Still, they promised to drop in
one day and see me. I will probably follow up with them, since they did seem

interested in what I had done with the Abernathy project, and they do have five grandchildren!

The next two guys I met were a lot of fun! Jonathan and Sidney are two computer executives who have adopted a little girl from an Eastern European country and are planning to adopt several more children over the next few years. Their house is almost as big as the Abernathy's, but not really suitable for a growing family without serious work on the interior spaces. I spent a lot of time with them, talking about the possibilities I saw for changing some surface details of their home and editing their collection of Art Deco furniture: All that slippery marble and authentic furniture is not the best for young children. I suggested replacing the flooring with matte-finished slate tile and their incredible furniture with pieces children could use without anyone falling and getting hurt or ruining anything so valuable. They asked so many questions! They, too, want a specially designated area of the house for the children to live in, separate from the "adult" areas. They loved the tree-house concept and wondered what I might be able to do for them. Sounds like they might be possibilities, too—huh, diary?

Toward the end of the party, I met Tracy and Michael Barnett. They liked my "whimsical" approach, as they called it, and wondered if I could design a jungle motif for their family playroom. They did tell me they were interviewing other designers but that they had never seen anything like what I had planned for the Abernathy house. We talked for some time, and they took my card. They said I should definitely call them when I got a chance because they would like to talk further about their project, and I said I would.

So, those were some of the better prospects I met at the party. Some folks just took my card and wandered off before I got a chance to talk to them. I got sidetracked talking to the three couples I just mentioned. Maybe I should have gotten around and talked to more people. I wonder if it's worth following up on any of the three? They all seemed so nice, but I don't want to waste a lot of time and energy if they won't come through with projects! Anyway, I'll write more soon. I have to get back to work!

Question

2. How would you classify the prospects Lee met at the party? Were all of these the "hot" leads that she believes them to be? Explain why you think they might or might not be so. Complete a Contact Management Worksheet (Form 7.2) for each potential client. Then suggest to the designer in writing which client prospect appears to be the most promising and why you think so.

CONTACT MANAGEMENT WORKSHEET

Date of contact _____   Office call _____

    Name _____   Ad _____
             _____   Source _____
                                     Date _____

Address _____   Personal contact _____
             _____   _____
             _____   _____

                                Where _____
                                       _____
                                       _____

                                Referral from _____
                                       _____

Needs
or
reason
for
inquiry _____

        _____

        _____

        _____

        _____

        _____

        _____

Follow-up

        Send information _____   Appointment date _____

        Call-back date _____   Appointment time _____

NOTES

Lead type

Hot _____ (Immediate need)

Warm _____ (Needed soon)

Cool _____ (Needed within year)

Other _____ (Interested)

Follow-up with referral _____

CONTRACT INTERIOR DESIGN CASE STUDY: THE CASE OF THE SHOUTING SURFER

For decades, a McDowell Bunga-Board was "the" surfboard for surfing afi-cionados. During this time, there was only one place in the entire world to get these brightly colored boards—often sporting airbrushed images of Hula girls dancing across cresting waves or twin red pineapples—and that was at "Richie" McDowell's little shop in the Ocean Beach section of San Diego, California. Named Kowabunga, after the cry of pioneer surfers in the 1950s as they rode the large waves, the store attracted legions of fans seeking the handmade, one-of-a-kind boards they deemed to be "totally awesome."

The shop where these boards could be obtained remained practically unchanged for over 30 years. A former gas station situated next to a pub-lic beach, it was only a few hundred feet from the Pacific Ocean—so close, in fact, that it was not uncommon for seagulls to fly around the shop be-fore blissfully perching on surfboards displayed on sawhorses out front. McDowell and his wife covered the station's original white color with the cheapest paint available, a strident green; then in freehand he printed the store's name in red over the garage's two roll-up doors. Over time, bright green and red became the store's "totally awesome" colors. It was also not uncommon for professional surfers to donate trophies they won while rid-ing McDowell's boards to the shop as tokens of appreciation. These me-mentoes remained proudly displayed even after they had been tarnished black by the salty sea air. Store regulars knew to just help themselves to the free soft drinks found in an old-time icebox painted the same green color and placed right in the middle of the store. Other decorative ele-ments inside the store included straw mats and palm fronds fastened over the cinder-block walls in an effort to make the place look like a "totally awesome" tropical hut.

The success of the surfboard shop surprised the couple, who never thought of themselves as businesspeople, and each year thousands of fans snapped up the boards as soon as they were produced. In 1999, McDow-ell and his wife decided to retire and sold the shop to Malcolm Watkins, a longtime collector of Bunga-Boards and a wealthy California investor. Watkins also bought the legal right to use all the names and images, such as the wave-dancing Hula Girl and the double-pineapple motifs that ap-peared on the surfboards. Sensing that surfing and surf-related clothing would be popular with teens and young adults, Watkins was inspired to expand the Kowabunga concept from the single store into a multistore empire of surf-themed clothing and accessories stores that could be found in shopping malls throughout the United States.

By completing many retail projects over the eight years your firm has been operating, you and your business have developed an acknowledged expertise not only in planning, designing, and producing stores, but also in defining shopping experiences through architecture and design. Having seen previous projects produced by you and your firm, Watkins has selected you to translate the Kowabunga concept from the one little beach-front store to a series of stores soon to be found in major shopping malls throughout the United States. Watkins is planning to capitalize on his investment in the business to the extent that he wants to have 50 to 60 stores, each of approximately 5,500 rentable square feet, in various malls; and he has begun negotiations with mall developers to lease more than 300,000 square feet of retail space, itself a major business deal.

This project will not only be the largest commission you and your firm have ever received, but also promises to have the most visibility among consumers. The first phase of the project will be to conceptualize, plan, and execute the beta-site, or prototype store, to be built in a popular Las Vegas, Nevada, shopping mall. This store will be seen and used by thousands of tourist shoppers each day, and will further be used to measure consumer response to the store's design concept as well as how efficiently the store layout is able to handle large volumes of sales. The estimated time for realizing this first store is a tight twenty-four months away; but the goal is to have the store open by May 1, in two years, to take advantage of the numbers of tourists visiting Las Vegas throughout the summer months. The May 1 date happens to coincide with your firm's ten-year anniversary, when you and three of the other firm principals first began operation. This project has an estimated budget of around $10 million for completing only the prototype store, the highest amount allocated for a single prototype store project on which you have worked. The firm accountant noted that the development of future stores in this series means that your firm should anticipate a stream of income over the next five years sufficient to finance increased hiring and office-space expansion.

To announce this tremendous accomplishment, you have determined that your firm should distribute a press release. This press release may serve as the basis for a feature story in an architecture or contract interior design trade journal that will be read by your professional peers. On your firm letterhead, which lists contact information for your firm, you provide information necessary to inform your press contacts of this exciting new commission. First, you indicate that the release is "For

Immediate Release," in other words, you want to let these media contacts know that the information is time-sensitive and currently relevant. Your goal in the press release is to communicate how you intend to bring the Kowabunga concept from its current limited application at one site to multisite installation throughout the United States. Furthermore, you want to convey how winning this commission is a major accomplishment for you and your firm, and one that should pave the way for many more like it. As you begin writing the release, you should remember that it is not an advertisement for a business. While it does have to mention the names of the firm and principals, the primary purpose of a press release is to provide enough timely information to serve as the basis for a feature story in a publication. In the press release you are drafting for this project, you should seek to convey the following:

1. You want to represent the spirit of Kowabunga. You seek to do this in the prototype store by incorporating the colors, images, and sounds found in the first Ocean Beach shop. Your initial idea is to use industrial garage doors as the point of entry into the shop, as in the original store, and to use the same green and red colors, although modified to "read" better in an indoor setting. In the press release you want to describe how you will incorporate other elements from the original Kowabunga store, such as the red-lettered signs, the old surfing trophies, the ice box at the center of the store, vintage Bunga-Board surfboards, the images of the hula girl and twin red pineapples, the straw-covered walls complete with seagulls, and even Richie McDowell's favorite phrase, "totally awesome."

2. You also want to make known the importance of the project, in terms of its magnitude and its effect on your firm and its future. For example, the number of future stores, the total estimated amount of square footage they will encompass and the beta-project budget and timetable are all details you wish to include. The other firm principals want the press release to stress what the project will mean to the firm, emphasizing the firm's age; and, for professional reasons of your own, you want to make clear that you are the designer to whom the project was awarded.

3. In order to accomplish the task of writing a press release, you refer to other projects on file in your office and note that past press releases typically answered the following questions in the course of making public the firm's past accomplishments:
   ◆ Who?
   ◆ What?

- When?
- Where?
- Why?
- How?

4. Think for a moment about how you can incorporate all the factors discussed here in a multiparagraph press release, at the same time taking account of the key information transmitted in the firm's past press releases. In sum, your press release should make it known that for both you and your firm the Kowabunga commission is "totally awesome"!

PART THREE

YOU AND
YOUR CLIENTS

Part 1 of this text, "You and Your Work," introduced you to the professional practices of interior designers, whereas applications to the practice of interior design such as the general principles of business law, accounting, management, and marketing were detailed in part 2, "You and Your Business." After reviewing and responding to questions in each chapter's Professional Practices Portfolio and Strategies-in-Action Projects, you should feel more confident about your ability to incorporate the skills you have learned in the creative work you enjoy so much.

You are about to begin part 3, "You and Your Clients." This part of the text discusses objectives and processes that will enable you to achieve goals that are specifically related to the work of interior designers. Chapters 8 through 11 are interrelated. Each chapter articulates a particular step in the process of learning what services an interior designer needs to perform to satisfy the requirements of the project, including the selection of realistic and profitable ways of charging for those services. You have already been introduced to fundamental project management concepts. Part 3 revisits the process of project management in more detail so that you can clearly understand the role of project management within the broader context of interior design work. Finally, part 3 shows you how to define your relationship with your clients through the use of written contracts for your design services.

Chapter 8, "Defining Your Services," introduces and explains the scope-of-services concept, which is the basis for your relationship with your clients. As you will see, the exact nature of a project must be defined before a designer assumes responsibility, much less begins work on it. Developing a project's scope-of-services analysis requires you to correlate the results clients seek with creative and management tasks to create meaningful project work plans.

The importance of a detailed work plan becomes especially clear when designers consider methods of charging clients for the services outlined in the scope-of-services analysis. Chapter 9, "Charging Your Clients," describes how you may derive effective compensation strategies from your analysis of the project. Those methods will enable you to adequately pay yourself for the work you agree to complete for clients.

While finished projects differ in appearance and function, the process involved in producing such unique results is substantially similar from project to project. The scope-of-services analysis will come into play again as you learn how the tasks identified in your analysis fit into the formal project management scheme introduced at the beginning of your study of professional practices. Chapter 10, "Managing Your Client's Project," explores project management techniques in greater detail.

You likely recall earlier discussions of contracts or legally enforceable agreements. Chapter 11, "Defining the Client Relationship," demonstrates how design contracts may be constructed on the basis of a scope-of-services analysis to include terms related to charging for services and project management. Whether you use a letter of agreement that you prepare yourself or a standard-form contract available from professional associations, your understanding of the terms of these agreements is an extremely important aspect of your relationship with your client.

Part 4 of the text will address your role as a vendor, or seller of design merchandise, as well as your relationship with other vendors and service providers. Exploring options for professional development available to interior designers is the subject of the final part of the text. Meanwhile, as you begin your study of this part of the text, think about what procedures a designer might implement to complete even a small project.

CHAPTER EIGHT

DEFINING
YOUR SERVICES

The term analysis of scope of services has such importance that it should be posted prominently in every interior design office and planted firmly in the mind of every designer.

HARRY SIEGEL AND ALAN SIEGEL

WHY THIS CHAPTER IS IMPORTANT TO YOU

You are now acquainted with four fundamental sets of skills required of interior design professionals who participate in businesses. And you have learned the ways that interior designers incorporate those skills into their own practices. This chapter is important to you because it will teach you how to identify and describe the interior design services you provide to clients. The description of the scope of your services is one key aspect that defines your working relationship with clients. To help you perform this important task, this chapter will explain:

1. How the term *scope-of-services analysis* may be defined and its place in the project management scheme;
2. How designers traditionally—and now not so traditionally—obtain project information in order to determine the services they provide; and
3. The importance of carefully negotiating a scope-of-services analysis with your client.

The chapters in this third part build on the scope-of-services concept detailed here. Before you begin your study of this chapter, ask yourself how you might go about defining your services and what information you need to know about the client, the site, the environment proposed for the project, and even the "feel" of the project itself.

PROFESSIONAL PRACTICES PORTFOLIO

After completing this chapter, you should be able to answer the questions that follow. Include your responses in a professional practices portfolio that you should keep as a handbook for your later use.

1. Define scope-of-services analysis in your own words. Can you explain it to someone who is unfamiliar with interior design?
2. How have interior designers traditionally gained information about their clients' needs for projects?
3. Describe some modern ways in which design professionals gain information about client needs, and explain the process of interpreting that information.

INTRODUCTION TO SCOPE-OF-SERVICES ANALYSIS

As you know from the introduction to part 3, chapters 8 through 11 are interrelated. Chapter 8 begins your study of client relationships by exploring the basic reason clients engage interior designers: for their services. What kinds of services are offered by designers? How have designers traditionally analyzed their clients' needs and wishes to determine what services they need to provide, and how is this activity changing? As you will come to learn, the kinds of services offered greatly influence the methods designers use in seeking compensation for their services. Scope of services also affect management of the projects. Finally, a definition of services must be included in the written contracts for design services entered into by designers and clients.

During the course of your design education you have probably come across the term scope of services, or perhaps you have heard of a designer preparing a scope-of-services analysis. Maybe you wondered about the meaning of this term, since it seems so integral to the work of an interior designer and is so frequently mentioned that it seems to need no definition. First, the scope-of-services analysis is not necessarily a formal project document, although it is a part of the contract with the client for design services. What is important for you to know is that the **scope-of-services analysis** is an evaluative process necessary for the designer to understand the client as well as the client's wishes and needs for a proposed project. Once a designer determines that it would be appropriate (and potentially profitable) to participate in the project, the scope-of-services analysis may then be formally incorporated into the written agreement between the designer and client. Before defining the scope-of-services analysis and detailing what is involved in its processes, consider its relation to the concept of estimating.

ESTIMATING

As part of your interior design education, you need to learn the skill of estimating. Much of that study involves learning methods of quantifying the dimensions of individual spaces and items and then calculating the costs required to modify them in particular ways. A simple example of this process would involve estimating what is required to paint the exposed wall surfaces of a space.

1. First, you would determine the dimensions of the space.
2. Then determine the product cost (the amount of paint required to cover the space multiplied by the cost of the paint).
3. Next determine the application costs (the amount of time required by the contractor multiplied by the monetary rate charged for the work).
4. Consider all these factors and reach a conclusion about the cost and time required for the proposed modification, which you then present to the client.

The scope-of-services-analysis process is essentially also an estimating process. And while it is similar to the smaller-scale estimating procedures with which you are familiar—as in estimating what is involved in painting a wall—you should be aware of an important distinction.

Estimating paint amounts and application costs may be tedious, but it is relatively easy to do. Spaces can be measured these days with extreme accuracy: you need only hold up an electronic device that can store the dimensions in memory, so nothing even needs be written down. In most locations, paint and contractors are easily available and affordable as well. In short, many estimating processes involve obtaining information that is readily available. Whereas designers do interpret obvious factors in a scope-of-services analysis—such as what clients profess they need—they also consider latent, or less obvious, details about a project. These may include the clients' personal expectations regarding results and the role they envision for the designers who are carrying out the projects. Designers also use scope-of-services analyses as ways of anticipating problems that might possibly hinder project completion (an underlying project consideration). With this context in mind about the scope-of-services analysis, how might a working definition of the term and its related process enable you to better understand and apply it?

EVALUATING CLIENT NEEDS

When designers and clients initially meet, designers need to translate what clients are really asking them to do in realizing proposed projects. Sometimes that translation involves determining what specific activities will be required of designers to bring the projects to fruition after interpreting the emotional nuances of and solving concerns expressed by the clients. This is certainly true of residential interior design, in which a designer and client often build a close personal relationship. In these circumstances, the practicalities of carrying out a project may be underemphasized by designers and lost entirely on clients, all of whom may have their own reasons for wanting to see the projects realized. Contract interior designers, alternatively, may seem to be code breakers in understanding a prospective client's needs. Often, these designers have only a Request for Proposal (RFP) in front of them from which they must decipher clients' most important concerns about projects. On that basis alone, contract interior designers must intuit how to practically address those needs as they carry out the project. Designers in both areas of practice rely on the scope-of-services analyses in planning how to transform clients' ideas into finished spaces.

DESCRIPTION OF THE PHYSICAL SPACE

A scope-of-service analysis may be thought of as having two basic parts: a description of the physical space, often referred to as the subject space or property; and a description of the specific results the designer is agreeing to bring about on behalf of the client. The description of the physical space can be a statement reading simply "the entire home," as in the final version of some letter of agreements for residential interior design. Of course, a description of subject property for a nonresidential project is often much more detailed, with references to spatial dimensions quoted on blueprints or schematics. The description of subject space or property, whether destined for private or commercial use, should be as specific as possible to avoid any misunderstanding or confusion. If spaces flow into each other or opinions could reasonably differ about what is, in fact, the subject space—for example, a residential living room that segues into an entryway or an office waiting area leading to an attached hallway—then the designer's description ought to include a statement about the project's underlying intent. If the client intends to have design work in only the living room, for example, that should be specified in the initial scope-of-services analysis and finally in the language of the contract between a designer and client. Similarly, a scope-of-services analysis for a commercial space should note the physical coordinates of the subject space.

DESCRIPTION OF THE DESIGNER'S DUTIES

Once the physical description of the project spaces is finalized, the designer needs to consider how to realize the client's goals for the project. After completing forms such as the Client Information Worksheet (see Form 1.5), you should have enough information to describe what needs to be done to meet these project goals and what duties you, as the project designer, are going to assume.

At first, this description of duties may be very informal, even presented orally to clients. The better practice would be for the designer to write out the project activities in list form. As designers gain experience in handling projects, the informal outline may take a specific form in which project tasks and the designer's duties are organized within the context of formal project management phases.

OBJECTIVES TO CONSIDER

By now you should have a sense of the importance and content of a careful scope-of-services analysis. You may be surprised to learn that the process of conducting this analysis is easily learned. In fact, it may well become second nature to you fairly quickly. This chapter identifies three objectives to master that will help you in this task.

1. Conducting an informal evaluation of the project and what it entails
2. Selecting appropriate methods of gathering project information, and identifying relevant information according to tangible and intangible goals
3. Obtaining client buy-in before finalizing the scope of services in contract form

PROCEDURES AND PROCESSES FOR
DEFINING YOUR SCOPE OF SERVICES

What do you think is involved in carrying out the first of these objectives? Conducting an informal evaluation of the project and its characteristics is an important threshold concern a designer should address. At early client meetings, there are likely to be numerous suggestions and comments about client goals and project requirements. In the excitement of undertaking a possible new project, it is important for the designer to gather this information and record it in such a way that it may be easily referenced and evaluated later. The many forms found throughout this text enable you to easily record project information as you obtain it. Another easy way to record information is to take written notes during these early discussions. The main thing is to record the information in a useful way, since you will refer back to it countless times during the development of the project.

EVALUATING A PROJECT AND WHAT IT ENTAILS

What information about a project should be of special concern as you begin to assess what it involves and how to bring it to completion? As part of the scope-of-services analysis process, you should focus on the following two factors in completing information worksheets or taking notes:

◆ The kind of project that is being proposed and its size
◆ The amount of research and resources required to understand project concerns or to meet client wishes or needs

Type and Size of Project

Certainly, there is no hard-and-fast rule for determining what kind of project is easier to complete than another. For example, the design of small retail spaces clearly intended for nonresidential use will likely take much less time and effort on the part of a designer than residential projects of any real magnitude. However, small projects are not always easy projects: a living-room concept requiring only custom-made furniture and elaborate built-in features may be extremely difficult to realize; and large projects, such as hotel installations utilizing existing items, may be fairly easy to implement. The purpose of identifying both the kind and size of project being proposed is to determine whether a designer is realistically able to handle such a project.

A designer's ability in this regard may depend on several factors, including the timetable for completing the project. A designer involved in multiple projects within the same time frame, even if they are in different stages of administration, is quite simply a busy designer. Such a designer might conclude that he or she is not able to take on another project after conducting an informal scope-of-services analysis. Other concerns relate to a designer's ability to work within the time and budget constraints proposed by the client. A designer may not be able to accomplish what the client wants given the time and budget available.

Furthermore, a client may require inordinate amounts of the designer's time while vacillating about design choices, or, worse yet, second guessing the designer; the client may simply demand the designer's involvement excessively. As a result, the designer may conclude that he or she does not have the ability to juggle the client's demands along with the project's demands. Subjective impressions formed in these early assessments are also important to consider when deciding whether to take on a project. For example, a designer may conclude that he or she would not be able to work with a client in a business relationship.

From an objective perspective, however, designers need to conclude, during the course of these processes, whether they have the professional ability to carry out a project without jeopardizing either the project or their reputations in the community. In this text's Residential Interior Design Project Simulation, Lee was asked to complete a large children's room project as her first job after graduation. An argument could be made that while the young designer may have had education enough to carry out the project, she lacked previous experience with large projects of this kind. However, one could make an equally strong argument that the designer's association with a retail store specializing in work related to the children's room project provided her with enough resources to carry out such a project. Perhaps you will be faced with a similar situation in your design career and will need to figure out whether you should take on a project. While conducting your initial scope-of-services analysis and learning about the client's project goals, ask yourself whether you are able to complete the project given your education, experience, time commitments, and perceived relationship with the client.

Research and Resources

With respect to the research and resources required to both understand the project and meet client goals, both are important concerns answered during the early scope-of-services processes. Many times, clients will seek designers' services because of their expertise or the style for which they are known. Such renowned designers usually have firsthand knowledge of what it takes to complete similar projects and do not require much specialized research of products or tradespeople. They frequently have available a network of suppliers and contractors on which they can call. Whether a new project will permit designers to draw from their network of sources is also addressed in the scope-of-services analysis. What this means for the less experienced designer is that client goals requiring a great deal of research into territory with which the designer is unfamiliar may result in problems once the project is under way. The scope-of-services analysis reveals the extent to which the project requires a strong research component, among its other tasks.

Understanding of Client Goals

The early stages of a project bring out all the client's hopes, desires, and fears. The designer's task is to sort out the client's desires from what is actually needed to complete the project. The issue of supervision offers an example. Clients may want designers to provide a level of project supervision that is unwarranted by the actual nature of the project. In that circumstance, a designer has to persuade the client that such oversight is not needed. On the other hand, clients sometimes wish for the installation of features requiring extensive modifications to, or reinforcement of, the original structure. For function and safety of the space, the designer should point out to the client the necessity of including additional provisions for less obvious support mechanisms and to also engage the assistance of other professionals—especially architects or engineers—to aid in that task. Reaching conclusions about project requirements require designers to understand the implications of what clients wish for and to convince clients of their necessities.

METHODS OF GATHERING AND ASSESSING INFORMATION

Interior design projects require information in order to come to fruition because varied and specific information is required to determine the scope of a designer's services on a project. To meet the changing demands of modern interiors, designers must be familiar with innovative ways of collecting this information. This is a vanguard area of interior design.

Useful information gathered in developing a scope-of-services analysis usually includes the physical dimensions of a project's subject space, the project goals, its end users, and how they are anticipated to use the space. These factors are then analyzed by designers to produce spaces that are functional and attractive at the same time that they take into account health, safety, and welfare needs. Recent trends, however—in fields as far-ranging as technology and interior design education—suggest that, increasingly, there are other goals to meet. These goals require yet additional information for designers to consider when developing a thorough scope-of-services analysis on a project.

In identifying these additional goals, IDEO, the noted design firm based in Palo Alto, California, has become an innovative force in many different disciplines, including architecture, consumer product innovation, and technology. Its influences can be seen in a diverse number of business settings including retail, communication technology, and, in particular, health care. The firm's approach is to enhance the experience of consumers in using the products and facilities it researches as a consultant.

Toward that end, IDEO strives to imbue these items with characteristics their research has identified as desirable. For example, the group found that young automobile drivers perceived authenticity as a desirable characteristic of their car buying and operating experience. To arrive at these insights, IDEO developed unique information-gathering methods to pinpoint how to imbue their products with such experiential qualities. It is important to recognize that consumers now expect products and services to provide positive, authentic experiences. How has the interior design industry responded to such trends?

"Environmental poetics"—"creating memorable and inspirational spaces that address aesthetics and humanism," or "the 'art' of design that focuses on the meaning, emotion and spirit of place"—has been identified as an important concern that should be addressed by interior design education (ASID 2004). The relevance of this concept is in line with the IDEO approach of meshing experience with product and facility design. This trend of imbuing experience or emotion into product and design offers great opportunities for expanding an interior designer's scope of services. The issue for designers, however, is whether traditional ways of gathering information are sufficient to achieve these intangible, but nonetheless very real, design results. How might one, for example, identify emotions that could then be translated into usable interior spaces?

Traditionally, interior designers have asked clients to simply tell them about the qualities they want the completed design to feature. Designers also usually rely on their own detailed observations of their clients' current environments and objects in order to identify what elements to retain or further develop. Other ways of gathering information include the use of questionnaires or personal interviews—particularly in contract interior design projects, when large numbers of employees will inhabit a work space, much information is sought out regarding the uses to which the space will be put.

As entrenched as these methods are, they are not without limitations. Clients and employees may not understand the full implication of the questions asked of them and so give partial or meaningless answers. And personal biases may skew the interpretation of results. Or, quite simply, the subjects participating in this type of research may not feel like they are a part of the overall design process and thus may view it as cumbersome and annoying rather than as a means for bringing about a positive outcome. In order to gather information that is both useful in achieving a project's end results and flexible enough to engage interview respondents, something more is required. To that end, the IDEO developed a series of observational and prototyping techniques that hold particular promise for use in developing interior design that is responsive to the physical and emotional needs of end users. Techniques such as the ones described here permit interior designers to gather information that they can use to expand their scope of services and produce spaces that are also experiential. Following are some of these approaches developed by IDEO.

BEHAVIORAL MAPPING In this technique, spaces are photographed for a series of days to understand how a space is being used and to catalog the range of emotions elicited by users in the space. One important implication of this approach for interior design is that it can serve as a neutral, objective way to report the actual uses to which a space is put, free from subjective interpretations. Used as a way of evaluating existing spaces and identifying problems that will be addressed in the scope-of-services analysis, this technique also has the advantage of being less intrusive than interviews and questionnaires.

BODYSTORM This dramatalurgical approach to information gathering involves first identifying different kinds of users and consumers, and then acting out scenarios showing how they will interact in a space.

CONSUMER JOURNEY As the name suggests, this technique involves cataloging every interaction of a consumer or user in a space.

EXTREME USER INTERVIEWS This technique involves having those who know very little or a great deal about a product, service, or, in the case of interior design, a space evaluate their experiences with these items.

SHADOWING This technique involves following subjects as they interact in spaces.

STORYTELLING This technique prompts people to talk about their own experiences in using an item.

UNFOCUS GROUPS In this approach, the traditional focus group—usually made up of a target group—is modified so that a wide variety of people, not only a targeted few, are interviewed.

These unique ways of gathering information can be incorporated within the context of interior design so that interior designers can expand their scope of services to account for factors such as emotion and experience.

Once information has been gathered and assessed, it is important that designers obtain what is referred to as client **buy-in**, which is when clients agree to designers' scope of services before finalizing everything in contracts for design services.

PROBLEM-SOLVING STRATEGIES
IN SCOPE-OF-SERVICES ANALYSIS

Since you are a professional, your clients will expect you to solve problems for them. Also as a professional, you will have to understand and solve problems that the client creates for you. Suggested changes offered by a client to a designer's scope of services are one such problem area. Resolution of these concerns in large part depends on which stage in the designer/client relationship the modification is requested and how well the designer is able to negotiate with the client. Many of the questions regarding changes to a designer's scope of services are addressed in the design contract or letter of agreement binding a designer and client. But what of suggested additions or subtractions made by a potential client before a contract is signed?

Consider these kinds of changes to a scope-of-services analysis commonly requested by clients and some strategies for resolving them.

PROBLEM Prior to signing a contract for design services, a client asks the designer to omit the task of installing items at the project site; the clients' reasoning is that he or she can follow the designer's layout without having to pay installer's costs or pay for the designer's time (when the designer is being compensated at an hourly rate).

STRATEGY Clients understandably do not want to pay more for services and goods than absolutely necessary. Because a designer and client have not yet formally agreed to work together, designers (theoretically) could agree to this limitation in their scope of services as part of the give-and-take of pre-contract negotiations. The issue addressed here is the timing of the change. No final bargain for services has yet been struck that requires the designer to take part in the final installation of the project. A designer could agree to this proposed limitation on his or her services and have the contract written to reflect it.

As a point of negotiation between a designer and client, a designer may need to first empathize with the client about the need to keep project costs low, but then simply refuse a subtraction of this kind. Eliminating some fundamental tasks in an attempt to save some money will endanger the project's outcome. How a project looks after final installation is a crucial test of a designer's professional skills. Agreeing to a provision of this kind, even at a client's request, is likely to result in disaster for both the project and the designer's reputation. Therefore, agreeing to a client's requests to limit services that will likely affect the outcome of an entire project should be refused even at the pre-contract phase.

Are there any kinds of changes, notably subtractions, to which a designer might agree during the pre-contract phases of a project? Of course, facts and circumstances vary greatly according to a designer's area of practice and geographical location. One situation in which designers might consider limiting their scope of service (assuming they are compensated on a basis other than commissions earned from goods sold) occurs when the client has greater buying power than the designer. Institutional and government clients may have far greater procurement abilities than the designer. In such instances, the designer may agree to evaluate the institution's cadre of vendors to identify those most likely to provide appropriate goods. In addition, the designer may also write product specifications and review received merchandise for compliance to the specs. Again, suggested subtractions, even at the pre-contract stage, to the scope of services should be carefully evaluated by the designer based on their reasonable effect on the overall project.

PROBLEM During early negotiations, the client requests the designer's presence at the project site daily, a requirement the designer does not feel is necessary or even possible to provide.

STRATEGY Suggested additions to a designer's scope of services, if ultimately agreed to, may be as onerous as subtractions, especially if their inclusion is not really necessary in order to complete the project as agreed and scheduled. The Residential Interior Design Project Simulation considers this very topic. As a point of negotiation, the designer should attempt to find out the reason for the client's requests. Perhaps this is the first time a client has engaged the services of a designer and is insecure about the outcome. Addressing the source of the suggestion as soon as possible may be the designer's best strategy for coping with unnecessary additions.

REFERENCES

Alderman, Robert L. 1997. *How to Prosper As an Interior Designer*. New York: John Wiley & Sons.

——. 1982. *How to Make More Money at Interior Design*. New York: Whitney Communications.

Allison, John, and Robert Prentice. 2001. *Business Law: Text and Cases in the Legal Environment*. 3rd Custom ed. New York: Thompson Learning.

American Society of Interior Design, 2004. *The Interior Design Profession: Facts and Figures.*

Berger, C. Jaye. 1994. *Interior Design Law and Business Practices.* New York: John Wiley & Sons.

Coleman, Cindy, ed. 2002. *Interior Design: Handbook of Professional Practice.* New York: McGraw-Hill. (See, in particular, scope-of-services chart, pp. 483–91, for a detailed perspective on the scope-of-service analysis.)

Crawford, Tad, and Eva Doman Bruck. 2001. *Business and Legal Forms for Interior Designers.* New York: Allworth Press.

Cushman, Robert F., and James C. Dobbs, eds. 1993. *Design Professionals Handbook of Business and Law.* New York: John Wiley & Sons.

Duffy, Frank. 1997. *The New Office.* London: Conran Octopus Ltd.

Geiger, Helene. 2003. *Project Management Fundamentals.* New York: Element K LLC.

Gould, Frederick E., and Nancy Joyce. 2002. *Construction Project Management,* pp. 115–28. New York: Pearson Educational.

Holland, J. Kent, ed. 2003. *Construction Law & Risk Management: Case Notes and Articles.* McLean VA: Ardent Publications.

Kelley, Tom, and Tom Peters, (with Jonathan Littman). 2001. *The Art of Innovation: Lessons in Creativity from IDEO, America's Leading Design Firm.* New York: Doubleday.

Knackstedt, Mary V. 2002. *The Interior Design Business Handbook.* 3rd ed. New York: John Wiley & Sons.

Piotrowski, Christine. 2002. *Professional Practice for Interior Designers.* 3rd ed. New York: John Wiley & Sons.

——. 2004. *Becoming an Interior Designer.* New York: John Wiley & Sons.

Russell, Beverly. 2000. Breakfast with Beverly. *ISdesigNET.*

Siegel, Harry, and Alan Siegel. 1982. *A Guide to Business Practices and Principles for Interior Designers.* New rev. ed. New York: Watson-Guptill.

Thompson, Jo Ann Asher, ed. 1992. ASID Professional Practice Manual. New York: Watson-Guptill.

STRATEGIES-IN-ACTION PROJECTS

STRATEGIC BUSINESS PLANNING: BUSINESS SERVICES DESCRIPTION

Many people outside the interior design profession do not exactly know what an interior designer does or is supposed to do. To compound this surprising finding, many designers cannot adequately settle on a conclusive way to describe what they do as professionals (Russell 2000). Do interior designers enhance their clients' environments aesthetically or functionally? Maybe some combination of these two approaches applies. And how are designers expected to accomplish these tasks? Read the following short definition (see chapter 1) of an interior designer offered by NCIDQ: "The professional interior designer is qualified by education, experience, and examination to enhance the function and quality of interior spaces." Does even that description promulgated by the main accreditation body for the interior design profession raise questions about the services offered by an interior designer? What is meant by enhancing the function of an interior space? What is quality? Does this statement even address how a designer is to perform these tasks? Does the NCIDQ short definition help a nonprofessional to better understand a designer's role (see Box 1.1 in chapter 1)?

Considering that there is some lack of consensus about the role of an interior designer, imagine that you are trying to obtain funding for your interior design business from a bank or private investor. These potential investors in your business do not have a clear idea about what you or your business do. How and where do you go about describing your services? To inform readers of what your business will offer, a section of your written business plan must contain a thorough description of the functions your business is to perform. Usually styled "Services," or "Service Business Analysis," this section of your business plan informs decision makers about the activities your business will undertake for clients and how it will do so. Sounds easy.

Before you get started, remember that most other professionals or potential investors in your business who read your plan may not have an inkling of what an interior designer really does to complete a project. Perhaps they have seen the finished work of an interior designer before or have seen a television program in which a designer does a room makeover in a few days; they may even have a glossy shelter magazine on their office coffee table. But, other than this limited exposure to interior design, they have little knowledge about the design process. Others may just assume that being a designer is easy. After all, these outsiders to the design industry may even be proud of their own decorating efforts, which they may have accomplished without any help from a design professional. In short, most people outside the industry have no idea of the process of stages in which a designer analyzes, researches, and executes design options for a space. This section of your business plan must, therefore, perform another function besides merely describing what it is a designer does. This section must also teach these businesspeople why an interior designer follows procedures to complete a project.

As a practicing interior designer, you may well discover that different types of clients seek different outcomes from a designer's work. A residential client, for example, may be less concerned with the final cost of a project, but more interested in its visual attractiveness. On the other hand, a commercial client seeking a designer's services to finish and design large blocks of office space may value the efficient use of costly rented space more than its visual impact. Who were the target clients you identified in chapter 7 as those most likely to use the services of your ideal business? What do you think they will desire in the finished projects you execute for them? Do you think that the description in your business plan of the services you will offer should also include an explanation of how these services will benefit your client's needs?

There are several specific components you should include in the services description of your business plan.

1. Precise descriptions of the interior design services you will offer
2. Explanations of the process you will carry out to provide these services
3. Reasons why you will undertake these steps
4. Benefits that clients will receive for using your services

Before you begin your services description, read a preliminary draft of the services section for Imagination Unlimited. Do you think that the following draft includes all the necessary components of a business plan's description of services?

Imagination Unlimited is a full-service interior design firm and retail showroom offering the following: complete interior design concept realization and implementation. From initial client contact through final installation, our services will satisfy clients and meet their needs.

Based on your knowledge of the services section of a business plan, would or should you change anything? Would a client or a bank loan officer know what concept realization and implementation involve? What details might you add? (Hint: There are many.) Rewriting this preliminary draft may better prepare you for writing your own description of services.

RESIDENTIAL INTERIOR DESIGN PROJECT SIMULATION

Read the latest installment about the children's-room project that Lee is completing. How might the scope-of-services analysis be modified when the project expands well beyond what was originally intended—at least beyond what was intended by the designer?

Lee's Diary

Ugh! I knew when the phone rang at 7:00 A.M. it was going to be Mrs. Abernathy with another "Oh, by the way" thing for me to do. Sure enough! This time it was "Oh, by the way, we are going to need to do something about that room off the landing on the stairs right inside the children's quarters." What room? Huh?

As it turns out . . . I found out there is a space large enough, maybe about 9 by 11 feet at the most, located off a small landing (the stairway has several "turns" on it, this being the last). There is just one step down from that landing into the children's space. Because of the way it is situated, with its door facing the playroom, this "mystery room" visually seems to be a part of the children's space. But it's not, really. It's on a separate electrical and air-conditioning system from the children's rooms. I thought it was a closet and hadn't included anything at all about it in my proposal for the space. The subject never came up, and the door was locked when I visited the site to take measurements, so I just specified painting the door and the door frame to blend with the color palette of the playroom area and forgot about it. What I also did, unfortunately, was to include in my letter of agreement that my work was to include "the entire ground floor," which Mrs. A. clearly thinks this space is a part of. I told Mrs. A. I would meet her at the house to discuss possibilities. Maybe paint and a coatrack would solve the problem. . . . I hoped.

Well, no, in fact, that's not what she had in mind at all.

"I want this to be the gift-wrapping room," was the first thing I heard her say once she and I and most of the kids were all jammed into the box-filled storage room. She pulled out a picture from a Chicago showcase home featured in a shelter magazine and showed me what she had in mind. I didn't even know gift-wrapping rooms existed!

You would not believe the amount of cabinet detail the designer who did that project must have had to specify: individual, built-in cubbyholes for holding rolls of gift wrap; handmade Peg-Boards holding scissors and tape; tiny carved drawers with tiny carved knobs placed in a freestanding workstation, the top upholstered in felt (to protect the gift while being wrapped according to the caption); wooden shutters coordinating with the cabinet fronts; lighted shelves holding woven bins for ornaments—all with an antiqued white-on-white color scheme on the exposed surfaces that must have been applied by hand several times.

"So . . . how are you going to make this happen? I want it done along with the rest of the project," Mrs. A. said.

It didn't go so well after that.

I told Mrs. Abernathy I was supposed to only do the children's spaces. That did not include designing a gift-wrapping room as part of my services. She pulls our agreement out of her purse, puts it on top of one of the boxes, and points right to the language that says: "the entire ground floor of the premises."

"So, with that problem out of the way, how are you going to make this happen?" she asks again.

Well—what a mess—and I have only myself to blame with the language I used in the letter of agreement. Fortunately, Mrs. Abernathy's little phone rang, and she took the call, but not before saying, "Get back to me on this tomorrow with your plan. I want the same thing, but in celadon green and white."

How am I going to work it in to the existing project schedule, not to mention take time out to work up a budget and, honestly, the schematic cabinet drawings alone will take so much time? In ten minutes Mrs. A. just added probably several hundred hours of very tedious work to the project. I am going to have to do an enormous amount of research, measuring, and drafting just to get all the details she wants, to say nothing of the time it will take to actually find a contractor able to do this kind of work, plus a painter who knows how to apply the finishes correctly. Other than a couple of stools, there is no furniture component of this new add-on to the project. Remember, diary, I get paid based only on the retail method, which is the percentage we add at the store to our cost, the wholesale cost, of the actual products the client agrees to purchase and nothing else. I'd have to sell those stools at maybe $50,000 each to earn any profit from the time I'm going to need to spend. I'm going to need to ask the boss about this.

Lee's Diary

The owner of Imagination Unlimited just hit the roof when I told her what happened about the gift-wrapping room subproject Mrs. Abernathy requested. "There's no money in that for us. Don't take the job," she told me, "We do projects requiring things we can sell the client; we don't sell custom-made cabinetry." "Mrs. Abernathy didn't see it that way," I told her. She thought it was all part of the children's-room project, since it is, in her opinion, part of the ground-floor area, the area I said I'd complete in my scope-of-services analysis and put in the letter of agreement.

The owner just looked at me and said: "She wants a different project altogether from the one she hired you to do. You need to tell her how impossible her request is."

So, that got me thinking. Since I had a few hours before the meeting, I sat and thought about my options and came up with this:

I can't tell a client how crazy or impossible an idea they came up with right in the middle of project really is—even if it is out there. I'd create more problems for sure! She did have a point I have to reckon with: I did write "the entire ground floor" in the letter of agreement and in my scope-of-services analysis. I should have not only specified the physical space in which the project would be located, but I should have also said something about the scope of the project's intent. Maybe, just a quick sentence stating: "It is specifically understood the intent of this project is to complete play and living spaces for use by the family's children and no other." Then, put in the physical dimensions of the exact space and not used the word "entire"!

But future troubleshooting doesn't solve my current problem. This took several coffee drinks to figure out, but what I suggested to the client was this.

First, I did a little checking up. I called the interior designer who did the gift-wrapping room project in Chicago and actually got him on the phone! He laughed and said that ever since the photo appeared, his phone had been ringing off the hook from designers and others interested in the room. He told me he had an old-world-style German craftsman with three sons who specialized in that kind of work in his town. They were his exclusive contractors, in fact. Then he told me the owners of the show home had specifically agreed they wanted a room devoted to just gift wrapping. They were retirees with over fifteen grandchildren, with birthdays coming up all the time. The couple had given the designer an almost unlimited budget to work to produce the final effects. As for the budget for that one room, in fact, it was, as he put it, "in the very high five, almost six figures." For one little room! Then he gave me some advice: Tell the client what's involved in doing the work. I can tell you the price will scare them. Just try to work with what you have."

So, with all that in mind, I told Mr. and Mrs. Abernathy at our meeting what I had learned. The addition to the children's-room project was really a project in and of itself, one that needed a whole new project scope detailed and a new budget drawn up. I stood firm and also said that I would have to finish the first project before I could even think of tackling something like the new project Mrs. A. wanted; to take it on in the middle of the children's-room project would jeopardize it, and I might not get the children's room finished on time.

I also pointed out it was a very expensive—and permanent—allocation of space. It might not hold the family's interest over time nor could it be converted to other uses once the highly specialized cabinets were built in. I then suggested a relatively easy amendment to my original scope-of-service analysis that would make the room more of a general crafts room that could be used for several other things besides wrapping presents—a moveable work table and colorful little kid stools, a Peg-Board wall, things like that. The Abernathys thought my idea made more sense after I had explained the details to them. The cost factor took them both by surprise; they thought I could "just order the pieces and have them installed." Well, no . . .

Mrs. Abernathy approved the more abbreviated plan and said she would pay for the additional work and products involved. All I have to do now is write up an amendment to our letter of agreement explaining this change. She even called me her "clever cadeau"—whatever that is!

With the Abernathy family's assent to the installation of a less expensive craft room, Lee is faced with having to amend the original scope-of-services analysis created earlier for the playroom project. This will mean researching new and different products to use in the space.

Questions

This project allows you to combine your creative interests with your professional practices education. Using Form 8.1, describe the following new design tasks and items that have to be purchased to create the craft room. Gather appealing photographs or swatches and include them on the form.

1. Replace existing solid door with a ready-made one of textured, tempered glass.
2. Identify appropriate wall coverings such as grass cloth; same for woven-wood window treatment.
3. Locate and price baskets for holding wrapping paper and other supplies.
4. Get child-resistant wall plugs.
5. Locate an adjustable worktable, one that can be easily raised and lowered in height and rolled out of the way when not in use.
6. Purchase colorful chairs appropriate for children the same ages as the Abernathy's.

Having an easy-to-use reference will enable you to keep track of creative design elements that you can refer to later. Many designers keep

FIXTURES, FURNISHINGS, AND EQUIPMENT (FF&E) RECORD

Client _____   Job number/I.D. _____

Project address or reference _____

_____

_____

Item description	Number	Source	Intended use/placement

Swatches/photographs or descriptive media

such references to assist them in locating items for use on existing projects. When they come across items of special interest to them, whether they are intended for a current project, these designers like to have attractive items available for quick reference.

In addition to this task, you may want to draft a scope-of-service analysis for the proposed craft room project. By now you have an idea of the feel of the Abernathy project, as well as some specific information about the dimensions of the new space and how the family wishes to use it. Do you have enough information, or do you need more? Describe what needs to be done to make the tiny, white-walled room into a usable, attractive space for working on the children's craft projects.

CONTRACT INTERIOR DESIGN CASE STUDY: THE CASE OF THE DESIRABLE DORMITORY

Read the following case study and suggest ways the design team might solicit information from students about what dorm life is really like.

"Well, I'm stumped!" This, from an accomplished architect like Brad Jennings was quite an admission.

"We were awarded the University Dorm project and we still can't get a sense of what the students want and need from that facility, and time is running out on us getting a concept together. I'm going to need some outside consultants to help us with this one. It's been over twenty years since I lived in my college's dorm. I feel out of touch with students these days, and nothing we usually do is working here."

The firm's associate designers nodded in agreement with Jennings's statement. The state university system had awarded the firm the project more than three months ago and—still—the design team felt stymied by the project's lack of focus. By way of background information, the university system had become increasingly concerned about its campus housing. A great many students were currently forced to either pay exorbitantly high rents for private apartments near the university or drive long distances thanks to long commutes. Since the university had limited land available to devote to student parking and an even more limited budget for expanding shuttle-bus transportation, the logical alternative was to find ways to interest students in the benefits of living on campus. The main university dormitory was selected as the first of the four on campus to be renovated and expanded, spearheaded by the firm of

Jennings+Associates. The university's venerable Heritage Hall was to serve as the prototype for later work on the other three dorms; it would reflect both the pride its inhabitants feel in being part of the university's tradition of excellence while living in a facility that respects them as young, independent adults.

At least that was the university's stated intent in the press release they issued announcing the award of the project to Jennings. The real task of obtaining usable information to make that intent a tangible reality was an entirely different proposition. One associate recounted to the group the firm's first attempt.

"Remember when we sent questionnaires to the students?" asked Kimora Watanabe. "What a disaster! We sent 350 forms out, and got 27 back, and of those only 12 made any attempt to give us information we could use. Although I did get some great suggestions about how the school could better spend the renovation money."

"Yes, I recall that," said Jennings, "and the pizza party in the dorm's party room was completely ignored. I thought free food would draw a crowd, but maybe not in a room no one even thinks about, much less goes into."

"How about observation—watching how students live in the dorm and use the facility?" asked John Hamilton.

"You first on that one, Sport," said Jennings. "I remember what the conditions were like, living in a dorm. Besides, all of us are old enough to be these kids' parents. Can you imagine how happy they would be letting us just hang out with them and look over their rooms?"

"Eeew! What an image," responded Kimora.

"OK, so to recap, we have identified a consultant group of interior designers. These folks are going to get some concrete information we can use for the Heritage Hall project. What—specifically—do we need for them to get back to us with?"

"First, we have samples of two different kinds of chairs and tables we had identified as being budget-appropriate. We need to know which one of each will work best in this setting. We need to know how the kids will use these products," said Jonathan Hutchins.

"Right, and we also need to know how they get along in a 'modern' co-educational living environment: What are their issues with regard to privacy and safety?" said Kimora.

"And our biggest concern is space planning in this setting," said Jennings. "We need to expand the facility to accommodate a hundred more students, but we also can't just warehouse them in cubbyholes. So, we need to know how they like to set up their rooms and how they use, or don't use, the common spaces. No one uses the party room, as I found out. I also noticed they seem to like to congregate at the ends of the halls, where the windows are, to talk in small groups. That is until someone tells them to 'shut up' so they can get some sleep or study. I would be interested to know what the party room is really used for and what students would like for it to provide, and why the spaces at the ends of the halls are such a big draw. The windows do let in a lot of light, but there is no view to speak of. Yet I noticed students always clumped there, slouched in chairs 'borrowed' from other parts of the building."

"I hope these consultant folks are up to the task," said Jonathan.

Are you? Using methods discussed in this chapter, suggest ways the firm could gather the information they need to decide which furniture selections are most appropriate and to ascertain features to incorporate or avoid in the new facility. Draft a memo to the Jennings group explaining the following:

1. Why you believe the surveys were not effective
2. What methods you would use to gather the specific information the group seeks, and why they are indicated. Do note any pitfalls or problems you foresee in using any of your suggested approaches. Refer to the chapter's description of methods of gathering information on which to base your suggestions.

CHAPTER NINE

CHARGING CLIENTS FOR YOUR SERVICES

The design professions have struggled between the art and business of design for decades.

GARY E. WHEELER

WHY THIS CHAPTER IS IMPORTANT TO YOU

Designers generate revenue for their businesses by charging and collecting fees from clients. These fees are usually determined by things such as the services rendered by designers, the merchandise they specify and "sell," or a combination of these things. This chapter is important because it proposes a three-part strategy for you to use in setting your design fees, based on your business's needs and the specific services you provide. Using this suggested strategy should make the process less of an unprofitable art form and more the sound professional practice it can be. The fee arrangement is just one of the ways in which designers define their working relationships with clients. This chapter explores how fee arrangements, along with other issues, may be included in contracts entered into between designers and their clients.

PROFESSIONAL PRACTICES PORTFOLIO

After completing this chapter, you should be able to answer the questions that follow. Include your responses in a professional practices portfolio you can use as a handbook later on.

1. What are *direct/indirect overhead expenses*?

2. What is a *billing rate*?

3. What four basic methods may designers use when determining how to charge for their services?

4. In addition to being paid for their services, are there any other payment concerns that designers should be aware of?

5. What is an *invoice*?

6. What are *accounts receivable*? Are they related to *accounts payable*?

7. Describe the process of billing a client for services you provide.

8. What does it mean to *collect* payment?

9. To what extent do you believe the services of an interior designer add value to a project? How might you explain it to a client, and what concerns do you think the client might have about using such an approach?

10. Identify the charging method that you think will be most applicable to the kind of interior design practice in which you intend to participate. What factors about your business and the specific method of charging led you choose that approach over others?

INTRODUCTION TO METHODS
OF CHARGING FOR YOUR SERVICES

As you begin this chapter, envision yourself in the enviable position of having been selected as the designer responsible for the interiors of what, under your guidance, will become an impressive commercial space or private home. The design concept you proposed for this environment was deemed the best among all the presentations. Next, your new client asks how you will be compensated, or paid, for the activities you will perform to make that client's project a reality. How will you respond? What do you need to know about the needs of your own business and about the project itself before offering the most appropriate response? This chapter presents a three-part strategy for forming a profit-conscious and project-focused response to the important question of how you will charge your clients for your services as an interior designer.

OBJECTIVES TO CONSIDER

1. The first objective to master when determining design fees is knowing what to charge for your services. Simply put, what do you need to charge clients to satisfy your business's expenses and give you a *profit*, or financial surplus? In this context, determining the expenses your business incurs from its operation is a logical beginning step to take in planning for profitability. Are you aware of these expenses and the terms used to describe them? This chapter will identify these necessary expenses so that you can better understand the importance of choosing a financially appropriate method of charging for your services.

2. Once you have determined the costs of your business expenses, your next objective is to consider the methods typically used by designers who determine their fees. You should also understand how certain characteristics of a project can and should inform your final decision about which approach to use of the eleven methods discussed in this chapter. Most designers eventually select one approach for charging clients that they think is most suitable for their typical projects and that best enables them to earn profits. Knowing the range of methods available for determining fees for services enables a designer to select the most profitable fee structures in carrying out a range of different projects. Once you have ascertained your expenses and the range of methods available for charging for your services, you will know how to evaluate a project's potential for earning your business a profit; the expense obligations that need to be satisfied before any profit can be realized; and what characteristics of different kinds of projects could limit, or even eliminate, any possible profit. Understanding the relationship among these important considerations is necessary before selecting and applying a particular method of charging clients for your services.

3. Another objective of this chapter concerns knowing when to charge and collect fees for your services. Receiving payment of fees in a timely manner is crucial to both the designer's business and the project's orderly progression. Specifying appropriate times for the payment of fees and understanding the options available to designers with late-paying clients are important aspects of charging for your services. The following detailed discussion of these three objectives demonstrates how you can master their challenges.

UNDERSTANDING THE
FINANCIAL NEEDS OF YOUR BUSINESS

To determine what to charge for your services, you need to become familiar with several important financial accounting concepts and terms. You need to know whether the method you select for charging clients will adequately pay for the costs of providing those services as well as other business expenses. So you need to know how **income**, or financial increases, and **expenses**, or financial decreases, are handled and described.

HOW BUSINESSES CALCULATE REVENUE

During the course of their operation, businesses receive amounts of money paid by consumers for the goods and services produced by that business. These amounts are generally referred to by terms such as *income* or—for purposes of completing financial accounting reports, such as income statements—**gross revenue**. Of course, there may be other sources of income for a business, such as reimbursement for expenses or incentive payments. What is important is for you to be aware of these general terms used to describe the financial increases produced by a business. Income for an interior design business is typically derived from the design fees it charges and the merchandise it sells. Fees earned (and collected), proceeds from the sale of goods, and any other financial increases are added together to arrive at an amount referred to, for income-reporting purposes, as **total gross revenue**. Consider the following excerpt from the annual income statement of a small interior design firm:

Gross Revenue
    Fees for Services $375,000
    Sale of Goods $225,000
        Total Gross Revenue $600,000

Amounts noted as being gross revenues from fees for services are typically calculated using one of the methods described in this chapter. Contracts for the designer's services, discussed in detail in chapter 11, contain provisions related to how designers will charge for their services. Gross revenue derived from the sale of goods may also be determined using one of these methods or, when designers sell merchandise "off the floor" in a shop setting, from that source.

The amount of gross revenue is then decreased by a sum total of all financial adjustments. For example, interior designers who accept returns of merchandise from clients would note the dollar amount of that return, and then add it to other such adjustments to reach a total sum for all adjustments. That total is then subtracted from the sum of gross revenue to reach a sum known as **net revenue**.

Gross Revenue
Fees for Services $375,000
Sale of Goods $225,000
    Total Gross Revenue $600,000

Allowances and Adjustments $25,000
    Net Revenue $575,000

The amount of net revenue is important because it represents the sum, or total, of the financial resources produced by a business. This amount will be further decreased when both the costs of providing services and a business's operating expenses are considered.

HOW BUSINESSES CALCULATE EXPENSES

Perhaps you have heard the saying, "It takes money to make money." The money it "takes" is more formally referred to in accounting terms as **cost of sales** or, in businesses that primarily sell merchandise, *cost of goods sold*. These costs are added together to produce the total cost of sales.

Gross Revenue
Fees for Services $375,000
Sale of Goods $225,000
    Total Gross Revenue $600,000

Allowances and Adjustments $25,000
    Net Revenue $575,000

Cost of Sales
Fees from Services $65,000

Fees from Salc of Goods $35,000
    Total Cost of Sales $100,000

It is important to highlight the **fees from services** amount, listed here as $65,000. This amount is also referred to as the **direct labor expense**. What is involved in determining this expense, and why is it important that designers understand this concept when determining design fees? It may be simple to explain this concept if you first assume that the designers in this example are employed by a design firm or are independent designers who have specified their own annual salaries. In this case, further assume that such designers receive the following as their total annual compensation from their respective firms:

Annual Salary $25,000
Other Benefits (holidays, paid sick leave, ...$5,000
   health insurance)
   Total Designer Compensation **$30,000**

Why do you think the amount shown as the direct labor expense is $65,000 and not $30,000? Take a moment to consider what is involved in determining designers' compensation as expenses to their firms. How might these costs be calculated for income-reporting purposes? In this scenario, a designer works for a business a total of forty-eight weeks a year, or roughly eleven months, for a weekly cost to the firm of $625. This amount is often referred to as the **direct personnel expense** or **DPE**, incurred by a business for having a designer on staff. Annual salaries for designers vary greatly as do amounts spent by businesses on employee benefits. Here is an example of such expenditures for a hypothetical interior design organization.

Annual Salary $25,000
Other Benefits (holidays, paid sick leave, ...$5,000
   health insurance)
    Total Designer Compensation $30,000

$30,000 annual salary/48 weeks of work **$625**

As you can see, the designer "costs" the business a total of $625 a week in salary expenses: Given a typical forty-hour workweek, the salary expense incurred by the firm for employing the designer is $15.63 an hour.

$625 weekly rate/40-hour workweek **$15.63**

It should be noted here that this hourly rate is not the **billing rate** for the designer's services. *Do not confuse a designer's hourly DPE with the employer's billing rate.* The **billing rate** is the dollar amount charged per hour to clients for the services of a designer. The billing rate is customarily applied when a designer and client have agreed to the hourly-rate fee method. While the billing rate makes use of the hourly DPE rate, its calculation is more complicated. As a very general rule, the billing rate is approximately double the DPE, if that can help you better understand billing rate in relation to hourly rate.

During the course of a project, designers keep (or should keep) records of the amounts of time they devote to working on each of their projects. These amounts of time are then totaled and multiplied by the specific dollar amount determined to be a designer's cost to the firm. Here, for simplicity's sake, assume that a firm employs ten designers, each of whom costs the firm the same amount of salary, namely $15.63 per hour, and each of whom works the same amount of time.

Designer 1: 416 hrs × $15.63 . . . .$6,500

Designer 2: 416 hrs × $15.63 . . . .$6,500

Designer 3: 416 hrs × $15.63 . . . .$6,500

Designer 4: 416 hrs × $15.63 . . . .$6,500

Designer 5: 416 hrs × $15.63 . . . .$6,500

Designer 6: 416 hrs × $15.63 . . . .$6,500

Designer 7: 416 hrs × $15.63 . . . .$6,500

Designer 8: 416 hrs × $15.63 . . . .$6,500

Designer 9: 416 hrs × $15.63 . . . .$6,500

Designer 10: 416 hrs × $15.63 . . . .$6,500

Fees from Services **$65,000**

Savvy students will note that 416 hours of work, assuming a usual forty-hour workweek translates into these designers each working about ten and a half weeks, that is, approximately one-fifth of the year. This conclusion would mean that each designer received $35,000 for his or her work. More complicated income statements and discussions of costs would include larger numbers, of course. The point of this example is not the amount of time the designers worked or the amount of money they received, but rather to illustrate that the services of the designer cost the designer's employer a certain amount of money. This concept is very important to whatever method is used by designers to charge for their services. Without knowing the costs to the business, designers cannot realistically determine which method will be most satisfactory.

Cost of sales also includes supplies consumed during the course of the business's operations; telephone usage; amounts expended but not yet reimbursed; cost of goods purchased for use on projects; and transportation costs of those goods—in short all sums expended to provide design services and merchandise. It is important for you to be aware of the term **gross margin**, which is the difference in amount between net revenue and total cost of sales; here, that amount is $475,000.

Gross Revenue
Fees for Services $375,000
Sale of Goods $225,000
    Total Gross Revenue $600,000

Allowances and Adjustments $25,000
    Net Revenue $575,000

Cost of Sales
Fees from Services $65,000
Fees from Sale of Goods $35,000
    Total Cost of Sales $100,000
    Gross Margin **$475,000**

It is from gross margin that all remaining costs of a business are paid. These costs are referred to under the general term **operating expenses**. These are all the expenses required to operate the business, including the salaries of workers who support the activities of the design staff; rent paid for the office or studio space; utilities; and office supplies, to name just a few. You should also be aware of what is known as **indirect expenses.** These are the expenses a designer incurs in the course of completing a project that usually come about because of events or situations outside a designer's control. For example, a designer assumes responsibility for a project of a kind they have not done previously. Who pays for the time the designer spends researching unfamiliar design issues and learning to make appropriate decisions? Often, a designer cannot bill a client for time spent in activities such as these unless a client has agreed to pay a fee. In cases where a client has not agreed to pay a said fee, the time and costs to a business are absorbed as indirect expenses. You may better remember the concept of indirect expenses by noting time is only money to designers' businesses when they are able to adequately charge clients for it; if they are not able to do so, then time becomes an expense to those businesses and a limitation on the amount of gross profit they ultimately earn. Interior design is an expensive profession to pursue. Keeping each of these expenses as low as possible to be able to function and attract new clients is a key concern of managers in large firms as well as individual practitioners. Their success at managing expenses becomes evident, or appears lacking, when the total of all operating expenses is subtracted from the amount of gross margin. As a final note, the amount of net income is further reduced by taxes levied on a business.

Gross Revenue

Fees for Services $375,000

Sale of Goods $225,000

    Total Gross Revenue $600,000

Allowances and Adjustments $25,000

    Net Revenue $575,000

Cost of Sales

Fees from Services $65,000

Fees from Sale of Goods $35,000

Total Cost of Sales $100,000

    Gross Margin $475,000

Operating Expenses

  Non-billable salaries $40,000

  Rent $25,000

  Supplies $5,000

    Total Operating Expenses $70,000

Net Income **$405,000**

This overview of the accounting concepts used in calculating and describing the financial needs of a business is important when setting design fees for the following reasons:

◆ You need to know how the sometimes considerable amount of net revenue generated by a designer or an entire design business can be

DEVELOPING AN EFFECTIVE METHOD FOR CHARGING CLIENTS

Determining the Direct Personnel Expense Multiple

Step One: 1.0

For simplicity, begin with 1.0, since salaries form the basis of personnel expenses.

Step Two: ____

The multiple also takes into account expenses besides salaries. Add the amount of salary to the amount of indirect expenses, then divide by the amount of salary (the total of this calculation should be a number greater than 1.0).

Step Three: ____

After expenses, the relationship profit has to salaries forms the last component of the DPE multiple. Divide the stated amount of profit by the stated amount of salary (the total of this calculation should be less than 1.0).

Step Four: ____

Add the three steps above to reach the DPE multiple. The resulting number should be between 2.0 and 3.0. Is yours? As you complete this step ask yourself these questions. Can a design business manipulate the components of the DPE multiple in ways that affect the business's ability to meet expenses and profitability goals? How might doing so affect the business's competitiveness? These are important decisions inherent in the use of the hourly rate approach using a DPE multiple.

Deciding on a Billing Rate

Step One: ____

Add the amounts of salary and benefits paid and divide by the total number of weeks worked. This amount is the Direct Personnel Expense of the worker to the design business, expressed not as a multiple, but as an actual dollar amount.

Step Two: ____

Divide the DPE you determined above by the average amount of time available each week that is able to be billed to clients. This is the amount per hour it "costs" the design business to retain the services of a worker receiving salary and benefits.

Step Three: ____

The "cost" above is not the amount charged to the client; to determine that, you next need to use the DPE multiple and the hourly rate above. Multiply the two to get the client billing rate.

substantially eroded, or even eliminated, after cost of sales and overhead expenses are calculated. You now understand the meaning of accounting concepts such as *revenue, cost of sales, operating expenses, gross margin*, and *net income*. These terms and concepts are intrinsic to the charging methods described in this chapter.

◆ The concept of DPE, or *direct personnel expense*, is important in determining the hourly rate that a designer or design firm charges clients for design services (see Form 9.1).

Understanding the full scope of a business's financial needs is a lengthy process. This discussion has placed less emphasis on categorizing the many possible examples of overhead expenses and how they may be calculated. Accountants and office administrators with responsibility for the finances of a design firm can and do provide guidance to practicing designers on how to handle such issues. Above all, taking active measures to reduce or keep these expenses as low as possible is an important goal for achieving greater profitability for a firm. Enhancing the profitability of interior design businesses is an important goal to consider when establishing design fees, as further discussed in the following section of this chapter.

UNDERSTANDING HOW TO
CHARGE FOR YOUR SERVICES

The second major objective of this chapter is to introduce you to the specific methods designers use to charge for their services and assess potential projects for profitability. The latter process requires that designers recognize typical characteristics of projects that can and do influence their completion and also indicates whether a commitment to that project will prove to be a profitable use of designers' time and resources. Table 9.1 summarizes the different approaches discussed in this chapter.

To help you to learn and recall the different methods of charging for your services, they can be categorized according to their four general characteristics as follows:

◆ Rate-based methods
◆ Sale of merchandise–based methods

- ◆ Combination methods
- ◆ Other methods

The following discussion provides a capsule explanation of each method, including a phrase to help you recall it. The text then presents a more complete explanation of how each method operates as well as the kinds of projects most appropriate for each method. Finally, the advantages and disadvantages of each approach is noted.

Is there any one method of determining how to charge for services that is best for a designer to use? The answer to this frequent question depends on many factors. The method that is best understood by a designer may not be best able to satisfy this chapter's first objective—namely, meeting the expenses of a designer's business and producing a financial profit. Be receptive to the benefits of each of the following approaches. As you gain experience working with clients and projects, you will be able to recognize situations where one method rather than another will allow you to earn a greater, but still reasonable, profit from the expenditure of your time and talent as a design professional. For that reason, think of the methods described here much as you might a book of textile swatches: They are materials available for use on the project for a reason. Once you understand the nuances involved in using each method, and have learned the financial needs of your business by calculating its various expenses, you may form your own strategy for determining how to charge clients for your services.

RATE-BASED METHODS

Two major ways of determining fees for design services are considered in this category, notably the **flat** or **fixed fee method** and the **hourly fee method**. Their names give you a sense of how they operate. What may be less obvious, however, are the nuances distinguishing how they are calculated and how they are used.

Fixed Fee

Using this method, designers receive an agreed-upon amount, or flat fee, usually paid in increments, for their services. This approach is based on a designer and client agreeing at the outset that the designer will receive a defined fee as compensation for his or her services. Usually, this amount is stated in the designer's contract for services as a total dollar figure not to exceed an agreed-upon amount. Typically, the fee is paid in installments as successive phases of the project are completed, and it does not include costs for the designer's purchase of merchandise. In addition, **reimbursable expenses**, which can include travel to the project site and incidental expenses that may be incurred in many ways, are typically billed separately. The designer who selects this method must have experience with similar kinds of projects in order to accurately estimate the single price to place on the services necessary to complete the project, and which will also provide a gross profit to the firm when costs and expenses are subtracted from the fixed amount of income earned.

When to Select This Method

This approach is usually considered when two factors are present. First, a client wants to know the cost of a project before work on it begins. Second, designers who choose this method will have such a thorough understanding of both the scope of the proposed project and the costs and expenses involved in running their businesses that they can estimate the appropriate fixed fee that they can afford as compensation. Designers who routinely work on similar kinds of projects—for example, restaurants—maintain records of their costs in terms of salaries paid to design staff members; the time it took those designers to complete prior restaurant projects; and the business expenses incurred in implementing those projects. These records are sometimes referred to as **historical records**, since they document project costs over a period of time. Records of this kind are extremely valuable to design businesses, especially those that meticulously record the amount of time spent by members of the firm in completing projects. As a side note, as a new practitioner, you will probably dislike the process of keeping time records. It takes time to write down what you do and how long it takes you to do it. As an experienced interior design professional, however, you are more likely to understand the value of such records, since they provide valuable information about the time it takes you and members of your staff to perform various project tasks—time that costs the firm in terms of salary expenses. These costs must be more than compensated by revenues earned by the business if it is to earn a profit.

Advantages

It is appropriate to use this method when designers are aware of the historical costs of completing similar projects. If designers use that data well,

TABLE 9.1 Comparing Methods of Charging Clients for Your Services

Method	How Designer Charges Clients for Services	Best Suited for Projects	Concerns About Using
1. Cost Plus Percentage Markup	Increasing net merchandise cost by preset percentage	Involving extensive amounts of merchandise purchases; when designer/firm seeks a competitive advantage	Percentage used usually less than in retail method; less remunerative if percentage used does not fully provide for designer's efforts
2. Discounting of Percentage Off Retail	Decreasing merchandise MSRP by preset percentage	Involving extensive amounts of merchandise purchases	Discount may not provide enough gross margin to fully compensate for designer's services
3. Fixed Fee	Billing one set amount for work performed (plus other expenses)—sometimes called a *flat fee.*	Where final cost of project, as completed, is at issue before work has begun	Amount charged must take into account actual time and expertise required to complete project as bid; could result in substantial loss for designer/firm
4. Hourly Fee	Multiplying time spent on client's project by a billing rate, then charging client that amount (plus other expenses)	Involving extensive consultation time and preparation of drawings and documents	Must be based on adequate DPE to fully compensate designer/firm; "not-to-exceed" amount should be considered to address cost concerns
5. Percentage of Merchandise and Product Services	Multiplying an agreed-upon percentage by amount of final project cost (including merchandise and some construction costs)	Where clients purchase their own merchandise	Project revenue earned from designer's/firm's services exclusively; percentage used must be adequate to cover actual time, expertise required
6. Square Footage	Multiplying project square footage by a dollar amount derived from past projects	Where extensive information exists about past similar projects; when designer/firm is experienced with similar projects	Amount charged must take into account actual time and expertise required to compensate designer/firm, dollar amount used must be competitive

7. Retail Cost	Charging full amount of MSRP on merchandise used for project	Requiring designer to make many purchases of merchandise and other project-related items	Can be highly remunerative to designer/firm, but project cuts can greatly affect gross margin and amount earned
8. Value-Added	Convincing client the designer's services/experience are superior to others	Where designer/firm is well known or established, with substantial portfolio of similar projects completed	Client must see expertise as an added contribution to project, with less concern about final project cost
9. Cost Plus Percentage Markup with Fixed Fee	Charging a single fee for services and increasing merchandise costs by a set percentage amount	Where designer/firm seeks compensation for design services and for merchandise specified and purchased for project	Fixed fee must be adequate to compensate for services; usually cost of merchandise is less than retail amount; client may be concerned about designer receiving "double" fees
10. Cost Plus Percentage Markup with Hourly Fee	Multiplying a percentage amount by number of hours worked and increasing merchandise costs by a set percentage amount	Where designer/firm seeks compensation for design services and for merchandise specified, purchased for project	Rate amount must be adequate to compensate for services; usually merchandise costs less than retail amount; client may be concerned about designer receiving "double" fees
11. Service Consultation Fee	Charging a single dollar-amount fee for discussing ideas, usually not including drawings or purchases; limited time commitment for designer	Where designer desires to share ideas and make suggestions about possible design solutions	Designer should agree with client about specific scope of discussion and amount of work expected before undertaking; may be a good tool for developing later business

they can earn their businesses a profit by seeking a flat fee that more than covers costs and expenses. Furthermore, accepting a flat fee might be an incentive to a prospective client to do more business in the future. In short, the fee structure may allow the firm to distinguish itself in a particular marketplace.

Disadvantages

The fixed fee approach requires a great deal of preparation to use. The success of this approach is also very dependent on the accuracy of a project's budget. If designers have a wealth of data about the costs incurred by similar projects, they can conclude whether the client has set aside a viable amount for the project under consideration. This approach will probably not adequately compensate a designer if the project requires excessive purchase of merchandise or if the scope of services that a designer will have to perform has not been precisely defined. When a project requires that a great many purchases be made, other methods for setting design fees would likely result in greater profits. Situations in which a designer will be called upon to complete many tasks on an ad hoc basis or projects that require a designer to spend a lot of time with a client are not likely candidates for use of this approach.

Hourly Rate

Using this approach, a designer receives a fee based on the amount of time spent working on a project multiplied by the billing rate. This method of charging for services is perhaps the most familiar to those who have engaged the services of other professionals. Designers charge clients an amount determined by multiplying the number of hours they spend working on that client's project by a billing rate, a dollar amount calculated to compensate for firm expenses and desired profits. The Contract Interior Design Case Study explores the process involved in determining the billing rate.

When to Select This Method

The main reason to use the hourly approach in charging for your services is that it compensates designers for use of their time. Thus, it is appropriate in situations that require large amounts of time to be spent in providing design services, consultation, or preparation for the project.

Advantages

This approach has the chief advantage of flexibility for a designer. At the start of a project, it is often difficult to adequately assess the amount of time or the kinds of activities that will be required of a designer. Using the hourly approach, designers receive compensation for their work despite these uncertainties.

This approach has one advantage not readily apparent, but related to its flexible nature: It can provide a way for a designer to more easily exit a project. Of course, legal counsel about the effects of contract provisions should be consulted, since laws differ among jurisdictions. However, by carefully drafting the hourly rate provision in contracts for design services, designers may be able to simply bill clients for services rendered as of a particular date, without further obligation to continue working for those clients.

Disadvantages

The flexible nature of this approach can be intimidating to clients who fear design fees may become quite astronomical. For this reason, designers using this approach should insert not-to-exceed clauses in contracts for their services. This approach in particular requires designers to keep extensive time records, a process that is antithetical to some.

SALE OF MERCHANDISE-BASED METHODS

Historically, interior designers have used the merchandise they specify and sell to clients as the basis for determining their compensation. The following four methods are classified in this way.

Retail Method

Under the **retail method**, fees for a designer's services are derived from charging clients the manufacturer's suggested retail price for project merchandise—typically, double the net price paid by a designer. The fee for a designer's services, such as programming activities and schematics, is derived from the difference between the amount a designer initially paid for merchandise (the *net* price, also referred to as the *cost* price) and the price at which a client purchased that merchandise from the designer.

When to Select This Method

As you would suspect, projects in which large amounts of merchandise will be purchased would be ideal candidates for use of this approach. However, even if a proposed project requires a designer to purchase many items, it is important to fully consider the scope of services. Any profit that might have been earned from proceeds derived from large purchases may be more than offset by the extensive amount of time required to provide other project services.

Advantages

This approach offers the greatest possibility of earning a designer the most profit.

Disadvantages

Interior designers, especially those with residential practices, have historically used the retail method for setting fees in which they specify both products and the final prices that their clients will pay for them. However, some question the practices of selecting and setting prices for design merchandise, as reflected in the following statement: "The practice of selling furniture and accessories as the key compensation method is under attack by many sources. . . . The issues of protecting the health, safety, and welfare of the public are in conflict with the segment of the profession that is compensated primarily through the sale of products" (Wheeler 2002). What do you think is the conflict to which the writer refers?

Implicit in Wheeler's argument is the idea that designers using the retail approach have an incentive *not* to specify the most appropriate product if it will not garner the most profit for them. This criticism may seem valid when it appears that designers can take advantage of clients because they have superior access to merchandise offered by a manufacturer. Wheeler's criticism may even apply to designers who charge an hourly rate for their services, especially when they routinely sell so much of one manufacturer's merchandise that they receive substantially preferred pricing and considerations such as expedited delivery. Even when these designers pass on some savings to clients or when clients themselves place orders directly with manufacturers, there is still an incentive for designers to use a single manufacturer's products. If certain products are especially pleasing to clients they may patronize a designer who provides them even if other products may be more appropriate for client needs, or are more readily available or produced in a more ethical manner.

Cost Plus Percentage Markup

The fees earned by designers using the **cost plus percentage markup method** are based on increasing net cost of project merchandise by a percentage typically less than the percentage used in the retail approach. When learning about this approach, remember designers increase the amount they paid for merchandise before reselling it to clients. The retail method is extremely expensive for clients, many of whom may be less interested in using a designer's services without having some concession in the pricing of merchandise. Using the cost plus percentage markup method, a designer adds a percentage amount to the merchandise cost that is substantially less than the 100 percent used in the retail approach. Interior design businesses that set fees this way decide which percentage best fits their needs and will provide them with an adequate profit. Otherwise, this approach is similar to the retail approach.

Discounting of Percentage Off Retail

Designers who use the **discounting of percentage off retail method** to determine design fees decrease the manufacturer's suggested retail price of merchandise by a set percentage. Designers lower the retail cost when using the discounting of percentage method, whereas they increase the retail cost when using the cost plus percentage method. Typically, a designer's cost price is much less than the manufacturer's suggested retail price. Under this approach, designers lower the manufacturer's suggested retail price by some percentage; this is the equivalent of putting the merchandise on sale for the client.

As with the retail approach, this method is appropriate when large quantities of merchandise need to be purchased. It shares with the retail method the same advantage of earning a large gross profit for a designer's business provided that the fees also satisfy the costs of services provided for the project.

Percentage of Merchandise and Product Services

To determine fees using the **percentage of merchandise and product services method**, a designer estimates an appropriate percentage of the cost of project merchandise and services and multiplies it by the amount of a client's budget for the project.

COMBINATION METHODS

Cost Plus Percentage Markup with Fixed Fee

Designers who use this approach charge a set or fixed fee as compensation for their services and increase the price of any merchandise they sell by some percentage amount above the cost they paid.

Cost Plus Percentage Markup with Hourly Fee

Designers using this approach charge an hourly fee as compensation for their services and increase the price of any merchandise they sell by some percentage amount above the cost paid by the designer. Designers using these approaches essentially have chosen two methods of charging clients: a fixed fee or hourly rate they believe will cover their expenses and that will pay them for the merchandise they provide.

When to Select These Methods

These methods of charging clients may be appropriate for projects that involve many activities on the part of the designer. When designers understand the financial needs of their businesses, particularly expenses, they can accurately estimate what flat fees at hourly rates will cover those expenses.

Advantages

These approaches probably best compensate most designers, who usually provide both services and merchandise.

Disadvantages

These approaches can be confusing for a designer who does not understand how their use can affect his or her business's profitability. They can also be confusing to clients who believe they are being charged twice for the same services or merchandise.

OTHER METHODS

Square-Foot Method

In the **square-foot method** the amount of project space—square footage multiplied by a calculated dollar amount—is used to determine a designer's compensation. Using data from previous projects, it is possible to derive a monetary amount that a firm could charge that would provide a profit to the firm; that amount would then be multiplied by the project's square footage to arrive at a designer's fee.

Advantages

When accurate records can be used to determine the dollar amount to be charged, and market conditions allow for use of this approach as well as the specified dollar amount, it may be profitable for a firm to use this method.

Disadvantages

This approach may be extremely lucrative in locations where the services of designers are so highly valued by consumers that the monetary rate per square foot can be kept high. On the other hand, market conditions may be unfavorable when the rate that designers would have to charge for their services in order to show a profit would be unattractive to potential clients. In addition to geographic factors, economic downturns also determine whether to use this approach.

Value-Based Method

The **value-based method** allows designers to charge a premium for their services based on some intangible benefit they are perceived to provide to the client for the project. Such benefit might be the designer's expertise, or the fame that the designer enjoys. According to Nila R. Leiserowitz, ASID 2004, this method of charging clients will be the preferred approach in the future:

> the interior design profession will develop value-based compensation. The traditional fee model of cost per square foot has not worked well for our profession. . . . Interior design fees will be divided into two portions. One portion will be fees for delivery of design from programming through construction administration. The second portion will be fees based on value-added services and work environment performance.

ASSESSING A PROJECT'S POTENTIAL FOR PROFIT

You must be aware of more than just the needs of your business in order to determine what to profitably charge for your services. Of course, you need to completely understand the demands of your project and to estimate what will be required for you to complete it. Think for a moment about two important factors that affect the work of interior designers: the time at their disposal for professional activities and the merchandise their clients purchase from them. Assessing a proposed project's potential for earning a designer a profit involves balancing these two factors to find an approach that best compensates a designer.

Considering the following questions as you approach each newly proposed project can give you a better idea of how your time will be spent during the course of a project—time for which you should find a way to be compensated. Before determining how to charge for your services, consider which methods of charging clients will best pay you for engaging in your interior design activities. What other factors are critically important for the project and should also be considered when assessing a potential project's potential for profit?

1. *What kind of project is contemplated, and how many project stakeholders are involved?*
   Interior design work may be applied in either residential or commercial installations. In residential work, there is usually only one or, at best, a few stakeholders who have an interest in and input into the project. When approaching residential projects, the designer needs to assess the magnitude of the project and the extent to which stakeholders wish to be involved. Large-scale interior design projects can involve either the construction of a completely new structure or substantial renovation of an existing building. In both instances, it is highly likely that the designer in charge will be required to meet frequently with the clients as well as many other professionals, such as architects and general contractors, during the course of the project. Small-scale projects may involve only selected spaces in an existing dwelling and thus require the designer to spend less time meeting with other professionals and clients.
2. *How experienced are you with projects of the kind you are considering?*
   If designers have a great deal of experience with certain kinds of projects, they will need to do less initial research to undertake it. Often, time spent on initial preparation is not time the designer can bill to the client as a direct expense.

3. *How experienced are your potential clients in working with you and with the process of interior design?*

Clients who have not experienced the scope of interior design projects or who want to be extensively involved in the process are clients who will demand the greatest amount of a designer's time. The expenses required for such large expenditures of time can make a project unprofitable for a designer.

4. *Will buying merchandise be necessary to complete the project, and if so, who will be responsible for making the purchases?*

Large purchases of merchandise can be profitable sources of revenue for a designer. In those instances, a designer should consider using any of the purchase of merchandise-based methods of charging for services.

5. *What is the scope of services offered by a designer?*

Projects for which a designer has agreed to provide a full range of services, from programming to contract administration, will require substantial expenditures of time. In those circumstances, a designer may wish to combine an hourly or flat fee with a purchase of merchandise-based method.

KNOWING WHEN TO CHARGE
AND COLLECT FOR YOUR SERVICES

Any strategy related to determining business revenue must take into account the timeliness of payments. Few interior designers can (or should) allow unpaid invoices to accumulate after billing clients for the services they provide or the merchandise they sell (see Form 9.2 for an example of a purchase invoice). Unfortunately, clients may not be so concerned about paying the balances, or totals, listed in their designers' receivables accounts. For these reasons, you should be especially aware of the need to specify to clients—before it becomes problematic—when you expect to receive payment of the fees you charge. Most contracts for services entered into by designers and their clients spell out payment terms, as you will note in chapters 10 and 11. You should also know when and how to initiate payment from clients; how professionals charge clients for permitting them to delay payments; as well as basic aspects of formal collection practices.

PURCHASE INVOICE

| COMPANY NAME |
| Address |
| City |
| Phone No. |
| Fax No. |

Date _____
Invoice Number _____

INVOICE

Payment Due Upon Receipt

To _____
_____
_____

Reference _____
_____

In accordance with the Contract for Design Services, dated _____, the following purchases have been made as of the date of this invoice in furtherance of the referenced project.

Description	Unit Price	Quantity	Extended

Please remit payment within ____ days of the date of this invoice. Late payments will be assessed a charge of ___% per month.

Subtotal	_____
Sales Tax	_____
Total	_____
Deposit Paid	_____
TOTAL DUE	_____

ACCOUNTS RECEIVABLE, CREDIT, AND INTEREST

Amounts due to designers from clients are classified according to accounting principles as designers' **accounts receivable** (**accounts payable**, from clients' perspective). Each design business develops its own policies for handling situations where clients owe a design firm for services or for merchandise purchased on clients' behalf. Many firms cannot financially afford to allow any balance due from clients to remain unpaid, while others are able and willing to allow the client to pay these balances within a certain amount of time. Usually, firms not able to provide extended payment terms require payment of amounts due when billed. Firms extending credit to clients by allowing them to delay payment typically request it within thirty, sixty, or ninety days after the balance is billed. Why might these firms extend credit for a specified period of time?

State laws often allow businesses that extend credit to charge for this service by charging **interest**, or a percentage of the total amount due, as compensation to the business for allowing these amounts to remain unpaid (see Form 9.3). Theoretically, had the amounts been paid, the design business could have used the monies for other opportunities, which were lost when the business extended credit. This interest expense can be a viable source of revenue for the business, since amounts collected can be added to the business's gross revenue amount to increase its net revenue.

BILLING AND COLLECTION PROCEDURES

Interior design businesses intent on maintaining profitability through timely receipt of fee payments develop effective billing and collection procedures. The billing process involves preparing invoices (see Form 9.2) and making them available to clients for payment as soon as possible after the fee for service or for merchandise is incurred. This is followed by initiating follow-up procedures with clients when payment is not received within a specified time. Attempts to obtain payment for amounts due are generally referred to as **collection practices** and are further controlled by the laws of the state where the interior design business is located. Collection practices may be implemented informally by a designer or the financial administrators of a designer's business. This usually takes the form of letters (see forms 9.3 and 9.4) and phone calls to a client to request

FORM 9.3. LETTER REQUESTING FEE PAYMENT

REQUEST FOR FEE PAYMENT

COMPANY NAME
Address
City
Phone No.
Fax No.

Date _____

**ACCOUNT
PAST DUE**

To _____
    _____
    _____

Reference _____
           _____

This is to inform you that payment on the following account has not been received as of the date of statement. Please remit payment within ____ days of this statement, or contact us so that other payment arrangements may be made.

All invoices not paid within the provisions of the Contract for Design Services dated _____ will be subject to a monthly service charge of _____%.

Invoice Date	Invoice Amount	Interest Charge	Invoice Total Amount
		Total Amount	Now Due _____

Thank you for your prompt attention to this matter.

_____

payment of fees due or to make other arrangements for payment of at least a portion of the amount. These practices may be more formally implemented by attorneys or collection agencies who have expertise and success in collection. Usually, businesses that resort to using formal collection services pay for doing so in the form of an hourly rate to attorneys and a percentage amount to collection agencies.

As important as it is for designers to know the financial needs of their businesses, the methods of charging for their services, and project factors affecting profitability, receiving timely payment of fees is crucial for designers since their own expenses have to be satisfied whether fees due them are paid on time. Assessing the ability of clients to make timely payments of fees charged is another factor designers should consider when setting their fees.

FORM 9.4. COLLECTING PAYMENT: CHARGING INTEREST ON UNPAID ACCOUNTS

INTEREST ON UNPAID ACCOUNTS

COMPANY NAME
Address
City
Phone No.
Fax No.

Date _____

SECOND NOTICE

To _____
_____
_____

Reference _____
_____

This is your **second notice**. Payment on the referenced account still has not been received as of the date of this statement.

Please remit payment within ____ days of this statement, or contact us so that other payment arrangements may be made.

All invoices not paid within the provisions of the Contract for Design Services dated _____ will be subject to a monthly service charge of _____%.

Invoice Date	Invoice Amount	Interest Charge	Invoice Total Amount
	Total Amount	Now Due	_____

Thank you for your prompt attention to this matter.

_____

REFERENCES

Alderman, Robert L. 1997. *How to Prosper as an Interior Designer*. New York: John Wiley & Sons.

Berger, C. Jaye. 1994. *Interior Design Law and Business Practices*. New York: John Wiley & Sons.

Coleman, Cindy, ed. 2002. *Interior Design: Handbook of Professional Practice*. New York: McGraw-Hill.

Knackstedt, Mary V. 2002. *The Interior Design Business Handbook*. 3rd ed. New York: John Wiley & Sons.

Siegel, Harry and Alan Siegel. 1982. *A Guide to Business Practices and Principles for Interior Designers*. New rev. ed. New York: Watson-Guptill.

Wheeler, Gary E. 2002. "Financial Management," in *Handbook of Professional Practice*, ed. Cindy Coleman, p. 161. New York: McGraw-Hill.

PROBLEM-SOLVING STRATEGIES

Consider the following scenarios. Then suggest the method of charging for a designer's services that you believe would be most appropriate based on your understanding of this chapter. There may be more than one approach that could reasonably be applied. State your reasons for making your choices. As you consider these scenarios, you may discover similarities to your own ideal business. Completing this exercise may help you complete the Strategic Planning Project that follows.

1. "I have clients who just want ideas and suggestions about how to design a few rooms in their homes. How might I charge for providing that service?"

2. "My client's project will likely involve the purchase of a great deal of new furniture, but little of my time in other matters, since we agreed that the scope of my services on the project would be limited. What method of charging for my services might I specify?"

3. "Help! My clients are new to interior design and are not even sure what they want me to do. The project is one that promises to be quite extensive—if the clients ever decide on anything. What method of setting fees might work in this case?"

4. "I am a well-known specialist in small-sized medical facilities such as day clinics. I have expertise in completing these facilities quickly and less expensively than most of my competitors, who lack my education and experience. What methods might I use to determine my fees that take into account the valuable contribution I make to my clients' businesses?

5. "Are there any advantages to charging on an hourly basis for my time, as do lawyers, accountants, and other professionals? It does seem like a lot of work to keep track of the time spent on projects."

STRATEGIES-IN-ACTION PROJECTS

STRATEGIC PLANNING PROJECT

The business plan project that has occupied you for some time now has sought to inspire your curiosity about the kind of interior design venture that would be the best showcase for your interests. As you are aware by now, that entity must be organized in realistic, profit-conscious ways. When you present your completed plan to others, they will probably not know how interior designers make money, that is, how they generate income for their businesses. As you also know by now, a business's potential viability is extremely important to those whom you approach for financial assistance. The purpose of this section of your business plan is to provide an overview of the particular ways in which designers charge clients.

This section of the business plan project begins simply enough by describing in your own words the four basic methods designers traditionally use to determine how they will charge for their services. Include as much detail as you can, and be sure to use your own words in writing the description. You may title this addition to your business plan "Setting Fees for Interior Design Services" and devote several pages, if necessary, to your description of these methods.

There are two main reasons for preparing this exercise. First, you will be called on by those interested in financially assisting your business and particularly by clients to explain how you propose to charge for your services. Clients will point to provisions in your contracts for design services related to determining fees and ask you to explain how those provisions operate. This exercise will help you to do so because it provides an opportunity for you to mentally process information discussed in this chapter, interpret it, and then explain it in your own way. Second, this exercise relates to the profitability of your business. Think of the profitability—and longevity—of your business as an important goal of each and every project you consider. You know that your interior design business must earn more than just enough to satisfy paying expenses, or costs, if you are to remain in practice. The methods you choose to use when charging clients for your services may determine whether you reach that goal. In fact, as you assess prospective projects and their potential for earning a profit for you and your business, you should consider which method of charging for your services might be the most applicable. To do that, you must understand these methods as completely as possible.

RESIDENTIAL INTERIOR DESIGN PROJECT SIMULATION

In this section of the project, Lee asks your help with matters related to receiving payment due for her work on the Abernathy children's room project.

Lee's Diary

With some clients it's never easy, and with the Abernathy family it is always a question of time. What that means is everyone and everything has to wait until the couple decides they have to "deal with" something, as Mr. Abernathy might say. Well, someone needs to deal with the invoices—the bills we keep sending them! The owner of the studio has told me I need to collect the fees that are due. Not only that, the owner pointed out to me what's written on the back of all of our purchase orders and invoices: "Interest at a rate of $1^1/_2$ percent per month will be charged and added to any balance due if payment is not received within 30 days after the date of invoice (see Form 9.4)."
Well, here we are at day #31, and I've sent a second notice with the interest figured on the following three items:

1. Two chairs @ $112.50 each
2. A table lamp @ $75.00
3. 55 yards of fabric @ $35.00 a yard

As you can see, this is just one more thing to finish!
Come to Lee's assistance, and using Form 9.5, determine what the Abernathy family owes for the merchandise with the interest expense added and with a sales tax rate of 8.25 percent.

CONTRACT INTERIOR DESIGN CASE STUDY: THE CASE OF THE CALCULATING CONSULTANTS

Brad Jennings and his group at Jennings + Associates remain busy with the State University dorm project. You will recall that this group of ar-

FINAL NOTICE OF OVERDUE FEES

COMPANY NAME
Address
City
Phone No.
Fax No.

Date _____

FINAL NOTICE

To _____
_____
_____

Reference _____
_____

Invoice Date	Invoice Amount	Interest Charge	Invoice Total Amount
_____	_____	_____	_____
_____	_____	_____	_____
_____	_____	_____	_____
_____	_____	_____	_____
		Total Amount	Now Due _____

We have previously requested payment with regard to the above-referenced account.

Those requests have been ignored. No other payment arrangement has been made as of the date of this statement.

Under the provisions of the Contract for Design Services dated _____ and signed by you, we must inform you that this matter will be turned over for collection within _____ days of the date of this notice should you not pay the full amount shown owed or contact us to make other arrangements.

We value you as a client and will work with you as best as we are able to bring your account current and prevent further collection activities. However, you must contact us for us to do so.

Please be aware you will incur additional legal and court costs should we be forced to pursue this matter through the collection process. Your credit rating may be damaged as well.

You may prevent this matter from being turned over for collection by contacting:

Name _____
Phone No. _____
Fax No. _____
E-mail _____

Thank you for your prompt attention to this matter.

_____

chitects and interior designers were retained to plan the renovation of the university's venerable Heritage Hall campus dormitory. You are on the team of consultants hired by Jennings to assist his group to resolve a variety of design-related issues. Prior to beginning work with the Jennings group, you and your other team members determined that your compensation for working on the dorm project would be based on an hourly rate of the kind described in this chapter. That is, the fees you would charge the Jennings group would be based on the amount of time you spent working on matters that Jennings referred your team, an amount in hours that would then be multiplied by a percentage rate. The Jennings group agreed to your team's use of this method but requested that your group prepare a memorandum describing how your team would determine the hourly billing rate charged. Using Form 9.1, Developing an Effective Method for Charging Clients on page 300, you will determine your billing rate, then, in accordance with Jennings's request, draft a short memo describing your finding. Be sure to attach your completed worksheet to the completed memo.

As you approach this project, there are several issues to consider. Under the hourly rate approach, the amount of time spent by a professional is multiplied by *something* to reach the specific amount that will be charged to a client. That something is called a multiplier, specifically the Direct Personnel Expense multiplier, and determining it will be the first issue you will resolve in this project. Then, using suggested amounts of time your team would likely have spent on consulting activities related to the dorm project, you will resolve the second issue of determining what to specifically charge the Jennings group.

Using Form 9.1 to determine the DPE multiplier first, assume each member of the consulting team receives the same amount of salary, $40,000; expenses of the group that cannot be billed to any client, known as *indirect expenses* are $12,000; the consulting group wishes to earn, total, a profit for the year in the amount of $20,000.

Then calculate the hourly billing rate using the form. The number of weeks a designer works in a year and the amount of time they work in a typical forty hour workweek varies greatly according to their situation and habits. Assume, however, members of your group work a total of fifty weeks a year and, on average have twenty-five hours actually available to bill to clients. Using the salary facts above, further note your consulting group pays staff an additional 25 percent of salary in the form of expenses, or $10,000.

In approximately seven steps, you will have determined how this particular group should charge their client for their services as design consultants. However, this approach is one you can use in your own practice. The key to using the approach suggested by this form is to maintain detailed records of all your expenses, set realistic profit goals, and maintain accurate time records throughout the tenure of a project.

CHAPTER TEN

MANAGING YOUR CLIENT'S PROJECT

A happy client is the best client.

KATHY ROGERS

WHY THIS CHAPTER IS IMPORTANT TO YOU

Managing interior design projects effectively requires that practitioners orchestrate the completion of a series of detailed, interrelated tasks. Throughout this process, designers must not only undertake or initiate specific activities, but also know how to document the initiation, progress, and completion of the tasks. This chapter is important because it will explain to you why designers need to use project management skills in their practices and what tasks and documents are necessary in carrying out each of the five project phases typical of all but the most unusual interior design projects. As a practical matter, understanding the process of project management should better enable you to define your working relationship with clients when preparing contracts for your services, the focus of chapter 11. From the perspective of a designer's working relationship with clients, proficiency at project management is a skill that can help a designer keep clients sufficiently happy to be good for his or her business.

PROFESSIONAL PRACTICES PORTFOLIO

After completing this chapter, you should be able to answer the following questions. Include your responses in a professional practices portfolio that you use as a handbook for your later use.

1. What is project management, and what are its five phases?
2. What are the characteristics of each of these phases?
3. What are construction documents, and how do they compare with other schematics prepared in the course of an interior design project?
4. What are *specifications*, and how do they relate to contract documents?
5. What are examples of concerns clients may have during project management and how may a designer address them?
6. With the aid of information learned in this chapter, complete Form 10.1, the Project Management Outline. Then include it for reference in your portfolio.

INTRODUCTION TO
MANAGING INTERIOR DESIGN PROJECTS

This chapter will examine the phases through which an interior designer guides projects from initial information gathering to final installation and project close-out or completion. What are the reasons that interior designers might have for using a formal methodology such as the one described here? Aside from the most obvious reason—to get the job done—there are more subtle rationales for employing formal project management procedures.

Using project management procedures to organize tasks and using effective interpersonal communication allows designers to better inform their clients about the sometimes lengthy and complicated processes required to complete projects. Clients in both residential and commercial projects want to know the status of their projects at any given time, including what activities will occur next. Perhaps the worst response designers could give to their clients is to say they don't know what is happening next. Being aware of the sequence of project demands within the scope of the project management procedure explained in this chapter enables designers to clearly explain a project's progression to their clients.

PROJECT MANAGEMENT OUTLINE

Phase	Associated Tasks	Relevant Documents
Programming		
Schematic Design		
Design Development		
Contract Documents		
Contract Administration		

Another important reason for working within an organized project framework is apparent in contract interior design projects. When business decision makers allocate a portion of a company's financial resources to interior design projects, those resources are no longer available to address other business concerns. A designer should be able to allude to project management techniques in justifying the use of company resources and ensuring those decision makers that they will obtain tangible results from the project. For example, designers rely on project management techniques to gain information about working conditions and activities in order to demonstrate to stakeholders that project results will promote worker satisfaction and efficiency.

Undertaking projects should be financially profitable for an interior designer. Knowing what is required to complete each phase of a project can help designers to determine how to charge for their services. Consider, for example, a designer who routinely relies on an hourly rate for compensation. In this method, the time required to carry out project management tasks, such as preparing contract documents, determines how design fees accrue. However, not all projects require the same amount of work from a designer; for example, he or she may have to perform very little formal project management in some projects. When designers ascertain that a project will require less time to manage it phases through completion, they can then better assess which method of charging for their services, as described in chapter 9, might be more profitable. Lack of knowledge about project management tasks may mean that a designer is working for extended periods of time without being compensated because he or she could not foresee necessary expenditures. In such cases, the project will not likely be financially profitable for the designer. However, in addition to these financial concerns, designers develop ideas and concepts that inform and guide the vision of the project shared by both designers and clients who are working together. How might project management techniques influence the development of these intangible, ephemeral, yet significant aspects of a project?

DESIGN INTENT AND THE PROJECT MANAGEMENT PROCESS

Interior design projects typically can be divided into five phases. During the course of a project, designers initially conceive and, considering client input as well as time and budget constraints, continually refine the design they have selected to meet the goals of the project. **Design intent** is a concept best defined as making up the set of decisions made by designers to address the aesthetic and functional issues that are critical in the project. These issues are identified as a result of the factual information gathered by a designer as well as a client's input. Obtaining this necessary information is one of the goals of the first phase of project management.

THE FIVE PHASES OF PROJECT MANAGEMENT

Interior design projects begin with what is usually referred to as the **project programming phase**. At this stage, designers gather information about their clients' goals for the project and the reasons for selecting those goals. After discussing the project and the terms of their working relationship, designers and clients formally agree to work with one another by entering into a contract for the designers' services.

The **schematic design phase** sets in once designers and clients formally agree to work together. It is at this stage that a designer uses the information gathered during the first phase to develop the initial design intent, or concept, on which the entire project will be based. As you will see, there are many tasks involved in developing a responsive, factually-based concept for an interior design project.

Finalization of a project's design intent occurs during the subsequent **design development phase**. At this stage, the options presented for consideration during the schematic design phase take shape as specific features of the design to be completed. Also during this phase, designers prepare written specifications for merchandise to be purchased, reflecting final product choices made by designers and clients. Designers also inform clients of the costs likely to be incurred in ordering specified products and services, and decisions may be adjusted as a result. The final expression of a project's design intent is thus subject to financial constraints.

The **contract document phase** is, as the name suggests, the stage where appropriate documents are drawn up to communicate the design intent to those providing the labor needed to complete the project. It is also the stage in the project where purchase orders for the merchandise specified during the prior phase are submitted to vendors, along with any additional specifications and instructions. The project's design intent at this stage is considered to be fully determined, since any subsequent changes are likely to affect the schedule and cost of the project.

It is during the **contract administration phase** that the design intent of the project is realized. At the conclusion of this phase, a designer's efforts to program the project to meet the needs of a client become apparent. All products and services, as specified and ordered by a designer and approved by a client on the basis of estimated cost and schedule, have been brought together for the benefit of the installation and realization of the project. However, this phase does not typically end with project installation, but continues until all invoices and bills have been certified and paid and project evaluations have been conducted. The process of project management, especially the role of budget preparation and scheduling, can thus influence the final expression of a designer's intent, as well as any number of design decisions made during each of the project phases. A knowledge of the phases of project management, including the appropriate junctures for decision making, will benefit a designer's ability to bring the project to fruition as well as to recognize when to assess or recommend options, or propose alternatives, that satisfy the project's design intent.

THE ROLE OF THE PROJECT MANAGER

Project management thus far has been presented primarily as a function of a designer in charge of the project. It is true that designers frequently are the designated professionals, "of record" who agree to carry out the management responsibilities required to complete a project. Particularly in large projects, however, specifically designated project managers may be responsible for carrying out project management tasks. These professionals frequently—although not always—have expertise in construction practices and in working with other professionals, such as technical consultants, who provide highly specialized services.

Although designers who accept project management responsibilities and designated project managers ultimately have many of the same goals in mind, notably completion of the project in a timely and budget-conscious way, project managers perform specific tasks that may be distinct from those assumed by a designer managing a project. These specific tasks include the following activities:

- Working with the in-house design team responsible for the project to ensure timely and correct submission of project documents, such as specifications and construction documents
- Identifying other professionals, such as contractors and consultants, and assist in soliciting and evaluating the proposals, bids, and other documents they submit for consideration
- Acting as liaison with the client by obtaining information relevant to the project. In many instances, the project manager acts as the linchpin between a client and design team, contractors, consultants, and others retained for the project.
- Where indicated by applicable state and local laws and by the terms of the agreement between the client and project manager, evaluating the quality of the specified products and supervising the completion of required work
- Maintaining project budget and schedule documents and providing status reports as needed or as called for in any service contract
- Performing administrative duties, such as maintenance of project files and documents

A thoroughly detailed list of activities performed by project managers is not within the scope of this study. From this overview, however, you can take note of what project managers typically are *not* called upon to do: provide design services such as space planning, product research, or writing of specifications. Whether the designer or a specially designated project manager is responsible for completing the actual project, both must be attuned to the tasks and documents that are characteristic of each phase of the project management process.

THE ROLE OF PROJECT DOCUMENTS

This chapter also presents documents that designers may use throughout the course of managing an interior design project. These documents, such as notes taken to help with decision making, are kept for a designer's own use in facilitating project tasks. Other documents, such as detailed construction drawings, concept boards, or other forms necessary to communicate a project's design intent to a client and others are usually referred to as **deliverables,** since they are intended to be shared with users other than a designer or design firm.

OBJECTIVES TO CONSIDER

With this basic overview of the project management process in mind and an understanding of some of its more relevant terms and concepts, this chapter will consider the specific objectives of each phase of this process in greater detail. In so doing, the discussion will focus on the following:

1. Tasks that designers must accomplish in each phase of the project
2. Documents that designers employ to manage each stage of the project, enabling them to record and interpret data and information as well as the project's progress

PROGRAMMING PHASE

The *programming phase* may be defined as the stage at which a designer obtains and interprets information in order to develop a project's design intent. How can designers accomplish this critical task and prepare for the phases of the project that follow?

ASSOCIATED TASKS

Interior designers have a great deal of information to accumulate, record, and interpret during the course of a project. This is particularly true at the very beginning of a designer's association with a potential client. During the programming phase, a designer engages in some of the following typical tasks:

1. Conducting interviews with residential clients in order to ascertain the project's functional and aesthetic needs. With regard to nonresidential clients, the designer may prepare and evaluate written survey forms completed by project stakeholders, such as office workers, in order to gain insight into the project's organizational demands.
2. Obtaining existing floor plans, construction drawings, or related media that can help a designer in preparing space plans during subsequent phases of the project.
3. Identifying any existing items that may be used with appropriate modification in the design space or to obtain information needed to

specify new items. In residential projects, for example, it is common for clients to request that designers use some of the existing furnishings or objects owned by the client. On the other hand, items used in commercial spaces may not be suitable for use in the new project, although they can inform designers about their efficiency and appearance.

4. Conducting visits to the site of the proposed project, measuring the space, and assessing its present condition and location for later project-planning purposes.

5. Preparing budget and schedule estimates based on the goals of the project and the level of design and construction skills it will require to be realized. For example, completing an elaborately detailed suburban living room or a historical restoration can and probably will require substantially greater amounts of project resources than most public spaces intended for commercial use. During the programming phase, the designer takes note of these issues and shares them with the client.

6. Conducting research in order to ascertain how—and whether— designers will assume responsibility for the project. An important activity for designers at this stage is to ask themselves what knowledge they will need to obtain in order to complete the project. Certainly designers gain expertise over time in handling specific kinds of projects. However, each project is different and has different restrictions placed on its completion by a host of applicable laws, as well as building and safety codes. The needs and requests of clients also differ from project to project.

During the course of early project programming, designers also indicate whether services provided by other professionals, such as artisans, craftspeople, and expert consultants, will be necessary to carry out aspects of the project that a designer is not able to perform. In summary, the programming phase includes the following tasks:

- Reviewing initial project requirements
- Documenting project requirements
- Preparing project budget/schedule
- Determining physical/budgetary feasibility
- Providing written program of requirements

ASSOCIATED DOCUMENTS

In earlier chapters, you were introduced to some of the activities designers perform during this phase of project management. You were also acquainted with a number of forms that might be used to facilitate those tasks and also enable you to gauge the progression of a project from its inception to conclusion. Given this basic knowledge, you can now consider in greater detail the documents that are typically generated during this first project phase. Documents associated with the programming phase include the following:

- Any of the note-taking and information-gathering forms to which you were introduced in the first Residential Interior Design Project Simulation (see chapter 1).
- Proposed letters of agreement developed by the designers that will be used in contracting their services on the project. Chapter 11 fully sets out the provisions of these documents as well as the rationales for their inclusion.
- The transmittal form (Form 10.2), which may be used throughout the entire project-management process and is included for your reference and as a possible model for your own form. This project document may be used in a variety of different ways, such as a cover letter for faxed documents as well as mail and hand delivery of other documents.

As you are aware, a major purpose of the programming phase is to accumulate and retain project information in assessible ways. Many designers now enter such information into their computers as text narrative or on electronic spreadsheets for later retrieval and possible transmission to others involved in the project.

Unless designers and clients have agreed that designers will conduct programming activities as part of a design study separate from their contract for services, the programming phase in residential projects usually begins when the two enter into an agreement for a designer's services. In nonresidential projects, especially when a designer has submitted a proposal in response to a published RFP, the programming phase may begin after a designer or design firm has been retained by a client. This first phase of project management is distinguished by its focus on information gathering. The use of that information by designers is the subject of the subsequent phase.

TRANSMITTAL COVER LETTER

COMPANY NAME
Address
City
Phone No.
Fax No.

Date _____

Number of Pages _____

To _____   From _____
   _____   _____
   _____   _____
   _____   _____
   _____   _____

Job No./Reference No. _____   Client _____

Project Location _____

Please Do the Following:
_____

Add to project file _____   Keep for your information (as requested) _____

Review and return _____ Comment _____

Distribute to the following _____   Other action required _____

_____

The following is enclosed or transmitted:

Transmitted via:
_____

Fax (total pages including this one)   Courier _____   UPS _____
USPS _____   Delivery confirm _____   By hand _____   Interoffice _____
        Forwarding co. _____   Other _____

Notes/Comments/Instructions
_____
_____
_____
_____
_____
_____

SCHEMATIC DESIGN PHASE

Once the relationship between a designer and a prospect has been formalized by means of a contractual agreement, so that a prospect has now become a full-fledged client, the interior design project enters into what is referred to as the *schematic design phase*. At this stage, designers use the information they have obtained in order to develop the first comprehensive design concept for the project.

ASSOCIATED TASKS

As this phase begins, a clear division in project-related tasks become apparent. In addition to those tasks necessary to actually complete the project, there are tasks required to support project completion. For example, this phase is usually considered the stage in the project when designers start to prepare preliminary diagrams and drawings indicating their design concept. Designers also make initial selections of furniture and other merchandise that will be submitted to clients for approval. As part of this process, designers prepare the first series of time and cost estimates for the fabrication or procurement of these items. That task is an example of an activity necessary to support the project's completion. The tasks associated with the schematic design phase may be summarized as follows:

- Preparing preliminary functional diagrams
- Reviewing alternative approaches to the project
- Preparing space allocations/utilizations
- Preparing design-concept studies
- Submitting preliminary cost estimates

ASSOCIATED DOCUMENTS

During this phase, designers are responsible for preparing initial design sketches and floor plans, as well as sample boards showing selections for products, colors, textures, and finishes.

In addition, designers prepare initial estimates of the materials, labor, and the associated costs necessary in order to complete as accurately as possible a budget for the project in its next phase. Designers may prepare **estimates**, or initial determinations of project-related costs, for a wide variety of products and services they intend to incorporate in the project. As a practical matter, a designer should make clear to a client—by means of informal communication as well as the specific terms of the written agreement for a designer's services—that estimates of project costs are approximations made by a designer using the best, most recent information available. Final costs of these items and services may vary as a result of many factors outside a designer's control. See Form 10.3 a cost-estimating worksheet. The schematic design phase is perhaps best characterized as the stage when the designer makes initial design decisions and takes action to support those decisions. The next phase involves further refinements of those tasks.

DESIGN DEVELOPMENT PHASE

This is, in essence, the stage in which the project is refined and finalized. The *design development phase* of a project begins once the plans and estimates generated in the previous phases have been approved by a client. The main goal of the previous stage is to establish the concept or design intent of the project; the purpose at this stage is to fine-tune those details and establish the final set of project characteristics.

ASSOCIATED TASKS

During this stage, a designer presents the updated cost estimates for items and services needed to complete the project as programmed and planned. From a practical standpoint, this is the time when a designer should also review with clients the project costs related to delivery and installation. At this stage the costs of the project become more apparent to the client. In addition, estimated arrival and completion dates for desired goods and services may not coincide with either the project budget or schedule. The challenge for the designer here, in order to receive the approvals necessary to move the project into its next phase, may involve further research to find products and service providers more appropriate for the actual project budget and schedule.

Whether the project is residential or commercial, the designer must attend to many external details, such as the constraints related to project compliance with public health, safety, and building codes. Only after such

WORKSHEET FOR ESTIMATING LABOR AND MATERIALS

Description

Materials Included	Est. Labor	Est. Cost	Act. Labor	Act. Costs	Budgeted	Var.
	Unit price X quantity and other	Labor rate X time and other	See final invoice	See final invoice	Per master budget	Positive/ negative
1.						
2.						
3.						
4.						

Description

Materials Included	Est. Labor	Est. Cost	Act. Labor	Act. Costs	Budgeted	Var.
	Unit price X quantity and other	Labor rate X time and other	See final invoice	See final invoice	Per master budget	Positive/ negative
1.						
2.						
3.						
4.						

Description

Materials Included	Est. Labor	Est. Cost	Act. Labor	Act. Costs	Budgeted	Var.
	Unit price X quantity and other	Labor rate X time and other	See final invoice	See final invoice	Per master budget	Positive/ negative
1.						
2.						
3.						
4.						

details are considered do designers make final presentations to clients of their refined selections and plans as well as revised budgets and schedules. Although adjustments are made throughout the duration of the project as designers and clients gain more information, it is at the conclusion of the design development phase that the major creative, functional, and technical aspects of the project become set.

The tasks associated with this phase include the following:

- Preparing documents to fix/describe the final project
- Completing documents to reflect final project appearance/function
- Recommending colors/materials/finishes as necessary
- Preparing presentation boards and related materials
- Advising on cost-of-work adjustments

ASSOCIATED DOCUMENTS

During this phase, designers are required to complete drawings and schematics indicating space allocations and placement of furniture and equipment. They should also present their accumulated swatches of textiles and other project merchandise.

During this phase of a project, interior designers typically produce three kinds of documents, construction drawings, schedules, and specifications. Construction drawings are, as you are undoubtedly aware, items such as floor plans and elevations that depict the location of geographical landmarks defining the subject space. Schedules, with which you may also be familiar, are graphics that convey information about project characteristics not readily apparent from construction documents, such as architectural finishes to be applied or location of light fixtures. In addition, designers note in specifications the exact characteristics of labor and merchandise destined for application in the project. Consider this latter aspect and how writing of project specifications fits within the larger context of managing an interior design project.

Labor and merchandise for a project may be obtained through any of two basic means. These include contracts entered into with specific service providers or vendors by the designer or client at the suggestion of a designer. Alternatively, the scope of the project (or, as with publicly funded projects sponsored by government or military entities requiring it) may call for use of a process known as competitive bidding. Under this approach, different service providers and vendors submit binding offers (known as "bids") to provide requested goods and services. The project's client then selects from among those bids to choose those resources to be used. Regardless of which approach is used, designers are responsible for describing in writing the merchandise and services planned for use. Usually, designers perform this task during the design development stage. From your other interior design study and related experiences, you may already know these written instructions (Piotrowski 2002) are referred to as specifications, or less formally as "specs." According to one source specifications are: "written to describe the details of the materials to be used, delivery and storage of those materials, installation methods, and acceptable workmanship for installation. Specifications work in concert with the graphic information presented on the drawings" (Ankerson 2004). Because of their prevalence and, hence, importance to interior designers, the different types of specifications and the manner in which they may be organized should be noted as well as their relationship to other contract documents.

Specifications may be classified as follows: descriptive, performance, proprietary, and reference. Considering the most basic characteristics of each should make clear how and why these different approaches are used. A descriptive specification is one in which designers provide detailed written notations about the tangible, physical characteristics of items or features sought. These specifications are made without a designer's reference to any one particular manufacturer or source, only to required features. A written instruction for a "black plastic laminate counter top 3' wide by 8' long with a 1" bull nose edge" in which a particular brand or manufacturer name was not further specified, would be a simple example of this kind of specification. This form of specification allows a vendor or service provider, not a designer, to choose the source for the item or service. The performance specification is similar to descriptive specifications in that both make no mention of any one particular source for an item or service. Whereas the descriptive specification relates physical attributes of items and services sought, the performance specification notes what the selected item or feature must do, that is, what function it must carry out. If, in the example above, a designer further noted the countertop must be able to withstand the application of heat up to a certain degree, again without specifying a source or brand name, then it would be a performance specification. To gauge the appropriateness of the selected item or feature, the required performance criteria should be ones capable of measurement and evaluation. In this example, that might include noting the specific degree of heat tolerance required for the project.

Often, lay people refer to items by a commonly used brand or company names. Designers carry this practice further through the use of proprietary specifications in which they particularly describe a product, by its specific name or model number. You can probably think of several examples of proprietary specifications just from recalling design products you like. Due to the exact nature of this kind of specification, by necessity the name of the maker or source as well as the exact way in which that resource refers to its products must be included in the specification. The final type, the reference specification, relies upon characteristics and standards set by such sources as the American National Standards Institute (ANSI) or the American Society for Testing and Materials (ASTM). These sources set minimum performance requirements for acceptability of a variety of products. For interior design purposes these standards include flammability of textile products or wear resistance for floor coverings.

With the knowledge of the basic types of specifications used by designers, it is next important to consider how those specifications are organized. Within the professional interior design community, the most commonly used way of organizing product specifications is with the approach developed by the Construction Specifications Institute (CSI). Discussions related to the preparation of contract documents include a more lengthy description of the CSI approach. This approach utilizes three categories, or levels, to provide first the basic requirements and information about project products in the General Requirements section. Next, in a section devoted exclusively to the desired products for use on a project, a detailed description of those to be used is noted. Finally, the manner of installation of the product is noted.

As you can see, designers consider a great many details during this phase of completing a project. What is important for you to remember, however, is that when preparing information about a project through the use of drawings, schedules, and specifications, that information should act together "as a coordinated whole" (Ankerson 2004) in which information is conveyed consistently and without contradiction or omission.

CONTRACT DOCUMENT PHASE

As the name implies, the *contract document phase* of the project is largely devoted to the preparation of working documents. The construction documents prepared at this time are "created to communicate a design project to contractors for pricing and ultimate construction," and thus "provide clear, complete, and accurate communication regarding the design intentions of a project" (Ankerson 2004). This phase may be best thought of as the stage when the design intent is carefully communicated to the service providers and vendors involved in the project. How might that task be accomplished?

The documents related to the contract document phase are more highly detailed and technical than those created during the design development phase. Drawings at this stage are usually drawn precisely to scale, with each sheet precisely and consistently organized so as to prevent any misinterpretation. These documents may illustrate the plan of ceilings and placement of mechanical systems, other equipment, and partition walls. Schedules in rendered, not written, form are other construction documents generated at this time. These typically indicate where surface finishes will be applied or the placement and direction of doors and windows. Great care must be taken in preparing these drawings, since they are used not only as models to guide the construction of the space, but also as the basis for seeking competitive bids for construction services as well as bids for fixtures, furnishings, and equipment destined for the project. These documents are thus considered as part of the contracts for services and FF&E. Interior designers working on small projects may suggest which general contractors are able to provide the construction necessary to complete the project. In more complicated projects, where a designer is retained to work as a designer/specifier, the designer prepares all final deliverables, such as construction drawings, for use by the project manager.

There is some divergence in design literature as to whether the designer places orders at the conclusion of this phase of the project (Knackstedt 2002) or during the next project phase (Piotrowski 2002). Regardless of a project's stage, virtually all writers on interior design agree that purchase orders for merchandise (see Form 10.4) should not be placed with vendors until they have been presented to and reviewed by clients and all necessary authorizations and initial payments have been obtained. In this way, designers will not incur any financial liability for purchasing items without full client authorization if some change in a client's situation should occur (Alderman 1997).

For your review, consider some of the following tasks associated with the contract documents phase:

◆ Preparing final working drawings/specs
◆ Advising on further cost adjustments

PURCHASE ORDER FORM

Order No. _____

Date _____

Sold to _____
_____
_____
_____

| COMPANY NAME |
| Address |
| City |
| Phone No. |
| Fax no. |

Ship to _____
_____
_____
_____

How to ship _____

Terms _____

Item #	Quantity	Description of Item Ordered	Unit Price	Extended

Subtotal: _____
Delivery Charges _____
Tax _____
Total _____
Deposit _____
BALANCE DUE _____

- Obtaining necessary approvals/permits
- Qualifying vendors/suppliers/contractors
- Assisting clients in assessing bids for project
- Assisting in preparing/awarding FF&E bids
- Placing orders for FF&E, given final client approval

CONTRACT ADMINISTRATION PHASE

After the designer receives formal client approval for necessary construction work and purchases, the final phase of the project begins. The contract administration phase is where it all happens; more specifically, it is the stage during which the entire project is completed and its outcome evaluated. Unlike other stages of the project, which a designer of record is primarily responsible for completing, the role of a designer during this phase may be limited by several constraints.

CONSTRAINTS ON A DESIGNER'S FUNCTIONS

The first constraint imposed on the activities of designers during this phase is contractual in nature. In some instances, designers agree to be responsible only for developing the project's design intent or concept and for preparing construction documents and their attendant specifications. Given that scenario, responsibility for completing the project rests with a project manager, an individual or business hired to implement a designer's plans.

The other constraint is imposed by laws. Usually, laws of the state in which a design project is sited control issues such as whether a designer who is not a licensed general contractor may assume responsibilities for supervision of construction and project installation. In instances where designers are not allowed to perform these functions without a license, it is usually the role of an appropriately licensed general contractor to complete contract administration activities. Even in states where a designer is legally able to perform these tasks, there may be other legally based reasons for wishing an appropriately licensed general contractor complete them. For example, designers may wish to limit any liability they might incur in supervising the work of others. Many clients seek legal recourse against designers when construction tasks are not completed correctly, when injuries occur, or when there is property damage. As a result, some designers may stipulate in their contracts that the client—not the designer—is responsible for the selection, retention, and payment of fees to any general contractor or subcontractor that the client wishes to employ. Within this framework, designers work with clients to review the progress of construction work. They also advise clients about necessary changes, adjustments, and repairs, which need to be implemented by the project's general contractor. For contractual and other legal reasons, a designer's role may therefore change during this project phase.

ASSOCIATED TASKS AND DOCUMENTS

At this stage of the project, the activities of others are required to bring about its completion. Usually in small residential projects, designers may either strongly suggest project workers, such as general contractors or subcontractors, whose previous work designers have seen and deemed satisfactory; or designers may ask clients to locate these service providers. As projects gain in complexity, however, and especially in projects where governmental agencies are the client of record, service providers are retained through what is referred to as the *competitive bidding process*. Within this context, the client solicits responses from service providers—sometimes from any who wish to respond in open selections, or from only those previously identified and qualified to respond in closed selections—by publishing an invitation to bid containing project details. This is usually followed by a series of instructions to bidders about the required form of submitted bids. Designers are usually responsible for assisting clients in this aspect of contract administration by preparing and evaluating bid documents for publication and approval. In a typical project in which a designer is responsible for preparation of bids but not actual supervision of construction, the role of a designer may be more consultative in nature as designers and clients work together to assess the progress of the project. In some cases, a designer may be tasked with only supervising the ordering and delivery of products destined for project use (see Form 10.5), whether those products are procured by a designer, provided by bidders, or purchased through resources, such as in-house governmental purchase offices directed by a client.

Once a project is at or substantially near completion, designers conduct what is referred to as a *walk-through* with a client—or representatives of a client—to note any errors in workmanship that need to be

FINAL INSTALLATION INVENTORY

Page ____ of ____

Date _____

Job Number/I.D. _____

Client _____

Designer/Firm _____

Project Address or Reference _____

Room or Space

ITEM	Vendor/Contractor	Style/I.D.#	Dimensions
	Source	Colorway	Repeats
Year/Date			
Photo #			

Room or Space

ITEM	Vendor/Contractor	Style/I.D.#	Dimensions
	Source	Colorway	Repeats
Year/Date			
Photo #			

Room or Space

ITEM	Vendor/Contractor	Style/I.D.#	Dimensions
	Source	Colorway	Repeats
Year/Date			
Photo #			

Room or Space

ITEM	Vendor/Contractor	Style/I.D.#	Dimensions
	Source	Colorway	Repeats
Year/Date			
Photo #			

Room or Space

ITEM	Vendor/Contractor	Style/I.D.#	Dimensions
	Source	Colorway	Repeats
Year/Date			
Photo #			

(continued)

Room or Space

ITEM	Vendor/Contractor	Style/I.D.#	Dimensions
	Source	Colorway	Repeats

Year/Date

Photo #

Room or Space

ITEM	Vendor/Contractor	Style/I.D.#	Dimensions
	Source	Colorway	Repeats

Year/Date

Photo #

Room or Space

ITEM	Vendor/Contractor	Style/I.D.#	Dimensions
	Source	Colorway	Repeats

Year/Date

Photo #

Room or Space

ITEM	Vendor/Contractor	Style/I.D.#	Dimensions
	Source	Colorway	Repeats

Year/Date

Photo #

Room or Space

ITEM	Vendor/Contractor	Style/I.D.#	Dimensions
	Source	Colorway	Repeats

Year/Date

Photo #

SWATCH SAMPLES/PHOTOGRAPHS

corrected. Usually stickers or pencil marks are used to mark the location of a problem, which is then indicated on a document referred to as a **punch list**. Form 10.6 is an example of a punch list.

Contract administration is the phase of a project where its many facets come together to build, install, and appoint the space in accordance with the project's design intent. To determine the effectiveness of these efforts, many designers, especially those working on commercial projects for the use of a variety of people, conduct post-installation evaluations of the completed environment. These evaluations typically assess user's perceptions of the space and seek input about any adjustments or refinements that could enhance user efficiency and enjoyment. For your reference, the contract administration phase typically includes the following activities:

◆ Assisting with final bids
◆ Job-site management if no project manager is required
◆ Placing orders for FF&E, given final client approval
◆ Maintaining project management records
◆ Visiting job site periodically to review program
◆ Supervising installation process
◆ Assisting in determining substantial completion of tasks and payments/ releases
◆ Conducting post-occupancy evaluations/adjustments

Project management is a process complicated by the interplay of many different factors. Not only must designers understand details related to identifying and specifying tangible goods for use in the project, but also understand how to provide detailed written and drawn instructions in ways understood by other professionals. In addition to the technical aspects of project management, there is also a decidedly interpersonal factor. During the course of a project, designers may be called upon to work with clients, architects, engineers, consultants, general contractors and subcontractors, among hosts of others, each with differing levels of education and expertise. Designers are assisted in their work in such complex environments by first learning project management information of the kind described here, and by then developing their own strategies based on that information for organizing the progression of events, tasks, and documents that result in successfully completed interior design projects.

PUNCH LIST

Page ____ of ____

Date _____

Job Number/I.D. _____

Client _____

Designer/Firm _____

Project Address or Reference _____

Surface Finish Conditions

Contractor	Noted on site: Y/N	Sticker Color	
Room/Space/Location **FLOOR**			
Description		Accepted	Noted
Condition As Noted			

Contractor	Noted on site: Y/N	Sticker Color	
Room/Space/Location **FLOOR**			
Description		Accepted	Noted
Condition As Noted			

Contractor	Noted on site: Y/N	Sticker Color	
Room/Space/Location **TRIM**			
Description		Accepted	Noted
Condition As Noted			

Contractor	Noted on site: Y/N	Sticker Color	
Room/Space/Location **TRIM**			
Description		Accepted	Noted
Condition As Noted			

Contractor	Noted on site: Y/N	Sticker Color	
Room/Space/Location **WALLS**			
Description		Accepted	Noted
Condition As Noted			

Contractor	Noted on site: Y/N	Sticker Color	
Room/Space/Location **WALLS**			
Description		Accepted	Noted
Condition As Noted			

Contractor	Noted on site: Y/N	Sticker Color	
Room/Space/Location **EQUIPMENT**			
Description		Accepted	Noted
Condition As Noted			

(continued)

Contractor		Noted on site: Y/N	Sticker Color	
Room/Space/Location	**EQUIPMENT**			
Description			Accepted	Noted
Condition As Noted				

Contractor		Noted on site: Y/N	Sticker Color	
Room/Space/Location	**EQUIPMENT**			
Description			Accepted	Noted
Condition As Noted				

Contractor		Noted on site: Y/N	Sticker Color	
Room/Space/Location	**EQUIPMENT**			
Description			Accepted	Noted
Condition As Noted				

Contractor		Noted on site: Y/N	Sticker Color	
Room/Space/Location	**WINDOW**			
Description			Accepted	Noted
Condition As Noted				

Contractor		Noted on site: Y/N	Sticker Color	
Room/Space/Location	**WINDOW**			
Description			Accepted	Noted
Condition As Noted				

Contractor		Noted on site: Y/N	Sticker Color	
Room/Space/Location	**DOOR**			
Description			Accepted	Noted
Condition As Noted				

Contractor		Noted on site: Y/N	Sticker Color	
Room/Space/Location	**DOOR**			
Description			Accepted	Noted
Condition As Noted				

Additional Notes or Comments:

TROUBLESHOOTING
STRATEGIES FOR PROJECT MANAGEMENT

Where a designer is engaged to simply present suggestions or to have informal discussions with a homeowner, each party may go its separate way with little consequence should either decide to have no further association with the other. This lack of formal, binding agreement between the parties has both positive and negative implications for a designer.

At this stage, residential interior designers should take particular care to ascertain whether clients have reasonable expectations about the outcome of projects and designers' ability to bring about desired results. For example, do clients understand the expensive and time-consuming nature of interior design? Often, potential clients have seen and been impressed by finished projects, but have little idea of the time and money required to produce highly customized items or dramatically finished spaces. Designers should listen for clues that indicate whether the budget for the potential project is in line with the desired results; they should also pay attention to clues about the projected completion date. Many prospective clients foresee schedules that may be patently unrealistic given their design expectations and the resulting demands placed on designers.

After learning about a client's expectations, how might a designer address the issues a client has raised? At this early stage, it is important for a designer to have some idea of a strategy for handling a potential client's concerns. In particular, a designer should pay attention to a client's expectations. Are they realistic, given a designer's abilities and the projected budget and time constraints? The answer to these questions may either bless or doom the project before it has even begun. Designers should be extremely careful in discussing projects; they should not agree to accept a project when they do not have the expertise to complete it and when the proposed budget and completion schedule are unrealistic. As you learned in chapter 3, designers should not assume responsibility for a project when they lack the experience and knowledge required to complete it. Yet, how can designers gain experience and learn new professional skills if they don't take on projects that present some new challenge or difficulty?

Some writers have suggested that designers consider the 80/20 rule when deciding whether to take on a new project (Knackstedt 2002). According to this rule, designers should accept projects in which 80 percent of the required work is readily familiar to them from past experience, and no more than 20 percent requires unfamiliar work. This approach is based on the idea that a designer's financial profitability diminishes the more the designer assumes new project tasks, such as background research required to learn about a project. In many instances, a designer may not be able to adequately bill a client for all the time required to learn about new sources or performing new tasks. Of course, a designer's final decision depends, among other issues, on a designer's comfort level with a project and its desirability. An easy project probably does not exist; and, moreover, no two projects are ever exactly alike. As a result, even well-educated designers, who have extensive prior experience working on residential projects may find themselves having to solve unforeseen problems during what may have looked like the most innocuous project.

With this knowledge in mind, designers may advise their clients regarding specific project concerns such as the following:

1. Whether a designer believes that he or she is able to accomplish the project and can perform tasks such as keeping the client routinely informed of a project's progression, given constraints placed on a designer's time and energies by every project for which a designer is responsible
2. Whether the proposed budget is adequate for the amount and kind of work the project will require
3. Whether the time schedule proposed for completion is realistic given the project goals
4. Whether the designer will have to spend a great deal of time researching particular products or services necessary to complete the project
5. Whether the method of compensation proposed is appropriate, given the tasks a designer needs to perform and the amount and kinds of merchandise a designer needs to procure to complete the project
6. Whether any project management issues—for example, potential project delays—appear relevant based on goals a client wishes to accomplish.

Possible project delays may occur when a designer specifies a particular item around which an entire design concept depends—a large custom-made rug, for instance, destined for use in either a hotel lobby or residential living room. If that item is delayed or becomes unavailable, the entire installation process planned for the space in the latter part of the contract administration stage may be delayed as the site sits empty.

The major objective of project management is to address the needs of a client. These needs may be explicitly expressed by a client—"I want a blue living room"—or inferred by a designer from facts about a project—"From what you've said about needing a large conference room, we'll have to reconfigure the room using space from the entry area." However project goals are determined, accomplishing them in an objectively reasonable manner is an important task requiring project management skills. Another important objective of project management is to enable designers to earn a sufficient, reasonable profit that justifies the use of their talents and time.

REFERENCES

Alderman, Robert L. 1997. *How to Prosper As an Interior Designer*. New York: John Wiley & Sons.

Allison, John, and Robert Prentice. 2001. *Business Law: Text and Cases in the Legal Environment*. 3rd Custom ed. New York: Thompson Learning.

Ankerson, Kathy S. 2004. *Interior Construction Documents*. New York: Fairchild Books.

Berger, C. Jaye. 1994. *Interior Design Law and Business Practices*. New York: John Wiley & Sons.

Coleman, Cindy, ed. 2002. *Interior Design: Handbook of Professional Practice*. New York: McGraw-Hill (See especially, pp. 483–91.)

Knackstedt, Mary V. 2002. *The Interior Design Business Handbook*. 3rd ed. New York: John Wiley & Sons.

Piotrowski, Christine M. 2002. *Professional Practice for Interior Designers*, 3rd edition. New York: John Wiley & Sons.

Siegel, Harry, and Alan Siegel. 1982. *A Guide to Business Practices and Principles for Interior Designers*. New rev. ed. New York: Watson-Guptill.

STRATEGIES-IN-ACTION PROJECTS

STRATEGIC PLANNING PROJECT

Business decision makers reviewing the plan for your ideal interior design venture will want to know many details about the services you propose to offer. In particular, they will want to know how interior designers work, how designers bring about the private and public spaces they and others experience. In this section of your strategic business plan, you will provide these interested executives with an overview of the step-by-step procedures a designer carries out when overseeing an interior design concept from early stages to fruition.

In real life, once you are a practicing interior designer, it is likely that you will have to explain to clients—repeatedly—the steps that make up the project management process. Writing a succinct narrative that describes project management, should enable you to better explain this complicated process to clients in the future.

RESIDENTIAL INTERIOR DESIGN PROJECT SIMULATION

As you recall from previous simulations, Lee has planned a unique tree-house concept for the children's living spaces. Carrying out this arboreal vision involves the designer's coordination of many purchases and services to bring it into full bloom. In this portion of the Residential Interior Design Project Simulation, the designer calls upon you to help them estimate the effect of several of design decisions. For this project, you will need Form 10.3, Designer's Estimating Worksheet for Labor and Materials on page 337.

Lee's Diary

Of course, Mrs. Abernathy called today! This time, she was concerned about the amounts due on one of the invoices the contractors tendered today. She wants to know "where we are, budget-wise," as she put it. She is concerned with the cost of constructing the tree house/play platform anchoring the common area of the children's space. In particular, she wants to know more about the effect on the project's budget of constructing the raised wooden platform. "It just seems like a lot for a deck, don't you think, Lee?" she asked. So, what to do?

The two items Mrs. Abernathy is so concerned about are actually quite different in more ways than just what they are, now that they are completed. First, the raised wooden platform did require a great many supplies to construct, but not much in the way of specialized labor to do so. We did not have to hire a special carpenter, but it did require more workers than initially planned in order to be done on time. On the other hand, making the tree trunk required relatively little in the way of supplies, but a great deal of labor to produce according to spec. Here's what I mean, and thanks, diary, for letting me jot this all down. It helps me to know what to do!

About the platform, the final invoice from the contractor for the lumber and labor to construct it came to $300.00 for the wood and $400.00 for the construction labor. Let's look at the initial numbers I used to estimate this to see if we are in trouble (Mrs. Abernathy's term) or not. Consider the wood; I specified standard decking wood, which is available at most lumber yards. Because of the angles of the deck and my idea of limiting the amount of board seams, while still achieving what should look like a deck in a tree house with some texture to the finished surface, I estimated $250, total cost for just the wood. I further estimated it would take a total of five hours at $13.75 an hour for one worker to construct the raw platform according to my floor plan. The contractor used five workers for the job.

Working with Lee's numbers above and Form 10.3, what are the actual costs of wood and labor in comparison to the budgeted amount?

CONTRACT INTERIOR DESIGN CASE STUDY: THE CASE OF THE DESIRABLE DORM

What factors do you think make for a successful project, especially if it is intended to have a great many different users, as with a public space? In this case study, you will identify and describe some of these factors. In the process, you will gain some idea not only of the tremendous effect designers have on shaping interior spaces, but also their influence on those who work to realize these large-scale projects as well as those who use or simply observe the completed environments. To complete this project you will need Form 10.7, the Project Stakeholder Assessment. You will also need an image of a completed interior space intended for larger scale public use (not provided in this text).

Put yourself in the figurative shoes of a person listed along the left-hand side of the form. Ask yourself, for example, what might make your designated space a successful project from the perspective of a passerby who steps in to get out of the rain? How does your space appear to have satisfied, or not satisfied, a user such as that. Referring to the project goals you have lisetd, consider the client and others, such as the general contractor and subcontractors. Try to focus on the little things, not obvious goals such as meeting the project budget, or the like. Think about what might make the project a success in the eyes of a variety of people, ranging from the client to the security guards on duty at the security desk.

As a savvy design student and soon-to-be practitioner, you would be right to wonder about these concerns, since early project programming activities may have anticipated some of these issues. Or did they? The goal of this project is to help you to recognize the importance of analyzing the needs and desires of a space's end users. Such analysis enables you to better anticipate and account for these needs when you begin new projects, for example, during the initial programming phase. After you complete Form 10.7, share your results with others and compare your findings to theirs. In this process, you engage in that same kind of dialogue that you will experience with your designer peers and with your clients.

PROJECT STAKEHOLDER ASSESSMENT

Project Stakeholder	Goals of Project
Client	
General Contractor	
Allied Professional #1	
Allied Professional #2	
Subcontractor(s)	
Vendor(s)	
Artisans/Craftspersons	
1. Direct Users	
2. Incidental Users	
3. Observers	

(continued)

Goals Achieved	
Goals Not Achieved	
Goals Achieved	
Goals Not Achieved	
Goals Achieved	
Goals Not Achieved	
Goals Achieved	
Goals Not Achieved	
Goals Achieved	
Goals Not Achieved	
Goals Achieved	
Goals Not Achieved	
Goals Achieved	
Goals Not Achieved	
Goals Achieved	
Goals Not Achieved	

CHAPTER ELEVEN

DEFINING THE
CLIENT RELATIONSHIP

God is in the details.

MIES VAN DER ROHE

WHY THIS CHAPTER IS IMPORTANT TO YOU

Contracts can seem intimidating and difficult to use. From your study of the previous chapters, however, you should already have some idea about the content of interior design contracts, including an analysis of the project's scope of services, method of charging clients for those services, and the procedures by which a designer intends to manage a project. This chapter is important because it will show you how these and other factors come together to form *contracts*, or *enforceable agreements*, that define the working relationship between designers and their clients. This chapter will explain to you when and how to present contracts for your services; what specific provisions to include in your contracts; and how contract provisions and terminology are applied within the context of an interior design practice. As you complete the chapter projects, you will further realize how the contract details examined in this chapter animate designers' relationships with their clients.

PROFESSIONAL PRACTICES PORTFOLIO

After completing this chapter, you should be able to answer the questions that follow. Include your responses in a professional practices portfolio that you keep as a handbook for your later use. You may wish to add your own notes to help you understand what certain design contract provisions mean or which provisions might require your further study.

1. How would you define a contract for interior design services?
2. What is the *Statute of Frauds*, and how is it related to interior design contracts?
3. What are two common forms of interior design contracts?
4. What is *enforceability*, and what elements must be present for that concept to be applied to a document purporting to be a contract?
5. What are three basic objectives to consider when working with contracts for interior design services?
6. When should proposed contracts be presented and negotiated with prospective clients?
7. What is *contract negotiation*, and what is involved in the process of negotiating contract terms?
8. What basic elements are necessary in all design contracts?
9. What contract terms represent the importance of defining the services you propose to offer?
10. What contract terms represent the important ways in which you propose to charge clients for your services?
11. Generally describe the following terms, and state the reasons why their inclusion in design contracts is important: *arbitration*, *disclaimer of liability*, *assignment* and *delegation*, and *integration* of contract terms.
12. In addition to seeking advice about the use of specific contract terms, what other topics would interior designers seek legal advice for to understand if they want to protect their businesses against legal claims?
13. What is the difference between *mediation* and *arbitration*?

INTRODUCTION TO DESIGN CONTRACTS

As you recall from your study of previous chapters, *contracts* are agreements that courts of law will enforce, or hold the parties to their provisions, because certain conditions have been met. A designer's promise to render specified services and a client's promise to pay for those services can form the basis of a valid or enforceable contract. **Enforceability** refers to the ability of a court of law to uphold such promises if it determines that certain elements were present.

REQUIREMENTS OF A DESIGN CONTRACT

As this chapter will demonstrate, a **valid** contract is one whose provisions can be enforced by courts of law. The following specific elements are usually necessary for courts to find the presence of a contract:

1. *An offer to do or not to do some specific activity*
   An interior designer's offer to provide services to a prospective client indicates the presence of a contract.
2. *An acceptance of that offer by another party*
   That something more for contract formation purposes is called an acceptance, which is usually thought of as a willingness on the part of the person to whom an offer was made to adhere to the terms contained in a proposal. The **acceptance** must be to the exact offer as made—or else it is usually considered a **counteroffer**—an offer made for the purposes of negotiation, not contract formation, when additional or different terms are proposed. A prospective client may accept the offer of an interior designer, for example, by agreeing to pay for the services offered by that designer.
3. *Capacity*
   Both the party making the offer and the party accepting the offer must have the legal ability (referred to as **capacity**) to enter into contracts. Capacity may indicate whether parties are of sufficient legal age to enter into contracts, sometimes referred to as reaching the **age of majority**, usually 18 or 21 years of age, or having sufficient mental capacity to understand the consequences of their actions.
4. *Mutuality*
   For a contract to be in effect, there must be **mutuality**, or *mutual assent*, sometimes also referred to as a meeting of the minds. One legal writer has described this as the presence of a valid offer and acceptance (Crawford 2001). What this requirement means is that both parties agree—and understand they agree—on the exact terms of their relationship.
5. *Consideration*
   With respect to contracts, **consideration** means that something of legally sufficient value was exchanged between the two parties.

Courts of law in contract-related disputes where this factor is an issue usually look to see if each party gave up something sufficiently valuable. Consideration is usually found when there exists a promise for a promise. That could mean a promise made by a designer to perform certain services for some amount of money to which the designer's client has agreed by promising to pay for those services.

6. *Legality*

The **legality** of a contract refers to its having a valid, legal purpose. This requirement may seem to have little implication for interior design, since design is not an activity usually considered criminal or contrary to public policy interests. However, with the increasing number of laws controlling who may engage in interior design work, especially practice laws now present in several states, practitioners without the appropriate state credentials to engage in interior design work risk having contracts for their services found void by the courts. There are other important implications of the legality requirement to note. Interior designers are not allowed to legally engage in activities that should be legally performed by architects or engineers. Nor should they prepare and carry out plans for designs that violate health, safety, or building codes.

MUST CONTRACTS BE IN WRITING?

The early common-law Statute of Frauds, which was discussed in chapter 4, addresses this concern. According to that doctrine, an agreement containing terms clear enough for courts to ascertain that performance of that agreement's subject matter was intended to be completed within a year from the making of the agreement do not have to be written down to be enforced. In other words, oral contracts may be found valid by the courts. It is questionable business practice, however, to rely on oral agreements for services as complicated as interior design.

In addition, under the terms of the Uniform Commercial Code, which has incorporated principles from the Statute of Frauds, contracts involving the sale of goods valued at $500 or more are required to be in writing for those contracts to be enforceable. The import of this provision is simply that by having a written agreement when a designer sells an amount of goods worth at least $500, a designer may successfully seek payment for the merchandise. If, in the course of completing a project, a designer is also responsible for selling merchandise to a client, it is highly likely the price of the goods sold will be substantially greater than the threshold amount. From both a practical and legal perspective, it is a better professional practice for designers to always have in place written contracts for their services.

FORMS OF DESIGN CONTRACTS

What common forms do contracts for interior design services take? There are basically three forms of design contracts: the letter of agreement; the standard form agreement; and the custom contract.

Letter Agreements

Perhaps the most informal type of contract is the **letter agreement** since it often takes the form of a letter, with a body of correspondence following an opening salutation (see Form 11.1 for a generic example of a letter agreement. The terms in this letter are discussed in subsequent sections).

Standard-Form Agreement

These agreements often take the shape of a blank form on which a designer fills in requested information. **Standard form agreements** are often formulated by professional organizations for use by their members. They are proprietary to those organizations and require payment of a fee each time they are used. Such agreements may be organized differently from the examples represented in this chapter; however, they contain many of the provisions described here. This kind of agreement typically favors designers by indicating specific ways for clients to pay designers for their services as well as providing for **remedies**, or monetary penalties owed to designers by clients who do not perform their responsibilities according to the terms of the contract. Sample interior design contracts can be found at the ASID website (www.asid.org). This organization makes a variety of forms available for practitiones for a fee. Consultation with a legal expert about the use of any contract is always advised.

Custom Contract

In very large projects, especially commercial ones, clients and designers may request attorneys to prepare **custom contracts** especially for use in

FORM 11.1. LETTER AGREEMENT FOR INTERIOR DESIGN SERVICES

(Date)

(Name of Interior Design Business)

(Address)

(Contact Information)

Dear (Prospective Client):

Thank you for selecting (name of interior design firm) for your interior design project. The purpose of this letter is to describe the terms and conditions under which we will render interior design services. Before signing, please read this letter fully and carefully. You are welcomed and encouraged to consult with an attorney of your choosing should you feel further clarification is necessary. If the terms of this letter are satisfactory to you, please indicate your choices as appropriate throughout this agreement, then sign on the line above your printed name under the word "Agreed" found at the conclusion of both copies, and return one copy for our records. Once signed, this letter will become a binding contract for services between you and this firm.

Cordially,

(name of individual representing the firm)
(name of interior design firm)

Agreed: _____
(Prospective Client's Printed Name) _____
Date: _____

a particular project. In the event that a designer's own legal advisers do not prepare the contract that is ultimately used by both parties, it is extremely important for a designer's own attorney to review the terms of a contract. Many times attorneys include provisions or language that may favor their client's interests over those of others, such as a designer.

A PERFECT CONTRACT?

Given the emphasis on a contract's terms or provisions as well as the different forms they might assume, is there such a thing as a perfect contract? In other words, is there a way to draft a contract that is best for protecting the interests of interior designers when working with clients? Many legal writers consider that there probably is not (Alderman 1997). Those same sources, however, do suggest that any proposed set of agreements be reviewed by an attorney before the parties formally agree to enter into them.

OBJECTIVES TO CONSIDER

Like most students of interior design about to enter working life, you are probably interested in knowing the simplest methods for handling contracts, which you could then use as soon as possible. What is the role of a contract in the project management process, how do designers discuss contracts with prospective clients, and, for that matter, what specific provisions should be included in interior design contracts? Keeping in mind the goal of making this complicated area of professional practice easier to understand, this chapter identifies three objectives for you to master when working with design contracts.

KNOWING WHEN TO PRESENT CONTRACT PROPOSALS TO PROSPECTIVE CLIENTS

Designers need to be aware of the practices involved in initiating the contract process while meeting and working with prospective clients. As you might suspect, the procedures used in residential interior design differ from these in commercial projects. Within the context of residential interior design, designers and prospective clients may meet and become acquainted in any number of ways—for example, through introduction by a mutually acquainted referral or through a prospect's knowledge of a designer's work.

During this early stage of a prospective project, a residential designer will engage in activities such as interpreting the needs and wishes of a client and suggesting how these interpretations could be applied to a project site. At this introductory stage, designers do not generally receive compensation unless they enter into a **design study fee agreement**; however, these early services teach designers a great deal about both the client and the project that might lie ahead. For example, at this stage a designer learns about the project budget and proposed time frame for completion, and whether a designer will have to generate working drawings because of the absence of blueprints. Designers may request financial information from the prospect and ask for permission to initiate a credit check. Many financial institutions can assist businesses with the task of obtaining credit information about prospective clients, provided the inquiry is appropriately authorized according to the institution's established procedures. It is important for designers or their firms' accountants to learn from these sources what is required to perform credit checks. It should be noted that some prospects object to making known the state of their finances. If so, designers need to decide how comfortable they would be working on what might be a very expensive project without knowing if prospective clients can afford their services.

During this time, designers indicate the terms by which they structure their working relationships with clients. This can be done informally, through oral communication with the prospect; or a designer can provide a blank contract form for the prospects to review with their legal advisers. The process and ramifications of negotiating the provisions to be included in a design contract are discussed next.

KNOWING HOW TO PRESENT YOUR PROPOSED CONTRACT TO PROSPECTIVE CLIENTS

Once designers and clients agree that they wish to work together and further negotiate the terms that will define that working relationship, then both may sign a proposed contract and so formally initiate the interior design project. However, if a designer had discussed in only general terms how to structure the working relationship, then at this time, the designer may present a proposal that states in writing the terms and conditions discussed earlier with the client. That proposed contract may take the form of a letter of agreement, a blank standard form contract, or, if necessary, a contract drafted by the designer's legal counsel. Similarly, clients might have their own attorneys prepare a proposed contract for use in the project. Although prospects and designers of residential projects may meet in any number of different ways and the contracts for design services they enter into may come about in different ways, once they sign a proposal and create a valid, enforceable contract, they both share the obligations described in that contract. Typically, the schematic design phase of a project, in which initial design choices are made, begins once designers and clients formalize their working relationship by entering into a contract.

Nonresidential, or contract, interior designers obtain clients in different ways than do residential practitioners. In a typical instance, a designer or firm working on a nonresidential project will respond to a formal written request for proposal (RFP) by an entity seeking design services. These requests are likely to be formally published in journals of record or through specific institutional sources. RFPs may be found by perusing journals devoted to commercial architecture or construction as well as U.S. government agency websites. Responding to these requests can involve lengthy preparation and research to decipher the needs of these institutional prospects. Again, the designer or firm is not likely to receive compensation for this preparatory activity.

After the institutional client receives proposals submitted within an establish time frame, that client reviews the submissions, interviews successively narrower sets of respondents, and then offers the project to the candidate determined to the most appropriate and capable of completing the project within its guidelines. At this stage of the process, a designer and a institutional client enter into a contract for a designer's services. Once they have a contract, designers may then engage in more formal programming activities, such as conducting interviews with the intended users of the space and obtaining working documents such as blueprints and other schematics; this information is not typically available while the initial design proposal is being prepared.

KNOWING HOW TO NEGOTIATE CONTRACTS

Presenting your proposed contract to prospective clients through effective negotiation techniques can be an obstacle for designers, especially young design professionals eager to obtain new projects. Negotiation, when referring to contracts, means the parties involved engage in a continuing discussion of possible terms and conditions intended to define as fully as possible how those parties will or will not be obligated toward the other. How might you—as one of those eager, young professionals—approach the intimidating task of contract negotiation? Consider why this task can be so challenging. On the one hand, you want and need to obtain new clients and, further, want the project experience to be beneficial for both you and the client. On the other hand, it is sometimes very difficult to know beforehand whether a decision you make when you accede to the wishes of a prospective client is a sound one. The challenge for young designers when negotiating is, simply put, based on your concern about later regretting having acceded to a client's wishes. Some requests by clients should trigger an immediate decision to *not* proceed with a particular client. For example, as a condition of letting a designer work on their project, prospective clients may demand that the designer accept a flat fee unreasonably small considering the scope of the project proposed; or a client might require a designer to agree to time-saving ideas such as leaving to the client contract administration–related tasks such as project installation. These are somewhat unreasonable demands, to be sure. Rather, other more subtle requests may require a designer's use of negotiation techniques.

How do you think experienced designers might handle contract negotiation? For many veteran interior designers, the process is straightforward: They do not negotiate. Many, in fact, present a proposed contract to prospective clients with a take it or leave it attitude and, furthermore, are not willing to vary from the terms found in their contract forms except to insert specific names and dates. Some designers, especially those with predominately residential practices, can be quite blunt about how they will not agree to clients purchasing merchandise destined for the project on their own along with any number of activities that, depending on the fee structure, can limit the amount of commission the designer might earn. This approach may work for some designers, but it does have consequences. The first result, of course, is that designers may repel clients who are intimidated by them. Also, clients who do agree to work with designers using this tactic may feel like engaging in litigation against a designer should problems develop during the course of a project. Not all designers, of course, take this approach. Instead, practitioners take a more consultative approach with prospective clients, reviewing the details of proposed interior design contracts with clients so that both parties understand the meaning of the provisions of those proposals. Designers using this approach then usually ask the prospect if they are comfortable proceeding under the terms of the proposal. While this may seem like a more reasonable approach since clients cannot claim they were not informed about the demands of the project, it is not without consequences as well. Notably, prospects may become frightened by the cost and amount of time necessary to complete the project. As a result, they may not choose to work with a designer who uses this approach. Deciding on the best tactic to use in presenting a proposed contract to a client requires you to assess what you know to be the requirements of a project in light of the need to obtain not merely clients, but clients who remain satisfied with the project you complete for them.

Should you think prospective clients and their project are worth your time and energy to pursue, what steps might you take to prepare for negotiating a contract for your services? Gathering and understanding information is one important first step. Read the entirety of the proposed contract. Understand its terms yourself, so you will know the implications of what they mean and, perhaps more important, what their omission might mean for you. To help you in this task, a section of this chapter is devoted to annotating, or explaining thoroughly, the meanings of specific provisions commonly found in design contracts. Furthermore, gain as much information as possible about project costs and schedules. You cannot be browbeaten into accepting lower fees or commission rates by a prospective client if you know what will actually be required to realize your scope-of-services analysis for the project. Make clear, of course, that any costs or time frames you propose during the negotiation process are estimates and subject to change, even if those estimates are based on the most recent information you can gather. Of course, providing detailed information of this kind can result in the prospective client walking away from negotiations. Nevertheless, it is undoubtedly the better practice for a designer to make clients aware of what is involved in interior design work than to hide or simply ignore such issues.

Your prospective clients will likely share their concerns with you regarding the project. Anticipating these concerns and learning how to address them are important skills inherent in the negotiation process. Again, having information available is a key to handling most concerns. Prospective clients are simply not usually aware of what it is that designers do. This text includes projects that help you to clearly explain the many tasks that designers perform. While many prospects may think, for example, that a designer who seeks compensation under the *retail* approach, with no additional design fee charges, is earning considerable revenue from the project, these prospects may not know how revenue earned is easily consumed by the enormous expenses incurred by the designer. Other concerns that you can expect prospects to voice relate to merchandise costs. Interior design can be an extremely costly undertaking. That fact should be made clear to clients, along with the value they receive from having products made to order or selected to conform to project needs and the client's particular desires.

Scheduling and time constraints are concerns of residential prospects, but can be especially important issues on commercial projects. Information about the length of time required to complete highly similar projects can be inserted in responses to RFPs, and can be cited during the negotiation processes attendant to a designer or firm obtaining the contract project.

SELECTING THE SPECIFIC PROVISIONS TO INCLUDE IN INTERIOR DESIGN CONTRACTS

For a variety of reasons, it is important for you to recognize and understand the provisions commonly found in interior design contracts. For example, several provisions are necessary to create an enforceable contract, whereas the inclusion of other terms protects designers in specific ways. Your challenge may lie in remembering what the different provisions seek to accomplish and why they should be included in a contract. In order to help you to recall these terms and their functions in contracts, they are grouped and annotated in the following way.

1. *The names of the parties to the agreement*

    It is important for both a designer and client to be specifically and recognizably identified by name and by including information such as the address where they may usually be found. Most agreements provide spaces in which to insert this kind of information about all parties to the agreement:

    The parties to this agreement are (*insert name of designer*), "Designer," and (*insert name(s) of client*), "Client."

2. *The specific services the designer will perform*

You will recall that a complete and detailed analysis of the scope of services must be completed by a designer and agreed to by a client. It is helpful to organize this section in terms of project phases. The sample contract excerpted here is by no means inclusive of all this section might contain. Rather, it is included to show you how this provision may be organized and the type of language commonly used in a contract to express the scope-of-service intent.

Scope of Services

Designer agrees to perform the following work:

_____

_____.

Project Phases in Scope of Services: Designer agrees to perform the following services in order to plan, manage, and complete the project described above:

Program Stage (information and planning stage): Designer agrees to meet with Client to determine project objectives, observe and record existing characteristics of subject area(s), measure dimensions of subject area(s), and prepare drawings or renderings depicting proposed design plan for subject area(s). Recommend merchandise purchases and identify construction work necessary to carry out proposed design plan. Other services Designer agrees to perform for this project include:

_____

_____.

Unless specifically requested, Designer will not prepare a proposed project budget. If Client requests a proposed budget, Client agrees that any such budget prepared by Designer is for estimation purposes only and is in no way a guarantee of availability of goods and services so noted, nor is a guarantee of final price of those goods and services and, furthermore, is no warranty of fitness of those goods and services for any particular use or purpose or guarantee of quality.

Schematic Design Phase: After acceptance of proposed design concept, Designer agrees to prepare working drawings for use by others describing the following areas of subject property: _____.

Upon Client's approval of these drawings, Designer agrees to submit drawings for competitive bids to contractors of Client's choosing made after consultation with Designer. Designer agrees to prepare orders for project merchandise and construction tasks. Designer agrees to submit those orders to Client for Client approval prior to making any such purchase or engaging any such construction professional. In addition, Designer agrees to perform the following tasks at this stage:

_____

_____.

Project Management: Designer agrees to make on-site inspections of project progression on the following basis: _____. Designer agrees to be available to consult with Client about project progression, status of orders and contractors, and conformity of purchased goods to specifications made. Designer agrees to be available to consult with Client about the conformity and suitability of project construction to plans and whether such construction is of suitable quality. Designer agrees to the following as well: _____

_____.

Designer agrees to make project presentation within _____ days after this agreement becomes effective, or alternatively within _____ days after Client provides the following: _____

_____. After final approval of design concept, Designer agrees to do the following (please indicate):

___ Begin project and undertake all reasonable efforts to continue project OR

___ Undertake these steps:

_____.

Projected date of completion of project and availability for occupation is scheduled for:

_____.

Contract Administration: Designer agrees to make any reasonable effort to carry out the completion of this project within the time set for its completion . . ."

3. *How the designer will be paid for services*

This can be quite a lengthy provision in a design contract. As you recall from chapter 9, not only is it important for designers to select a method of charging clients for their services, but also take care to see that payment from clients is received in a timely manner. The purpose of the billing and collection process, also described in chapter 9, is to ensure that the designer is paid or that the designer is compensated for delays in payment by receiving additional fees known as *interest*. Considering these factors, this provision should contain:

◆ *The amount of retainer paid for the services of the designer*

Client agrees that Designer's project retainer for services to be rendered will be in the following amount: _____.

◆ *A description of way(s) in which the designer will be compensated*
Refer to earlier discussions of charging methods (see chapter 9). Those methods may be based on several different ways of computation, and their provisions would appear here. Frequently used methods of charging client include the following:

Rate-based methods such as fixed-fee and hourly methods
Sale of merchandise–based methods, including the retail, percentage of merchandise and product services, cost plus percentage markup, and discounting of percentage off retail
Combination methods involving cost plus percentage markup with fixed fee and cost plus percentage markup with hourly fee
Other methods of compensation, including the square foot, value-oriented, and consultation methods

A sample of this contract provision might read:

Client agrees that Designer's compensation for project services rendered will be calculated according to the following method: The difference between any discount Designer may receive for merchandise purchases and the full retail/list amount, plus ___ % of any project construction costs.

◆ *Timeliness of payment*
This section should also contain a statement to the effect that the designer expects payment for services or purchases within a specified period of time after being billed. Typically, interior designers require payment upon receipt, or specify a set number of days within which they expect to receive payment.
◆ *When and according to what percentage interest payments on outstanding amounts owed are due and are to be computed*
Usually most design contracts consider interest charges to accrue after a certain number of days from the date of the invoice and

specify a percentage rate such as 1.5 percent of the outstanding amounts due, although that rate may vary according to the cash-flow needs of a designer's practice as well as general business practices in a designer's community. It is important to note that without including such provisions, designers can be prohibited from charging interest.

4. *Date contract was signed by designer and client*
Stating the intended duration of a project is also useful, as noted in the previous excerpt from a sample contract.

Projected date of completion of project and availability for occupation is scheduled for: _____.

5. *Signatures of parties to contract*
It is especially important that any contract for interior design services contain the signature of the party to be charged, a term taken from the Statute of Frauds. Since it is usually a designer who offers his or her services, and a client who then accepts and agrees to pay for those services, it is the client who is usually considered the party to be charged under the terms of contracts for interior design services.

THE SUBJECT MATTER OF A CONTRACT

Once you are familiar with these basic contract terms, it is important to consider the following provisions, which reflect the real-world environment of interior design. Their inclusion is not usually a legal necessity. Once the basic terms legally required of contracts are in place, designers may choose whether to incorporate additional terms. On the one hand, many designers do not want to present clients with contracts of intimidating length. On the other hand, contract terms that thoroughly reflecting an assessment of issues arising during the course of a design project are the most effective protections available to designers in defining their working relationships with clients. The following inventory of contract terms are useful in effectively managing your client's interior design project. The topics of these provisions are also the themes of chapters in part 3 of this text.

DEFINING YOUR SERVICES

A description of an interior designer's scope of services is a specific requirement of a valid and enforceable contract. As you also know from your interior design studies, a description of the space or area subject to a designer's services is necessary in order for designers to formulate an appropriate program for use of the space. Contracts for design services almost always contain such a description, although parties may enter into an agreement for design services before deciding on the subject area. This may seem like an obvious provision, which requires little more than a scant reference to a location in a residence or commercial building. However, failure to include a detailed site identification can lead to misunderstandings between designers and clients about the full scope of a designer's activities. This provision may read as follows:

Identify the exact area that will be subject to the services performed by a designer.

The design contract should describe precisely the areas that will be affected by a designer's work, as in the following excerpt from a sample contract:

Subject Area of Services
This agreement concerns only the following areas of Property described above and no other: (*Include as many areas as necessary.*)
Physical address of site subject to designer services: _____
First area:
_____ Measurements: _____
Sq. Footage: _____ Blueprint references: _____
Projected Use and Occupancy Number: _____

CHARGING YOUR CLIENTS

To be enforceable, contracts must specifically spell out the manner in which designers will be paid by clients for their services. However, designers will incur a host of expenses during the course of completing a project. Inclusion of the following provision is one way designers may obligate their clients to reimburse those expenses.

Client Reimbursement of Expenses

Interior designers should make clear in their agreements with clients that clients must reimburse them for any and all expenses they incur as a result of working on behalf of those clients. As you might suspect, there are many different ways in which this provision could be interpreted. Be sure to read the entirety of the following sample provision to note the different ways in which designers and clients may agree to handle purchases. Interior designers often complain that clients do not pay according to the terms of their agreements with them. To prevent that from happening in your practice, it is advisable to discuss with prospective clients the importance of compliance with provisions of this kind in order to prevent a project from stalling when payments are not made. You will also notice that provisions of this kind should specifically appoint a designer as a client's agent for purchases to limit the possibility of clients later successfully claiming that a designer had no authority to make project purchases on their behalf. In addition, this provision should spell out that it is the client, not the designer, who is responsible for shipping and other charges incidental to project purchases.

Project Purchasing Arrangement: Designer and Client agree that for purposes of completion of this project only, the following will control the purchasing arrangement of project merchandise and services:

___ Designer tenders payment for merchandise and construction ("Option 1"), or

___ Client tenders payment for merchandise and construction ("Option 2"), or

___ Designer tenders payment for merchandise only; and Client tenders payment for construction only ("Option 3"), or

___ Client tenders payment for merchandise and construction after Designer places all purchase or work orders ("Option 4").

___ Other arrangement as follows: _____

_____ ("Option 5").

In the event Designer is to tender payment for either project merchandise or project construction services under the terms of Options 1 and 3, Client agrees to give advanced written authorization and make payment according to the following percentages before Designer will tender payment for same. Client expressly understands and agrees that any order for any project merchandise or any project construction cannot be cancelled by Client for any reason. Client agrees to pay IN FULL for the following merchan-

dise, or classes of merchandise: _____ ;
Client agrees to pay ___% deposit for other merchandise, such as _____ and ___% deposit for construction. Client agrees to pay the full balance due for these purchases before delivery or installation, but in no event later than project completion and occupancy of subject property by Client.

Client agrees to provide written authorization to Designer to appoint Designer as Client's sole agent for project purposes and for approving Designer's project purchases (Option 4).

Client agrees to provide Designer with copies of all invoices, purchase orders, work orders, and documents related to the purchase of project merchandise and services (Options 3 and 4).

Client agrees that Client shall be responsible for paying any and all taxes, fees, duties, tariffs, packing, and shipping charges.

Price Escalation Provisions

For many reasons, the final price of any one item of specified merchandise as delivered, or any group of items so specified, may differ substantially from the price initially quoted by a designer and approved by a client. In order to be protected in the very real chance that this could occur, designers should include language in their letters of agreement or formal contracts that reads as follows:

> Designer cannot and does not guarantee that the actual final price of any merchandise presented to the client will not vary either with respect to any one item or with respect to the aggregate of any item.

MANAGING YOUR CLIENT'S PROJECT

1. *Client's responsibilities to designer and project*
   It is important that the contract for design services defines what both parties understand to be the role of the client in the project. Of course, making timely payments is one responsibility discussed previously; but there are other responsibilities, which a designer should seek to include in design contracts. Read the following provision, and consider how its omission in a contract might hinder a designer's ability to complete a project.

Client Responsibilities

Client agrees to cooperate with Designer throughout this project to effect its successful completion within the time frame set forth in the agreement. Client further agrees to provide the designer with reasonable access to the subject property.

2. *Project document ownership rights*

Many interior designers, whether their practice has a residential or commercial focus, have the desire to own drawings, graphic schedules, and written specifications (among other documents) they produce to complete a client's project. Many clients, however, also wish to own these documents, perhaps believing they are included in the total amount of services to which they have agreed, or concerned that ownership of them by others may jeopardize their safety and security. If a designer believes it is their preferred practice to retain ownership of documents indicating the design intent of the project and sources used to procure necessary items, the designer should make sure any proposal for their services is included from the start. Following is an example of this kind of agreement:

"It is specifically understood and agreed by the parties to this agreement for design services that _____ (the interior designer) shall own any and all documents, whether of a graphic or written nature, produced during the course of this project as well as any and all rights to use and/or reproduce them."

3. *Mediation and arbitration agreements*

Taking contract disputes through the court system can be an expensive and lengthy process. For that reason, many contracts for design services specify a two-part procedure for both parties to follow in the event that disputes arise. The first part of the process usually calls for the dispute to be heard by a neutral, third-party **mediator**, who will gather information about the cause and nature of the dispute, and then negotiate a resolution. In the event the mediator fails to resolve the issues, these provisions further allow for the matter to be considered by an **arbitrator**, whose decision about the outcome of the dispute is binding on the parties.

Now that you are aware of the differences between these two methods of dispute resolution, you will be better able to recognize and understand the meaning of contract provisions reading as follows:

Mediation: "In the event of a dispute arising from this contract, the parties, Designer and Client, agree that prior to initiation of legal proceedings, any and all matters under dispute shall first be submitted to mediation, the terms of which are further agreed as being only advisory in nature and nonbinding on the parties."

Arbitration: "In the event of any disagreement or dispute between Designer and Client under the terms of this contract, that disagreement of dispute shall be subject to arbitration. Any such arbitration shall further be conducted by a third-party arbitrator mutually agreeable to Designer and Client and whose conclusion shall be binding on the parties as well."

4. *Force majeure clauses and the impossibility of performance*
There are events that neither designers nor anyone else can control. This provision addresses the issue of those instances where "acts of God" (**force majeure**) or other actions render it impossible for a designer to complete a project. These provisions typically read as the following sample taken from a contract:

Designer is not responsible for, nor liable for, any damages resulting from the occurrence of any of the following: delays caused by Client, vendors, or contractors that result in delay of any performance or activity of Designer. Furthermore, Designer shall not be responsible for any delay or damage occurring from fire, natural disaster, strike/unforeseen work stoppage, act of public authority, force majeure, or any and all causes beyond the reasonable control of Designer. Designer agrees that Client shall not be responsible for any delay or damage occurring from fire, natural disaster, strike/unforeseen work stoppage, act of public authority, force majeure, or any and all causes beyond Client's reasonable control. In the event of delays caused by any of the above-mentioned events, any and all performance of the parties shall be excused while pending with no recourse for any breach or damage accruing.

5. *Disclaimer of liability*
Designers perform their services in tandem with other professionals, such as architects, general and independent contractors, engineers, and consultants. This provision of interior design contracts is intended to limit the extent of a designer's liability for the actions

of others. **Liability** is a legal concept related to finding of fault by courts of law; also related is the concept of **damages**, which courts can award when fault is found. The intent of these provisions is to limit the possibility of a designer having to pay monetary damages caused by the faulty actions of others or by happenings beyond a designer's control. These provisions typically contain language such as that in the following excerpt.

Client expressly agrees that Designer shall not be responsible for the following:

Any actions or failures to act on the part of project merchandise suppliers or contractors; any defect of any item purchased for the project other than those specified by the designer; any changes made by the client or contractor that were either not specified by the designer or were made without the designer's consent; any latent defects of any item of merchandise purchased for the project, or any defect caused by any action or failure to act on the part of any project contractor; any defect or problem resulting from the use or placement of project merchandise, such as the effects of fading, wear, fraying, or abrasion.

6. *Administrative contract provisions*
   Legal concepts defining how contracts should be interpreted and their terms implemented have developed throughout centuries of use. These concepts can now be found in the specific contract provisions of most modern contracts, including those for interior design services. The sections that follow are examples of contract provisions describing what the parties intend their working relationship to be and how other provisions in the contract are to be interpreted.

7. *Assignment and delegation of contract*
   What might happen if a client sold a residence or a commercial facility during the course of a designer's work for that client? Or what might happen if something unforeseen resulted in either a designer or client being unable to perform the obligations of the contract? Provisions of this kind protect a designer in the event the contract right of one party is either *assigned*, or transferred by an outside agreement; or *delegated*, that is, given to another party. Including provisions of this kind ensures that both designers and clients have some say about who may be the other party to the agreement.

Neither party to this agreement for interior design services may assign, delegate, give, or in any way convey or transfer their interest to another without the express written consent of the other party to the original contract dated _____.

8. *Integration of contract terms*

   The *integration* provision of the kind excerpted here is one with which you may not be readily familiar; yet it is a centuries-old contract principle, known as the *parole evidence rule*. Much of its history and the implications of its use are of limited importance to designers, but its basic tenet is significant. According to that principle, written agreements, such as design contracts, will be considered by courts of law as the final expression of the terms to which the parties agreed. Courts will not consider as persuasive any other oral or written terms to which the parties might have assented if those terms differ from or contradict those found in the written agreement. According to this provision, the terms of a final, contract are those that the parties must have intended to be bound by with regard to their respective obligations. Of course, parties to a contract can mutually agree to change contract terms through the use of a **contract amendment**. Typical provisions of this kind read as follows:

   This agreement represents the entirety of the understanding between Designer and Client. No other agreements or representations, either orally or in writing, exist or have been made between the parties. This agreement can only be modified in whole or in part by a writing signed by both parties so stating any new and/or additional terms.

9. *Severability*

   Suppose that a portion of a design contract were found to be unenforceable. Should the remainder of the contract *fail*, or be found unenforceable as well? In general, contract provision of **severability** states something to the following effect:

   If any provision of this agreement shall be found to be invalid or unenforceable, the remaining provisions shall remain valid and in force and in effect.

10. *Termination of contract*

For many reasons clients may not be able to complete an interior design project. However, designers should not be left uncompensated for the services they have rendered when clients wish to, or must, dissolve the contract relationship. Provisions of this kind typically state that the parties agree at the outset of the contract that it may be terminated upon written notice given within a specified time period, and that the client further agrees to pay the designer for all services rendered prior to the termination date as well as reimbursement for any project expenses. Inclusion of this provision in a contract permits designers to seek enforcement of the payment and reimbursement terms in courts of law should the client not honor the agreement. Typically, these sections contain language similar to the following excerpt:

This agreement may be terminated by either party upon the other party's default in performance [that is, one party to the contract failed to act according to the terms of the agreement], provided that termination may not be effected unless written notice specifying nature and extent of default is given to the concerned party and such party fails to cure [that is, "make good" on their part of the contract] the default within _____ days from the date of the receipt of notice. Termination shall be without prejudice to any and all other rights and remedies of Designer. Client shall remain liable for all outstanding obligations owed to Designer and for all items of merchandise, interior installations, and other services on order as of the termination date.

Suspension is a concept related to *termination* since clients are sometimes not able to continue to participate in an interior design project, although they still intend to finish the project. A project may be suspended when clients fail to pay for services within a specified time period, making the designer unable to continue work until they pay their fees. After a set period of time, the designer may be permitted to terminate the agreement under the contract terms.

The exact language of suspension provisions can mirror the summary description above. As you review the language of design contracts, however, you should note some suspension provisions effectively give either party not just the designer, the ability to halt completion of a project until the other has acted in accordance with the agreement.

11. *Amendment of contract*

As you will learn in the following discussion of problem-solving strategies, contracts may be changed through the use of written amendments. Both parties, of course, would have to agree to any changes in contract terms and separate consideration exchanged between the parties. This provision recognizes the potential need to change initial contract terms during the course of a project. Typically, such provisions state that all amendments must be in writing to be valid. Provisions concerning contract amendments can read as follows:

This agreement between Designer and Client can be modified only in writing, signed by both Designer and Client.

12. *Controlling jurisdiction*

The laws of the various states differ, sometimes markedly, from each other. In an effort to prevent confusion as to which state's laws might apply in the event of a contract dispute, the parties to the contract may agree that the laws of a particular state will govern the outcome. Some contracts simply provide that the laws of the state where the designer's principal place of business is located will apply. The advice of legal counsel is necessary to determine the advantages and disadvantages of specific state laws when resolving contract matters. You can identify this section of a design contract by the following language:

The laws of the State of _____ shall govern this Agreement.

PROBLEM-SOLVING STRATEGIES IN WORKING WITH DESIGN CONTRACTS

Learning about contracts can be confusing at first. On the one hand, recalling their basic elements—*legality, capacity, offer, acceptance, consideration,* and *mutuality*—is undoubtedly quite easy for you. However, understanding the way contracts really work in business dealings can be much more difficult. Part of the difficulty is that many interior design students have not been exposed to contracts containing the kinds of provisions discussed here, and they have never had the opportunity to use them in their work. This chapter has attempted to show how the combination of elements usually found in design contracts may define your working relationship with clients. Yet, something else remains. What strategies, based on the realities of that working relationship, should you employ in your daily practice to protect yourself against possible legal claims brought against you by clients and others? Of course, the facts and circumstances of each designer's practice are unique, in terms of the specific activities and projects in which a designer chooses to engage as well as the provisions of the law of the states and localities where they work. That said, designers should keep in mind a number of problem-solving strategies when working with contracts in their practices.

CONTRACT TIPS

Contracts for interior design services, as you know, must have a legal purpose. Thus, any contract into which designers enter during the course of doing business must contain provisions for only services legally permissible for the designer to perform in that jurisdiction. Designers should take care to ensure that their contracts contain language (or client expectation) requiring them to submit plans of a structural, or load-bearing, nature, which an architect or engineer would be better qualified to do. In states such as California, that limitation is expanded to also prohibit a designer from submitting plans of a seismic nature, which usually requires the assistance of geological engineers. Other states, particularly Louisiana, publish an entire list of activities in which interior designers cannot engage in the course of their work, including tasks related to planning electrical and plumbing systems. Other common prohibitions are related to the supervision of construction work during and after its completion. Some jurisdictions specifically require those who perform such tasks to hold licenses or permits issued by that state. Many clients of interior designers expect them to oversee construction work. If designers choose to perform that task, in states such as Florida that require a separate general contractor license, they would need to obtain such a license or the legal right to do that work, in addition to any authorization necessary to perform for interior design work. If, however, designers do not wish to assume that responsibility, they would have to indicate their legal limitations to clients and ensure that any contract for their services does not obligate them to engage in prohibited activities.

What do you think happens when interior design contracts contain provisions for services in which the designer cannot legally engage? How might courts of law interpret those provisions? One legal consequence of the inclusion in contracts of provisions of this kind is that such terms are typically considered by courts to be **void** or legally unenforceable. This is distinguished from voidable contracts in which one of the parties chooses not to honor the contract's enforceable terms. Many contracts contain a special provision indicating that if any portion of the contract *fails* for legal reasons—for example, is found unenforceable—then remaining portions of the agreement are still binding on the designer and client. A more difficult legal issue involves situations in which interior designers are found by courts to have actually engaged in prohibited conduct. Performing tasks that only a general contractor is legally permitted to do is one way designers have been found to have acted outside the scope of their profession. The consequences of engaging in prohibited activities differ according to the state in which the designer practices. Penalties can, in general, be quite harsh, and include payment of fines, imprisonment, and forfeiture of fees related to such work. For these reasons, it is extremely important that designers understand what services they can and cannot offer to perform in interior design contracts.

TIPS FOR BUSINESS PRACTICES

Contracts do not exist apart from other business practices and realities faced by designers. A common goal of businesspeople, including designers, is to protect their businesses and property from the effect of any legal claims brought against them. Accordingly, designers, especially those just starting in practice, should consult legal professionals to inform them about crucial issues and business practices. Legal advisers may be helpful in the following activities:

◆ Research and counseling concerning state laws that might prohibit, limit, or are otherwise relevant to the practice of interior design in a particular state.
◆ Review of proposed agreements to understand their possible ramifications as well as suggestions for their correction and modification. Of course, the implications of all contract provisions can be important. Designers should seek specific counsel about the

effectiveness of limitations of liability with regard to the designer as well as the designer's attempts to disclaim liability for acts of third parties. Jurisdictions differ in how such provisions are interpreted and enforced.

◆ Advising on the form of business organization most appropriate to protect the interior design firm, such as choice of the Limited Liability Company (LLC) or corporate form. The form of organizing an interior design business, along with carefully worded contracts, can protect both designers and their businesses from the effects of legal claims. Legal counsel qualified to advise on these matters can be of great benefit to young designers.

◆ Suggesting the types and amounts of insurance coverage appropriate for the activities in which the interior designers engage.

There are certainly many concerns that designers might raise with their legal advisers. The issues discussed in this chapter show how a legal understanding of contract provisions in conjunction with other business practices may be used to protect designers and their businesses from legal claims.

THE ROLE OF A DESIGN AGENT

As you have learned in this and other chapters, interior designers are usually appointed by design contracts as agents for their clients. This agency relationship allows designers to purchase products and engage the services of other professionals on behalf of their clients. With the agency relationship in place, it is extremely important for designers to fulfill the duties it imposes. Obedience, loyalty, providing information, and working with reasonable diligence and skill are examples of those duties. Some activities in which designers engage would likely be found to violate an agency relationship with clients. One example would be the practice of ordering merchandise or authorizing work under the auspices of a client without obtaining a client's approval. Another activity that could be found to violate the agency relationship with clients is to ignore the client's budget schedule in carrying out a project. As a practical matter, designers should refrain from ordering merchandise prior to receiving written authorization from the client. They should also strictly adhere to the budget and schedule constraints specified in interior design contracts.

CONTRACT AMENDMENTS

Perhaps you received the impression that contracts cannot be changed or modified in any way. However, during the life of a contract—that is, the period between its formation and final performance—frequently is necessary to make changes to contracts. Adding or modifying an original contract's terms is enacted through the use of **amendments**. Assume, for example, that a contract left out an important provision of the kind discussed in this chapter. If both parties to the contract agree to the inclusion of this new term, and put in writing both the new provision and their signatures indicating their agreement to it and separate consideration such as additional amounts of money exchanged between the parties, then the new terms become enforceable as contract terms. An amendment should be dated and reviewed by legal advisers for its effect on the entire contract.

Your ability to formulate problem-solving strategies in working with contracts will develop over time. The tips noted here may serve as your introduction to problem solving in this complex field. The projects that follow should be of further assistance.

REFERENCES

Alderman, Robert L. 1997. *How to Prosper as an Interior Designer*. New York: John Wiley & Sons.

Allison, John, and Robert Prentice. 2001. *Business Law: Text and Cases in the Legal Environment*. 3rd Custom ed. New York: Thompson Learning.

Berger, C. Jaye. 1994. *Interior Design Law and Business Practices*. New York: John Wiley & Sons.

Coleman, Cindy, ed. 2002. *Interior Design: Handbook of Professional Practice*. New York: McGraw-Hill.

Crawford, Tad and Brock, Eva Doman 2001. *Business and Legal Forms for Interior Designers*, New York: Allworth Press.

Knackstedt, Mary V. 2002. *The Interior Design Business Handbook*. 3rd ed. New York: John Wiley & Sons.

Siegel, Harry and Alan Siegel. 1982. *A Guide to Business Practices and Principles for Interior Designers*. New rev. ed. New York: Watson-Guptill.

STRATEGIES-IN-ACTION PROJECTS

STRATEGIC PLANNING PROJECT

By means of contracts for design services, designers establish the working relationship they will build with clients. Those contracts are developed through the formal conversations, or negotiations, between designers and clients. During negotiations, both designers and clients interact in order to better understand the activities required of both parties to satisfy the terms of their agreement.

Decision makers who review plans for proposed businesses are interested in knowing what procedures are involved when designers negotiate proposed contracts with potential clients. Remember, these decision makers are considering whether to advance sums of money or lines of credit to the business venture you seek to establish. If prospective clients are not interested in working with you, you will probably be unable to repay any of these sums. In this section of the plan for your ideal interior design business, describe the steps involved in contract negotiation and suggest how you will address the concerns of prospective clients about entering into contracts for your services as an interior designer.

RESIDENTIAL INTERIOR DESIGN PROJECT SIMULATION

Lee has been too occupied with the children's-room project to do much writing in her diary. Lee has also been preoccupied with another problem. She failed to include a provision in the original contract related to ownership of project documents, such as schematic drawings she has completed. On the one hand, she wants to keep them, since they are her original work product that she would like to include in her portfolio. On the other hand, her extremely affluent clients are concerned about protecting their privacy and about possible security risks should the drawings, which depict features of the house, fall into the hands of a criminal. Because of the lack of an agreed-upon contract provision determining ownership of the drawings, the resolution to this issue remained uncertain for some time.

Mr. Abernathy has called Lee with this suggestion: the designer may keep and use all the drawings in her work but must remove the Abernathy name from the drawings before the project is completed. Lee tells you that she agreed to the proposal but is confused about what to do next. "He told me," she says, to "write up an amendment to the original contract and send it over for us to sign." "What do I do now?" she asks you.

Question

At your suggestion, Lee begins a memorandum to the Abernathys titled "Contract Amendment." What other suggestions, based on the understanding of contract amendments you gained from this chapter, could you make about details to include in the memo?

CONTRACT INTERIOR DESIGN CASE STUDY: THE CASE OF THE DESIRABLE DORM— CONTRACT PROVISIONS MEMORANDUM

Your consultation on the University Dorm project has been immensely helpful to the Jennings Group. In this final project with the group, you will explain to them in a written memorandum why it is important to include certain provisions in their contracts for design services.

Brad Jennings had been in practice for many years; yet contracts for the firm's services remained a problem for him. As a businessperson, he was interested in finding the best language to use when drafting contract provisions that would protect the firm against legal claims as much as possible. Yet, also as a businessperson working in a highly competitive area, he knew that to present one-sided contracts to clients, which protected the firm too much, would result in losing clients who might think they were being exploited. For that reason, he would like you, as a consultant to his firm, to explain the intent of the following three contract provisions and why the firm should not let clients talk them out of these provisions during the negotiation process. The group will then forward your comments to the firm's attorney for use when writing the first draft of a contract that the group will propose to the university. Can you fully answer the following questions about the three provisions of concern to Jennings?

Questions

1. *Disclaimer of responsibility*
Should there be a limit to the occurrences for which an interior designer is responsible? What might those events be, and what language might you

include in a contract for your services expressing a disclaimer of responsibility?

2. *Limitation of liability for act of third parties*

Why might an interior designer such as Jennings want to include such a provision in a contract for design services. Identify who these third parties might be in your memorandum and which of their activities might require the inclusion of a contract term such as this one?

3. *Mediation and arbitration provisions*

What is the difference between these two activities? Who might be responsible for selecting and compensating the professionals carrying out these two processes?

PART FOUR

YOU AND
YOUR RESOURCES

In part 3 of this text, you learned the importance of developing effective methods for working with clients on projects as well as the specific skills that enable you to do so. Another factor affecting your ability to work well with clients is how well you are able to work with other professionals. After all, as a project's interior designer of record, you are sometimes the only link between your client and these resources. Who are these professionals on whom you will rely to make your concept for an interior design project a reality?

These resources likely include vendors from whom you directly purchase merchandise on behalf of your clients for subsequent resale to them; or they are suppliers who submit bids to provide goods for project use. Other professionals on whom you will rely include those who provide services or labor, such as independent and general contractors. Chapters 12 and 13 explore your relationship with these important resources.

Chapter 12, "Working with Vendors," discusses how you can interact effectively with vendors. It identifies important objectives for you to consider, among them learning how to access merchandise vendors, many of whom may not sell to the general public; and understanding policies and terms that define how these vendors price and deliver merchandise. The chapter projects should intrigue you as well. The Strategic Planning

Project enables you to identify a selection of vendors appropriate for your ideal interior design business. In the Residential Interior Design Project Simulation, you will be able to assist Lee place an order for a textile product, and then help to prepare an invoice for that purchase to present to the project client. Finally in the Contract Interior Design Case Study, you prepare a short statement concluding why the study's interior design firm might or might not choose to work directly with vendors in light of the firm's goals and the practical realities of business life.

Chapter 13, "Working with Service Providers," explores how to develop and manage your relationship with those who carry out project tasks. This involves becoming familiar with the different service providers typically used in interior design work. Interior designers need to know how and when service providers become involved in a project. And they must know how to document different aspects of their relationships with service providers. This chapter also introduces important documents used by designers and shows you how these documents function during the course of a project. The Strategies-in-Action projects have two goals. The first involves writing an executive summary of your ideal interior design business as you conclude the text's Strategic Planning Project. In the Residential Interior Design Case Study, you help Lee draft a change order for use by the project's general contractor. Finally, in the Contract Interior Design Case Study, you draft a statement for a fledging interior design firm concluding why the group should or should not be directly involved in the selection and management of project service providers—again, given the goals the firm seeks to accomplish and the realities of modern business life.

Understanding the intricacies of working with vendors and service providers, and learning to apply critical concepts in this context, can help you form your own strategies for better serving your clients' interests. This knowledge may also contribute to your profitability as an interior designer.

CHAPTER TWELVE

WORKING WITH VENDORS

Interior design is complex—as an art,
as a profession, and as a business.

HARRY SIEGEL AND ALAN SIEGEL

WHY THIS CHAPTER IS IMPORTANT TO YOU

Part 4 of this text explores your relationship with trade sources that provide merchandise and services necessary to realize your design concept for a project. **Vendors**, the subject of this chapter, are trade sources offering for sale products such as textiles, furniture, light fixtures, and accessories—to name just a few. Obtaining the most appropriate merchandise for a project means that designers must first assess vendors not usually open to the general public and then communicate with these sources using the business terms that they use. Because designers, particularly those who specialize in residential projects, frequently earn the majority of their project revenue from selling merchandise they purchase to clients, it is also necessary for the designer to understand the process of obtaining and pricing products. Chapter 12 explores these aspects of interior design work. Knowing how to work effectively with the resources discussed in this chapter and in chapter 13 may allow you to perceive your professional business practices in a new light.

PROFESSIONAL PRACTICES PORTFOLIO

After completing this chapter, you should be able to answer the following questions. Include your responses in a professional practices portfolio that you keep as a handbook for your later use.

1. Describe the purposes of specialized merchandise market centers and how interior designers may access them.
2. Distinguish between *product-pricing* and *product-selling* terminology.
3. What are some examples of product-pricing terms?
4. What are some commonly used selling-price terms?
5. Describe trade and cash discounts and how they affect product prices.
6. Distinguish between sales and use taxes.
7. What does it mean when the term FOB/factory is used by a shipper, and what concerns should an interior designer have in such instances?
8. What is the purpose of a vendor's "terms and conditions of sale"?
9. What is a purchase order, and describe how it functions.

INTRODUCTION TO WORKING WITH VENDORS

This chapter identifies objectives designers need to master in order to interact professionally with vendors. First, a designer must know how to gain access to vendors. Since many vendors operate in the wholesale format, serving only designers and others such as retail sellers offering merchandise to end users, an interior designer should be aware of the procedures and documentation required to gain admittance to these "trade only" showrooms and merchandise marts. In addition, knowing the terms vendors use in the selling and delivery process is a critical skill. Nothing creates problems more than failing to understand and correctly apply sales terms in commercial transactions. As you may recall from chapter 4, "Understanding Law and Your Business," a special set of contract-related laws, known as the Uniform Commercial Code (UCC), applies to the sale of goods. This chapter builds on that introduction by describing how that code operates specifically in the sale and purchase of merchandise. Another objective is to understand the process of pricing, selling, and delivering products. Clients usually assume that designers are proficient in obtaining the products they want to use in a project. In addition, designers' pricing policies have a direct bearing on the profitability of their businesses. These two concerns should be reason enough for designers to master this task. Knowing what vendors expect before working with them can help you reach the goals you set for a project. Finally, common sense—borne of this knowledge, experience, and interpersonal relationships can be very helpful in troubleshooting problems with vendors before they occur.

OBJECTIVES TO CONSIDER

In this chapter, you will learn to master several important objectives related to working with vendors, or those individuals and companies providing the items you will use to complete projects. These objectives include the following:

1. Gaining access to vendors
2. Knowing basic sales and delivery terms used by vendors
3. Understanding how interior design products are priced
4. Learning to troubleshoot problems related to vendors

After explaining the main objectives in learning to deal with vendors, this chapter discusses the procedures involved in pricing products, followed by an account of the purchasing process from ordering an item through delivery for installation. Defining this process should let you know what to expect after you place an order with a vendor. Writing or placing clear, unambiguous orders is the critical link between project concept and realization. But before that order can be written, a designer must have access to those offering goods for sale. How can a designer gain entry into a vendor's place of business?

OBTAINING ACCESS TO MERCHANDISE VENDORS

Whether you ultimately focus your interior design practice on completing residential or commercial projects, you are undoubtedly aware of the importance of obtaining appropriate products for use in those projects.

One factor contributing to the success of any kind of project may well be your ability to locate and obtain furniture, textiles, light fixtures, window and floor treatments, accessories, and other items conforming to your specifications. Thus, identifying where vendors of these items may be found as well as learning procedures for accessing them are important considerations for interior designers.

MERCHANDISE "MARTS" AND DESIGN CENTERS

Furniture and design product shows have long been a tradition in the interior design industry. The popularity and convenience afforded by what were once only occasional exhibits featuring different makers or sellers of goods in one central location spawned an interest in and establishment of venues where such goods might be found on a full-time basis, particularly by professionals, such as interior designers, architects, and retail merchants. These places are now known by different names, but are generally referred to as merchandise marts and design centers. Two characteristics distinguish these selling situations from regular retail malls.

Perhaps the most significant feature of design-industry marts and centers and the showroom practices of individual merchants contained in them is that these are for the most part *wholesale* establishments. This characteristic means several things. First and most obviously, prices shown to professional purchasers there are usually not retail prices, such as the manufacturer's suggested retail price (MSRP). Such prices are those shown to consumers in a retail shop. Wholesale prices for products are typically much lower than retail prices. They are usually increased by their eventual reseller, such as an interior designer who first purchases them at a mart or center then adds a percentage amount to what they paid to determine the final amount they will charge the project's client.

In addition to featuring items offered at wholesale prices, another characteristic inherent in wholesale establishments is that professional purchasers patronizing them must show they have the necessary credentials required by state and local governments for reselling the merchandise obtained there. Although such requirements also vary, as a general rule, most users of these special selling venues must show proof of having a valid state-issued certificate permitting them to collect state and local sales tax from endbuyers of items obtained at a mart or design center. It may also include showing proof of a use tax permit. These requirements are especially applicable to those operating retail establishments. Designers and architects, on the other hand, showing current certification to practice may obtain admission to that center on that basis alone, as with the Dallas Market Center located in Dallas, Texas. Furthermore, proof of current membership in state or national design organizations such as the ASID, or the IIDA or, if an architect, the AIA also qualifies individuals for admission. Lacking either a state certification or proof of organizational membership, anyone who desires to access marts or centers must follow procedures of the kind described above that show the individual is in the business of reselling merchandise.

Because of these features, most marts and centers and the showrooms found there are predominately open only to design professionals, a situation referred to as *closed* showrooms with access made available only to the *trade*. This practice also varies and in many respects is changing. Some manufacturers now maintain an *open* showroom policy in which consumers from the general public are permitted to enter to look at items found there and, if permitted to purchase, accordingly charged retail prices. Even *closed* showrooms may permit non-professionals to enter under certain circumstances. These situations typically require that the showroom have a policy whereby clients of interior designers may enter to view, but not to purchase, merchandise. This can occur either with the designer being present or with a designer's letter, usually written on business letterhead, introducing a client to a showroom and indicating that client is working with that designer. As noted, there is a marked trend toward the open policy as manufacturers and vendors seek to capitalize on both the wholesale and retail consumer markets. However, there are a great many showrooms, particularly those featuring textiles and textile products and highly exclusive furniture items that remain resolutely closed to retain consumer perusal and purchases.

UNDERSTANDING MERCHANDISE PRICING

In order to do business with vendors, designers must first become familiar with the terminology used in buying and selling merchandise. Several of the key terms are *net price, wholesale, cost, list price, manufacturer's suggested retail price (MSRP)*, and *selling price*.

PRODUCT-PRICING TERMS

Wholesale price is thought to be the price at which one vendor (the wholesaler) offers merchandise for sale to another merchant (for example, an interior designer). Usually, the wholesale price is not the price at which the wholesaler offers merchandise to public consumers. Interior designers who purchase goods at wholesale, may then either charge clients an amount equal to the wholesale amount they paid for the goods or charge clients an amount marked up by some percentage above the initial wholesale amount. The decision to pass savings on to a client or to charge a client a higher amount may be based on the method by which a designer and client have agreed a designer will be compensated for his or her services, or any other agreement related to how a designer will provide merchandise.

The **list price** is often thought of as being the manufacturer's suggested retail price (MSRP). What is important for you to remember is that whether referred to as *list* or *MSRP*, this price is that which is offered to the buying public; those who are non-merchant consumers. In general, a *list price* or MSRP is double the *wholesale price*, although merchandise pricing policies differ among merchants and according to different circumstances. For example, companies selling merchandise to others for subsequent resale cannot require any other vender under the terms of federal law to charge only a fixed amount for merchandise. Thus, the MSRP may or may not be the final price at which consumers pay for goods. Many designers will offer items to clients at a price that is discounted, or lower than retail prices, a practice referred to as **discounting from retail**. A designer who uses that approach to price items select a percentage reduction amount and apply it to the MSRP to determine a client's cost. The **net price** is the amount typically representing one-half of the MSRP.

Markup from cost is another way designers may determine product costs. Historically, interior designers have earned their entire compensation for work on a project through this method, especially when their scope of services indicated a great many product purchases. Quite simply, designers would add a percentage amount to the cost they paid and then charge their clients that increased amount. In this way, a product that cost a designer $1,000 would be charged to his or her client at $2,000, assuming a 100 percent markup rate from cost.

Gross margin refers to the difference in dollars—known as **gross margin dollars**—between the price at which an item is sold by a designer and the cost of that item to a designer. When that amount is divided by the selling price, a gross-margin percentage is obtained. Gross margins are important for designers who base their compensation solely on selling merchandise, since this amount represents the compensation for their design work and is their only source of income to pay operational expenses.

Designers may select whatever percentage amount they desire when setting a price; considering that many still earn most, if not all, of their income from the sale of goods and not from separate design fees, it seems logical that designers choose to earn the highest gross margin amounts possible. The difficulty with any method of establishing a selling price is determining how much the market for interior design services in any location can bear product costs. While 100 percent markup from costs may be among the most beneficial ways for designers to charge for products, there may not be enough clients who are able to pay such high prices for them to sustain their practices.

DISCOUNT TERMS

As an incentive to encourage further business, many vendors offer **discounts**, or reductions, to wholesale purchasers from the suggested retail price. Two common forms of discounts are those referred to as trade discounts and cash discounts, both of which reduce the final cost of merchandise purchased by interior designers. Based on their business practices, interior designers may sell the merchandise to their clients at the discounted cost, which is lower than the suggested retail price; or they may sell an item to clients at the original suggested retail price and thus recoup a higher amount of profit.

Discounts may be offered based on different considerations. **Trade discounts** are reductions offered to design professionals. **Quantity discounts** are offered based on the number of items ordered; a fairly large number of purchases are usually needed to trigger the price reduction, and frequently the more items ordered the larger the percentage discounted.

Prompt payment for items ordered is another consideration for vendors to offer price reductions. These are referred to as **cash discounts**. Frequently terms such as **5–10 Net 30** or **2–10 Net 30** appear on invoices or bills if cash discounts are offered. Respectively, these terms mean that the purchaser may take 2 percent or 5 percent from the total cost price if the bill is paid within ten days of receipt of the invoice, with the total amount of the invoice due within thirty days of its receipt. This discount is taken only after all other discounts have been figured.

TAX TERMS

Whether or not a vendor extends discount terms to designer who purchases merchandise, it is inevitable that there will be tax consequences for which some party to the exchange must be responsible. State and local governments assess taxes in order to earn revenue to support the function of those entities. They do so through the imposition of two kinds of taxes generally referred to as sales and use taxes. You are probably familiar with the **sales tax** from your own store purchases: In addition to the price you pay for an item, an additional charge is frequently added to that cost, usually a percentage of the total purchase amount. The store's addition of that tax derives from its holding of a **resale license**, although the term varies. This permit allows a store to pass on any state and local sales taxes it would have had to pay to a purchaser—a designer, in this case. An interior designer needs to have the same ability to pass on sales taxes to his or her clients. As you know, imposition of sales taxes increases the cost of a final product. In addition, accounting for sales taxes and making sure they are collected on required transactions is an operating cost for a business.

If you have purchased goods out of state to be shipped to your home or, as is typical today, you have purchased goods on the Internet, you are aware that you likely paid no sales taxes. You are also not subject to paying tax for using such items in your home state. The situation is different, however, for businesses that purchase goods out of state or on the Internet: States impose what is referred to as a **use tax** when those same goods would have been subject to sales tax in a user's state. In addition to a sales tax license, a business would also need to obtain a use-tax permit or certificate.

Merchandise must travel from a vendor's distribution site or factory to a designer before it can be used in a project. Who do you think is responsible for the costs of such transportation, and when might ownership of the merchandise be legally considered to have passed from buyer to seller? Specific provisions of the Uniform Commercial Code (UCC) adopted by many states consider these and related issues.

DELIVERY TERMS AND COSTS

Descriptions of merchandise frequently include the notation **Free on Board (FOB)**, followed by the notation *factory* or the name of a destination city. With regard to the delivery of merchandise, FOB indicates that a vendor is responsible only for the costs associated with placing goods with a *common carrier*, such as a train or a commercially operated truck. The remainder of the description addresses which party, vendor, or purchaser is responsible for payment of shipping charges. It also determines when actual ownership of the goods may be said to have occurred, according to the UCC. The notation *factory* indicates that ownership of merchandise passes from a seller to a buyer at the factory once the goods are placed with a carrier for transportation. This implies that a buyer must usually pay the cost of transporting the goods from a vendor's factory to his or her location. Of course, in those instances delivery charges must be added to the final cost of the merchandise. In addition, this notation indicates that the buyer, not the seller, bears the risk of loss or damage to merchandise once it leaves a vendor's factory. Shipping insurance—another cost—must be added to the final cost of such merchandise.

The FOB designation could also be followed by the notation *destination* or by the name of a specific city. In that case, a vendor is considered to retain title and ownership of the goods after they leave the factory throughout the transportation process until the goods are received at a purchaser's location for receipt. There are usually no associated delivery costs to be borne by a purchaser, since a vendor pays for delivery under this FOB notation.

Freight Prepaid is another shipping-related term of importance. In an effort to limit the extent of any possible liability that might result from retaining ownership of merchandise during its transportation and also to reduce the costs of insuring the merchandise, some vendors will use the notation *Freight Prepaid* to indicate that ownership of the goods passes from a vendor to a purchaser once the factory places the goods with a carrier for transportation. While a buyer in this case assumes liability for any damage that may occur to the goods during transport (and may still be responsible for any insurance charges), a seller agrees to pay the costs of transporting the goods from the factory to the buyer's location. This payment of transportation charges is usually considered a form of incentive for a buyer to assume the *risk* of transporting the goods in exchange for having the actual transport costs borne by a seller.

INSTALLATION

Once the merchandise has traveled from a source factory to its destination, it must be stored for use, then further transported, and either placed or installed at the project location. These activities have some important consequences that may bring about increased product prices. Obviously, storage and insurance expenses are incurred when merchandise must be held until use. Also, charges accrue for the costs of the physical labor necessary to transport merchandise to the project site, unload and uncrate it, and then place or install the item. Simple placement of an item requires workers to follow instructions and consult charts prepared by a designer for that purpose. Installation, however, usually implies that some type of specialized labor or knowledge of product application is required in order for the product to function as intended. Common sense would suggest that overhead lighting fixtures, for example, are not considered fully installed and functional if they are simply removed from a crate and left on the floor. This section has summarized the ways in which product costs may be determined. The next section of this chapter considers some of the issues that arise when interior designers work with both vendors and clients.

PROBLEM-SOLVING
STRATEGIES FOR WORKING WITH VENDORS

Working with vendors will undoubtedly be one of the most fascinating, although occasionally frustrating, aspects of your work as an interior designer. It is fascinating because you will actually get to see, touch, and experience objects available to very few others. This is especially true if you intend to practice in the field of residential interior design. However, even if you choose contract interior design work where you specify products for installation but rely on clients and others to complete the purchasing process, you will have to be familiar with vendors, their products, and their business practices in order to make informed, appropriate choices. As you will discover, when unacceptable merchandise arrives, working with vendors to rectify any problem may become, as one designer notes, "quite maddening." The adage "there are no guarantees in life" also applies to working with merchandise trade sources, so it becomes a designer's job to take the necessary steps to prevent problems from emerging in the vendor/client/designer relationship. What are some potential sources of problems, and how might they be avoided—or at least minimized?

THE VENDOR/CLIENT/DESIGNER RELATIONSHIP

As is true in other aspects of interior design, direct communication with clients about vendors and the merchandise they sell is an important first step in troubleshooting. An unhappy client who refuses to pay for an item may jeopardize future relationships with a vendor, thus preventing or hampering your ability to work with that seller on future projects. As a result, it is important to understand client concerns about vendors and their wares. Clients often cannot even comprehend how expensive designer merchandise really is, especially if items are custom-made or specially ordered. Former clients of an interior designer in the Austin, Texas, area explained how surprised they were to learn, after the fact, that they could have purchased a luxury automobile for the same price as a rug specified by their designer. The clients called the vendor themselves, flatly refusing to pay the bill presented to them by the designer since they believed they had received an incorrect invoice. When the clients learned from the manufacturer's representative that the balance due was, in fact, the correct amount, the clients had to substantially adjust the project's budget and schedule after paying for it. "Sure it is a beautiful rug. Who wouldn't want it in their home?" said the clients. "But the designer never, ever talked price. He just told us we could afford it, which would have been true if we hadn't also needed furniture to go with it. That rug threw off the entire project's budget." The clients never again worked with that designer on other projects, nor did they send him referrals. Should the designer, in your opinion, have alerted these clients to the exorbitant cost of the rug, perhaps showing them other options to prevent the problem. Had the designer revealed the rug's price, it would have probably also avoided the clients' direct and somewhat heated interaction with the vendor.

BUDGET ISSUES

Some designers have clients for whom budget issues are at best secondary. These clients may never consider an item's cost as a disruptive concern and may even go so far as to instruct the designer not to give them any prices at all. Other clients, however, are very apprehensive about prices and want detailed information before they receive an invoice. By asking questions such as, "Are you comfortable with how expensive this will be?" and actively listening to clients' responses, you may better handle issues of product cost. Another approach is to show the client a range of options. Many interior designers develop value ranges of the merchandise they show to clients, grouping different manufacturers' goods together according to price. For example, these designers may develop a budget-range list of vendors that offer goods acceptable for shorter-term use as well as a list of vendors that offer a premium range, or one-of-a-kind product range, for long-term use. With a designer's assistance, a client can then choose among those vendor lines that are within that client's project budget. Contract designers frequently use this approach, making sure to receive a client's *sign-off*, or authorization, as protection from budget-issue claims later.

INFORMING CLIENTS ABOUT VENDOR POLICIES: CANCELLATION OF ORDERS

Making clients aware of vendor policies early in the design process is another troubleshooting strategy. You should already be familiar with the term invoice, a bill or claim for amounts of money due. Invoices may be issued for the purchase of products or rendering of services. This chapter includes a Terms and Conditions of Sale Outline (see Form 12.2 on page 415). The full text of these terms are often found on the back of invoices. As to the condition of sale, clients should be informed that a common practice among vendors is not to permit cancellations of an order—or part of an order—once it is accepted (usually after receipt of a signed order form and payment of an initial deposit). Vendor policy further states that once an order is accepted, the purchaser is liable for the entire amount due. A client's remorse or change of heart about a particular item, or even about the entire project proposal, may come into play when a client decides to *back out* of a purchase. This is a highly problematic situation for designers, who are caught between clients who are not likely to pay the balance due on an order and vendors who will not honor cancellations.

Several strategies are available to avoid or ameliorate this situation. First, it is absolutely critical that a designer receive written and signed confirmation from a client regarding every purchase planned for a project, even before a vendor is involved. This is done with a formal document sometimes referred to as a **confirmation of purchase** or **sales agreement**. The purpose of this document is to protect designers from possible claims brought against them by their clients. Governed by laws relating to contracts for the sale of tangible goods, the sales agreement must indicate in sufficient detail prices, quantities, and other relevant information to specifically identify the purchased products. Second, a designer who has a long and successful history of working with a vendor may be able to negotiate a resolution to this problem. Vendors usually want to accommodate designers and continue to receive their business. But this is not always the case. A designer may not always be able to recoup any of the initial deposits. Ultimately, a vendor's decision to consider, much less grant, cancellation of an order may depend on whether the vendor has already made preparations to produce custom-made products or to ship items that are available or in place. It may be easier to convince a vendor to cancel a recently placed order when such preparations have not begun. Cancellation of orders following placement is a challenging issue for designers.

Vendors whose products are in demand may accept merchandise from cancelled orders or returns, as long as merchandise is in a condition suitable for subsequent resale. Items such as door and plumbing hardware, light fixtures, appliances, and other such equipment are types of merchandise that may possibly be returned to vendors. Vendors that accept cancellations and returns also usually impose a **restocking fee** based on a percentage of the order amount—for example, the common percentage is 15 percent, although percentages vary among different vendors. Making clients aware of this fee early in the design process is critical. It is also important to note that changes in product selection may cause additional costs.

COMMUNICATING WITH CLIENTS ABOUT COSTS

Are your clients new to the design process as well as to you and your style of working? Or are your clients familiar with your work and undertaking their second or even third project with you? Your responses to these questions may make your communication with clients easier when dealing with vendors and other trade sources. As unappealing as it may be, you simply may have no choice but to find a less expensive source if you believe that a client would be unwilling to follow through with certain purchases. Use common sense, too: No one, however affluent, desirous of a particular item, or in love with a particular maker's products, enjoys surprises. Ensuring that surprises do not occur will greatly enhance your clients' perceptions of your abilities and their overall satisfaction with you and the projects you complete for them.

During your practice as an interior designer you may find yourself in something of a quandary about discussing merchandise costs with clients. Few clients truly understand why design products cost as much as they do, and once they learn those costs, that information can scare them from authorizing their purchases. To circumvent this occurrence, many designers remain vague about merchandise prices. In all fairness, however, many designers themselves do not know what final costs may be. Designers working in competitive bidding situations also face this concern as the interplay of factors such as the project's overall budget and type of specifications used will be influential in both the price of and the final merchandise selected for use. Designers, whether their practice focuses on residential or commercial projects, do need satisfied clients in order to remain in business. Clients' perceptions of satisfaction may be enhanced if they believe merchandise costs were disclosed as fully as possible by a designer and ultimately reflect the quality of product received.

Vendor prices may increase after your order has been placed. Such changes, furthermore, can occur without prior notice. Believing that they have kept to their side of the bargain, clients may refuse to pay the difference between the price you originally quoted and the new, higher price. To avoid having to assume what may be a substantial cost or otherwise risk jeopardizing a project, make sure that your contract, or letter of agreement, with the client makes clear up front that the client—not the designer—is responsible for all product costs; this includes costs incurred as a result of a vendor's price adjustment after the product was ordered and before delivery.

COMMUNICATING WITH CLIENTS ABOUT TIME ISSUES

In addition to issues related to price, few clients really understand the time involved in preparing products of the quality specified by designers. Often, an item will pass through many different hands during the lengthy course of its creation. Alternatively, many items may take considerable amounts of time to produce in specified quantities. In either case, the amount of time may seem unreasonable or unnecessary to clients. As a result, designers should be aware of the need to communicate with clients about time issues before they become a problem. Ask clients about whether they would be willing to wait for a particular product and choose vendors accordingly.

Specifying products on hand for immediate delivery or ready-made products that require no customization is another way to troubleshoot time issues. This method may also be indicated for projects that must be completed on a tight schedule. Of course, this kind of specification may prevent project delays, but the items when installed may distinguish neither the project nor the designer in the eyes of the client. In general, practicing interior designers note the degree of customization an item requires, the distance an item has to travel, and whether an item is a textile product as factors bearing on the length of time required for production. If time of delivery is an issue to your clients, it is better to inform them of potential delays as soon as possible. As an example, a designer asked a fabric company's showroom representative to make clear to the client before placing an order that it would take a considerable amount of time before the desired Italian-made upholstery fabric could be produced and delivered. The client nevertheless consented to the purchase; after a year of many phone calls to the designer asking about its whereabouts, the fabric finally arrived. Some clients understand that the length of time required to produce an item may help to make the product unique; other clients do not. Discovering your clients' attitude toward this issue and acting accordingly when choosing vendors or products is a strategy for troubleshooting time problems.

TROUBLESHOOTING PROBLEMS WITH SPECIFICATIONS

An item arrives matching your specifications, even matching its description on the vendor's order form and other paperwork; yet, somehow, the item or some component of the item is off. Perhaps the fabric color differs in gradation on various sections of a sofa although it still can be said to be the specified color. The client then asks you how the problem might have been prevented and what you intend to do to remedy it. Troubleshooting this type of problem with a vendor requires planning on your part. First, plan your specifications with extreme care, and select vendors that you know will work *with* you, not against you, to correct problems.

Vendors assume that you, as a professional interior designer, understand and follow procedures. Troubleshooting problems involving specifications requires that you know what questions to ask vendors, both before and after making your specifications. First, you need access to the best information available in order to make decisions. Ask vendors for their most recent swatches of textiles and finishes, which are still fresh in appearance and not overly handled. This way, you can get the best sense of an item under consideration. Look at the sample from different angles and in different lighting before specifying on paper. Some lighting schemes cause colors to fade almost to invisibility or to garishly stand out. Even a classic piece of furniture may look awkward when viewed from some angles. If possible, really get to know the product from more than a photograph or tiny swatch before proceeding with your design. Also acquaint your client with the look of the product so that they will not be surprised should they see the item before it is properly installed.

Once you have identified a particular product you wish to order from a vendor, ask the vendor's representative how to ensure the arrival of a product that looks like the sample from which it was selected and specified. One simple—but not foolproof—way to bring this about is to make sure that the item ordered is specified in the same way in all documentation. For example, a product spec should read the same on both the written order form and the invoice, as well as on every other document you provide to the vendor.

This attention to detail when you place orders also extends to the degree of detail in the specification. With textiles this may mean asking to reserve a certain amount of fabric from a particular dated or numbered dye lot; or, on very large jobs, asking to reserve an entire dye lot's production for your project. Leather products of any kind can be particularly troublesome, for the delivered product may vary substantially in appearance and texture from the swatch you handled to select it. These variations are usually caused by differences in the ways skins absorb tanning treatments, processing techniques, and dyes. Alert clients to these facts before ordering, and ask vendors if they can supply cuttings from specific hides to be shown for final approval before construction of a product begins. With respect to furniture pieces ordered from very high-quality manufacturers, it may be possible to specify a particularly consistent craftsperson or workshop to produce the product. Ask company representatives what they can do to help in this matter. Also find out whether they have had problems in producing particular items, or received complaints from other clients about an item you are considering. If so, that may be a warning to consider alternatives. Many vendors source the goods they sell from a variety of makers and then sell them under a single vendor's name. For example, a fabric house may obtain trimmings from a variety of smaller producers according to availability or pricing. These makers may produce items that are very similar but not exactly alike. One way to troubleshoot is to ask every possible question about sources for the items you select, including whether vendors rely on their own trusted sources.

DEVELOPING GOOD RELATIONS WITH VENDORS

Sometimes bad things happen to good designers, to borrow a phrase. Through no fault of a designer, a product may arrive that is in some way wrong and needs to be adjusted or replaced. Again, while there are no guarantees that a vendor will work with you to correct problems with a product, one way of troubleshooting such issues is to develop correct, good relationships with your vendor sources. Granted, this may be difficult to accomplish; but consistently paying bills on time, correctly specifying products that you order, and working with vendors' schedules as closely as possible are some ways to maintain a mutually beneficial relationship. Reliable clients may be few and far between, and many trade sources will work to accommodate conscientious designers who have already written and paid for many orders in order to obtain future business from them.

The importance of developing good relations with vendors is underscored if you consider the situation facing designers who do *not* have good reputations among vendors. Some sources flatly refuse to work with, or offer credit to, designers with a prior history of sketchy payments. Other vendors will work with troublesome designers only on a pro forma basis, requiring them to pay in full for merchandise before an order can be initiated. In such cases, a designer may be left with a limited range of vendor options. Clients may also ultimately bear the brunt of their designers' poor status with vendors, especially if vendors require full payment with no credit terms. Clients who work with designers in such circumstances will pay more up front throughout the course of their projects.

WHEN THE CLIENT IS THE PURCHASER

As an extreme form of troubleshooting vendor relationships, a designer might choose to not resell items to clients at all. In other words, the client could control the buying relationship with vendors and become the front-line party responsible for dealing with them. Large corporate clients and governmental agencies, for example, may have purchasing departments and personnel responsible for procuring items for those entities. In those instances, a designer (who may be an employee of an architectural or engineering firm) could still have a great deal of responsibility in handling the purchasing process and, ultimately, the relationship between the client and vendor. In such cases, a designer usually acts as a consultant for a client when selecting trade sources. The designer is also the one who specifies products and prepares orders.

When a client is the purchaser, troubleshooting requires a designer to have expert market and product knowledge to evaluate whether particular vendors can produce the kinds and amounts of goods a client desires. A designer must be able to evaluate product quality and justify choosing one maker's item over another's, even if the items are substantially similar. Prior experience with vendors and products may be the best way to prevent problems from emerging in relationships with vendors. Troubleshooting in these circumstances also means protecting the designer from future problems stemming from a client's purchases. Contracts or letters of agreement with clients who will make purchases should clearly state that a designer is not liable for purchases made by a client that differ from the items specified by a designer. Designers should diligently oversee their clients' purchases to make sure that products meet their specifications.

SHOPPING WITH CLIENTS

For many clients, shopping is almost a full-time occupation. They often want to personally accompany designers to trade-only showrooms and merchandise marts that are the source of so many delightful products. One issue facing a designer is whether to take a client along on these trips. Sometimes it is necessary for a client to accompany a designer to view products available only in showrooms. Many designers have no problem with a client's presence on these trips and even encourage it. However, some clients may attempt to purchase the identical or similar goods on their own and thereby bypass having to pay the designers' markup. Designers need to gauge whether their clients or vendors might be willing to act in this way. Do you know both a client and vendor well enough to be assured that they won't cheat you? This issue can arise in the context of visits to art galleries and antique dealers, sellers of one-of-a-kind items, or sources that offer items for sale to both the design trade and the general public. It can also refer to situations where products are sold *off the floor,* and not custom-made for a project. At the outset of a designer/

client relationship, a contract or letter of agreement should specify that once a designer has introduced a client to a vendor, that client is obligated to pay the designer a commission based on a percentage of every purchase that the client consents to place with that vendor or places personally during the course of the project and some period thereafter.

What may be considered shopping by a client is work for a designer—work for which a designer should receive compensation. Interior designers are often surprised when clients refuse to pay for time spent with designers visiting showrooms, especially when such trips resulted in no purchases. Troubleshoot this issue directly with a client by indicating that these trips are a designer's equivalent of going to the office. And include contract language making it clear that time spent with a client visiting vendors will be billed at a certian rate per hour, even if a designer also receives a commission based on purchases or charges by a flat rate for services. In this way, designers protect themselves from clients who believe the designer's working time is freely available to them, including trips to showrooms that have no relevance to their project.

DEALING WITH GOODS DAMAGED ON DELIVERY

Most vendors do not ship the merchandise they sell, often relying on shippers or freight forwarders to move merchandise from the seller's place of business to the place where it will be installed. Some large manufacturers will ship goods directly to a designer. In either circumstance, a difficult reality exists for designers: what to do with goods damaged in transit. This is the typical situation: Upon arrival a piece appears to be damaged in some way, with perhaps a scratch or other blemish spoiling an otherwise acceptable item. The manufacturer claims that the goods were in perfect order when turned over to the shipper, while the shipper claims that the goods must have been damaged before they arrived for delivery. It is a designer's responsibility to resolve this matter. One way to troubleshoot this issue is for a designer to do business only with those shippers who are insured against such claims; or, as an additional cost to be borne by a client, a designer can obtain shipping insurance on the item. As a general rule, once products are paid for in full, their ownership resides not with a manufacturer, but with a buyer, whether it is a client or designer. Shipping insurance is one way to mitigate possible losses, but as noted, it is an additional expense. In some cases, you may need to consult an attorney about how to proceed.

Most of the purchasing transactions in which you engage with vendors will no doubt begin and end satisfactorily. Clients will usually respect the integrity of the purchase process. Most clients, in fact, have neither the time nor the desire to cheat a trusted designer. Your projects will have positive outcomes because of your efforts in troubleshooting these kinds of issues. As you start and develop your interior design practice, network with other designers to become familiar with their best and worst vendor experiences. Learn which vendors consistently support the design community, and how designers have solved particular problems they faced in working with vendors and clients. Should you experience reservations about the quality or integrity of a vendor, discuss your concerns with your clients both orally and in writing, and ask them whether they want to do business with that vendor. Receiving a client's written authorization to order from a questionable vendor after you have informed them of your concerns is one way of troubleshooting liability issues that may arise from a vendor's poor performance.

As in most aspects of interior design, education and experience are the practical keys for beneficial interactions with those who sell merchandise. Equally important is the human factor: Merchants offering goods for sale and representatives of large manufacturers are people too. A designer should take steps to develop open, honest lines of communication with members of the sales community regardless of a designer's level of expertise. In fact, young interior designers can informally learn a great deal about how the design industry really works through helpful vendor sources.

FORMS USED WHEN WORKING WITH VENDORS

The following discussion focuses on a selection of forms interior designers can expect to use when working with vendors. Form 12.4, a product research and evaluation worksheet on page 418, may be used by designers for their own reference to note and compare the characteristics of products.

SAMPLE ACCOUNT APPLICATION

Almost without exception, every vendor creates and uses an account application form similar to Form 12.1. The purpose of this form is to obtain

SAMPLE ACCOUNT APPLICATION

Date _____

ACCOUNT APPLICATION

VENDOR COMPANY NAME
Address
Phone No.
Fax No.

Name of Applicant _____

Address _____

Phone No. _____ Fax No. _____
Cell phone No.

Name of Business/DBA _____

Address _____

Phone No. _____ Fax No. _____

ATTACH BUSINESS CARD HERE

Sales Tax No. _____ **State** _____

Expiration Date _____

Credit Information

ONE   Name on Card _____

        Card No. _____ Expiration Date _____

        Card Type _____ Card ID No. _____

TWO   Name on Card _____

        Card No. _____ Expiration Date _____

        Card Type _____ Card ID No. _____

Additional Applicant Information (Check one)
_____ Interior Designer   State _____   Number _____
_____ Architect   State _____   Number _____
_____ Interior Architect   State _____   Number _____
_____ Retail Store   Address _____
_____ Other   Specify _____

relevant business information about a prospective wholesale, or *trade*, purchaser. This information is usually used to determine whether the prospective purchaser has obtained valid current state and local sales tax certification, along with any other credentials required of wholesale buyers by the vendor/company and applicable law.

TERMS AND CONDITIONS OF SALE OUTLINE

Perhaps best thought of as a vendor's *rules and regulations*, documents such as Form 12.2 are also created and made available by virtually every company that provides merchandise. This outline lists common provisions and summarizes their typical language. Although it is admittedly difficult for designers to read and understand the terms and conditions of sale for every vendor they work with, it is critical for designers to be aware of these documents and their provisions prior to ordering merchandise. Since the purchasing experience is likely to be relatively new to you, an outline of these provisions is included here (see Form 12.2) for your reference. Take the necessary time to discuss its provisions with a classmate to check that you have a viable understanding of Form 12.2.

PURCHASE ORDER FORM

Form 12.3 is the document vendors use to receive initial orders for merchandise. While the particular forms used by individual firms vary considerably, purchase orders do contain several very important elements that you should understand. The first relates to the quantity listed in the order. Under the terms of the UCC, which governs the sale of tangible goods, a precise statement of the quantity of goods involved in a contract is one of the necessary conditions for a contract's validity. An additional *core* element is, as you would expect, the specification or identification of the desired product. Information contained on the purchase order will be used throughout the purchasing experience. Errors made in purchase-order specifications or descriptions may be difficult or impossible to change later on in the project. For that reason, precisely identifying products is necessary, even to the extent of listing catalog pages or photograph numbers, or for custom-made products, listing the exact style or color number used or suggested by a vendor.

TERMS AND CONDITIONS OF SALE OUTLINE

As you read the terms and conditions of your chosen vendor/company, consider its provisions. Describe in your own words what each section seeks to do.

After you have completed this form, explain to friends what each section provides, and answer any questions they may have about how it might affect them if they were your clients.

Introduction to Terms and Conditions Forms
Purchaser/Orderer/Buyer: Designer or client, depending on agreement between the two
Company/Vendor/Seller: Entity selling merchandise

Limitation of Liability
> In what ways has your chosen company defined the kind of relationship it is willing to have with those seeking its products?

No Alternative Terms
> How does this phrase appear to affect purchasers?
> What importance does this place on purchase documentation?

No Cancellation Policy
> Do you see the importance of obtaining your client's sign-off on your final design concept?

Quotes, Prices, and Payments Policies
> How long does your chosen company honor quotes?

Sales Order, Acceptance, Payment, and Deposits
> When are payments due with respect to orders?

Incomplete Sales Orders and Production Scheduling
> What constitues an incomplete order?

Change-Order Specifications
> Does your chosen company permit change orders? If so, under what conditions?

Abandonment and Collection
> What do these terms mean with respect to purchasing products?

Shipping and Delivery
> Who is responsible for these activities?

Storage Fees
> Do you see how this provision can add to product costs and the importance of delivery scheduling during the contract administration phase?

Return Policy
> Under what conditions, if any, will your chosen company accept returns?

Claims
> Does your chosen company permit arbitration of disputes?
> What other claims provisions are there?

PURCHASE ORDER FORM

Order No. _____

Date _____

COMPANY NAME
Address
Phone No.
Fax No.

Thank you for your order. Please be advised we will also require $ _____ or _____ % of balance due before we may begin processing this order. All **COMPANY** terms and conditions of sale apply to this purchase order. After this order is acknowledged, **NO CANCELLATIONS WILL BE ACCEPTED. Purchaser remains liable for full purchase price. All delivery dates are approximate and subject to change without notice.**

Item Description		Unit Price	#	Other Costs	Extended Total
	SKU/Id. No.				
Item Description		Unit Price	#	Other Costs	Extended Total
	SKU/Id. No.				
Item Description		Unit Price	#	Other Costs	Extended Total
	SKU/Id. No.				
Item Description		Unit Price	#	Other Costs	Extended Total
	SKU/Id. No.				
Item Description		Unit Price	#	Other Costs	Extended Total
	SKU/Id. No.				
Item Description		Unit Price	#	Other Costs	Extended Total
	SKU/Id. No.				
Item Description		Unit Price	#	Other Costs	Extended Total
	SKU/Id. No.				
Item Description		Unit Price	#	Other Costs	Extended Total
	SKU/Id. No.				

Ship to _____

_____

_____

_____

Bill to _____

_____

_____

_____

_____

Subtotal _____

Tax

(____%) _____

Shipping/
Handling _____

Insurance _____

Other _____

Payment Information

Name on Card _____

Credit Card No. _____ Type _____

3-digit _____ Exp. Date _____

Check No. _____ Acct. No. _____ Bank _____

Total

Deposit _____

Amount Due _____

Delivery Date _____

After a purchase order is submitted, vendors usually send what is known as an **acknowledgment** on a separately generated form. That document confirms the item that a vendor understands has been ordered by a purchaser. Errors can be corrected at this stage—for example, when acknowledgment terms do not match the terms of the original purchase order. Such errors may be corrected by contacting vendor representatives within the specified time period in the acknowledgment. A designer needs to make sure that the client signs the confirmation (assuming its terms are correct) so that the order can be processed by the vendor company and so that the contract is legally enforceable.

Once orders are processed, vendors generate another document—an invoice or bill—requesting payment of the amounts due. An invoice usually accompanies delivered merchandise and requests payment within a specified period of time. Following receipt of invoices from vendors, designers send clients separate invoices requesting payment for the goods received.

PRODUCT RESEARCH AND EVALUATION WORKSHEET

Designers come in contact with a great many products during the course of completing a project. The selection of any product will have an impact on a project overall, particularly on a budget, since prices for goods will affect a project's financial resources once a product is purchased; it will also determine the range of products available for use in a project. This means that a designer must choose products that can best satisfy project goals and, at the same time, adhere to project budget and schedule constraints. That *optimization*, or ongoing review of design options (Coleman 2002), is the purpose of documents such as the Product Research and Evaluation Worksheet (Form 12.4). Using this form will enable you to note the characteristics of a product and then assess the impact of its selection on a project's budget and schedule.

REFERENCES

Alderman, Robert L. 1997. *How to Prosper As an Interior Designer*. New York: John Wiley & Sons.

PRODUCT RESEARCH AND EVALUATION WORKSHEET

Client _____ **Job No./I.D.** _____

Project Address or Reference _____

Type/Purpose/Function of Project Item _____

_____

_____

Product Source Alternatives

Product _____ Selected | **NO** | **YES**

Brand/Maker of Product: _____ Style/SKU No. _____

Evaluation   Functions   Budget

Pro	Con	Est. Price	Budgeted	Variance

Contact _____ Phone No. _____
Address _____ Fax _____

Product _____ Selected | **NO** | **YES**

Brand/Maker of Product: _____ Style/SKU No. _____

Evaluation   Functions   Budget

Pro	Con	Est. Price	Budgeted	Variance

Contact _____ Phone No. _____
Address _____ Fax _____

Product _____ Selected | **NO** | **YES**

Brand/Maker of Product: _____ Style/SKU No. _____

Evaluation   Functions   Budget

Pro	Con	Est. Price	Budgeted	Variance

Contact _____ Phone No. _____
Address _____ Fax _____

Product _____ Selected | **NO** | **YES**

Brand/Maker of Product: _____ Style/SKU No. _____

Evaluation   Functions   Budget

Pro	Con	Est. Price	Budgeted	Variance

Contact _____ Phone No. _____
Address _____ Fax _____

Coleman, Cindy, ed. 2002. *Interior Design: Handbook of Professional Practice*. New York: McGraw-Hill. (See particularly chart on pp. 132–33, 136, and 762.)

Knackstedt, Mary V. 2002. *The Interior Design Business Handbook*. 3rd ed. New York: John Wiley & Sons.

Meyer, Alfred W. 1993. *Sales and Leases of Goods*. St. Louis: West Group Publishing.

Sampson, Carol A. 2001. *Estimating for Interior Designers*. New York: Watson-Guptill.

Siegel, Harry and Alan Siegel. 1982. *A Guide to Business Principles and Practices for Interior Designers*. New rev. ed. New York: Watson-Guptill.

Turner, William. 1981. *How to Work with an Interior Designer*. New York: Watson-Guptill. (Although dated, this book explains to the nonprofessional consumer how interior designers work as well as aspects of the designer/client relationship. In particular, see pp. 130–32 for a discussion of costs and cost concessions given by vendors to designers. The photographs form a unique visual resource of residential and contract interiors completed in the 1970s and early 1980s.)

Woodhead, Lindy. 2003. *War Paint: Madame Helena Rubinstein & Miss Elizabeth Arden, Their Lives, Their Times, Their Rivalry*. New York: John Wiley & Sons. (This text describes the extensive social network of these two pioneers of the modern beauty industry, including Miss Arden's affiliation with early interior design practitioner Elsie de Wolfe; in particular, see pages 67–68 for a "behind-the-scenes" description of de Wolfe's work on the Colony Club project.)

STRATEGIES-IN-ACTION PROJECTS

STRATEGIC PLANNING PROJECT

As you have progressed through this series of plans for your ideal interior design business, you have undoubtedly thought a great deal about what must be done to make that business a success. As an interior design student, you have learned the importance of resources that enable you to carry out your design intent for a project. Considering these two factors, this segment of your strategic planning project asks you to identify five vendors or manufacturers whom you think would be appropriate resources for your planned business. These vendor resources may sell furniture, fixtures, equipment, and textile products; in short, they may include any vendor or maker whose products you would prefer to select for the interior design projects on which your business will focus. After identifying these five resources—noting their names, the showrooms where their products are displayed, and other venues where the merchandise is sold—present a brief history of each vendor company, including the products for which it is best known. Finally, explain in detail why these vendors and the products they provide are appropriate resources for your business.

RESIDENTIAL INTERIOR DESIGN PROJECT SIMULATION

The Abernathy project has been a challenge for Lee. After you read the latest installment of her diary, respond to concerns she has raised.

Lee's Diary

Another day in project paradise! The items for the children's spaces have been arriving almost daily. The store has a separate warehouse where I can keep them until installation. If we ever get that far! Here's the scoop on Mrs. Abernathy's latest tirade. First, she wants to see me today, ASAP, on the double, so I schedule her for 11:00 A.M. When she gets here, I see that she's clutching an old interior design magazine. I mean, the magazine is at least twenty years old. So, here goes: "Lee, you have got to cancel that order we placed last week for the upholstery fabric on the big sofa that's going to go in the kid's space on the wall opposite the tree house. I want the sofa, but I want it covered in this."

With that, she opens the magazine and shows me an advertisement for a famous fabric company's Spring 1982 collection, featuring a beautiful green-and-white glazed toile print depicting—get this—children playing in a tree house! It was stunning and visually appropriate for the space, and even treated, according to the ad, to resist stains. So it might function well, too, although I told Mrs. Abernathy that anything with a white background around children won't stay white for very long. I also asked her if she knew what she was asking me to do: cancelling a fabric order placed five days ago with one company after sending a check for pro forma payment (the entire amount due up front), then coming up with a fabric another company probably hasn't had in production for decades, then changing the upholstery order on a sofa made by a third company. And hoping it all can happen on time so that the sofa can be installed with the rest of the project!

"Call the company right now, and see what they can do to get the green and white toile; I'll wait."

So, with that, I first went to the company's Web site and perused its online catalog. Although I didn't see exactly that same print, I did notice several others that likely went through the same production process as the fabric Mrs. A. had in mind. I called the company's main showroom in New York and, after identifying myself, asked the representative there about the fabric.

"Frolic," the representative said.

"I beg your pardon," I said.

"The print's name is Frolic, and it came in three colorways: green, as you saw, blue, and red. Let me see if it's still in production."

"It's called 'Frolic,' and he's checking," I told Mrs. Abernathy. "Oh, really! No kidding, I'll tell my client."

After I hung up, I told Mrs. Abernathy what the representative had told me. Yes, the chintz was still in production, but it was available in their production facility in France. And the company requires payment up front in full, with delivery promised in 12 to 15 weeks, which would barely be enough time to get it to the sofa maker for the upholstery workroom to meet our scheduled installation. Then followed the three words I have come to dread.

"Make it happen," Mrs. Abernathy said. "Oh, but see if I can get my money back on the other fabric I ordered a week ago, first." I didn't even have a clue about where to begin to tell Mrs. Abernathy what this change meant. Maybe you can help me explain it to her. Help!

With this most recent installment comes a host of new problems for Lee to contend with. Consider the issues raised in the following questions. How can Lee best advise her client of the implications of the changes she has requested.

Questions

1. What are some issues Lee might raise with regard to cancelling the original order for fabric she placed on Mrs. Abernathy's behalf?
2. Considering the tight schedule for the project and the length of time estimated for delivery of the new fabric, what issues might Lee raise to Mrs. Abernathy about the advisability of making this change?
3. If Mrs. Abernathy still insists on using the substitute fabric, do you think that Lee should document in a letter to Mrs. Abernathy her concerns about the possible consequences of waiting for the new fabric on the project schedule?

4. Should Lee obtain her client's signed consent to the changes in fabric and schedule?

Try to draft a consent letter, using the following format:

1. State what the client has requested the designer to do.
2. State the possible effects of such a change on the project, both in terms of increases in the project budget and possible delays in project completion.
3. State several reasons why those effects are likely to occur.
4. Conclude by noting that in signing and dating the letter, the client agrees to the changes and understands their effects on the project's budget and schedule, including the projected date of completion.

Complete Form 12.3, a purchase order, using the following information:

1. The company will require payment in full of the net, or wholesale, product price, including taxes (if any) plus shipping and handling charges.
2. "Frolic, green" is referred to by the manufacturer as 05-1982-123-G.
3. The sofa in question has the following dimensions:
Width: 106 inches
Depth: 41 inches
Height: 35 inches
   You may use your estimating skills to calculate the approximate yardage of fabric needed to cover the sofa, assuming it will have no skirt or need excess fabric; or you may use the following Customers' Own Material (COM) requirement provided by the company: 20 yards.
4. The setup fee for producing the fabric is 10 percent of the fabric's net cost before shipping, handling, or taxes are figured.
5. The fabric's net, or wholesale, cost is $55 a yard, and the suggested retail cost is $110.
6. There is no sales tax from the manufacturer to Lee, since it is an out-of-state purchase; however, Lee will have to charge Texas sales tax when billing Mrs. Abernathy for the final amount. The tax rate is 8.25 percent in their location.
7. Shipping and handling as well as insurance total $325.
8. Lee must apply company pricing policies and charge Mrs. Abernathy the suggested retail cost of the fabric.

After completing the company purchase order form, assist Lee in drafting an invoice, or bill, that will indicate the entire amount of payment she should seek from Mrs. Abernathy. Use Form 12.5, sample invoice number 5312 from Imagination Unlimited, to do so.

CONTRACT INTERIOR DESIGN CASE STUDY: THE CASE OF TOO BAD AND TO BUY

Interior designers historically have acted on behalf of their clients when working with vendors. In a traditional scenario, designers of both residential and commercial interiors specify products for use, place orders directly with vendors for their selected items, and then charge clients using the methods described in this chapter. Whereas this approach is still in use, it can and does create problems for designers. This case study explores how one firm assesses these problems and concludes with your proposal for drafting the new firm's purchasing policy to address these issues.

INTERIORA is the name chosen by three interior design entrepreneurs for the new business they propose to open together. All three had worked independently for several years after receiving their degrees, and they met at a local chapter meeting of a professional organization to which they belonged. Jonathan Kelley, Samantha Bruce, and Renee Fields had each sought to join forces with other, like-minded designers to form a practice in the highly competitive commercial interior design market in Houston, Texas. The competition was especially problematic for individual nonresidential designers, especially those whose preferred market niche was working with owners of small and midsized businesses on office and retail projects. Their varied experiences working on similar projects and their shared interest in bringing *green* or *sustainability* concepts to the attention of local small businesses seemed to make the trio an ideal match. Sustainability is a concept of importance among members of the design/build community that stresses "meet[ing] today's needs without compromising the ability of future generations to meet their own need" (Coleman 2002). Sustainability is achieved by using products made up of environmentally responsible materials and reducing the amount of unnecessary waste generated during the course of a project, among other activities. After a series of meetings to discuss their proposed business, the three designers found they shared the same outlook on how their nascent business should operate—except for one thing.

INVOICE NO. 5312

IMAGINATION UNLIMITED   Date
123 Texas Drive
Austin, Texas 78731

Description	Price	Quantity	Extended

Subtotal _____

Tax _____

TOTAL DUE _____

"But that's what designers 'do,'" Jonathan told the group. "Designers have always been responsible for purchasing from vendors."

"I agree that's what a designer did 'do' previously," said Samantha, "but the times are-a changing, and how we work with clients needs to reflect it. We've agreed that we're going to emphasize charging an hourly rate for our services and not charge based on the cost of the merchandise we specify anyway."

"True," said Renee, "under our suggested flat-rate hourly billing plan, our clients will have no economic incentive to buy on their own, since we add no profit to the product costs we pay, only taxes and shipping costs, and even pass on whatever discount we are able to negotiate with the vendor. But Jon does have a point. Our clients are going to be small business owners—like us—with no time and interest in handling the project purchases, which they're going to think we should be doing anyway."

"They expect a turnkey operation from us. That means not having to deal with any third parties at all. They hire us to work with the sellers directly," said Jon.

"OK," said Samantha, "let's think this through. First, our clients probably don't have the time or interest to look on their own for items we specify. I give you that; but they're going to be businesspeople themselves, and they'll have the means and the incentive to sue us if we act for them and buy directly from vendors, then resell, and something goes wrong. We do the specs, then we hand them off to work with vendors. They sign their own contracts and orders with sources and leave us out of the process except for having us check merchandise for compliance with our specifications. That's my idea for this."

"Well, Sam, I hate to say it, but liability is a fact of life now, whether we or the clients buy the products. It's a question of money, sure," said Jon, "but what if they pay only for an initial design consultation, then tell us they'll find the items and try to do the project themselves since we weren't going to do the buy-side of it anyway. We get no project—and no fees—or we get the project and the headache of dealing with them when they don't want to buy from our sources, but from whoever the heck they want to. If we buy from vendors ourselves, we keep control."

"Let's think about something," said Renee. "The commitment we set out in our mission statement says we will work to instill sustainable concepts whenever and however we are able. Vendors are a big part of that. I mean, all of us know that it's one thing to specify sustainable products; but the vendors— the product makers—actually make sustainability happen. So we have a disjoint here, as I see it: We understandably don't want to deal with liability issues, the legal reality of being sued by clients when vendors mess up. You're right about that, Sam. But Jon has a point, too, in that we face other kinds of

constraints: We lose control of the decision-making process when we opt out of working directly with vendors, letting clients deal with them directly by submitting orders and payments to the vendor, even if we write the spec. When it comes right down to it, we can only tell a client what to do then. No matter how we define our relationship with clients in our letters of agreement, noting that we won't be responsible for problems arising from products or vendors we didn't specify, the reality is that if the client pays, it's the clients, not us, who call the shots with the vendors and choose the products they want—not necessarily the choices we think, or hope, or even tell them they should make. Even if sustainable products cost no more than others and are just as easy to get in some cases, if something sways a client to make a decision contrary to what we suggest, there's really nothing we can do about it. We'll have to live with, or deal with, the consequences for the project.

"Well, put that way," said Sam, "it may be just too bad for us and our business if we're going to buy directly from vendors on behalf of clients and some problem comes up. Or it may be too bad for sustainability, or anything else for that matter, if clients are left to buy merchandise on their own."

This case study has posed a difficult policy decision for the fledgling firm to consider, one that's not easy to resolve. The group has turned to you to draft a policy for how the firm should deal with vendors. Which of the arguments presented, combined with the knowledge you have gained from this chapter—especially the section on problem-solving strategies—do you find most persuasive? In a short paragraph addressed to the group, suggest a specific course of action for the new firm to follow: Either the designers should contract directly with vendors, or their clients should do so, using specifications and other documents that designers provide. State why you think your policy would provide the preferred course of action for the firm.

CHAPTER THIRTEEN

WORKING WITH SERVICE PROVIDERS

Knowledge comes, but wisdom lingers.

ALFRED, LORD TENNYSON

WHY THIS CHAPTER IS IMPORTANT TO YOU

As covered in chapter 12, designers require the assistance of other professionals, such as vendors, to complete their projects. Designers also need to rely on those who provide construction and design-related services, such as carpentry or surface finishes. This chapter introduces you to the ways in which designers interact with service providers. This knowledge is important since it enables you to understand basic concepts, documents, and issues involved in the design process. This aspect of an interior designer's work is challenging because a project's completion and its success depends largely on activities outside a designer's control. That is, interior designers may specify what service providers need to accomplish, but in many situations they may be unable to directly control their work. This overview offers information necessary to enable you to form your own strategy for making wise decisions when working with service providers.

PROFESSIONAL PRACTICES PORTFOLIO

After completing this chapter, you should be able to answer the following questions. Include your responses in a professional practices portfolio that you keep as a handbook for later use.

1. Who is a *general contractor*, and what role does he or she play in completing work specified by an interior designer?

2. Who is a *subcontractor*, and what is his or her relationship to the general contractor?

3. If you were speaking to a client who did not understand the contracting-for-services process, explain how the process typically operates.

4. Why might an interior designer decline responsibility for hiring and supervising the activities of *service providers*, such as general contractors and subcontractors?

5. Even if a designer declines to work directly with service providers, explain how and why designers should be careful when recommending their services to clients?

6. What is *competitive bidding*, and how is it conducted. Why might a client be interested in this method of retaining service providers?

7. What documents are associated with the competitive-bidding process, and what role do designers play in preparing them?

8. Distinguish an *addendum* from a *change order*. Who or what is responsible for each document, and when is the use of each of them indicated?

9. When, in the course of a project, are the activities of service providers typically called upon?

10. What ways can interior designers prevent or limit potential problems that may occur when working with service providers?

11. What does it mean for a service provider to be *bonded* and *insured*, and why should a designer be interested in a service provider's characteristics?

12. What is a *chain of command* as it relates to project management and relationships with service providers? Why might a designer be interested in establishing a communication process involving workers and clients?

INTRODUCTION TO
WORKING WITH SERVICE PROVIDERS

Designers enhance the function and appearance of interior environments by specifying the physical attributes that will characterize a space once it is completed. In addition to a designer's work, the labor of others is usually necessary to bring about any modifications required by a designer.

Who are these important workers who provide the services necessary for realizing a designer's specifications? How do these service providers interact with both a project's interior designer and client? This chapter seeks to provide you with an understanding of concepts, terms, and issues relevant for the relationship among clients, designers, and service providers, so that you may better know how to manage its intricacies and avoid common problems that occur.

OBJECTIVES TO CONSIDER

Working with service resources involves perhaps more details than other interior design processes and procedures with which you are already familiar. In understanding the following objectives, you will gain an appreciation for the terms and concepts you will use in this process, along with the tasks that you, as an interior designer, will face as well.

1. Classifying and locating service providers
2. Working with service providers
3. Avoiding problems when working with service providers

CLASSIFYING AND LOCATING SERVICE PROVIDERS

Who are the service providers who help to carry out an interior designer's plans? Among these professionals are general contractors, craftspeople, and independent contractors.

GENERAL CONTRACTORS

Perhaps the most common example of a service provider with whom interior designers frequently work is the **general contractor**. A GC, as general contractors are sometimes known, may be an individual operator or an entity employing a large number of people. General contractors traditionally perform the following tasks:

◆ They enter into contracts with design professionals, home owners, building owners, and others for the purpose of erecting a physical structure or modifying an existing one according to contractually defined specifications and as otherwise required by law.

◆ They retain the labor of other service providers with specialized skills and knowledge of some aspect of the construction process. Those hired by general contractors are usually referred to as *subcontractors* and are responsible for completing tasks such as structural framing; installing plumbing apparatuses; wiring electrical systems; installing wiring or heating, ventilation, or air-conditioning (HVAC); applying architectural finishes; and installing surface treatments such as wallpaper, tile, and carpet. It is a general contractor's responsibility to handle questions and problems relating to service providers.

General contractors frequently organize as a form of corporation, such as a limited liability company (LLC). This form of operation is selected (see chapter 4) in order to protect the personal assets, or property, of its founders from financial claims arising from legal and other actions. In many jurisdictions, general contractors are required by law to have a license permitting them to engage in construction work. Sometimes general contractors will also engage the services of specialized secondary contractors for work that requires particular training or equipment to perform. Certain types of masonry or brick work as well as interior cabinet making and installation are carried out by secondary contractors.

CRAFTSPEOPLE

Related to specialized secondary subcontractors are other workers, referred to as *artisans* or *craftspeople*, who provide unique project services. If you recall from the Residential Interior Design Project Simulation for chapter 8, the ornately carved cabinets found in the fictional gift-wrapping room of the Chicago showcase home that so captured Mrs. Abernathy's attention would in real life likely have been created and installed by woodworking artisans. Muralists, metalworkers, glass workers, and others who specialize in producing one-of-a-kind design features are among this group of service providers.

INDEPENDENT CONTRACTORS

General contractors, subcontractors, artisans, as well as interior designers, may be classified as independent contractors. As you recall, an independent contractor is a worker who is classified according to certain

Internal Revenue Service (IRS) requirements. Unlike employees, whose work process is controlled by others, independent contractors control the way in which they perform the work they are retained to complete. Whatever entity, be it a person or company, that pays the independent contractor controls only the final result of those labors. This is important as you learn more about ways to troubleshoot possible problems that may arise in this area.

HOW TO LOCATE SERVICE PROVIDERS

Clients frequently ask interior designers to suggest the service provider best able to carry out an entire job or some aspect of it. Designers themselves in some instances may not only specify a particular outcome, but also specify—as an express condition of their participation in the project—the service provider who will carry out the work. Knowing service providers and the quality of work they produce is an important part of a designers' function. How might designers go about locating service providers? Among the ways of finding contractors and other workers, designers first rely on their own experience and research. In most communities, the work of residential contractors and craftspeople is on display and easily ascertained in a variety of ways: signs in the yards of homes being built or renovated; charity tours of private homes where the contributions of the many workers involved are acknowledged; advertisements in local shelter publications; and even word of mouth. The identities of nonresidential contractors are also easily available. Completed buildings usually acknowledge on their cornerstones service providers such as general contractors, as do the large signs bearing the name of the contracting company seen at most construction sites. Building owners and managers frequently maintain lists of service providers who have worked on a structure's original construction and interior finishing or on subsequent renovations.

RESEARCH AND EVALUATION

After locating individuals and companies that offer interior design–related construction services in their community, designers usually conduct further research to find providers whose work is most applicable to a project. For example, a residential designer may require the assistance of a service provider capable of precisely installing European-made kitchen cabinets, whereas a designer specializing in hospitality and restaurant work will likely seek a service provider capable of installing large industrial appliances. In addition, designers usually consider those service providers whose working styles and abilities communication are best suited to the designer's. On the basis of this ongoing research and evaluation, interior designers frequently develop a list of service providers available in their community whose work they deem appropriate and acceptable for use. Although a designer's identification of potential service providers is extremely important, it should not occur apart from other considerations, however. Input from clients about the characteristics they desire in these project participants also plays a factor in the outright selection of a service provider or in deciding whether to extend an invitation to bid a project, a process discussed in this chapter. Together, designers and clients might agree that important criteria include a service provider's overall reputation in the community; ability to complete jobs in a timely manner without excessive cost overruns; and whether the service provider requires the assistance of unionized workers and has the skills necessary to work within those constraints.

The importance of this ongoing research and dialogue when evaluating the qualifications and performance of service providers cannot be overemphasized. A designer's responsibility to a client as a design professional is to make the best recommendation possible. That involves learning as much as is reasonably possible from available sources about a service provider's previously completed work. Obviously, a designer cannot predict exactly how a service provider might or might not carry out some future project. It is not clear whether a designer would incur legal liability as a result of difficulties arising from the actions of a service provider that he or she recommends. That would depend on the specific circumstances and actions as well as the relevant laws in effect. However, if designers failed to do research about the competence of a service provider they have recommended and if, consequently, they lacked knowledge about the nature and quality of a service provider's work, they would come under scrutiny by legal decision makers as part of a determination.

REFERRALS, RECOMMENDATIONS, AND BIDS

Many interior designers develop close working and personal relationships with service providers, especially in the area of residential interior design.

Within the design and service community, obtaining a steady amount of new business is critical to the long-term success of both designers and contractors. The ability to refer rewarding and profitable business to each other is a factor in fostering the development of their respective businesses and relationship. Referrals and recommendations may be of some importance in nonresidential interior design work as well. However, because of the special process of decision making and awarding projects in this area, they have less influence. In contract design work, decision making usually rests with a group of people—a committee, for example, whose members may have never heard of a particular service provider and may be less impressed by oral recommendations. Projects in this area are also awarded on the basis of written bids, a process discussed in greater detail later in this chapter. Usually bid amounts submitted by many different general contractors are received and reviewed by decision makers who give preference to a particular contractor based on the bid, not the project designer's past relationship with a particular contractor. Armed with this general understanding of the factors underlying the designer/service provider/client relationship, you are now ready to explore the dynamics of the working relationship among these principals in a design project.

WORKING WITH SERVICE PROVIDERS

Working with service providers can become quite complicated, since many different people participating in complex relationships are involved. A straightforward method of learning to work with service providers is simply to consider the components of the process in the sequence in which they occur. Obviously, the service of providers has to be obtained before they can work on projects. Thus, the first objective for designers to master is to learn how general contractors and subcontractors are retained. Once selected, these service providers must work together or work directly with clients or the designers retaining them. With that in mind, interior designers need to be aware of the ways in which service providers traditionally organize their activities in carrying out tasks. Many of these workers are usually classified as independent contractors, who have sole control over the way in which they work. Those who hire independent contractors may exercise some control over their completed work through payment for these services. Thus, designers also need to be aware of how service providers are paid for their services during the course of performing their work.

During the design development phase, designers typically complete project specifications and budgets. Once that phase is completed and a designer receives final client approval, a project enters the contract documents phase. It is during the contract document and contract administration phase that designers, clients, and service providers interact. Essentially, the *creative* part of the project, where its aesthetic and functional characteristics are determined, is complete once the contract administration phase begins. The goal from then on is to tangibly realize the project concept. As you learned in chapter 12, purchasing and installation of products are necessary when completing a project. The activities of service providers responsible for carrying out a designer's construction and design-related specifications are another important part of that process.

During the contract document and administration stages, designers, vendors, and service providers become actively involved in a project and work together. Of course, the actual retention of service providers may be somewhat fluid, depending on the circumstances of a project and the service provider marketplace. Particularly popular service providers, for example, or those few who are available in a particular area, or artisans who require long lead times between commissions may need to be retained months in advance. Waiting until the later phases of a project to hire these workers may be impractical for its timely completion. In such cases, service providers may have to be reserved as early as the completion of a project's programming stage.

HOW TO RETAIN SERVICE PROVIDERS

As the contract documents phase evolves, interior designers and clients must decide on how to retain service providers for work on a project. In some instances—small residential interior design projects, for example—a client may simply go with a provider recommended by a designer. In that case, designers prepare written specifications for a service provider to follow, but may not participate in hiring the service provider even if he or she is highly recommended. It may be a client who enters into a contract with a service provider and therefore agrees to pay that service provider directly. Designers then usually contract with their clients to serve as consultants in matters related to the supervision of labor used on the project. In some states, interior designers are legally permitted to do no more than that unless they are also licensed to work as general contractors. Notwithstanding these laws, ask yourself whether designers should even be directly involved in hiring service providers. Why, for example, might many designers refuse to perform this task on behalf of their clients? The following troubleshooting section explores a designer's legal liability for becoming directly involved in this aspect of his or her work.

During the contract administration phase, designers may be responsible for overseeing the completion and quality of specified construction-related work. While nothing usually prevents a designer from doing a walk-through during and after construction, informing clients about what he or she observed, and working with clients to request necessary changes, a designer's ability to hire project workers as well as plan and supervise the actual construction process may be controlled by various laws. These laws passed by individual states dictate who may directly engage in construction-related activities and specify the credentials required. In some states, interior designers may directly hire project workers and supervise their activities, while in others states, designers have legal constraints imposed on their ability to do so. States such as California and Florida, for example, require a general contractor's license to plan and supervise construction projects and other workers. Because states impose serious penalties on those who engage without appropriate licensure in activities defined as supervisory, it is critical for interior designers to understand how the laws in their chosen locations affect them in this context.

When determining the scope of services for a project, designers consider its degree of complexity and negotiate their role in managing its completion accordingly. Among the options a designer has in this regard is the choice of performing only design focused activities such as programming, design development, and product selection. With this approach, a designer and client agree a designer will not assume full responsibility for contract administration activities, or may take on minimal ones, perhaps only preparing documents that will be made available to service providers. On the other hand, the agreement may call for a designer to continue being involved in a project through the contract administration phase. Even a designer who does not directly hire service providers may assist clients in a variety of other ways. In the next section, "The Competitive Bidding Process," you will learn how interior designers, particularly those concentrating on commercial projects, may expand their scope of service to include fairly complex managerial tasks as well as design-related ones.

THE COMPETITIVE-BIDDING PROCESS

On very large residential and contract design projects, a highly structured process is frequently used to secure services. This process is sometimes informally referred to as the *bid*, or *bidding process*, or what is formally known as the **competitive-bidding process**. This process allows a project's client to assess the ability of various service providers to perform project tasks within a project's financial budget and time frame. Bidding is usually a formal procedure, which may be administered by a project's interior designer or design team, depending on the contractual relationship between a designer and client. Before continuing to describe this process, it is important to clarify language frequently misused with regard to bids and estimates.

The purpose of the bidding process is to solicit a number of offers obligating service providers to complete project tasks under certain conditions. Recall that an *offer* is a formal element of a contract. Once a client accepts a bid and payment has passed between the parties, both a client and service provider may be found by a court to have entered into a valid contractual relationship. Tasks sent out for receipt of bid may be large functions (such as working as the project's general contractor) or relatively small ones. The size of the job *bid out* is not the primary concern.

Bids state a dollar amount that a service provider will charge to complete a task. These bids are analogous to contract offers, among which project decision makers ultimately choose one. Once accepted by a client, the amount and conditions stated in the bid submitted by a successful service provider are binding on both parties. Later in the project, service providers and clients cannot by themselves change the terms of an accepted bid unless both parties agree on new terms, and the contract between the parties is formally amended to reflect the change. The stated bid amount, as proffered by a general contractor in response to a formal request, is extremely important. If a project's budget is to satisfy completion costs, service providers must perform their work at the cost stated in the bid. As a result, project clients may require a form of insurance, called a **bid bond**. In brief, this is a form of protection for a designer's client and is issued by third parties, usually a specialized company or banking institution known as a **surety**. A bid bond is the surety's guarantee that bid work will be completed at the price stated. Designers whose practices make use of the bid process should be aware whether instruments such as bid bonds are commonly used in their specialty.

Bids and Estimates

Bids and estimates are frequently confused. Usually, **estimates** are used for negotiating purposes between the parties before reaching a final price that is incorporated into a contract for services. The forms shown and discussed in this chapter include Form 13.1, a model to use when requesting estimates from prospective service providers, as well as Form 13.2, an estimates log in which to note their receipt. Form 13.3, a contractor log, is designed to record information from service providers retained for a project. Another aspect of the contract document phase involves responsibility for procuring the permits necessary for work to begin. Cities, counties, and other governmental bodies interact with the design-build project during this phase of the process.

Steps in the Bidding Process

Returning to the formalities of the competitive bidding process, it is important to understand the procedure and the terms used to describe it. The competitive bidding process begins with the accumulation by a client or design team of contract and interrelated documents. Although this chapter focuses on service providers, the same process of competitive bidding can be used by vendors of project merchandise as well.

1. *Invitation to Bid*
   Publication of an invitation for competing construction service providers to submit bids for a project is the first step in the competitive bidding process. Usually, a statement of general conditions is also made available, in which a client provides information such as his or her name and the legal rights and responsibilities of the parties once a contract is awarded, or *let*, to any particular service provider. Standard forms stating general conditions are usually available from such organizations as the AIA, the ASID, and the IIDA. Invitations to bid specify the qualifications required for consideration as a service provider and, among other elements, provide a deadline for receipt of the bids submitted.
2. *Instruction to Bidders*
   To ensure uniformity and fairness in the bid process, an instruction to bidders provides information about the form in which bids should be received.

FORM 13.1. ESTIMATE REQUEST

ESTIMATE REQUEST

Name of Designer or Firm   Date _____

Address   Return to _____
City, State, Zip Code   _____
Phone No.   _____
Fax No.   _____

To   _____
            _____
            _____
Attention _____

Project Address or Reference _____
_____

This is a request for an estimate of your services to complete the referenced project.
This information will be used ONLY as an estimate for the cost of the services requested.
You may be asked to submit a formal bid at a later date, the terms of which will be incorporated into a
contract for your services.
Please complete, date, and sign this estimate and return to the above contact by _____.
              Thank you for your interest and consideration in this matter.

Description of Services   Estimated Costs

Subtotal _____
Applicable Sales Tax _____
Shipping/Handling _____
Estimate Total _____
Deposit Required _____

Date of Estimate   _____

Contractor Signature _____

PROJECT ESTIMATES LOG

Client _____ Job Number/I.D. _____

Project Address or Reference _____
_____
_____
_____
_____
_____
_____
_____

Client Contact Information _____

Product/Service Requested	**Vendor/Contractor Information**
Description	
	Name _____
	Address _____
	_____
	_____
	Phone No. _____
	Fax No. _____
	Attention _____
	_____

Subtotal _____	Date Estimate Requested _____
Applicable Sales Tax _____	Date Estimate Received _____
Shipping/Handling _____	Estimated Delivery/Completion Date _____
Estimate Total _____	Notes _____
Deposit Amount _____	
	AWARDED, Date NOT AWARDED

Product/Service Requested	**Vendor/Contractor Information**
Description	
	Name _____
	Address _____
	_____
	_____
	Phone No. _____
	Fax No. _____
	Attention _____
	_____

Subtotal _____	Date Estimate Requested _____
Applicable Sales Tax _____	Date Estimate Received _____
Shipping/Handling _____	Estimated Delivery/Completion Date _____
Estimate Total _____	Notes _____
Deposit Amount _____	
	AWARDED, Date NOT AWARDED

PROJECT CONTRACTOR LOG

Client _____ Job Number/I.D. _____

Project Address or Reference _____

_____

_____

_____

_____

_____

Client Contact Information _____

Vendor _____

Address _____ Phone No. _____

_____ Fax No. _____

Subject	Documents		Costs		Schedule		
	Date	Type/I.D.	Bid	Modified	Begin	Due	Finalized

(continued)

Project Contractor Log (continued)

Vendor _____

Address _____   Phone No. _____

_____   Fax No. _____

Subject	Documents		Costs		Schedule		
	Date	Type/I.D.	Bid	Modified	Begin	Due	Finalized

3. *Tender (or Bid) Form*

The form on which a service provider offers a formal price for completing a project is referred to as the **tender** or *bid form*.

As you might suspect, changes and corrections may be necessary to documents tendered by both a client and service provider prior to awarding a contract. Any change made by a client prior to awarding a project is typically referred to as an **addendum**. Addenda typically modify contract documents, and are necessary when discrepancies, ambiguities, and incorrect information are found in any of the original project solicitation documents. It is usually necessary for each identified bidder to receive notification of these changes. Changes made by a client *after* a project contract has been awarded are referred to as **change orders**.

Change orders have a significant impact on the course of a project. Clients will often direct their request changes orally to a subcontractor, without expressing their concerns to the general contractor. It is important that all changes requested by a client are made in writing and delivered through the designer to the general contractor or directly to the general contractor. Change orders can greatly affect a project's budget and time schedule and thus its completion date.

AVOIDING PROBLEMS WHEN
WORKING WITH SERVICE PROVIDERS

Working with service providers is an integral part of an interior designer's job. Unfortunately, many legal issues can arise during this phase, which are critical for the designer. The following problems typically emerge at this phase of the client/designer/service provider relationship.

◆ *The client does not wish to hire an appropriate service provider, such as a general contractor.*

Some clients refuse to hire general contractors, believing that by not doing so they will keep project costs as low as possible. In these instances, designers have two choices: either accept responsibility for supervising the project themselves or refuse to work on the project at all. Both options are, from a designer's perspective, not particularly desirable. On the one hand, unless a designer and client have agreed that the designer will receive an hourly fee for performing services as a contractor, there is little likelihood that the designer would earn enough to even cover expenses when working as both a designer and general contractor on a project. In these circumstances, the designer's commissions—assuming that fee structure is used—would not generate enough revenue to compensate the designer for the amount of time spent on a project. On the other hand, walking away from a project would also result in the loss of revenue and even possibly negative word-of-mouth generated about the designer. Ultimately, however, a designer may be asking for trouble during the later phases of a project if it becomes overwhelmingly complicated. Project selection is a difficult task for any professional, since the need to generate business revenue is always present; however, choosing to take projects that hold little promise for profit is not good business and, furthermore, may incur legal liability.

◆ *The designer is not qualified to act as a general contractor, either legally or because of lack of experience.*

Many states require individuals who supervise, manage, or otherwise oversee construction activities to hold special state-issued licenses. Failure to obtain proper licensure can result in designers facing legal action brought by their clients, fines, and even imprisonment, as well as professional censure. Before choosing to act as general contractors, designers should know whether and how they may legally do so.

◆ *The designer directly contracts with service providers who default in their obligation in some way.*

Interior designers provide clients with information about service providers, and they may also hire and work directly with them or with others selected by a project's client. They are not, however, a client's guarantors or insurance when a service provider does not perform as contracted or does negligent work. As you recall, *negligence* refers to actions that fail to meet a standard of reasonableness. How may designers formally protect themselves from legal claims of negligence? The contract for an interior designer's services—after being reviewed by a legal authority with expertise in state laws—should include what is referred to as a **disclaimer**. The purpose of these clauses is to note specifically that a designer assumes no responsibility for the actions of any service provider hired to work on the project. In addition, legal authorities can best advise a designer about which types of *errors and omissions* insurance they should carry to protect themselves from possible claims arising from the actions of service providers even when disclaimer language is used.

PROBLEM-SOLVING STRATEGIES

When service providers become involved with your projects, you will have many questions about how to work effectively with them and your clients. Following are some questions you might ask, along with answers culled from the advice of experienced designers: How can I avoid horror stories such as clients making important changes without my input—or, even worse, without my knowledge—or demanding that changes be made "here and now"?

You need to learn all you can about how such matters are handled in your area, by asking either other design practitioners or legal sources. Design and construction literature addressing this issue usually suggests clarifying the chain of communication at the start of the project. When a designer has engaged a service provider directly, all matters should be communicated through the designer and not directly to the service provider. If clients have retained a general contractor on their own, any changes recommended by a client or designer after inspecting a service provider's work should be transmitted through the general contractor in the form of change orders. Implementing a clear and orderly pattern of communication among project participants, even if a client sometimes objects, may prevent these problems from emerging.

- *To what extent could I be found at fault for recommending a service provider, such as a subcontractor, who does not perform a job well?*
  Sources believe the answer depends on who engaged the service provider in the first place. Part of the determination would likely depend on whether a designer hired and paid a service provider or merely suggested one of several providers a client might choose to work with on a project. Designers who directly retain and pay a service provider who proves to be problematic may face legal claims brought by their clients.
- *What are some questions I should ask a legal expert about working with clients and service providers before I begin my interior design practice?*
  There are many relevant questions to ask about this aspect of interior design work. Take note of the following examples:
  - What steps should a designer take when organizing a business to limit exposure to liability in the event a client or service provider brings a legal action against the designer? For example, is it preferable to establish a corporate form of business?

- What role do errors and omissions (E & O) insurance policies play in protecting designers in the event of a negligence claim related to the designer's work? What companies offer such protection?
- What language can designers put in their contracts for design services that might limit the extent of their liability in the event of a legal action? Are contract terms claiming to hold designers accountable?
- How much investigation of service providers is enough? Ask an attorney to explain a designer's duties to clients with regard to making recommendations. What is considered reasonable?
- Are there ways to structure the designer/client relationship as well as design fees that might also limit designers' exposure in the event legal action is brought against them? Why do so many interior designers insist on being paid an hourly rate?

Any specific answers to questions such as these depend on the laws in effect in the location where you wish to practice. Since the factual circumstances of a designer's practice also varies considerably, few hard and fast rules and conclusions are applicable. As a practical matter, you should learn through consultations with lawyers and insurance experts whether and to what extent you can afford to be involved in working directly with clients and service providers. It is important to realize at this stage of your study of professional practices that you can find answers from reliable sources to your questions about working with service providers before major problems develop.

REFERENCES

Alderman, Robert L. 1997. *How to Prosper As an Interior Designer*. New York: John Wiley & Sons.

Allison, John, and Robert Prentice. 2001. *Business Law: Text and Cases in the Legal Environment*. 3rd custom ed. New York: Thompson Learning.

Asner, Michael. 2000. *The Request for Proposal Handbook: A Sourcebook of Guidelines, Best Practices, Examples, Laws, Regulations, and Checklists from Jurisdictions throughout the United States and Canada*. New York: McGraw-Hill.

Bagley, Constance E. and Craig E. Dauchy. 2002. *The Entrepreneur's Guide to Business Law*. 2nd ed. Mason, Ohio: South-Western.

Berger, C. Jaye. 1994. *Interior Design Law and Business Practices.* New York: John Wiley & Sons.

Coleman, Cindy, ed. 2002. *Interior Design: Handbook of Professional Practice.* New York: McGraw-Hill.

Goleman, Daniel. 2002. *Business: The Ultimate Resource.* New York: Perseus.

Holland, J. Kent, ed. 2003. *Construction Law and Risk Management: Case Notes and Articles.* McLean, Virginia: Ardent Publications.

Knackstedt, Mary V. 2002. *The Interior Design Business Handbook.* 3rd ed. New York: John Wiley & Sons.

O'Donnell, Michael. 1991. *Writing Business Plans That Get Results: A Step-by-Step Guide.* New York: McGraw-Hill.

Siegel, Harry, and Alan Siegel. 1982. *A Guide to Business Practices and Principles for Interior Designers.* New rev. ed. New York: Watson-Guptill.

STRATEGIES-IN-ACTION PROJECTS

STRATEGIC PLANNING PROJECT

In this final section of your strategic planning project, you will write an *executive summary* of the project. The executive summary appears at the beginning of your plan and will be the first thing reviewed by business decision makers, although it is usually the final portion of the plan written. The summary first describes the unique, specialized service that your ideal interior design business will offer to the market segment you have identified as being the business's target consumers. Then it describes how those consumers will benefit from using you and your firm's services. Finally, you will describe the skills and talents that you, as chief entrepreneur of the business, offer. And you will explain how your abilities and skills enable you to carry out the designated work of the business.

RESIDENTIAL INTERIOR DESIGN PROJECT SIMULATION

In this section of the strategies-in-action project, you can help Lee explain an interior design project's chain of command to her clients, particularly how changes in the execution of a project must occur through a change order. You will assist Lee in drafting a change order and calculating the effect of yet another suggestion made by her client, Mrs. Abernathy.

Lee's Diary

Well, other than the absolute riot that occurred on the project site, there's really not much to say.

Per our company's policy, the clients, not us, enter into agreements with general contractors to build projects like the Abernathy children's room. The general contractor they hired then contracted with the best subcontractors in town, really! With such a big budget and the amount of detailed work necessary for the project, he had to. One of those "subs" was a decorative painting team known for their ability to paint skies and clouds and—you name it, they can do it. They were supposed to paint the tonal, ombre-like effect on the walls and ceiling of the room, with clouds wafting overhead. According to what I heard, Mrs. Abernathy thought the clouds looked like "lumps of mashed potatoes" on the wall. And that's when the fun began!

It all started when she made an unannounced visit downstairs to see how the project was going. I told her that workers—even if, yes, she's ultimately paying for them—can't really do their best work if they feel they're being watched over. In fact, we have a standing appointment each evening to review the day's work. I told her that was the best way—leave it to the general contractor to handle the daily problems and so on.

So, anyway, she comes into the site while the painting crew is just "roughing out" the clouds—no detailing, no shadowing—and berates them for how clumsy, cheap, and cartoon-like their work looks, then asks if that's the best they can do considering what they're being paid!

OK, so if that's not bad enough, she then proceeds to dip a five-inch brush into (the wrong) paint and starts drawing circles on the wall surface, smudging the still wet "clouds" and other coatings in order to show them the "best" way to paint the cloud effect, the way she learned in a workshop in decorative painting she attended. She ruined their morning's work, insulted the best team of painters in town, yelled at the general contractor for hiring them in the first place—and was then surprised when the painters put down their brushes and walked off the project! Wait, it gets better.

The painter working on the now infamous "potato clouds" gave a ladder a good swift kick in frustration as he left the site. It must have been some kick! The ladder hit the wall nearby, shattering a built-in sconce light and gouging the entire surface of the southeastern wall as both the ladder and what was left of the lamp crashed to the floor.

Questions

1. Before reading further, can you identify the steps Lee took to prevent such a problem from happening?
2. Although the designer in all likelihood did as much as possible to avoid this situation, what actions would you recommend to solve the problem? Answer this question before learning about Lee's response in the following section of her diary:

Here's what I did to resolve at least some of the problems. First, we can't lose a "sub" this late in the project. I called the general contractor who was still pretty upset, but not so upset that he didn't tell me that I needed to control my client. I apologized for the problems and asked if the team was still at the site. He said that they were, so I personally paid for the entire group's lunch, and told the general contractor to give them my apologies and my assurance that it wouldn't happen again. Then, I called Mrs. Abernathy who was on her way to yoga class and asked her to please remember what I had said to her about the project chain of command: Everyone, including me, the designer, and her, the client, needs to go through the project's general contractor to resolve problems or address any concerns—any concerns, including "potato clouds." She said she would do that, adding that the whole incident was a misunderstanding on the part of the painters. She was just trying to offer helpful suggestions, and "since we are all professionals," the painters should have understood. I told her I'd be in touch later with the paperwork we needed to set the problem right. And that's what I face now! I need help sorting all this out.

First, there is the issue about estimating the repairs caused by the morning's activities and their effect on the project budget and schedule. Fortunately, we don't have to replace the wallboard—it just needs a good tape-and-float repair—so I'll need to complete a change order authorization (see Form 13.4) showing what I estimate to be five hours of labor by one of the wall crews. Then, I have to describe the repair on the authorization. Hmm—repair effects of one temper tantrum? No, that won't do. I'll have to think of something. The rate for the one laborer is $13.50 an hour, and the supplies needed are on hand. However, the cost isn't the issue; it's the schedule! This repair will take a few hours to do, but it needs about a day to fully dry, then the wall has to be sanded down, primed, and repainted. Then, I need an electrician to install a new light after the wall is repaired. That will probably take another day or two. So, let's say it takes three days to fully repair those damages, meanwhile, the decorative painters can't work on the wall while it's being fixed, and they have another job already waiting for them once this one is completed, and our *extra day planned in the original schedule was taken up with what happened today.*

So, long story made short and sad, the painters are going to have to come back to the house to finish the damaged wall. That will add a total of a week— seven days—to the schedule. According to the general contractor, they can come back in three weeks. So, we were supposed to be done with the painting May 1. That means they'll be back to work May 21, then take a week to finish, so June 1. I'll need to get Mr. or Mrs. A's signature after I complete the form.

Using Form 13.4, document these changes, noting that the original contract the clients entered into was dated November 20.

CONTRACT INTERIOR DESIGN CASE STUDY: THE CASE OF TOO BAD AND TO BID

This case study continues the discussion that previously engaged the designer entrepreneurs of INTERIORA. The members of INTERIORA are still at odds in their beliefs about policies the new firm should adopt. The disagreement concerns whether the designers should agree to work as their clients' general contractors on projects for which they are hired. In fact, there is some concern about whether even to be involved in helping clients to select general contractors. As Samantha said, "If our clients use their own service people and contract with them directly, we stand less of a chance of getting into legal trouble." These designers will ask you to interpret their concerns in light of your new knowledge about this subject and then to draft a policy statement that you believe will best serve the interests of the group. You recall that the members of the firm wish to focus their practice on nonresidential work, particularly small offices and retail spaces, and desire to advance principles of sustainability in those projects.

"Well, let me say. . . . we all have enough experience to be the general contractor, and if we need any additional license, that's easy enough to get. I repeat, it's what designers have always done," said Jonathan Kelley.

"Didn't we just have this discussion?" asked Samantha Bruce. "We're back to the same issue. If we play active roles, this time in supervising construction, first, we probably can't charge enough to earn a profit for the firm

CHANGE ORDER AUTHORIZATION

Client _____ Job Number/I.D. _____

Project Address or Reference _____

The following changes to the above-referenced project are authorized as of notice date:

Description of Change(s) Authorized

Project Phase	Cost(s)		Scheduling	
	Original	Adjusted	Original	Adjusted

The contract for services, dated _____, is amended as follows to reflect these changes or is otherwise modified as follows with this change order:

_____
_____
_____
_____
_____
_____
_____
_____
_____
_____

This document modifies previous specifications or instructions and notes the approximate effect of the authorized changes on prior project budget and schedule estimates. All changes are approximate and may be further modified by other project requirements. These changes are based on additional information not reflected in original specifications or instructions or are made in accordance with revised plans.

Please sign and date this document to complete the authorization process and return to

_____

Authorized Signature _____

Date _____

because of the incredible amount of time that takes and, more to this point, doing so puts us clearly in line for legal liability."

"But," Jon began, "we have to be involved in the construction process anyway, especially if we intend to incorporate principles of sustainability in our work. First, we have to seek out workers, a general contractor and subcontractors, who are even aware of the issue, much less what is involved in making it a reality. Then we have to educate our clients about its importance, and then bring it all together by providing workers who can and are willing to do the things it takes to work in a sustainable way."

Renee Fields joined in: "Sam, we all know we can't just talk about being green and not be involved in the entire process. Say we specify a particular sustainable feature—so what, if we're not also actively part of the construction process: We know what products to use and how to use them, and we know the importance of planning for the recycling of construction or demolition waste. Without our participation, what's to keep an unknowing or uncaring sub from making use of incompatible products or processes? If we hold ourselves out to be focused on sustainability, then we should provide the services needed as well as the products."

"I hear you. I really do," said Sam. "But my issue is the liability involved. If we act as general contractors, even if we suggest workers for projects, then we're the ones who'll take the heat, if you will, when something goes wrong. My idea: We do the best we can to promote sustainable products and practices, but leave the client to pick whom they want as generals and 'subs.'

"Well, that's just bad service, Sam. Who would hire us, then?" asked Jon.

"I know," said Sam. "It's just 'too bad' for our business if we choose 'to bid' the contracting part of a project and something goes wrong. But if a non-green service provider bids on a job, it may be just 'too bad' for one of the reasons we decided to work together in the first place—to promote sustainability."

This case study has posed a difficult policy decision for the fledgling firm to consider, one with no easy answer. The group has turned to you to draft a policy for the firm to follow when dealing with service providers. Which of the arguments presented in this chapter, combined with what you learned particularly in the section on problem-solving strategies, do you find most persuasive? In a short paragraph addressed to the group, lay out a specific course of action for the new firm to follow: Argue that either designers themselves should contract directly with vendors or that they should request their clients do so and rely on designers to provide specifications and other documents. Then, state why you believe yours to be the preferred course of action for the firm.

PART FIVE

YOU AND YOUR CAREER

Your formal education may end when you graduate from college; however, you will need to have strategies for beginning and advancing in your interior design career. What kinds of activities will you have to engage in as you make the transition from student to professional? You will find out in the final two chapters of this text.

You are undoubtedly excited about undertaking your work as an interior designer. What steps do you need to take to access the professional opportunities you desire? Chapter 14, "Beginning Your Work Life," addresses those concerns. Accordingly, it focuses on topics you are probably interested in right now, such as completing a résumé and cover letter, compiling a portfolio, preparing for an interview, and participating in internships. Chapter 14 seeks to make you more confident and prepared when going through these professional rites of passage.

Once you have gained familiarity with these initial issues, you will come to realize your career lies ahead! What specific career options are available for interior designers, and what are the different kinds of businesses employing them? Chapter 15, "Planning Your Career," identifies career options for designers in a variety of professional settings from retail and wholesale establishments to architectural and independent interior design studios and academic institutions. Chapter 15 seeks to prepare you to effectively navigate the concerns faced by more seasoned design professionals. In particular, chapter 15 explores ways for you to develop your career by finding the focus of your career, understanding the importance of and procedures surrounding formal continuing education in interior design, and learning ways to prepare for your eventual retirement from active practice.

These two chapters bring together the Strategic Planning Projects found throughout this book by first asking you to prepare an assessment of your skills then by having you form a plan of action that will inform your career decisions and actions. Other projects will have you do things such as explore internships and research continuing education requirements. Finally, you will draft a professional practices memorandum based on your responses to the Professional Practice Portfolio questions in the proceeding chapters.

Your completion of this book and the many tasks it contains should give you reason to be proud of such an accomplishment and to have confidence that your abilities as an interior designer also contain an understanding of professional practice issues and strategies for addressing them.

CHAPTER FOURTEEN

BEGINNING YOUR WORK LIFE

The interior design profession is young, emerging
during the 1960s with new graduate courses and
increasing specialization in all fields of design.

ANNE MASSEY

WHY THIS CHAPTER IS IMPORTANT TO YOU

Part 5 of this text focuses on the steps you need to take to start and advance in your career as an interior designer. This chapter is important to you because it identifies and details four initial objectives to accomplish as you make the transition from student to professional. These goals include completing a résumé and cover letter compiling a portfolio, preparing for an interview, and learning about the purpose and structure of student internship programs. After working through this chapter, you will have completed a résumé and cover letter and taken the steps necessary to compile your portfolio. You will also be better prepared for the excitement of working as an intern in a design firm. With the knowledge you gain about how to prepare for working life, you can then focus on more advanced career planning presented in the final chapter of this book.

PROFESSIONAL PRACTICES PORTFOLIO

After completing this chapter, you should be able to answer the questions that follow. Include your responses in your professional practices portfolio.

1. What are the functions of a résumé, and what are its component parts?
2. What are the three basic forms of résumés, and when might each form be preferably used?
3. What is the purpose of a cover letter, and what are some basic types of cover letters?
4. What functions do portfolios serve, and what do they typically contain?
5. Why should designers keep portfolios current with their increasing levels of experience and expertise? How might designers accomplish this?
6. What important issues are related to conduct during employment interviews?
7. What are some reasons for participating in an internship program?
8. What is the typical structure of an off-campus internship program?
9. In what ways might an internship program require participants to document their activities?
10. According to this chapter's section on Problem-Solving Strategies, what actions should you take during the course of searching for a job in interior design?

INTRODUCTION: STARTING WORK AS AN INTERIOR DESIGNER

An exciting, challenging career in interior design awaits you after graduation. However eager you may be to leave school and begin your career, you will first need to acquire some skills that will enable you to enter the profession. These skills include completing a résumé and cover letter, compiling a portfolio that represents the range of your design talents, and preparing for a job interview. Many students seek out opportunities to participate in internship programs toward the end of their formal academic studies. If you are interested in taking that step on your career path, what might you hope to accomplish as a result of your participation in an internship program? What purposes do internship programs serve, and how are they typically structured to provide students with learning experience and appropriate academic credentials?

OBJECTIVES TO CONSIDER

This chapter explores the range of early career possibilities available to professionals new in the field. The interior design profession offers increasingly more specialized career opportunities to its practitioners. To participate in this dynamic environment, you must know how to access those opportunities through use of the kinds of skills introduced in this chapter. You will have taken steps toward starting your career by working through the following tasks:

1. completing a résumé and cover letter
2. compiling a portfolio representing the kind of work of which you are capable
3. preparing for an interview as well as an internship program

What do you think is the one career skill necessary to enter virtually all the professions? This chapter teaches you how to use that important skill yourself.

PREPARING A RÉSUMÉ

To gain access to future career opportunities, you need to be able to summarize information about yourself in a way that allows future employers and even clients to understand your background and capabilities. For this reason, professionals need to learn how to complete a résumé at or near the conclusion of their academic studies. A **résumé** has been defined as "a summary of somebody's educational and work experience, for the information of possible future employers. A résumé is typically used by people in all professions except academia and medicine" (Encarta 2004). Résumés focus on the written presentation of both academic accomplishment and work-related endeavors. Résumé writers typically emphasize achievements in either area, depending on the stage in their careers when they are completing or updating their résumés. As you proceed through this chapter, start to think about your major accomplishments in school and at work. Have most of your achievements been confined to your work as a student? Résumés also provide basic contact information as well as information about applicable honors or organizational affiliations. Given the broad categories of information they present, how might you begin the process of accumulating your personal information for use in a résumé?

DEVELOPING THE CONTENT OF YOUR RÉSUMÉ

As you know, a résumé traditionally contains specific categories of information, which are anticipated by those receiving and considering them. The physical layout is also expected to follow recognized and accepted guidelines. Although creativity and design skills are hallmarks of interior design, these talents are subordinate to the ability to describe yourself in clear, well-organized wording. You may have noted that résumés typically include the following elements. The emphasis accorded to any one element—such as educational information or work experience—and the order in which they appear, depend on the form selected for use by the résumé writer. Form 14.1 will help you organize the information that should appear on your résumé.

1. *Contact Information*
   Usually the very top of the résumé will present your name and address. Although this may seem obvious, if you are a student living on campus who will soon be moving to a different location, you need to carefully consider what contact information to present. Your goal should be to include personal contact information permitting an interested employer to communicate easily with you during the time you remain on campus and afterward. If you are not yet sure of your address after graduation, include the most accurate contact information available, perhaps using both your current address and the permanent address registered with your school. It may be necessary to retain a mailbox at a post office or a mail service in your new location. Electronic mail addresses and cellular telephone numbers can travel with you under some circumstances. Include them, of course, if they will remain active throughout the duration of your job hunt. You should indicate the personal nature of this

information, so that you are not contacted at any current place where you are employed.

2. *Objective or Professional Summary*

   Many students seeking a job early in their careers list a career *objective,* while those with more experience typically include a *skills* summary beneath their contact information on the résumé page. Job objectives usually indicate what position the professional is seeking—for example, an entry-level position as a member of a design team or a position as a junior designer. More experienced professionals, on the other hand, may focus on professional accomplishments such as the length of time in practice, a design-team leadership position, or a position that will give them business marketing and development experience. Résumé experts stress that both new and experienced professionals need to make clear that the objectives sought or skills summarized relate to the specific job that is being sought (Kennedy 2002).

3. *Education*

   New professionals should list their academic achievements (in reverse chronological order) directly following the career objective, whereas more seasoned professionals list their work experience (also in reverse chronological order).

4. *Work Experience*

5. *Skills*

6. *Honors and Activities*

7. *Professional Affiliations*

8. *References*

SELECTING A FORMAT FOR YOUR RÉSUMÉ

According to experts, résumés may follow a variety of formats, but the most common are the reverse chronological résumé, the functional résumé, and the combination or hybrid résumé.

The Reverse Chronological Résumé

This is perhaps the most commonly used method of organizing a résumé, describing both educational accomplishments and work history in the reverse order in which they occurred. In this approach, the most recent experience is listed first and the earliest experience is listed last. Typically, new professionals place educational accomplishments before work experience, since school activities have been their major and most recent focus. More advanced professionals who decide to use this approach list their work experience prior to their education, since many professionals have been out of school for some time and instead wish to highlight their work history.

The primary benefit of this approach is its wide acceptance. It is an effective method for designers who are starting out in their careers to highlight their educational accomplishments and note relevant extracurricular activities. At the same time, however, this approach highlights educational or employment gaps, which could be a problem for professionals whose histories are less sequential.

The Functional Résumé

The functional résumé shows what skills the applicant has acquired through education and work experience. Typically, résumé writers using this approach identify a series of skills or abilities and list them in their order of importance.

The Combination or Hybrid Résumé

This résumé combines the two previous approaches, typically focusing on skills, as does the functional résumé, and placing less emphasis on the sequential development of the writer. The list of academic accomplishments usually appears toward the end of the résumé and is organized in reverse chronological order.

After reviewing this discussion of résumé writing, complete Form 14.1.

COMPLETING A COVER LETTER

Perhaps you are new to the process of preparing résumés and cover letters. What could entice a recipient to consider reading your résumé? The main purpose of a cover letter is to interest decision makers in the skills and abilities you acquired during the course of your academic and professional life. It should engage the reader's interest in you as a professional and potential employee.

What do you think is the best way to approach a cover letter, since you may not even be aware of the specific job to which it could apply? Form 14.2 provides some strategies for writing effective cover letters. For

RÉSUMÉ WORKSHEET

After reviewing this chapter's discussion of résumé writing, complete this worksheet using your own information. You will then be able to complete a résumé using each of the formats described in this chapter.

1. Contact Information

2. Objective/Professional Summary

3. Education

4. Work Experience

5. Skills

6. Honors and Activities

7. Professional Affiliations

practice, consider the following classified advertisement that was drawn from actual job listings for entry-level interior designers. Using Form 14.2 as your guide, write a cover letter that would accompany your résumé if you were seeking this job.

> For more than thirty years, LJW Designs has enhanced commercial and residential spaces in the Dallas Metroplex area. As part of the firm's continued expansion we are currently seeking applicants for the position of Junior Designer. The successful candidate will possess a strong passion for design excellence, outstanding verbal/written skills, and the ability to work independently and as a team player. In addition, strong attention to detail, technical ability, and AutoCAD R14 through 2002 is a must. We offer an outstanding range of benefits, a beautiful working environment, and the opportunity to grow. Please fax or e-mail your résumé.

COMPILING A PORTFOLIO

Many interior design programs now include a class devoted to portfolio preparation under recent Foundation for Interior Design Education and Research (FIDER) accreditation standards. This emphasis reflects the important role portfolios play throughout a designer's career. This chapter's discussion cannot take the place of an entire class devoted to portfolio preparation, but it can prepare you for such a class or provide an otherwise convenient reference to assembling an interior design portfolio.

A **portfolio** is more than just a set of pictures, as a dictionary might describe it; rather, it is a visual synopsis of work that you have completed employing the creative and technical skills of which you are capable. It is an ongoing, progressive work because the level of your skills and project responsibilities will greatly increase over time. Review Form 14.3 for initial guidance on how to compile your portfolio. A new trend for developing portfolios includes the use of CD-ROMs and personal Web sites. If you choose this form of a portfolio, make sure that the user can access and navigate files easily.

PREPARING FOR AN EMPLOYMENT INTERVIEW

Your efforts at preparing a résumé and cover letter have paid off, and you have been selected for an interview by a prospective employer. You may

COVER LETTER WORKSHEET

Use this template to draft a résumé cover letter.

Your name
Your address
Area code and phone number
Other contact information as appropriate

Date

Title and name of person to whom you are applying
Name/title of company to which you are applying
Company/office address
City, state, zip code

Dear Mr./Ms.:

The first paragraph should tell the reader:
1. Why you are writing
   ("In response to your (advertisement, Web site posting, etc.), I am writing to. . . .)
2. What you are seeking
   ("to show my interest in and application for . . .")
3. The specific position you are interested in
   ("the position of (use the specific position title used by employer) . . .")
4. Your ability to practice interior design relevant to the state in which
   your registration/license will be held
   ("I hold the following interior design registration and affiliations . . .")
5. How you heard about the position ("I read of this opportunity . . .")

The body of the letter (two to three paragraphs, unless you have extensive experience to note) should spell out for the reader not only your education and experience, but also how they directly relate to the available position. One way to approach this may be to
1. Explain how your formal education is appropriate for the position
   ("I have earned a bachelors ot arts degree in interior design, as required in the posting")
   Explain further details about your education, such as honors and awards.
2. Explain how your previous internship experiences are appropriate for the position
   ("As an intern with Co. X, I gained experience relevant to this position by doing . . .")
3. Explain how your early formal work experience is appropriate for the position
   ("While working as a (name position), I performed the following tasks that enable me to perform this position's tasks of . . .")
4. Explain how your recent work experience is appropriate for the position
   ("As manager of projects similar to those referenced in the position, I . . .")
5. Address any concerns that might be provoked by your résumé or that you otherwise need to address. (This may be necessary if there are considerable gaps in your work history, for example.)

The final paragraph should include the following:
1. Thank the readers for their time and interest.
2. Express your availability for an interview, either in person or on the telephone.
3. Add a conclusion, such as "sincerely" or "thanking you for your consideration."
4. Leave signature space.
5. Write your signature.
6. Type your full name.

Add the following notation when sending a résumé:

Enclosure: résumé

FORM 14.3. COMPILING YOUR PORTFOLIO CHECKLIST

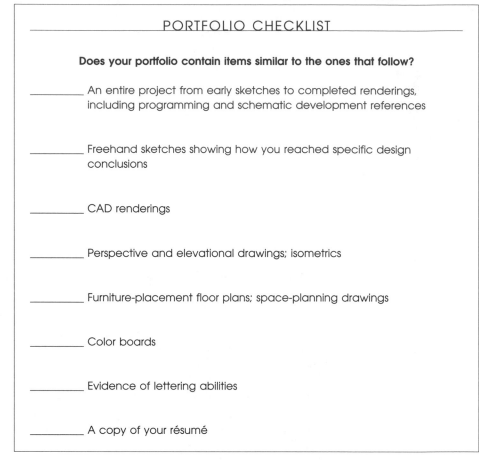

PORTFOLIO CHECKLIST

Does your portfolio contain items similar to the ones that follow?

_____ An entire project from early sketches to completed renderings, including programming and schematic development references

_____ Freehand sketches showing how you reached specific design conclusions

_____ CAD renderings

_____ Perspective and elevational drawings; isometrics

_____ Furniture-placement floor plans; space-planning drawings

_____ Color boards

_____ Evidence of lettering abilities

_____ A copy of your résumé

have been informed by mail (or e-mail) or by telephone. If you were notified by snail mail or e-mail, you were probably told by the prospective employer that you would receive a follow-up telephone call to confirm the date and time of your interview. In either case, therefore, your first notification of the interview process will come through telephone contact. Are you prepared to handle these initial preinterview encounters and use them to your advantage?

INITIAL CONTACTS WITH EMPLOYERS

These first phone calls are administrative in nature, seeking to know whether the applicant can participate in an interview on a specific day and time. The person tasked by the employer to call applicants may be an administrative assistant to the particular individual to whom you, if hired, would report; or he or she may be a staff member in the human resources department. Regardless of their exact role, these individuals may do more than just set times and dates; they may also ask you some preliminary questions so that the person conducting the interview will have more information about you and your qualifications. Before going further, consider what might be happening in your life when you receive such a call. Perhaps you are on campus talking with friends when your cellular telephone rings, or you notice the new message light blinking on your phone when you return to your apartment, tired, from class. All of a sudden, you have to talk to someone who in some way may be responsible for offering or denying you a job that you definitely want.

Although you may be involved in any number of activities when you receive a call to set up an employment interview, you want to make a very good impression on the phone. After all, the person calling may communicate with the person who will conduct your interview. You don't want to suggest that you are flustered and confused. Even these early encounters are opportunities to make a positive and memorable initial impression (Ingols and Shapiro 2003). For these reasons, it may be a good idea to get organized (Ingols and Shapiro 2003). How could you do that?

As you prepare and send out your résumés, along with appropriate cover letters, keep notes about the businesses and individuals to whom you have written. For example, on index cards of a size convenient for you to keep in your pocket or bag, note on one side the names of these potential employers, their contact information, and the dates you mailed your résumé. Note the name(s) of the people within the organization to whom you sent your résumé as follows.

Résumés sent to:
1. ArchDeco (1234 Studio Street, Los Angeles, California 90210); sent May 18, 2004 to Jon Jones. Phone # _____.
2. INTERIORA (5678 Design Drive, Burbank, California 90301); sent May 22, 2004 to Human Resources Department Phone # _____.

By keeping notes organized in this way, you will not have to recall on the spur of the moment to whom you sent your résumés. On the other side of your contact card, write easy-to-read synopses of your educational and work accomplishments as listed in the résumé you sent to these potential employers. Be sure to include specific information about your education, previous employers, and inclusive dates relating to your education and employment. This may seem unnecessary until you are asked by the person calling to set up your employment interview for this information. In the excitement of the moment, it is easy to forget the exact dates. Listing contacts on note cards is one easy method of preparing for interview success, even during the early stages of the process. Keep this card with you in your day planner, or enter the same kinds of information into your PDA—whatever means you have to keep the information available when you are busy with other tasks. In these initial contacts with staff and potential employers, you should also remember to convey your interest in working with them. You may be surprised how well your preparedness and enthusiasm are remembered.

Prior to the day of your interview, you will likely have much on your mind. Therefore, having an organized approach to prepare yourself for the interview will be extremely beneficial. As you review Form 14.4, the Interview Preparation Checklist, you can see how developing a method of preparation for interviews can get you ready and perhaps also help to quell some of your concerns by giving you something else to do besides worrying about whether you will get the job.

WHAT TO EXPECT DURING AN INTERVIEW

Once you have established a date and time for an interview with a potential employer and followed a routine that will prepare you for it, the time for that interview eventually arrives. The structure of interviews and how they are conducted vary by employer. In some instances, one person conducts the interview one-on-one with the job applicant. In other cases, two or more interviewers conduct a team, or group, interview. Applicants often will not be informed beforehand about which approach they will face when they arrive at the interview. Therefore, if you are an entry-level candidate, come mentally prepared to meet any number of interviewers. In many instances, the person directly supervising the position for which you are interviewing as well as other managers may be present. As you progress in your design career and seek positions requiring greater managerial authority and business decision-making skills, it becomes more likely that you will face multiple interviewers during a number of interviews, rather than one or a few interviewers in a single interview as do many entry-level candidates.

You may be surprised, too, that some interviewers may themselves appear to be less well prepared than you might have expected. Many have

INTERVIEW PREPARATION CHECKLIST

Appointment Preparation

_____ Have you confirmed your appointment with the appropriate contact person?

_____ Have you left your contact information, in case there is a change or delay, with the individual who will interview you?

_____ Do you know where the appointment is to take place and how to get there?

_____ Have you arranged for transportation, if needed?

_____ Do you have enough money for parking or transportation?

Personal Preparation

Your Portfolio

_____ Does your portfolio contain your name and contact information in case you have to leave it with the interviewer for later review? (Include a copy of your résumé as well.)

_____ Is your portfolio clean in appearance and neatly organized when opened?

_____ Have you repaired or replaced any damaged exhibits in your portfolio?

_____ Can you explain how each and every portfolio entry has prepared you for future work or how it relates to the position for which you are interviewing?

_____ Can you anticipate a discussion in which you describe your portfolio?

_____ What kinds of questions do you think will be asked about your portfolio, and can you answer them?

_____ Does your portfolio show you to be a problem solver?

Your Résumé

_____ Have you prepared your most recent résumé to take with you?

_____ Are additional copies of your résumé available to take with you?

_____ Can you explain how your résumé items (for example, education and work experience) have prepared you for future work or for the position for which you are interviewing?

_____ Can you explain any problems that may be presented by your résumé?

Your Appearance

_____ Do you have a suit that is appropriate for interviewing and that is comfortable, clean, and well-pressed? (Ask a trusted friend or sales associate for direction; if possible, see what others at the prospective place of employment are wearing.)

_____ Do you have shoes, purse, briefcase (as applicable) that are clean and comfortable? (Both your suit and accessories should be fairly conservative in appearance.)

_____ For men: Do you have a clean, pressed necktie that you can tie so that its tip touches your belt buckle?

had to squeeze the time for your interview into their own schedules and may not have been able to reacquaint themselves with details of your file prior to the interview. Work to make the interviewer in these circumstances understand your accomplishments and how they are a good fit with the position you are seeking. It may be helpful for you to review your résumé, section by section, before the interview is well along. Regardless of the specific interviewer or number of interviewers with whom you speak, it is important to stay focused on what brought you to the interview in the first place—the position offered by the business and the opportunity it presents for demonstrating how your accomplishments make you the best candidate for the job.

Interview Formats

The manner in which your interview is conducted may vary with different employers as well. Some interviewers use a dialogue-based approach, or a conversational style of interview, while others are more formal in their approach. Some interview styles can even be confrontational in their tone. This type of interview is generally referred to as a **stress interview**. Both the conversational and the stress approach is challenging; yet if handled well, both types of interview can provide applicants with an opportunity to show off their abilities to their best advantage.

Conversational-style interviews may not seem like interviews. In these instances, an applicant and the person or people conducting the interview talk about a variety of topics that may not seem to have anything to do with the available position or with any job at all. The thinking behind this approach is to get the applicant to open up, allowing the interviewer to see how their qualifications and skills relate to those required for the position or to enable the interviewer to get a sense of an applicant's ability to organize and take control of a seemingly random situation (Ingols and Shapiro 2003). If you encounter an interviewer who appears to use this approach, interview experts suggest that you try to turn these open-ended conversations into collaborations (Ingols and Shapiro 2003). Ask the interviewer about job responsibilities, the number of people to whom you would report—in other words, turn those open-ended, unfocused questions into a dialogue about the position and its responsibilities, which will also allow you to discuss your education and experiences in the context of those job requirements.

The **stress interview** approach is intended to be intimidating. The thinking behind this approach is that the interview in some way simulates actual conditions experienced by those working in the position for which you have applied (Ingols and Shapiro 2003). For example, many new designers have to contend with unyielding time pressure and the demands of conflicting interpersonal relationships in the workplace. The ability to handle confrontation and pressure may be what the interviewer is seeking to ascertain. In this type of interview, you are asked confrontational questions that require you to explain and justify every aspect of your résumé and portfolio in excruciating detail. Although all interviews seem to be challenging, the stress interview is specifically designed to test how applicants respond to grilling, or to rapid-fire questions about what the interviewer perceives as inconsistencies in statements or claims made by an applicant about his or her abilities. Detachment from this process as a personal attack and thorough knowledge of your résumé and technical abilities can help you to navigate through this trying form of interview.

As you advance in your career, you may likely come across other interview techniques. For more senior managerial positions, you may expect to be confronted with highly sophisticated questions based on behavior profiles the employer has developed to identify personal and professional characteristics believed to be most appropriate for a particular position. This interview style is usually referred to as the **behavioral** or **psychological interview**. Should you choose to apply your interior design background in a business rather than in a design-studio setting, you may encounter lengthy interviews, known as **case-study interviews**, that seek to gauge your ability to solve common business problems.

Regardless of the number of interviewers or the style in which the interview is conducted, you can expect that you will be asked questions. You can also expect opportunities to ask questions of your own to potential employers during the interview process.

Questions an Employer May Ask You

Consider, for example, the following sets of questions:

◆ Tell us about yourself and why you are interested in this position.
◆ What do you know about our business (or firm)?
◆ How did you learn about this position and about our business?
◆ Tell us why you are qualified for this position.
◆ What are your career plans and goals?
◆ What would you consider to be your greatest strength and greatest weakness?

- What do you consider your largest achievement and your worse mistake?
- What did you do to overcome your weaknesses and correct your mistakes?
- What about interior design excites you, and what got you interested in the field in the first place?
- Whose design work do you admire, and why?
- How do you feel when your work is criticized?
- Why should we hire you?

Are there any good answers to these inquiries? Of course, every interview situation is unique. What may work for one candidate in one interview may sound stilted and contrived in another. What should you remember to do when faced with questions such as these in an actual interview situation? It may help if you remember two concepts: *focus* and *needs*. Quite simply, remain focused on the position itself, *not* the personalities of the interviewers or even your own. Strive to present enthusiastic interest in learning what the employer expects and needs from anyone holding that position. Think about those needs. Many times, interviewers will run through a list of tasks or activities that they require the successful candidate for the position to perform on the job. If the interviewer seems unclear about what those needs are and what they entail, make sure that you find out during the process of learning about the position. Then, and perhaps most important of all, your response to any interview question—whether it is listed here—should demonstrate how your personality, knowledge, and technical skills make you the optimal candidate for the available position. This may be a lot to remember, but it should make it easier for you to answer any questions you are asked.

Questions to Ask an Employer

Employers expect you to ask questions of them as well. In fact, many employers like to see candidates exhibit an interest in their business. Although it is not a good idea to appear to immediately want to assume managerial tasks beyond the scope of the job for which you applied, or to present grandiose plans for a business that you know little about, neither is it wise to seem unconcerned about its growth and further development. Consider the following questions as possible inquiries you might pose to an employer, if they are applicable to your circumstances. When asking the following questions, develop a tone of collaboration, indicating an interest in helping employers meet goals they deem important.

- What specific responsibilities are expected of this position?
- To whom will the successful candidate report?
- What are your plans for the business in the near and more distant future?
- What characteristics do you think it is important for a candidate to have in order to be successful in this position?
- How many people are employed by this company, and how is the organization structured?
- What resources and opportunities does this company provide to employees to enable them to grow and develop as professionals?
- Are you interviewing many other applicants for this position?
- Do you need any other information from me to help you make a decision?
- Can I clear up any questions that emerge from a review of my résumé?
- When do you plan to announce your decision on this position?

With these questions in mind, you may have a better idea of how to interact with interviewers during the interview process. After reading the previous questions, can you think of an important question that has been omitted? The next section will provide the answer.

KEY INTERVIEW ISSUES

This text identifies three general areas of concern when it comes to handling interview questions. These issues relate to salary discussions; recognizing and handling questions employers are prohibited from asking job candidates; and some obvious, but sometimes overlooked, actions that employment experts universally agree should not occur during interviews.

Salary Discussions

Should you mention salary? If so, when should you bring up the topic? Should you simply take any amount offered? First consider this issue as it relates to the employment application and then to the interview.

Many employers specifically state that they will not consider employment applications that do not include current salary information. Others are silent on the matter. In the former instance, applicants may have no choice but to state the salary amount they currently receive or expect to receive if their application process is to proceed further. In general, however, and in the latter case, advisers suggest that you do not provide current salary information, since prospective employers can ascertain that information when checking the background of applicants. Since outright dishonesty about this or any other information will in all likelihood be discovered, attempts to inflate your current salary in an effort to raise amounts offered for a future position is discouraged.

Some applications ask the job seeker to supply an expected salary for the position they seek, and such inquiries are often made by employers during interviews. What should you do then? This aspect of employment negotiations requires some research on your part before you enter into any salary discussion. Many employment-related Internet sites as well as specific sites devoted to salary statistics provide a broad range of salaries for interior designers. In addition, the ASID publishes annual statistical reports that take note of salaries. If you are not already familiar with range of salaries offered to entry-level interior designers, some data is included here, based on the most recent (2002) statistics prepared by ASID. As you may know, California, Florida, Illinois, New York, and Texas, among others are states with the largest number of interior designers. According to ASID, the mean annual base salaries for junior designers in major metropolitan areas in those states are as follows:

Los Angeles, California: $34,339
West Palm Beach/Boca Raton, Florida: $30,281
Chicago, Illinois: $33,416
New York, New York: $35,507
Dallas, Texas: $31,418

As you conduct your own research about salaries, consider your employer's location (salaries may be lower in smaller cities that have less demand for design services). Also take note of the size of the design firm where you are seeking employment (many larger firms may offer more in the way of salary, but they also expect more of you). You can further gather salary information by consulting ASID and other sources, and, informally, by asking friends and others in the design industry.

Prohibited Interview Questions

There are some questions that are illegal, according to federal and state law, for employers to ask job candidates. Enforcement of these employment laws, should a formal complaint be filed and a violation found to have occurred, is carried out by such national agencies as the Equal Employment Opportunity Commission (EEOC) and by state employment and human rights commissions. In general, these laws prohibit questions related to age, ethnicity, religious beliefs, and gender. For example, specific questions about such topics as the applicant's exact age, place of birth, religious faith, or, with regard to gender, marital status or plans for starting a family fall into these prohibited categories. Employment advisers suggest that you either ignore such questions or ask the interviewer why such a question might have any bearing on the qualities necessary for an applicant to perform the job under discussion. If applicants believe they were subject to discrimination based on any of these grounds, they should consider seeking the counsel of an employment law specialist to determine whether to pursue formal actions against the employer through the appropriate enforcement agency.

What Not to Do in Interview Settings

Any candidate for employment is advised not to engage in two general categories of activities. The first category involves the use of body language that distracts the interviewer's attention from the applicant or wearing apparel that has the same effect. The focus should be on you and your accomplishments and not—according to business etiquette—on distracting behavior. The second category involves falsifying previous educational or work-related experience, which includes providing fictitious references that create a false impression about that experience. Many, if not all, employers perform background checks, through which they will likely uncover these issues. Uncovering falsehoods typically results in rejection of the applicant or dismissal in the event that a person was already hired.

PARTICIPATING IN INTERNSHIPS

According to its common dictionary definition, an intern is "an advanced student or graduate usually in a professional field gaining supervised practical experience." Internships, then, may include any that programs provide supervised practical experience. From your perspective, internship programs are exciting ways for you to experience working life while completing your education. Like many students, you are probably already anticipating the day you can begin your interior design career. A successful internship experience should ground that enthusiasm is an honest appraisal of how your knowledge and professional skills, including your interpersonal skills, will fare in a day-to-day working situation. Before exploring how internships are typically structured and overseen, consider some of the reasons why you might be motivated to participate in an internship program.

REASONS TO PARTICIPATE IN INTERNSHIP PROGRAMS

You probably have tons of ideas you want to try out: ideas about different projects you'd like to complete or ideas about working with other designers and clients. And since you have been planning your ideal interior design business throughout this book, you have ideas about the kind of business—particularly its focus and creative point of view—in which you want to be involved. Along that same line, you may have an idea about pursuing a particular career path or working with particular individuals or organizations. Most interns are not usually allowed to make important decisions, and some assignments may not seem very significant at all. Nevertheless, interns do get to see how design-oriented businesses are managed, and they learn about the work style of practitioners, even if the intern is responsible only for answering telephones. When approached realistically, internships can provide an opportunity to test the viability of the ideas you have about working as an interior designer.

Why Organizations Sponsor Internships

Internships also appeal to students because they provide work experience in a nonthreatening environment. Most internship supervisors at sponsoring businesses expect that student interns will require assistance with a variety of skills, from applying studio techniques to interacting with others in an office or studio setting. Although they do expect interns to be receptive and willing to learn, supervisors as well as other staff are often willing to help students polish rough technical and work-related skills in ways that they might not with respect to hired employees.

Why might they be more generous with interns? Firms and individual designers, or others who offer internships within their organizations, do so because they are willing and financially able to share their knowledge and expertise with a new generation of soon-to-be practitioners. Except as a portion of overhead costs, the work performed by an intern, whether he or she is paid, is not directly billable to clients. As a result, the business requires sufficient income to justify sponsoring an internship position instead of, say, upgrading the office's color copier. Additionally, the firm must allocate a portion of a regular employee's time to serving as an intern supervisor—a task involving direct interaction with an intern and frequently with an academic contact, such as an internship coordinator. In short, internships involve time and effort on the part of the firms offering them. However, many designers remember their own experiences, good and otherwise, as they made the transition from student to professional. The desire to make that process beneficial (not just easier) for future colleagues motivates these practitioners to be educators and mentors and thereby to assume the additional costs of the internship process. Of course, employers benefit from the services interns can offer to businesses. For example, interns provide an inexpensive or even free source of labor in instances where they receive no compensation for their services. Furthermore, interns can do routine office work or support work and chores not billable to clients. In this way, interns free paid employees from these tasks allowing them to do work requiring more professional skills. When interns do work directly on projects and that labor is billable to clients, the cost to the business of that labor is usually much lower than the cost of having a fully paid employee do it. Talented, motivated interns offer another benefit to the companies where they work in that they may not require constant supervision while performing at least some of their assigned tasks. Finally, and importantly for students considering internships, many of these programs serve as sources for entry-level hires. Interns are often strongly exhorted by their school's administration to respect the opportunity to participate in these programs. Knowing these basic facts about the costs and motivations behind employer-sponsored internships, can you better understand why businesses offer to work with interns?

Students' Considerations in Applying for Internships

Other reasons for seeking an internship depends on a student's needs and outlook. While it is true that some positions offer salaries to interns, money alone should not be the motivating factor for seeking and accepting internships. As a student, your disposable income is most likely limited. Tuition and supply costs, not to mention living expenses, probably consume most of the financial resources available to you. Although some internship positions do offer monetary compensation, often the salary will be more than offset by increased transportation and other costs required for participation in the program. The receipt of a salary may even have an indirectly negative effect on a student's finances, for example, limiting the possibility of need-based financial assistance for educational costs and requiring payment of income tax on amounts earned from participation in the internship. Before agreeing to take on internship responsibilities, students should raise these concerns with appropriate financial-aid advisers at their educational institutions and with human resources representatives at businesses offering internships. If an internship offers no paid compensation, students should determine whether they have the financial ability and the desire to take on the added costs and effort before promising to appear regularly at a specific place and time, dressed appropriately and ready to work, without the benefit of immediate income. Whether an internship offers some payment for your participation, the desire for experience, not financial compensation, should motivate your interest.

"It will look good on my résumé," many students give as a reason for selecting a well-known firm for an internship. A positive internship experience, which allows you to become involved in the work of a design firm or business, should be your goal, rather than a shopping expedition for names and titles to dress up your résumé. Business decision makers considering prospective employees are likely to follow up with references candidate provides, according to current hiring guidelines and accepted practices. Thus, vague recollection of a nondescript intern by a "name" designer would certainly be a less persuasive reason for hiring a candidate than a more positive recommendation from a lesser-known reference. Along the same lines, merely participating in an internship at the expense of solid academic performance in coursework might not have any later benefit either. Rather than seeking internships for the purpose of accessorizing a résumé, you should focus on using an internship to build a network of contacts with established design professionals; demonstrate consistent, thoughtful work habits; and display an ability to solve problems no matter how simple or mundane. Then you will be able to secure heartfelt references from established designers who genuinely want to help interns advance their careers.

Because internships involve relationships among you, your school, and a sponsoring business, what might these participants expect of an intern? In other words, how are internships typically structured, and what tasks might you be expected to perform in an internship program?

THE STRUCTURE OF INTERNSHIP PROGRAMS

Every internship program is unique, its format influenced by a school's established policies and by the business offering the internship. Some schools or interior design programs make no provision for an internship and offer no academic credit for work as an intern. If you face these circumstances, you need to consider whether participation in an internship program will conflict with your coursework and other obligations. However, many schools offer internship programs with academic credit; that is, students receive a grade on transcripts for their participation, as if the internship were a classroom-centered course. These programs usually specify student eligibility for participation, based on the number of academic hours and courses completed and possibly other criteria. Of course, the student must appropriately register and arrange payment for the internship course. When evaluating the merits of different internships, students should consider whether they can afford to pay for the opportunity to participate in a nonpaying internship, and, conversely, whether a paying internship will adequately reimburse them for course-registration costs.

The availability of interior design internships varies considerably, depending on factors such as a school's location, the overall economic climate, and the extent to which a school or an individual student has an established relationship with businesses that offer these programs. In a best-case scenario, a school would post internships available in interior design firms as part of an established internship program; in a worst-case scenario, students are responsible for finding a business willing to take on an intern and then must secure that internship position by themselves. As you are planning your interior design education, determine the extent to which an interior design program has an internship component and already established links to businesses offering internship positions. Assume for the purpose of this discussion that your school posts internship positions from a number of local employers. One of them reviewed your résumé, conducted a telephone interview with you, and then offered you a position in a summer internship program. What should you do next?

DOCUMENTING YOUR INTERNSHIP

Once you have been offered a position as an intern, you should obtain an internship handbook or other documentation detailing what activities you will have to perform, and by what specific dates, to receive academic credit for the internship. This book has already mentioned a number of people with whom interns will have to interact. These include an academic internship coordinator and a business's internship or on-site supervisor. You may also have to consult with an academic adviser at your school about your academic qualifications for participation in an internship program and the effect of your internship on your coursework or graduation date.

The academic internship coordinator is usually an instructor who is charged with conducting internships as regular coursework. To that end, coordinators frequently require participating students to complete information sheets, such as Form 14.5.

In addition, the coordinator may also require an intern to complete a learning objectives worksheet (Form 14.6), in which interns outline the goals they wish to accomplish by participating in the program.

Further requirements include completing and turning in weekly time sheets itemizing the activities that interns performed during the week. A sample of this document (Form 14.7) is included in this chapter for your review; if your internship coordinator permits, Forms 14.5, 14.6, and 14.7 may be modified for use in your internship.

In addition, a written report or series of reports is frequently required. In a typical academic program, at least two written reports, increasing in length and discussing different aspects of your internship, may be required—generally at the midpoint of an internship and at its conclusion. The academic coordinator will likely require that an intern supervisor complete an evaluation form. An intern may also be asked to turn in a journal describing what occurred at the intern site; an evaluation of the sponsoring business or studio; as well as a critique of the experience. Most programs require an intern to submit logs (see Form 14.7) indicating the amount of time spent performing various tasks. That said, what kinds of activities can interns typically expect to perform?

INTERNSHIP INFORMATION SHEET

Semester/Year _____
Internship Coordinator _____
Date of Form _____

Student Name _____

Internship Business/Company Name _____
Address _____
City _____ State/Zip _____
Phone No. _____ Fax No. _____

Internship Supervisor _____ **Title or Position** _____

Expected Start Date _____ **Expected End Date** _____

Work Schedule

Days (Circle)

Hours (From/To)

	Monday	Tuesday	Wednesday	Thursday	Friday	
				Total Weekly Hours		

This position is (Circle) **PAID** **UNPAID**

To the Student: Congratulations on receiving an internship position! Please read all applicable rules and policies and ask any questions you may have BEFORE your start date. Any questions should be directed to the school internship coordinator. Make sure that a completed copy of this form and your learning objectives form are on file with the coordinator and supervisor BEFORE your start date. It is also your responsibility to ensure completion and receipt by the coordinator of all internship documentation required of the supervisor. Best wishes on your internship experience.

During the course of this internship, you may be contacted at:
Address _____
City _____ State/Zip _____
Phone No. _____ E-mail _____

To the Internship Supervisor: Thank you for providing this internship experience for the student. Prior to the internship start date, please complete the following documentation:

_____ Institutional agreement(s) _____

_____ Internship Learning Objectives form with the student. The **student** is responsible for returning the completed form to the coordinator prior to the internship start date.

_____ Other documentation _____

If you have any questions, please contact the Internship Coordinator _____
at the following:
Address _____
City _____ State/Zip _____
Phone No. _____ E-mail _____

INTERNSHIP LEARNING OBJECTIVES

Intern Name _____   Semester/Year _____
                                                          Internship Coordinator _____

This worksheet is part of your agreement to participate in the internship program.
Please complete this worksheet, noting the five goals you wish to accomplish. You will use this to prepare internship reports or summaries.

I would like to know/be able to do the following as a result of this internship: _____
_____
_____

I will accomplish this by: _____
_____
_____

I will have succeeded when: _____
_____
Signature Internship Supervisor

I would like to know/be able to do the following as a result of this internship: _____
_____
_____

I will accomplish this by: _____
_____
_____

I will have succeeded when: _____
_____
Signature Internship Supervisor

I would like to know/be able to do the following as a result of this internship: _____
_____
_____

I will accomplish this by: _____
_____
_____

I will have succeeded when: _____
_____
Signature Internship Supervisor

I would like to know/be able to do the following as a result of this internship: _____
_____
_____

I will accomplish this by: _____
_____
_____

I will have succeeded when: _____
_____
Signature Internship Supervisor

I would like to know/be able to do the following as a result of this internship: _____
_____
_____

I will accomplish this by: _____
_____
_____

I will have succeeded when: _____
_____
Signature Internship Supervisor

INTERNSHIP TIME SHEET

Intern Name _____   For Week Ending _____
Internship Coordinator _____   Internship Location _____
Internship Supervisor _____   _____

Please indicate the amount of time you engaged in the following tasks during the subject week.
Use only the hourly method approved by an Internship Coordinator.

Tasks	Monday	Tuesday	Wednesday	Thursday	Friday	Overtime	Total
Catalog filing							
Sample/Swatch filing							
Telephone reception							
Correspondence							
Updating product info.							
Processing orders							
Office-wide meetings							
Workroom meetings							
Senior-staff meetings							
Client meetings							
Dealer/rep. meetings							
Rendering							
Manual drafting							
CAD work							
Blueprint work							
Researching materials							
Est. material amounts							
Physical measuring							
Space planning							
Furniture arrangement							
Color/material selection							
Concept board const.							
Construction-site visit							
Contractor meetings							
Installation time							
Assigned research							
Professional practices							
Other (specify)							
Total Hours							

Notes _____
_____
_____
_____
_____
_____
_____
_____
_____
_____
_____

Signature of Intern _____   Date _____
Signature of Internship Coordinator _____   Date _____
Signature of Internship Supervisor _____   Date _____

TYPICAL INTERN ACTIVITIES

Form 14.7, a time sheet, indicates typical intern activities. These jobs range from answering telephones to making visits to project sites to meeting with various staff members—clearly a gamut of different tasks. One of these activities is particularly noteworthy: the time spent engaging in professional practices. Depending on the sequence of the internship within an academic program, students may take a professional practices course after or concurrently with an internship. Student schedules may necessitate taking the course before the start of an internship. When students participate in internships prior to or during professional practices courses, the Professional Practices Portfolio that you prepared during your study of this—including chapter review questions and your responses— can help you during the internship. You may wish to have it available and as complete as possible so that you can identify the professional practices and related issues in which you participate. Just by reading this book's table of contents, you know these issues include business organization, ethics, business law, accounting, and interior design project management, among others. For example, interns participate in professional practice activities by sitting in on meetings related to marketing, firm management, project management decision making, and by preparing invoices with accounting managers. Conversely, if your course schedule requires you to take a practices course after you have completed your internship, be sure to keep detailed journals of your internship, so you have examples of the professional activities in which you participated available for use in class assignments.

STRATEGIES FOR USING INTERNSHIPS IN YOUR WORK

Your experience with the details of internship documentation will benefit you throughout your working life. Graduates are increasingly required to complete the Interior Design Experience Program (IDEP), administered by NCIDQ, to be eligible to take that organization's credentialing exam. Participation in IDEP exposes graduates to the extensive activities that NCIDQ has identified as comprising the practice of interior design. The program specifies both the kinds and numbers of activities necessary for exam preparation and, of course, subsequent practice. The IDEP requires, as part of its curriculum, that program participants keep detailed journal and record keeping documentation of the tasks accomplished by both participants and businesses or individuals supervising the work. In short, participation in an internship program can provide students with insights about how to function effectively in a supervised work program, such as IDEP. Much of the documentation and responsibilities of the two programs are similar; yet IDEP is more formal than the open-ended nature of most internships completed before graduation.

One important factor distinguishes the two programs. Under current NCIDQ rules, work experience that has also earned the participant academic credit is not considered as a participation requirement for IDEP purposes. Although working as an intern under these guidelines may not provide IDEP credit, internships still serve as the important first contact students have with the rigors of an interior design career.

Interns should expect to be called on to do a variety of tasks, some admittedly more interesting or satisfying than others—a characteristic of the working life of most professionals. Internships provide a way for students to experience this reality and develop ways of handling it. After getting a taste of the exciting challenges awaiting them, what should recently degreed practitioners consider as they approach the early stages of their careers?

PROBLEM-SOLVING STRATEGIES

A common problem faced by many students after graduation is finding jobs. Even experienced designers who want a change in their current employment face a similar problem. Both new and seasoned professionals embark on solving their problems by engaging in job searches. What should you and other designers consider while engaged in this process?

THE JOB SEARCH

Searching for a job, whether it is your first or fifth position, can be frustrating. This is because so many factors appear to be beyond your capacity to control. For example, economic conditions nationally and, particularly, locally—in the location where you would like to work—determine the availability of jobs in interior design; yet these factors cannot usually be affected by an individual. During times when design services are in demand—that is, when economies are strong and expanding—

jobs in design may be easier to obtain; yet those same jobs may be difficult to retain once conditions change and consumer interest lessens. In areas that have less expansive economies, there are simply fewer job opportunities available, since consumers in those locations may not perceive a need for interior design services. In both situations, difficulty in finding employment can be exacerbated by competition from a large number of designers seeking whatever positions are available. Is there a way to anticipate facing this kind of a job market when seeking employment?

The inherent uncertainty and feelings of rejection engendered by the job-search process only adds to the sense of frustration. Before beginning your job search, a key problem-solving strategy may be to first acknowledge that the process will make many demands on your time, energy, and psyche. Just recognizing the fact that seeking a job is a job in itself can make finding a desirable position all the more rewarding.

HOW TO LOCATE EMPLOYMENT OPPORTUNITIES

With that thought in mind, consider what basic options are available for discovering job opportunities in a location that holds your interest.

- Placement services offered by your school can include formal postings of available positions or even informal notices tacked to bulletin boards. Have you fully explored any of the services offered by your school?
- Classified advertisements are posted by employers for unfilled positions in local newspapers or posted on a newspaper's Web site. Do you check newspaper listings in the area that you are interested in working on a regular basis?
- Specific job listings are found through online Internet job-search engines, such as www.monster.com. In fact, some job-search resources now allow registered users to post résumés for potential employers' review, and they provide notification services when jobs in specified categories become available. Have you considered using any of these resources?
- Jobs are posted online at a specific employer's Web site. You undoubtedly have favorite individual designers, design firms, or lines of furniture/showrooms that appeal to you and your design approach. Have you checked any appropriate Internet sites to see what job options might exist with such potential employers?

- Magazines and other periodicals catering to the design trade and consumers of interior design services also are good sources for job postings. Trade periodicals, such as *Contract*, that are intended for a professional rather than a consumer audience are perhaps a more realistic source for employment information. Do you check out these sources on a regular basis?

- Indirect methods of obtaining information about job opportunities, such as word-of-mouth references or personal contacts, are also sources to consider. Interior design, whether for residential or commercial application, requires personal contact with other designers and participants. Have you identified several professionals who might assist you in your search for a job?

- You should look into personal marketing, should you choose self-employment. Have you thought about advertising your services? That might include producing and running a series of print advertisements and establishing your own informational Web site. These activities do require financial expenditures, possibly at a time when you have little to spare, and must be further maintained on a regular basis to have realistic possibility of attracting potential clients to your interior design business. Nonetheless, you should consider this method if you have the ability to conduct a personal marketing campaign.

- Professional associations, such as ASID maintain a job bank for use by their members. Have you considered joining a local chapter of such a group, among other benefits, to take advantage of this service?

- Registering with a headhunter. Advanced professionals in some instances may be approached by employment placement specialists known informally as *headhunters*. These recruiters are usually hired by design-related businesses to fill highly specialized positions. These might include the position of senior design director or other positions requiring demonstrated management abilities or business-generating skills on the part of the successful candidate. These employment specialists are paid on a commission basis, typically calculated as a percentage of the annual salary offered to a hired candidate by a client company. Recruiters typically keep files of professionals whom they believe they may be able to place, or find employment for, once their client has an available job. As a result, more advanced design professionals sometimes register—confidentially, of course—with headhunters. Headhunters also maintain their own list of potential candidates whom they might like to match with jobs offered by their clients in the future.

It may be necessary to use headhunters if you are seeking a highly specialized job, since many of these positions are not publicly posted. However, some of the practices engaged in by recruiters may not be appealing. Some headhunters require designers interested in finding more remunerative work through use of their services to register only with them and no other recruiters. This prevents established designers from knowing all the employment options that might be available. Recruiters receive a commission from an employer once a candidate is hired. As recruiters bluntly said to a candidate they considered highly qualified and desirable for placement, that person was "money waiting to be made" (for the recruiter, of course). The decision to work with or respond to headhunters is a personal one for a design professional. Although recruiters do have the incentive to gain repeat business if they are successful in keeping both the employer/client and the prospective employee satisfied with the outcome of their services, the amount of money they receive for those services may be an incentive as well.

These are some of the most common and obvious ways in which information about the availability of interior design jobs is transmitted. Most, if not all, of these methods are probably known to you, and perhaps you have at some time considered using them. What may be less obvious, however, are the guidelines to keep in mind when searching for a job through *any* means. Other texts found at local bookstores can also provide guidance on job-search techniques and possible employers in a given area.

GUIDELINES FOR SEEKING WORK IN INTERIOR DESIGN

A few techniques you might consider include the following:

- The job-hunting process takes time, energy, and patience. Do not get discouraged when you hear time and again that you lack the necessary experience.
- Network with others as much as possible. Ask about companies that and individuals who are hiring. Leave résumés with people whom you think might be interested in what you have to offer. In fact, try hard to develop your own pipeline of those who want to see you succeed and will work to make your name and availability known. For example, after you get to know people who work in showrooms and retail stores, you could simply ask them, "Who's hiring?" "What are they look-

ing for?" Clients of these vendors will often informally mention to them an interest in hiring new personnel. Your goal is to have them suggest your name in such instances. Similarly, if you have friends employed in the design industry—perhaps people whom you knew in school—make it known that you'd like to be kept in mind with respect to a potential job opening.

◆ Do as much research as possible on the interior design industry. It is, of course, important to keep up with new trends and products, new design points of view, and the like. However, also pay attention to the issues facing employers of interior designers, and consider what kinds of firms seem to thrive while others seem stagnant. In particular, look at the area in which you desire to practice. What services seem to be needed, and what firms provide them? If you are interested in contract interior design, you can keep up with the local commercial real estate market by reading business journals. Is there a surplus of office space remaining to be leased (and, thus, less of a need for services), or are old office spaces being sought out by clients to be made new again by designers or firms that provide renovation-focused services? Knowing the direction in which your industry is headed is critical for the success of your job search. The only way to understand that market is to research its existing conditions.

◆ Develop and maintain a job-hunt routine. What are you going to do each day to further your search? Create a schedule of tasks you commit to perform, much like routinely exercising, until you have found employment.

◆ Sometimes it is beneficial to have a friend with whom you can share the concerns that arise during this process—a person who is interested in you and your success. Try not to dwell on the setbacks, but focus on what has gone well despite the outcome. Sharing such matters with a friend can go a long way toward alleviating the anxieties and frustrations of the job-search process.

◆ Whether you choose to work for others as a valued employee or to work for yourself, is there any one thing to keep in mind when you are starting your work life and finding your place in the profession? Consider the successful designers with whom you are familiar. What skills or attributes do you think contributed to their success?

Most, if not all, of those professionals gained their success by identifying a need—maybe not in a formal way, but based on their own experiences or intuition—for a particular interior design approach or service that was not being met by existing practitioners. In short, they discovered a need for some kind of service and then found a way to satisfy the consumer's need or desire.

MEETING THE NEED FOR NEW DESIGN SERVICES

Consider what is currently being discussed about interior design in the world at large, and then ask yourself what innovative design issues might be interesting to consumers in your area. What is not being offered in your community that you think should be available? In this context, your research into the interior design industry will be of further benefit. The needs and, therefore, opportunities you identify can then develop into individual projects that can form the basis for your career—a career built on a succession of such projects.

As you conclude this chapter and start your work life, you may wonder about what career opportunities lie ahead for you. How, you might ask, can you find jobs or projects that will allow you to work in interior design? If this is your concern, think about the following scenario. Practicing designers are now expected to accomplish more than designing spaces that satisfy aesthetic principles only. According to design-education commentators, design studies also need to focus on exploring environmental design issues. This includes the teaching of sustainable concepts, deemed increasingly important as environmental problems accelerate (Harwood 2004). As you recall, the concept of *sustainability* refers to those practices that promote environmentally responsible designs and products (Odell 2002). How might a design practitioner find career opportunities in promoting the concept of sustainability, an issue now currently familiar to relatively few consumers?

Those same consumers, however, might very well be interested in how sustainable concepts could be applied to promote healthier living conditions for themselves and their families. Think about it: Health consciousness, or healthy living, is a topic widely discussed among consumers and prevalent in the media. Even everyday conversations focus on diet, exercise, and, for designers' purposes, ways that consumers may better make health-conscious choices in their daily lives. Perhaps you can be the design professional who is acclaimed for applying concepts of sustainability on a broad scale, in ways that appeal to a consumer's desire for healthier living and thereby make sustainable concepts as widely in demand as the most popular esthetic.

Whether you begin your working life as an employee or choose to work in your own business, beginning work as an interior designer involves identifying and exploring opportunities. These opportunities enable you to apply your design knowledge and skills in ways that satisfy a consumer's demands and solve their problems. The ability to use their skills to meet consumer needs enables designers to solve their own problem of finding and retaining work throughout their careers.

REFERENCES

Encarta® World English Dictionary. 2004. North American ed. Microsoft Corporation. Developed for Microsoft by Bloomsbury Publishing.

Curzon, Susan C. 1995. *Managing the Interview: A How-to-Do-It Manual.* New York: Neal-Shuman Publishers.

Hamadeh, Samer, and Mark Oldman. 2003. *The Internship Bible.* New York: Princeton Review.

Harwood, Buie. 2004. *Issues and Trends in Interior Design Education. The Interior Design Profession, Facts and Figures.* Washington, D.C.: American Society of Interior Designers.

Ingols, Cynthia, and Mary Shapiro. 2003. *Your Job Interview.* New York: Silver Lining Books.

Kennedy, Joyce Lain. 2002. *Resumes for Dummies*, 4th ed. New York: John Wiley & Sons.

Massey, Anne. 2001. *Interior Design of the 20th Century*, Revised and expanded ed. Thames & Hudson World of Art Series. New York: Thames & Hudson, Inc.

Odell, William. 2002. *Sustainable Design. Interior Design Handbook of Professional Practice.* Coleman, Cindy, ed. New York: McGraw-Hill.

STRATEGIES-IN-ACTION PROJECTS

STRATEGIC PLANNING PROJECT

In this chapter and in chapter 15, you are studying how to achieve your professional goals in interior design. In the Strategic Planning Project, which you completed in chapter 13, you presented in great detail the characteristics of what you thought would be an ideal business venture.

As part of that process, you discussed the focus of your business practice. What steps might you take now, while you are still a student, to make your participation in that practice a reality? The purpose of this chapter's Strategic Planning Project is to start you on your way to that exciting goal.

The process begins with an inventory of the many skills and talents you now possess as a result of your education, work experience, and other skills reflected in significant accomplishments. Résumés provide one type of assessment, but do not present the full range of your skills and abilities because they are typically focused on obtaining a job, which has characteristics defined by others. What about the job you described in the plan for your ideal interior design business, the one that would be the best showcase for your interests and talents? Since you defined the characteristics of that job, even its business environment, it makes sense now for you to take stock of your current abilities and skills to know what you will need to learn, accomplish, or experience to be qualified for that work. In this section, you will prepare that necessary inventory; and in chapter 15, using your completed Strategic Planning Project and the Personal Skills Assessment Worksheet (see Form 14.8), you will devise a plan of action to reach the professional business goals to which you aspire and have devoted much effort to describing. So, how might you assess your education and experience? Have your worksheet (Form 14.8) available as you begin this project.

1. *Summarize Your Accomplishments*
You will note that the first section of Form 14.8 contains three spaces for you to write down your academic, work, and significant life experiences and/or achievements. These section is devoted to just the facts, and you should list the activities chronologically, from the earliest to the latest. Remember, this section is intended for listing facts such as "graduated from High School of Performing and Visual Arts," "received bachelor's degree/associate degree in interior design (pending)," and "worked as sales associate in Furniture Store X as assistant manager."

2. *Skills Obtained from Accomplishments*
As a result of your academic, work, and life accomplishments, you are now able to perform many different tasks. Summarize those tasks in this section. For example, as a result of management-related accomplishments you may have acquired from working at a retail store, you are now able to oversee the work of a group of people. Or in your early high school education, you were able to learn technical skills, such as CAD abilities, over a period of years, so that by the time you reached college you had

PERSONAL SKILLS ASSESSMENT WORKSHEET

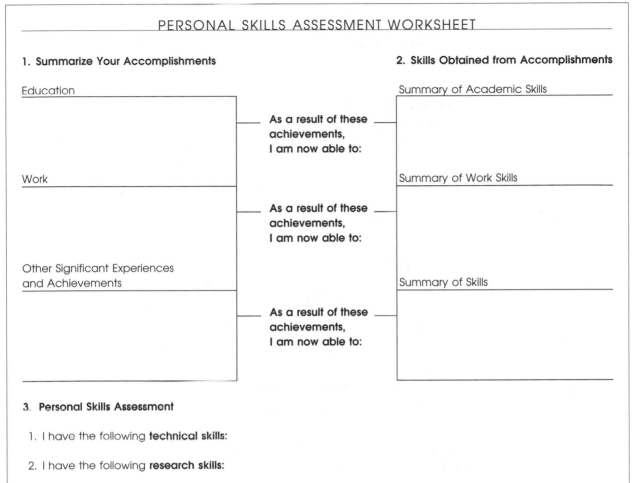

1. Summarize Your Accomplishments

Education

Work

Other Significant Experiences
and Achievements

As a result of these
achievements,
I am now able to:

As a result of these
achievements,
I am now able to:

As a result of these
achievements,
I am now able to:

2. Skills Obtained from Accomplishments

Summary of Academic Skills

Summary of Work Skills

Summary of Skills

3. Personal Skills Assessment

1. I have the following **technical skills:**

2. I have the following **research skills:**

3. I have the following **entrepreneurial skills:**

4. I have the following **leadership skills:**

5. I have the following **management skills:**

6. I have the following **interpersonal/interactive skills:**

7. I have the following **training/teaching skills:**

8. I have the following **administrative skills:**

9. I have the following **creative skills:**

10. I have the following **language skills:**

11. I have the following **marketing skills:**

12. I have the following **quantitative skills:**

13. I have the following **sales skills:**

developed advanced proficiency in that area. This section of the work-sheet asks you to provide a paragraph-long summary of the skills you obtained as a result of the accomplishments you identified in the summary of your academic, work, and life experiences.

3. *Personal Skills Assessment*

In essence, this section asks you to list and assess the personal and professional skills you indicated in your summary of skills. Your instructor can assist you by explaining in detail what each of the listed skills involves.

RESIDENTIAL INTERIOR DESIGN PROJECT SIMULATION

In your next-to-last encounter with Lee you will follow her lead in assembling your own portfolio, if you have not already done so. Because of her hectic schedule working on the Abernathy children's project, Lee has been so busy that she neglected keeping her own portfolio up-to-date. With your help, she will create order out of the chaos of drawings she has accumulated. And she will compile a portfolio that could then be used to attract future clients and perhaps even help her get her own ideal interior design job. As you participate in this project with Lee, you may be able to identify issues in your own portfolio that you should address before presenting it to others, especially potential employers. This simulation will help you make decisions about what to include and how to prepare a professional's portfolio. For this project you will need a blank Compiling Your Portfolio Checklist form (Form 14.3).

Lee's Diary

My first thought is "what a mess!" My portfolio, that is! After I got the job here at Imagination Unlimited, I forgot about it, and then after I got the Abernathy project—whew! There has been no time. I need to get it pulled together, that's for sure. I am going to stick with a portfolio of original drawings in the 14-by-17-inch format. At least for residential work, prospective clients seem to like to see full-sized work in, of course, good condition.

I have a list somewhere of what should be in the portfolio, and I'll follow that and really get this pulled together. I'm glad I have a real project like the Abernathy children's room to include in addition to the one I did as a senior. I need a full project—start to finish—in the portfolio, and the list I found will tell me what else. It's going to be some work to get this all done, but I think I need to keep it up-to-date now before it's too late.

Using a form like the one to which Lee refers, assemble items for inclusion in your own portfolio. Form 14.3, Compiling Your Portfolio Checklist, is included for that purpose. Before leaving this project, ask yourself what steps you might take to avoid being in a situation like Lee's—that is, allowing the pressure of current work to prevent you from actively developing your portfolio. Your portfolio is the most accessible window into your technical skills and an expression of your design point of view. It is also a record of accomplished projects. Doesn't it make sense for you to develop a plan for keeping it current?

CONTRACT INTERIOR DESIGN CASE STUDY: THE CASE OF THE INQUISITIVE INTERN

As you complete your study of interior design professional practices, you may soon have the opportunity to participate in an internship program offered by your school. What do you want to accomplish as a result of that activity? As a matter of fact, depending on the organization of your interior design program, you may have participated in an internship program prior to studying professional practices. If so, was your internship experience everything you hoped it would be? This case study seeks to do more than recount the facts of one internship experience. Instead, it is intended to get you thinking about what you want to achieve as a result of participating in your internship program. In other words, what do you want to get out of your internship? Or, better still, how will your internship help you reach the professional goals you ultimately wish to achieve? If you have already completed an internship, how did that experience help you to understand the interior design industry? Do you now have a better sense of how to blend your interests and abilities with those of others? Did you identify a mentor, or professional whose work—and manner of work—you wish to emulate?

This case will introduce to you to Jason Rensburg, and you will learn about Jason, his personality, and his professional interests as he embarks on his internship with the large architectural and interior design firm, Arch-Deco, based in Los Angeles, California. Then you learn more about the firm itself, its organization, its practice groups, and its design philosophy. On the basis of this information, you will assist Jason when he drafts a series of five realistic learning objectives he could hope to achieve as a result of participating in the firm's internship program. You will experience this process, or one highly similar, as you prepare for your internship.

- Students meet with an internship coordinator or administrator at their school to agree on objectives for them to satisfy as part of the experience. Both students and administrators consider the students' interests as well as characteristics of the businesses offering internship positions.
- They decide on specific objectives or skills for the student-intern to accomplish, and consider how the student-intern intends to meet those objectives or learn those desired skills during the course of the internship.
- The interns and the administrators decide what factors or criteria will determine whether those objectives or skills have been met.

You will assist Jason in determining whether he satisfied the objectives he has set out to achieve. To complete this project, you will require a blank Internship Learning Objectives form (Form 14.6).

If you participated in an internship program prior to this study of professional practices, you already know how that internship helped you to achieve goals you may have set earlier. Additional questions for students who have participated in an internship program are included in this case study as well. To answer questions, you will need to consult Form 14.6.

Designer Biography

Student: Jason Rensburg, age 22, about to complete his junior year at college

Major: Interior Design, with emphasis on commercial applications

Program: Four-year (120 credits), leading to a bachelor's degree at a large university located in Los Angeles, California

Growing up in Los Angeles, Jason was surrounded by and intrigued with the architecture and interior design indigenous to the city. When he entered college, Jason determined that it was interior design and its inherent ability to promote human interactions and influence behavior that interested him most. With that passion, he dove into the coursework of the interior design program. In his first two years of study, he completed the basics of design theory, drafting, and CAD training. In his second year, he studied and mastered advanced applications of these technical skills and prepared a sound portfolio of work for acceptance into upper-division interior design studies.

Jason was, by his own admission, happiest at the drawing board or when working with CAD in pursuit of developing his techniques in those media. The level of his technical skill was noticed by instructors, many of whom commented on his abilities. Some of them noted, however, that the projects he produced, although completed with a strong use of technique and attention to detail, were, as one instructor put it, "too ethereal" for real-world application. Many instructors recommended Jason pay closer attention to programming and design research classes.

Jason had no real experience working in a professional office setting prior to his internship. He was unsure about how interior designers obtained clients' and because he had not yet taken a class in professional practices, or even in business disciplines, he was not familiar with issues such as how to set design fees. He had seen a contract for design services once but had not read it. Like many of his classmates, Jason also disliked routine tasks, such as properly returning swatch books and cleaning up studio work space.

It was his extremely high degree of technical skill that made Jason's portfolio stand out for the school's internship coordinator. As a result, the coordinator suggested that Jason apply for one of four internship positions with ArchDeco, a locally-based architectural and interior design firm with offices in several major cities throughout the world and a combined staff of approximately 175 people. Jason was thrilled about the opportunity to work with such a large firm.

Firm Dossier

ArchDeco, founded 1979, Los Angeles, California

About the Firm (excerpt):

ArchDeco is a proponent of master planning and programming practices to ensure that its contributions to the collective built environment reflect the functional and human needs of those who experience them. The firm's practice has focused extensively on interpreting institutional concerns in installations including those sponsored by the U.S. government as well as those of private-sector clients, such as multinational corporations.

The Firm's Design Philosophy (excerpt):

ArchDeco is a client-focused, full-service architectural, interior design, and interior architectural firm. Projects are developed and carried out by client studios, a diverse group of professionals dedicated to fulfilling the range of services necessary to follow a project from first client contact through final entity evaluation.

Stephen Thomas, a principle with the firm, interviewed Jason and was impressed by his passion for interior design and his technical ability. He told Jason he would have some assigned tasks to perform as part of his paid internship. He also told Jason that he might assist in any practice group he wished, but recommended he try to work with as many groups as possible.

With those words, Jason went off to consider what the internship at ArchDeco had in store for him and what objectives he could share with the school's internship coordinator. As you consider possible objectives for Jason with Form 14.6 in front of you, identify five objectives for him to accomplish based on his interests, his strengths, and his weaknesses. Also identify the goals you would like him to achieve on the particular resources Arch Deco can offer. For example, Jason appears to have a limited understanding of how businesses of this kind operate financially. In this light, what might be a realistic goal for him to achieve while he is working at ArchDeco?

After you accomplish that first task, suggest ways for Jason to accomplish his objectives, again given his interests, strengths, and weaknesses, as well as the activities and mode of operations. For example, how might he gain a better understanding of the financial practices of design firms while still carrying out his assigned tasks?

Finally, suggest benchmarks, or measures by which Jason (and the school's internship coordinator) can conclude that he accomplished the objectives you identified for him. A logical way for Jason to measure his success in learning about the finances of the firm is for him to participate in the preparation of a financial or accounting spreadsheet and be able to explain its components and their importance.

If you have already completed an internship and have also completed the assessment of Jason's learning experience, ask yourself what different set of objectives you would define for yourself, knowing what you now know about internships. For example, did you learn something that you did not expect? What was it? As you have seen throughout this text, defining objectives and then assessing the extent to which they have been met are important skills for both student interns and interior design professionals.

CHAPTER FIFTEEN

PLANNING YOUR CAREER

Our life is what our thoughts make it.

MARCUS AURELIUS

WHY THIS CHAPTER IS IMPORTANT TO YOU

What career issues might you expect to encounter once you leave school? This chapter is important because it explores two objectives related to planning your interior design career: identifying options available to professionals who are making the transition from student to professional, and describing how you can develop your career over time. Leaving a professional practices course with an understanding of how to pursue meaningful, responsible work is perhaps the best way to conclude your study of this multifaceted subject. Once you have read this chapter and completed the final phase of your Strategic Planning Project, you will have learned how to start your career and, in the process, considered your own strategies for designing a business—and a life—in interior design.

PROFESSIONAL PRACTICES PORTFOLIO

As this book concludes, so does your professional practices portfolio containing review questions. Add the following questions and responses to your portfolio so you can review later.

1. Describe some of the benefits of practicing interior design in a retail or wholesale selling environment. What are the deterrents to doing so?
2. Why might working in a small studio setting be appealing to some interior designers?
3. Why might a small setting not be appealing?
4. What career issues are faced by interior designers who practice in large business settings, such as architectural and interior design firms?
5. What kinds of credentials are usually required of interior designers who are interested in pursuing academic teaching careers?
6. Where might you find information about wages and salaries of interior designers practicing in your geographic area?
7. What are CEUs, and how can you earn credit for them?
8. Do all designers face CEU requirements? Which designers do and do not?
9. What career decisions are particularly relevant to interior designers?

OBJECTIVES TO CONSIDER

There are an incredible number of career options available to interior designers. There are many different endeavors to which practitioners may apply their interior design education and expertise. And there are a variety of businesses seeking the services of designers. For example, people with interior design backgrounds may work in a range of diverse fields: as exhibition and display designers or as technical consultants in specialized areas such as fine art acquisition or compliance with legally mandated Americans with Disabilities (ADA) standards for public spaces. In addition, businesses that hire interior designers range from small locally operated studios to large international architectural firms that include interior design teams. In short, a career in interior design may take form in many ways and in many venues. In the presence of such career diversity, the challenge for students, including you, might be to identify which of these many options to pursue. Surveying the career landscape to learn what it has to offer, as this chapter does, will provide information that you can use to form your own plan for entering and finding success in the profession.

As if facing these issues were not enough, have you stopped to think about the career trajectory as a professional that you will develop based on your interests and work-related experiences? Perhaps everything about interior design seems fascinating to you; yet it is troubling in the sense that you may not know the right career choice for you. Conversely, you may already have an idea about how you will focus your career, based on your interests and by having worked through projects in this book such as the personal assessment and strategic business plan that you developed. Whether you know how to plan and develop a career direction in interior design, this chapter's objectives should help you assess the many options that are available to you when making such an important work and life decision. This chapter identifies and addresses two important career objectives for interior design professionals.

The first objective identifies career options available to interior designers, describing the kinds of jobs commonly filled by individuals with formal interior design education and the work settings in which these jobs may be found. Once you have identified the jobs and venues that are attractive to you, you may be concerned about situations that may come up in your career. Therefore, this chapter's second objective focuses on career development concerns such as continuing your education in interior design as well as recognizing and preparing you for two important milestones, those of changing the focus of your professional work and deciding to retire (concerns many practitioners have).

IDENTIFYING CAREER OPTIONS

The first career decision made by many students is whether they wish to practice interior design within the broad categories of **residential** work, which involves the personal dwelling spaces of individuals or families. Lee, who was portrayed in the Residential Interior Design Project Simulation, chose to work with residential projects. That project demonstrates the degree to which Lee is required to respond to the interests and concerns of her clients, usually by means of personal interactions. *Commercial* or *contract* interior design focuses on the modifications to physical environments destined for use by large groups of people and not intended for use as a permanent, personal dwelling. The Contract Interior Design Case Study aims to give you an idea of the breadth of different applications—gyms, restaurants, and college dormitories—that are subject to the professional attention of commercial, or contract, interior designers.

CATEGORIES OF INTERIOR DESIGN WORK

How can you choose between the two categories of design work if you are not yet sure in which area to practice? One way would be to focus on your interests and your education. Would you like to work in family settings and with clients like the Abernathys? Or does the thought of it make you unhappy? Also consider the kind of practice that is most suitable for your level of education. Many practitioners with two-year associate degrees find it difficult to find positions in large design firms that focus on contract design and are made up of architects and designers with a high level of formal education. However, a proven ability to secure lucrative projects may be a more persuasive factor than formal academic credentials. This chapter focuses on exploring three career avenues down which you may travel: seeking positions with retail and wholesale vendors, working in independent interior design firms or architectural firms that include interior design project groups, and seeking a career as a teacher in academic institutions.

RETAIL AND WHOLESALE VENDORS

If you visit retail and wholesale businesses in the design industry, you will undoubtedly meet interior designers who work there. **Sales associates** in retail establishments and **vendor representatives** (**reps**) at the wholesale level often have academic degrees in interior design. It makes sense that full-fledged interior designers would be hired by these businesses. These designers have been instructed in the formalities of product specification and end-use concerns, among other subjects. With this background, they are very well qualified to assist both retail and wholesale purchasers of merchandise. These venues may sell office and commercial furnishings or sell furniture to retail customers. Retail venues differ not only in the products they sell and how they operate, but also in how they compensate their interior design employees.

Dealer Showrooms

As you might suspect, the first of these businesses, sellers of office and commercial furnishings, provide merchandise that you commonly see in work environments—desks, office systems, and related items. Most of these sellers are considered to be **dealers** in one or a few manufacturers' products. Herman Miller, Steelcase, and Knoll, among others, are well-known, prestigious companies providing these goods that establish dealership agreements with other showrooms or open their own. Dealers in office furnishings typically have a staff of interior designers who are knowledgeable in topics such as space planning and who are capable of developing ways to use a manufacturer's products to satisfy the needs of end users. End users who buy the products and services of office furniture dealers include law and medical offices as well as businesses that require office landscapes to house numerous workers. Designers who are hired to work in this area need to have knowledge of commercial practices such as the competitive bidding process and standards of building construction as well as the state and local codes regulating commercial buildings.

Designers who are employed by dealers of office furnishings are usually part of a team or staff of designers who work together to complete a series of projects. Some designers may work on project issues such as space planning and schematic design preparation, while others focus on procurement of goods from a manufacturer by preparing and reviewing detailed specifications and purchase orders. Other designers may be primarily responsible for calculating and administering bids that a company submits. Together, these teams are usually called upon to present a dealership's design proposal for a space in conjunction with the individuals responsible for developing new client business.

In recent years, specialized dealers in a number of product lines have opened showrooms similar to those that showcase office furnishings for sale. Manufacturers of kitchen, bathroom, and closet components, sometimes of very high quality and correspondingly high retail prices, seek the services of professionally trained interior designers. Designers in this field often obtain specialized designation from professional organizations such as the National Kitchen and Bath Association. As with their office-furnishings counterparts, these designers frequently represent only one or, at the most, a few product lines. Typically, they are knowledgeable about planning the installation of their dealers' products in private dwellings and specifying customer-desired features such as cabinetry hardware and surface finishes, among other tasks.

For the most part, office-furniture dealers compensate the designers they retain by means of a salary and some benefits, perhaps participation in company-sponsored health plans. In addition, these designers may also receive a commission, or percentage of the sales price of certain types of merchandise they sell—usually accessory or selected items the dealer wishes to promote. Many entry-level interior designers seek employment in dealer showrooms so they can gain experience while earning a predictable income.

There are several drawbacks that designers should consider before choosing to work in dealer showrooms. The first may be the inherent limitations of the work itself. Designers in these settings often have little say about the projects that or the clients with whom they are required to work. In addition, these designers have to select only the products or services provided by the manufacturer that is represented by the dealership. Such constraints may become oppressive to designers who wish to be more fully engaged in selecting projects, clients, and products, as would a designer in private practice. The degree to which a designer requires a steady, salary-based income versus the ability to work more independently will influence the duration of a designer's tenure as a staff designer in a dealership setting. External economic factors are important influences as well. In robust economic times, when businesses have the resources to add to a company's workforce there is greater demand for design services to functionally and attractively place these new workers. Correspondingly, there is greater demand for interior designers who are interested in and capable of working in dealer showrooms. As consumers feel confident that they can afford amenities such as kitchens, baths, and closets, there is an increased demand for the merchandise and services of specialized dealer showrooms. Unfortunately, when negative economic factors result in less demand for a dealer's products and services, designers may find themselves out of work. Without a client base that they themselves established, designers in these settings may have difficulty obtaining work through personal referrals.

Retailers

Another category of possible employers are furniture and furnishings retailers. These venues focus on selling merchandise directly to consumers at retail prices. They may take the form of large freestanding stores or sections of department and specialty stores devoted to selling furniture, accessories, and decorative items. These retail venues offer a unique opportunity for young designers to gain experience working on complicated residential projects with clients they have attracted. This setting, moreover, allows these designers to establish a base of operation that can develop into their own interior design businesses. For example, a designer may develop a personal relationship with a store customer by assisting with several initial purchases or working on a series of small projects.

Some designers, in fact, develop a client following and client referrals that enable them to establish a lucrative career. Typically, these designers have strong selling skills in addition to their design education.

Designers working in this setting typically receive compensation in the form of an hourly wage combined with commissions they receive from selling the retailer's merchandise. This can produce high earnings for designers with an established clientele and business-prospecting abilities. Depending on the location of the store and the compensation percentages, designers can earn substantial incomes by operating out of retail stores. However, this kind of arrangement may be less remunerative for those who lack sales skills or the ability to weather periods of low earnings. Benefits, such as health-plan participation, vary, depending on the size and location of the retailer. The emphasis in these businesses is primarily on selling merchandise carried in the stores, which may not hold the interest of designers interested in more advanced applications of interior design research and practice.

Retail selling may prove limiting even to designers who otherwise enjoy personal contact with clients that they meet in this setting. For one thing, many stores limit the range of products that designers may select for their projects. It is not uncommon for stores to require designers who work there to specify only items off the floor, that is, already on hand, or that can be ordered only from the group of manufacturers that supply the store. This kind of arrangement works to clients' disadvantages as well, since clients are shown only merchandise that the store carries or can easily obtain, not necessarily items that may be better suited to their needs.

As you are aware by now, a designer provides many more services than simply making merchandise available to clients. Do retail stores require designers to charge fees for activities such as project management and generating schematics? Typically retailers do not, instead offsetting the expense of these activities (for which designers in other settings would have charged) against the revenue generated from the retail sales of merchandise. That markup could be equal to 50 or 100 percent of the wholesale cost of the merchandise. The markup amount is the source of a designer's commission as well.

INTERIOR DESIGN AND ARCHITECTURAL FIRMS

The practice of interior design takes place within settings other than retail vendors and independently owned design studios. Working in specialized interior design firms and architectural firms that include interior design practice groups provides another career option for interior designers. Are you interested in working in a more structured setting, in which employed designers have formal job titles and specific job requirements that they are expected to fulfill? Furthermore, how do you feel about holding a position in which you are expected to routinely identify and develop a succession of new clients for the business—an activity, by the way, that is often necessary before you can advance to senior-level designer? Jason, the design student whose internship experience was portrayed in the Contract Interior Design Case Study in Chapter 14, worked in such a firm.

ACADEMIC INSTITUTIONS

Among the career options for interior designers is the role of design educator. Along with other forms of practice, this area provides a great many options for career development. Academic institutions usually require postgraduate education and a Ph.D. degree. These positions interest designers who desire to focus on teaching and research in academic settings.

Opportunities also exist for practicing interior designers to teach part-time as adjunct, or nontenured, faculty. Typically, these positions are held on a term-by-term basis, when educational institutions require additional instructors. Adjunct faculty members receive financial compensation for their services but may possibly not be eligible for benefits. The attraction to these positions is that they allow practitioners an opportunity to share their knowledge with students and also to learn of advances in interior design education and research. If teaching appeals to you, consider discussing with your instructors how you might pursue working as an adjunct, or, should you decide teaching and research are your main interests, how you might pursue a full-time academic career in interior design.

DEVELOPING YOUR CAREER

Times and people change. In this regard, interior design practitioners are no different from other professionals. Unlike many occupations, however, interior design offers a diverse number of career options that practitioners may pursue when they decide that they, too, are interested in doing something different with their lives. What major career decisions might a designer face? What options exist for developing new careers in design, and what can designers do to prepare for career changes? This section focuses on three decisions that many interior designers are called on to make during their careers: first, finding a career focus; then, continuing their education in interior design; and finally, retiring from practice. Some of these career decisions are of immediate concern to you; others are less imminent.

FINDING AN INITIAL CAREER FOCUS

Are you unsure about what to do regarding your career in interior design—your professional life, for that matter? Try this idea: Step back from interior design altogether; think about the pastimes and activities you enjoy. Perhaps you like the excitement found in such settings as Las Vegas or in particular industries such as entertainment. Is your hobby related to collecting items of some kind? Are sports an interest of yours? Maybe your favorite pastime involves spending time with children. After asking yourself these and related questions, explore how interior design can enhance the enjoyment of those activities. What could you do as an interior designer to make others enjoy these activities, too? For example, how might you apply your knowledge of interior design to make auditoriums and entertainment venues more exciting, attractive, functional, and more accessible to a greater number of participants? That same question also holds for sports stadiums and arenas. Furthermore, how might you as an interior designer better serve other collectors? By applying the design skills you learned in your interior design studies, how could you design products for displaying and storing collectibles and art that are more beautiful and functional than those currently available? Finally, if you enjoy spending time with children and have an interior design education, how might you apply the space-planning principles you learned to better serve the many needs of parents, schools, and child-care centers? Many career advisers suggest searching for what motivates and inspires you, and then applying what you know to those inspirations when fulfilling them. A passion for interior design may have interested you enough to study it; discovering and pursuing ways to apply that passion may very well be the key to you career success. In short, employment options exist for designers in a wide variety of different industries and professions. If you are still deciding on your career focus, review Box 15.1 to get an idea of the many ways in which you can work in interior design.

CONTINUING EDUCATION IN INTERIOR DESIGN

Learning does not and should not stop once you conclude your formal education. Practitioners of most professions have long been required by laws governing their practices to keep abreast of changes by taking classes on a regular basis. These classes are typically referred to as **continuing education** courses. As you can see in Table 15.1, interior designers are now facing continuing education requirements in a number of states. Usually, state regulatory agencies deem it necessary for practitioners to take these courses to maintain their full professional, good standing and continue to practice. Interior designers who practice in states that have regulatory laws and professional oversight boards are now joining attorneys, physicians, accountants, and others who are subject to state regulations.

By now, you are familiar with the NCIDQ exam. One way you might prepare for it is a study course offered by many local chapters of the American Society of Interior Design to both members and nonmembers. The Self-Testing Exercises for Preprofessionals (or S.T.E.P. Program), usually a two-day series of workshops, offers study suggestions and opportunities to develop further test-taking skills, including preparation for answering both multiple choice and practicum portions. Information about times and costs of this program are available on the A.S.I.D. Web site (www.asid.org), or through local chapters. The NCIDQ offers samples of actual questions and practicum problems previously administered for a fee through its Web site (see the Publication Order Form, as part of the Examination Candidate Application and Handbook at wwww.ncidq.org).

PLANNING FOR RETIREMENT FROM PRACTICE

Individuals may practice interior design professionally as long as they are able or until they decide to retire. Of course, these are extremely personal decisions, which young practitioners are likely to view as too far removed from their current situations. But are they? This discussion focuses on a key issue in making retirement decisions: identifying ways to accumulate the financial means to retire. Because practitioners need to begin planning and saving for retirement even during the earliest stages of their careers, methods of initiating savings and investment plans may be considered by new designers who are recent graduates.

An interior designer who has been practicing for five years noted the importance of starting and regularly contributing to a savings account. Since

BOX 15.1. CAREERS LIST

CAREERS LIST

Many designers are self-employed or work in design or architectural firms. However, design skills are used in a number of industries. If you are thinking about a career in interior design, you may want to consider one of the following occupations:

ENTERTAINMENT
Design staff (in-house) for:
Amusement parks
Casinos
Movies
Television
Theaters/
   Auditoriums

GOVERNMENT AND INSTITUTIONS
Design staff (in-house) for:
Colleges, universities, and schools
Federal, state, and local government institutions
   (public buildings, schools, prisons)
Health care facilities (hospitals, clinics)
Medical supply companies
Medical furniture companies
Museum display designs
Hospitality industries (hotels, motels, restaurants,
   convention, and conference centers)
Senior housing
Special-needs housing

OFFICES AND CORPORATIONS
In-house design staff for corporations:
Office-design firms
Office-supply companies
Systems furniture dealerships
Real estate companies
Large developers with space-planning departments
Rehabilitation developers with in-house design departments
Freelance consultants for small firms
Staff space planner
Residences/residential developments

FACILITIES MANAGEMENT
Facilities Manager for:
Assisted-living communities
Health care facilities
Industry
Office buildings
Museums
Parks
Public buildings
   and universities
Real estate companies

MANUFACTURERS
Design staff (in-house) for:
Carpet and floor coverings
Fabrics/textiles
Furniture
Lighting
Wall coverings
In-house interior design staff
Marketing staff
Product design staff
Sales representatives
Trade-show exhibit design staff
Education
Product Design and Development
Product/furniture design

(continued)

BOX 15.1 (continued)

OFFICES AND CORPORATIONS (continued)
Children's spaces
Custom furniture design
Design to accommodate aging-in-place
Design for the physically challenged
Kitchen-and-bath designs
Window-treatment specialists

RETAIL
Colorists
Exhibit and display design firm staff
Home-fashion coordinator
Lighting design
Retail-store designer/space planners
Retail visual merchandising
Sales managers
Wholesale showroom designs

Adapted from ASID Careers List

this individual earned her living solely from commission-compensated sales, she noted the importance of having something to fall back on. Many business advisers suggest allocating a portion of each paycheck or commission check to a savings account plan offered by your bank or financial institution. The rates banks pay to depositors in the form of interest vary, as does the administration of these accounts. Nevertheless, accounts are relatively easy to set up and so you can make regular deposits. The challenge that savings accounts present, of course, is to ensure that you are routinely contributing to them, so that over time the benefits of the interest paid by the bank begin to compound. This means that the bank pays a set percentage amount of interest on what you deposited and on amounts of interest the bank previously paid as well. In this way, savings accounts can grow to become substantial retirement nest eggs.

In addition to opening and maintaining a savings account, interior designers may also consider making contributions to **Individual Retirement Accounts** or **IRAs**. There are two kinds of IRA accounts offered by banks and other lending or investment institutions. In very broad terms, the differences between the two relate to the tax benefits they offer. Under the laws in effect at the time this book was prepared, a traditional IRA taxes earnings from interest paid on contributions when it is paid out to the individual holding the account, usually during retirement.

TABLE 15.1
Understanding the CEU Process

1. Ascertain amount of Continuing Education Units (CEUs) required for renewal in state of practice.
This table contains a list of 24 states currently regulating the practice of interior design. Some have further established required amounts of **CEUs**—credits for completion of continuing education courses—that practitioners must satisfy to remain in good standing. Other states such as Colorado, Connecticut, Maine, Nevada, New York, and Virginia, as you can see have not, as of the date of this text, established continuing education criteria. New Jersey requires continuing education be completed every two years; however, students desiring to practice there and in Alabama are advised to consult appropriate governing bodies in those states to confirm exact requirements.

State	Hours Required	CEU credits	State	Hours Required	CEU credits
Alabama	YES	*See state requirements	**Minnesota**	24 hours every 2 years	2.4 CEUs/ 2 years
Arkansas	5 hours annually	.50 CEUs/year	**Missouri**	10 hours every 2 years	1.0 CEUs/ 2 years
California	10 hours every 2 years	1.0 CEUs/2 years	**Nevada**	NONE	
Colorado	NONE		**New Jersey**	YES	*See state requirements
Connecticut	NONE		**New Mexico**	8 hours annually	.80 CEUs/year
Florida	Not less than 20 hours every 2 years	2.0 CEUs/2 years	**New York**	NONE	
Georgia	12 hours every two years	1.2 CEUs/2 years	**Puerto Rico**	4.5 hours annually	.45 CEUs/year
Illinois	NONE		**Tennessee**	24 hours every 2 years	2.4 CEUs/ 2 years
Kentucky	12 hours annually	1.2 CEUs/year	**Texas**	8 hours annually	.80 CEUs/year
Louisiana	5 hours annually	.50 CEUs/year	**Virginia**	NONE	
Maine	NONE		**Wash., D.C.**	5 hours every 2 years	.50 CEUs/ 2 years
Maryland	10 hours every two years	1.0 CEUs/2 years	**Wisconsin**	9 hours every 2 years	.90 CEUs/ 2 years

2. Locate CEU designated classes offered by approved sponsor in your area.
3. Attend CEU class, and complete CEU documentation. Leave with sponsor.
4. NCIDQ receives completed CEU documentation from approved sponsor.
5. NCIDQ certifies to state accreditation board, or other appropriate authority, completion of CEU credits. Record is retained for NCIDQ's file.
6. NCIDQ certification of completion added to individual practitioner's file.

Usually registrants are notified if they require additional CEU credits for continued active status; however, it is a designer's obligation to obtain appropriate amount of CEU credits.

*State requirements are in process of change; check most recent requirements with agency responsible for oversight of interior design practice.

Table adapted from ASID Registration Laws, 2004

In addition, holders of IRA accounts may deduct the amount of their yearly contributions (up to certain amounts) when figuring their annual income taxes. If a traditional IRA plan is selected, it may result in retirees having to pay income taxes, which they may not wish to do; however, during the period they were making contributions to their retirement accounts, they often were able to use those contributions to lower the amount of annual income taxes they did pay. A **Roth IRA** lets you earn interest on contributions you make, which are not taxed when paid, or distributed, to you, assuming certain conditions are met. However, individuals holding a Roth IRA account cannot deduct the amounts of their contributions when figuring their annual income taxes. Again, consider the implications of this approach, since a retiree may not want to pay income taxes when he or she is no longer working.

Another type of retirement investment is a 401(k) plan. Under a "qualified plan" set up by an employer, employees deemed "eligible" may have a portion of their salary deferred, or set aside either before or after the employee pays income tax on that salary. Employers, then "match," or pay additional amounts of money to that portion contributed by employees, and may also share a percentage of company profits with plan participants. As these investments grow in amount, the employee does not have to pay taxes on these increases, known as "earnings." It is said that 401(k) investments are "tax-deferred" meaning employees are usually required to pay income taxes on amounts withdrawn from these plans. From the perspective of the employer, contributions made on behalf of employees are an additional cost, an important fact in which any business owner should be aware of. However, an important constraint placed on employee participants of 401(k) include limits, or "caps," on the percentage of contributions they may defer. There are also legal restrictions on when you can withdraw from 401(k) plans without incurring a financial penalty for doing so. Employees who are participants in such plans, who are under 59 years of age, are likely to incur such penalties. As you can see, investments are complicated but are important for young professionals to consider.

Advice about retirement accounts necessarily takes into account a great many personal issues affecting those who set up the accounts. This is especially true in instances where an individual wants to make investments in securities such as **stocks**, a form of partial ownership of a portion of a company usually referred to as shares. Another category includes **bonds**, which is a company's obligation to pay those who hold them. As you grow as a professional and approach the age when you consider retirement, your earlier decisions to save and invest for the future will be increasingly important.

REFERENCES

American Society of Interior Designers. 2004. *The Interior Design Profession: Facts & Figures.*

Bolles, Richard Nelson. 2003. *What Color Is Your Parachute? 2004: A Practical Guide for Job-Hunters and Career Changers.* Berkeley, California: Ten Speed Press.

Field, Shellcy. 2001. *Career Opportunities in the Retail and Wholesale Industry*. New York: Facts on File, Inc.

Goldsmith, John A., et al. 2001. *The Chicago Guide to Your Academic Career: A Portable Mentor for Scholars from Graduate School through Tenure*. Chicago: University of Chicago Press.

Green, Charles H. 2003. *Financing the Small Business: Raise Money for Your Business at Any Stage of Growth*. Avon, Massachusetts: Adams Media Corporation.

Jansen, Julie. 2003. *I Don't Know What I Want, but I Know It's Not This: A Step-by-Step Guide to Finding Gratifying Work*. New York: Penguin Books.

Lonier, Terri. 1998. Working Solo, 2nd ed. New York: John Wiley & Sons, Inc.

Piotrowski, Christine. 2004. *Becoming an Interior Designer*. New York: John Wiley & Sons, Inc.

Piper, Robert J. et al. 2000. *Opportunities in Architecture Careers*. New York: McGraw-Hill.

Salisbury, Dallas and Marc Robinson. 2001. *IRA and 401(k) Investing*. New York: D.K. Publishing, Inc.

STRATEGIES-IN-ACTION PROJECTS

STRATEGIC PLANNING PROJECT

For this chapter's Strategic Planning Project, you will devise a career development strategy personal to you, your interests, and your career goals. In this project, titled Developing Your Career Plan of Action (see Form 15.1), you will relate your current set of skills and abilities (as identified in Form 14.8, the Assessment of Personal Skills Worksheet) to the ideal interior design job you described in your Business Plan Project. By comparing the skills you have already obtained with those required for your ideal job or working environment, you can now begin to prepare for that ultimate career goal. On completing this project, you will know what further education and experience you need to reach that goal. You will need the following to begin:

1. Your completed Strategic Planning Project (chapters 1 through 13)
2. Your completed Personal Skills Assessment Worksheet (Form 14.8)
3. A blank copy of Form 15.1, Developing Your Career Plan of Action

After you have completed the personal skills assessment, you will have created an inventory of twelve skills that you obtained during your academic, work, and other experiences. In this project, you can compare those personal skills to the skills you will need to work successfully in your ideal interior design business.

Turning to Form 15.1, Developing Your Career Plan of Action, note the specific steps you will take to interpret your skills. True, this activity may appear at first glance to be a long process, but it goes fairly quickly since you are familiar with each of the steps from your work on the business plan project. Management skills as well as sales and selling skills have been discussed throughout this text; for example, the entire process of developing a business plan is a management activity, while sales and selling skills are explored in this chapter's discussion of careers in design showrooms and retail stores. For example, in the Strategic Planning Project found in chapter 6, "Managing Your Business," you described the characteristics of a position you would like to hold in your ideal interior design business. Fill in the appropriate blanks in Step One.

As you glance down the list of steps to take for this project, you will notice references to text chapters and corresponding business-plan tasks. For example, chapter 1 presented the initial brainstorming project, which was designed to stimulate your creative ability. That ability is probably highly developed when it comes to visual and spatial application. What about something as intangible as a business entity that may not even exist yet? Sometimes referred to as thinking outside the box, this ability is necessary to define a new direction in which to establish your ideal business. Reviewing your personal skills assessment, did you decide that your creative abilities included the capacity to conceive of an undefined concept? If you think that you need to enhance this type of creative ability, list the creative skills that you think are necessary and how you propose to enhance them. With respect to creative visualization and description of abstract concepts, refer back to chapter 8, particularly the Contract Interior Design Case Study: The Case of the Desirable Dorm, Part 1, and the discussion in chapter 8 on the innovative ways in which design groups such as IDEO enhance their creative decision-making process. Might learning more about such approaches enhance your own creative skills?

As you continue down the list you will find that other steps are straightforward, with easy correlations between the skills you identify in your personal skills assessment and what you describe as important or necessary attributes required for your ideal interior design business. Each step asks you to conclude—as a result of your working through each segment

FORM 15.1. DEVELOPING YOUR CAREER PLAN OF ACTION

DEVELOPING YOUR CAREER PLAN OF ACTION

Ideal Job Title and Description (see chapter 6)

Title _____

Description _____

_____

_____

YOUR CAREER PLAN OF ACTION

STEP		Chapter Activity	
One	Chapter 1	*Brainstorming Project*	I have identified the following **creative skills** necessary for the development of my career:

One — Chapter 1 — *Brainstorming Project*

Among the **creative skills** you have developed, do they include the ability to conceive of something as intangible as a business that does not yet exist?

_____ How might you enhance your skills?

_____ What do you think are important **creative (thinking outside the box) skills** for you?

I have identified the following **creative skills** necessary for the development of my career:

_____

I will do this by _____

Two — Chapter 2 — *Licensing and Regulation of Interior Design in Your State*

Among the **research skills** you have developed, do they include the ability to discover how you and your business will be affected by a variety of complex laws? Do you know how to contact professionals who can help you to interpret these laws?

_____ How might you enhance your skills?

_____ What important **research skills** might you need to develop?

I have identified the following **research skills** necessary for the development of my career:

_____

I will do this by _____

Three — Chapter 3 — *Mission/Values Statement*

Among the **leadership skills** you have developed, do they include the ability to work ethically while participating in a profit-oriented business?

_____ How might you enhance your skills?

_____ What important **leadership skills** might you need to develop?

I have identified the following **leadership skills** necessary for the development of my career:

_____

I will do this by _____

(continued)

FORM 15.1. (continued)

STEP	Chapter Activity	YOUR CAREER PLAN OF ACTION
Four	Chapter 4 *Legal Issues You Expect to Encounter in Your Business* Among the **administrative skills** you have developed, do they include the ability to incorporate legally imposed guidelines into the operating practices of a business? _____ How might you enhance your skills? _____ What important **administrative skills** might you need to develop?	I have identified the following **administrative skills** necessary for the development of my career: _____ _____ I will do this by _____ _____
Five	Chapter 5 *Sources of Financial Investment in Business* Among the **entrepreneurial skills** you have developed, do they include the ability to identify, seek out, and persuade others to invest in a business idea you have initiated? _____ How might you enhance your skills? _____ What important **entrepreneurial skills** might you need to develop?	I have identified the following **entrepreneurial skills** necessary for the development of my career: _____ _____ I will do this by _____ _____
Six	Chapter 6 *Specifying Job Activities* Among the **management skills** you have developed, do they include the ability to plan, design, and monitor the activities of others? _____ How might you enhance your skills? _____ What important **management skills** might you need to develop?	I have identified the following **management skills** necessary for the development of my career: _____ _____ I will do this by _____ _____
Seven	Chapter 7 *Developing a Marketing Identity and Budget* Among the **marketing skills** you have developed, do they include the ability to present a message about a business or service in such a way that it attracts new business? _____ How might you enhance your skills? _____ What important **marketing skills** might you need to develop?	I have identified the following **marketing skills** necessary for the development of my career: _____ _____ I will do this by _____ _____

(continued)

FORM 15.1. (continued)

STEP	Chapter Activity	YOUR CAREER PLAN OF ACTION
Eight	Chapter 8 *Defining Specific Services of Your Ideal Interior Design Business* Among the **language skills** you have developed, do they include the ability to write about highly detailed subjects in ways others can understand? _____ How might you enhance your skills? _____ What do you feel are important **language skills** you might need to develop?	I have identified the following **language skills** necessary for the development of my career: _____ _____ I will do this by _____
Nine	Chapter 9 *Explaining Four Methods Interior Designers Charge for Their Services* Among the **quantitative skills** you have developed, do they include the ability to determine the financial impact of your decisions on a business? _____ How might you enhance your skills? _____ What important **quantitative skills** might you need to develop?	I have identified the following **quantitative skills** necessary for my career that I need to develop: _____ _____ I will do this by _____
Ten	Chapter 10 *Providing an Overview of Interior Design Project Management* Among the **technical skills** you have developed, do they include the ability to systematically organize/plan the activities of others? _____ How might you enhance your skills? _____ What important **technical skills** might you need to develop?	I have identified the following **technical skills** necessary for my career that I need to develop: _____ _____ I will do this by _____
Eleven	Chapter 11 *Developing Contract Negotiation Techniques* Among the **interpersonal/interactive skills** you have developed, do they include the ability to engage in complex negotiation proceedings with clients and other professionals? _____ How might you enhance your skills? _____ What important **interpersonal/interactive skills** might you need to develop?	I have identified the following **interpersonal/interactive skills** necessary for the development of my career: _____ _____ I will do this by _____

FORM 15.1. (continued)

STEP	Chapter Activity	YOUR CAREER PLAN OF ACTION
Twelve	Chapter 12 *Identifying Appropriate Vendor Resources for Your Ideal Interior Design Business* Among the **training/teaching skills** you have developed, do they include the ability to educate others about the decisions or choices you have made so that they can assist you in your work? _____ How might you enhance your skills? _____ What important **training/teaching skills** you might need?	I have identified the following **training/teaching skills** necessary for the development of my career: _____ _____ _____ I will do this by _____ _____
Thirteen	Chapter 13 *Skills Addressed in Your Personal Skills Assessment* Among the **sales and selling skills** you have developed, do they include the ability to secure new clients and projects and to persuade others of the merits of certain products or services? _____ How might you enhance your skills? _____ What important **sales and selling skills** might you need to develop?	I have identified the following **sales and selling skills** necessary for the development of my career: _____ _____ _____ I will do this by _____ _____

of the business planning project—what you honestly believe to be the important skills you might need to develop to prepare yourself for work in your ideal interior design business. Only you know how easy or difficult it was to complete the different parts of the business plan project. For example, did you find it difficult to describe, clearly and in your own words, the interior design services your business will provide? Or might it be helpful to enhance your professional or technical writing abilities? If so, include your conclusions in the language skills section of your career plan of action.

As you can see, this project focuses on familiar topics; it asks you to interpret them in special ways. You may not yet know exactly how you will enhance the skills you have identified as requiring development. In a way, that is one of the goals of this project—to leave you with a series of personal objectives to highlight, pursue, and master to enhance your development as a well-rounded, goal-oriented professional. Consider trips to local bookstores or questions to ask of designers and coworkers as ways of gathering resources that will help you develop the skills your career plan of action has identified. After completing this project, if you have some ideas about where to begin to learn more about your areas of concern, use those ideas as a starting point and grow your plan of action from there. You could think of this plan of action as a course to follow in your personal journey from student to accomplished professional, developing a career that is ideal for you.

RESIDENTIAL INTERIOR DESIGN PROJECT SIMULATION

Lee has let you review the installation forms employed by her firm, Imagination Unlimited, to assess items used in a project. Complete this inventory of space you have already designed and with which you are familiar. This process will prepare you for documenting the items in a project that have been installed (see Form 15.2). This information may then be kept for later reference and estimating purposes. The final site survey notes the condition of every aspect of the space in detail. This information is usually shared with the service providers responsible for completing the work, such as an independent contractor or a general contractor who will then share the information with the appropriate subcontractor for possible remedy. Completed site surveys are also kept as project references and used to assess the performance of service providers whom you may wish to retain on subsequent projects.

FINAL INSTALLATION INVENTORY

Page ____ of ____

Date _____

Client _____

Job Number/I.D. _____

Designer/Firm _____

Project Address or Reference _____

Room or Space

ITEM	Vendor/Contractor	Style/I.D.#	Dimensions
	Source	Colorway	Repeats
Year/Date			
Photo #			

Room or Space

ITEM	Vendor/Contractor	Style/I.D.#	Dimensions
	Source	Colorway	Repeats
Year/Date			
Photo #			

Room or Space

ITEM	Vendor/Contractor	Style/I.D.#	Dimensions
	Source	Colorway	Repeats
Year/Date			
Photo #			

Room or Space

ITEM	Vendor/Contractor	Style/I.D.#	Dimensions
	Source	Colorway	Repeats
Year/Date			
Photo #			

Room or Space

ITEM	Vendor/Contractor	Style/I.D.#	Dimensions
	Source	Colorway	Repeats
Year/Date			
Photo #			

(continued)

Room or Space			
ITEM	Vendor/Contractor	Style/I.D.#	Dimensions
	Source	Colorway	Repeats
Year/Date			
Photo #			

Room or Space			
ITEM	Vendor/Contractor	Style/I.D.#	Dimensions
	Source	Colorway	Repeats
Year/Date			
Photo #			

Room or Space			
ITEM	Vendor/Contractor	Style/I.D.#	Dimensions
	Source	Colorway	Repeats
Year/Date			
Photo #			

Room or Space			
ITEM	Vendor/Contractor	Style/I.D.#	Dimensions
	Source	Colorway	Repeats
Year/Date			
Photo #			

Room or Space			
ITEM	Vendor/Contractor	Style/I.D.#	Dimensions
	Source	Colorway	Repeats
Year/Date			
Photo #			

SWATCH SAMPLES/PHOTOGRAPHS

While Lee is occupied supervising the installation of the final stage of the Abernathy project, she requires your assistance in explaining the continuing-education requirements prevalent in her practice state of Texas. In two paragraphs, explain the purposes of an interior design continuing education program and the requirements for practice in her state (see Table 15.1). Then, identify the state in which you intend to practice and describe that state's requirement. Also indicate if no requirements exist.

CONTRACT INTERIOR DESIGN CASE STUDY: THE CASE OF THE ACCOMPLISHED ASSOCIATE

For this final case study, you will need to have your completed Professional Practices Portfolio on hand.

Congratulations! Your abilities and diligence were recently rewarded with an offer of employment at an exciting firm. Your new place of work is the commercial interior design division of a large furniture retailer with many stores throughout the South and Southwest regions of the United States. This division is primarily responsible for completing executive-style offices of legal, financial, and other professionals. These professionals typically request environments that allow them to carry out work activities and provide a comfortable, attractive setting for client meetings. A team of five senior designers who have years of experience developing client relationships and completing projects is in charge of the division. In addition, eight junior designers—and you are now one of them—support the senior staff and are not, as yet, expected to secure new projects for the firm or to work on their own individual projects.

Although all the team members are accomplished, educated interior design professionals, the division's leader has come to you with a concern—and an initial assignment. "All our folks, except for you, have been out of school for at least several years. In fact, some of them came up through the ranks as salespeople and learned about professional practices, which they teach in school nowadays, in the school of hard knocks. What I would like for you to do," the director continued, "is to write a memo of around two to three pages that brings us up to date on some of the topics that are discussed in those classes." As your new assignment unfolds, it seems that the director would like your memo to cover one of the following topics:

1. What are some ethical considerations that an interior designer should understand, and to whom do these rules apply? Where do rules of ethics come from, and who or what enforces them? And what penalties can be imposed if these rules are found to have been broken?
2. How do legal issues arise from activities performed by interior designers? What issues of this kind should designers keep in mind when carrying out their work?
3. How may members of this team use contracts in providing interior design services? Describe what provisions must be included, according to legal authorities, for a contract to exist. What other provisions must be present for designers to more fully define their working relationship with clients?
4. What names are given to the formal stages of interior design project management, and what tasks are designers usually required to perform during each phase?

Recalling the Professional Practices Portfolio that you completed in your own professional practices course, your class notes, and your completed projects, select one of the topics proposed and start to work on your first assignment. This task represents your transition from student to working professional.

GLOSSARY

accept Agree to each and every term of an offer, making no change, and imposing no condition upon it.

acceptance Act of agreeing to an offer.

acknowledgment Document confirming an order and ensuring that a vendor correctly understands what exactly a purchaser has ordered.

active listening Paying close attention to someone's words to identify and evaluate the implications of what a person says.

actual damages Money awarded in a lawsuit that compensates an injured party for the actual amount of the financial loss the party incurred.

addendum Addition attached to a contract that covers changes made by a client after a contract is drafted but before it is signed.

advertising Methods of promotion that a designer or firm buys and pays for directly.

agency Relationship between an agent and a principal in which the agent represents the interests of the principal in a business relationship. *See also* agent; principal.

agent Party that acts for another party. *See also* agency; principal.

agreement Legally binding statement of what two or more parties promise to undertake.

agreement in restraint of trade Agreement in which one or more parties are restricted from engaging in certain competitive business activities. Such agreements violate antitrust laws.

amendment Written change to a contract to which all parties agree.

American Society of Interior Designers (ASID) Voluntary association that promulgates and enforces rules related to maintaining professional practices, such as ethics.

Americans with Disabilities Act (ADA) Law mandating that all new or renovated public and some private buildings be accessible to all individuals regardless of their physical abilities.

antitrust law Body of laws that curbs practices by monopolies designed to limit the ability of smaller, less powerful business entities to compete in the marketplace.

arbitrator Neutral third party who gathers information about the cause and nature of a dispute and decides on a resolution that is binding on all parties.

articles of incorporation Legal document that must be filed with the state when a corporation is formed.

balance sheet A financial accounting document used to show an entity's assets (property it owns or controls) and liabilities (obligations owed to others) at a specified, identifiable time.

behavioral interview Type of job interview in which the interviewer asks sophisticated questions based on behavioral traits the employer considers most appropriate for the particular position.

behavioral mapping Technique of collecting objective information about how a space is used by photographing it over a series of days and cataloging the range of emotions shown by people who are using the space.

bid Formal document in which a contractor proposes to complete a project at a stated cost.

bid bond Form of insurance issued by a third party that protects a client from loss if actual costs exceed estimated costs.

bid form *See* tender.

bilateral contract Contract that exists when one party makes a promise (usually a promise to pay sums of money) and, as a result of that first promise, another party promises to do something (or to not do something the party had a legal right to do) at some time.

binding agreement *See* agreement.

bodystorm Technique of collecting project information that involves first identifying different kinds of users or consumers and then acting out how they will interact in a space.

breach of contract Failure of a party to a contract to perform in the manner agreed to.

bribe Direct payment of some kind made to gain favorable treatment.

business entity Concern that exists to provide one or more services or products that is defined by its legal structure. Sole proprietorship, partnership, and corporation are types of business entities.

buy-in Client's assent to the final scope of service as described in the contract.

capacity Legal ability to enter into contracts.

case law *See* common law.

case study interview Type of job interview in which the interviewer describes possible job situations and asks questions about them to determine a job seeker's ability to solve business problems.

cash discount Price reduction given for paying the invoice within a certain amount of time.

chain of command Lines of authority within an organization.

change order Document authorizing changes that the client requests after a contract has been awarded and final documents have been signed.

close Point in the selling process when a prospect is asked directly to buy the product or service.

code of ethics Set of rules of professional conduct that members of a profession voluntarily agree to follow.

common law Legal principle that past decisions made by courts of law establish rules for making decisions about similar issues that may come up in the future.

common law of contracts *See* contract law.

comparative fault Degree to which a party to a lawsuit is at fault. Many states mandate that damages be apportioned based on comparative fault.

competitive bidding Process of inviting possible suppliers to submit bids on a project, comparing the bids, and selecting one supplier to perform the work.

complainant Person or organization that brings charges against another person or organization in administrative action.

complete performance Performance that satisfies every term agreed to in a contract.

confirmation of purchase Formal signed document confirming a client's agreement to purchase specific products and noting prices, quantities, and sufficient details to identify these products.

conflict of interest Situation in which someone has professional or personal loyalties, obligations, or financial interests that would make it difficult to act in an objective manner.

consideration Benefit one party to a contract gives to the other in exchange for a benefit received, as when one party pays a certain amount of money in exchange for the other party's performing a task.

consumer journey Technique of collecting project information that involves cataloging all the interactions a consumer or user has while in a space.

continuing education unit (CEU) Unit of credit for completion of continuing education courses. In states that license or certify interior designers, laws establish the number of CEUs practitioners must satisfy within specified time frames to remain in good standing.

contract Agreement made enforceable through legal action because certain requirements have been met.

contract administration phase Final stage of a project during which it is realized, bringing together all the products and services as specified and ordered by a designer and as approved by a client.

contract document Any of the papers that define a project, including drawings, plans, spec sheets, and schematic representations.

contract document phase Stage of a project during which appropriate documents are drawn up and purchase orders for the merchandise items are submitted to vendors.

contract interior design A term thought to have originated from this specialization's use of contracts and contractors. It generally refers to the practice of addressing accessibility, functional, and appearance issues related to spaces held open to the public or used for purposes other than an individual's dwelling.

contract law Body of laws that relates to legally enforceable agreements.

contributory negligence Negligence by an injured party in a lawsuit that was a factor in causing an injury.

conversational interview Informal type of job interview in which the interviewer invites the applicant to discuss various topics that may or may not seem to relate to the position.

corporation Legal entity that exists in its own right, apart from people who or organizations that own it, and continues after the owner(s) is (are) no longer engaged in it.

cost of sales All money spent by a business to produce sales income, including costs of labor, facilities, materials, supplies, transportation, etc.

counteroffer In contract negotiation, a proposal to add to or change the terms of an offer.

criminal conversion law Body of laws relating to exerting unauthorized use or control of someone else's property.

criminal law Body of laws that relates to preventing and punishing criminal acts. Actions involving violations of criminal law are brought by a governmental body.

critical listening *See* active listening.

custom contract Contract prepared especially for a particular project.

customer's own material (COM) A notation used when an interior designer specifies use of a textile product on an item different than those available through the item's maker.

dealer Wholesaler that sells the products of a number of manufacturers in a product category.

deceptive trade practice The making of any false or misleading statement by any seller of goods or services.

deliverables Documents, such as detailed construction drawings and related papers, concept boards, or any other form of media, that communicate a project's design intent to a client and to others.

design development phase Stage of a project during which a design is finalized and a designer prepares written specifications and cost estimates.

design intent Set of decisions a designer makes that seeks to address the aesthetic and functional issues a designer has identified for a project; design concept.

design study fee agreement Contract defining the services to be performed and the compensation for an introductory stage of a project.

direct labor expenses Total a company pays out to or for employees, including salary, benefits, and payroll taxes, etc.

direct personnel expenses *See* direct labor expenses.

disclaimer Contract clause stating that a contractor assumes no responsibility for the actions of any service provider hired to work on a project.

discount Reduction in the suggested retail price, usually a percentage off. (*See also* cash discount, quantity discount, trade discount.)

discounting from retail Selling a product at a price lower than the retail price.

duress Use of threats to induce entry into a contractual relationship.

employee Person who works under an express or implied contract that gives an employer the right to control the details of work performance. An employee is entitled to benefits offered by the company as well as unemployment and worker's compensation insurance should employment end or on-the-job injury occur.

enforceability In contract law, condition of having the attributes needed to make an agreement enforceable.

estimate Statement giving an approximation of the anticipated cost of work to be done.

estoppel *See* promissory estoppel.

ethics *See* code of ethics.

expenses *See* operating expenses.

extreme user interviews Technique for collecting project information in which those who know very little or a great deal about a product or service, or about interior design in general, or a specific space, are asked to evaluate relevant experiences.

Federal Trade Commission (FTC) Regulatory agency created in 1914 with the power to investigate and prosecute possible violations of antitrust laws.

FOB (free on board) Shipping term that indicates the point at which responsibility for the cost of shipping shifts from a vendor to a purchaser. This designation is usually followed by the notation factory or by the buyer's destination to denote the point at which responsibility between a seller and buyer shifts.

force majeure Event or circumstance that is beyond the parties' ability to predict or control; acts of God.

Foundation for Interior Design Education and Research (FIDER) Organization responsible for reviewing and accrediting interior design educational programs.

fraudulent misrepresentation Act of deliberately giving incorrect or misleading information about the terms of a contract.

Freight Prepaid Arrangement in which the seller names the carrier and pays the freight costs.

general contractor Individual or organization that takes on the overall responsibility for constructions or modifications of physical structures and retains the labor of other service providers with specialized skills and knowledge about some aspect of the construction process.

general partner Partner in a business who shares fully in the management of a business and has full legal responsibility for the consequences of actions taken by the business.

general partnership Business owned by two or more people who share equally the risks, decision making, and profits, and who are equally liable for the consequences of actions taken by the business.

gross margin Difference in amount between net revenue and total cost of sales.

gross revenue All money paid to a business for the goods and services it sells.

human resources Managerial functions related to coordinating the activities of workers.

idle production capacity Costs associated with one's services that must be met whether one is working for a paying client.

income All money paid to a business for the goods and services it sells.

income statement A financial accounting document used to report all the revenues (income) and expenses (costs) of an entity for a specified, identifiable period.

Interior Design Educators Council (IDEC) A professional association comprised of those who teach interior design. There are different categories of membership available including professional, associate, affiliate, and graduate student depending on an educator's interest and accomplishment.

independent contractor Worker who is hired by a company to produce a specific end product without close supervision and who is not entitled to company benefits or unemployment and worker's compensation insurance.

Individual Retirement Account (IRA) Type of retirement account that one can invest in up to a certain percent of one's earned income without paying taxes on either the amount deposited or the interest it earns until one withdraws it after retirement. Also known as a traditional IRA.

inferior performance Completion of a contract in a manner that greatly varies from, or is of a quality very different from, what was initially bargained for by the contracting parties.

instruction to bidders Document issued to all bidders on a project that contains information about the form bids should take.

interior decoration Vocation related to the furnishing and embellishment of a home.

interior designer Service professional who is qualified by education, experience, and examination to enhance the function and quality of interior spaces (as defined by the National Council of Interior Design Qualification).

invitation to bid Notice soliciting bids from competing construction service providers.

Invoice A claim for amounts of money owed, or a bill. An invoice may be issued by both manufacturers to interior designers and by designers to clients.

joint and severable liability Legally imposed arrangement in which the general partners in a business assume legal responsibility as a group and as individuals for the consequences of actions that are determined to have harmed others.

joint venture Partnership that exists for only so long as its members initially agreed it would continue or as long as a specific project takes to complete.

judicial committee Committee of a state board or national trade group formed to render decisions on ethics code violations and other related complaints.

kickback Money paid by a person or organization in exchange for having received some form of favorable treatment.

legality Condition of being valid for legal purposes.

letter of agreement Informal contract contained in the body of correspondence following an opening salutation.

libel Written statement that is false and is found to have injured another person's reputation and from which that person is found to have suffered some form of damage.

limited liability company (LLC) Form of business organization that combines the simplicity of a partnership with the protection against individual partners' assets offered by a corporation.

limited partner Backer who contributes funds to a business without making management decisions and whose liability is limited to the amount of money he or she invested in the business.

limited partnership Type of partnership in which some partners contribute funds and share in the profits but do not make management decisions.

line position Job that involves actually making a product or performing a service. In an organization chart, line positions are hierarchical, so one may move up the line to higher positions. *See also* staff position.

management Act of conducting, supervising, or controlling business affairs.

manufacturer's suggested retail price (MSRP) Price a maker asks, but cannot compel, the retailer to sell a product for.

market differentiation *See* market segmentation.

market segmentation Process of matching specific services to potential users.

marketing Process of planning and executing the conception, pricing, promotion, and distribution of ideas, goods, and services to create exchanges that satisfy individual and organizational goals (as defined by the American Marketing Association).

marketing analysis Process of identifying information about the particular services a designer or design firm can provide and the specific group of consumers to whom these services might appeal.

marketing plan Statement describing marketing goals and the means by which they are to be achieved, including budgets and schedules.

mechanic's lien (or mechanic and material man's lien) A legal impediment placed on real estate, which prevents sale to another owner until payment is tendered to a service provider who was not paid by the successive property owner.

mediator Neutral third party who gathers information about the cause and nature of a dispute and negotiates a resolution.

mission statement Short written description of the aims of an organization.

mistake Incorrect understanding of the terms of a contract.

mutual assent State of having all parties of a contract agree to accept the exact terms of a contract. *See also* undue influence.

mutuality State of having all parties of a contract agree to accept the exact terms of a contract.

National Council for Interior Design Qualification (NCIDQ) Organization that prepares and administers a commonly used qualifying examination to determine minimum competencies in interior design skills and knowledge.

negotiation Process of arriving at terms through dialogue and accommodation.

niche marketing *See* market segmentation.

nominal damages In a court action, relatively small award to the injured party, usually when any form of compensatory damages would be speculative or conjectural.

offer Contractual undertaking to do something that exists on the part of the parties when they are intent on entering into a binding agreement.

operating expenses Money paid out by a company in the course of doing business.

plaintiff Person or organization making legal charges against another person or organization.

portfolio Collection of representative examples of one's completed projects that functions as a visual synopsis of one's work and demonstrate one's creative and technical skills.

positioning *See* market segmentation.

principal (1) One of the people who have responsibility for the creative direction of a firm, interacting with important clients, and forming strategic plans concerning major firm activities; (2) party that engages and controls the work of an agent. *See* agency; agreement; agent.)

privileged Not subject to disclosure in a court action without the consent of the parties between whom information was exchanged; applies to conversations a party to the action has with a doctor, lawyer, member of the clergy, or spouse.

product liability law Consumer protection legislation regarding products deemed to be defectively designed, manufactured, or marketed.

programming phase Stage of a project at which the designer ascertains information about goals a client has for a project and reasons for those goals.

promissory estoppel Doctrine that prevents someone from acting in a certain way because he or she relied on someone else's promise not to act in that way.

promotion In advertising, method used to bring a message on behalf of a product, service, or organization to potential customers or the general public.

proprietary information Confidential information about a company's products, business, products, etc.

psychological interview *See* behavioral interview.

publicity A free promotional tool used for getting the message before the market.

punch list Document created when a project is, or is almost, complete, listing errors in workmanship that need to be corrected.

529

quantity discount Price reduction offered based on the number of items ordered.

rep *See* vendor representative.

request for proposal (RFP) A written document issued by potential clients used to solicit interest in, and suggestions from design practitioners about how they would address specific interior design needs, such as public spaces intended for large-scale use.

resale license Permit allowing a seller to pass on state and local sales taxes to a purchaser.

residential interior design The specialization of interior design practice that addresses functional and appearance concerns pertaining to non-public spaces used primarily for personal use and enjoyment.

restocking fee Fee, based on a percentage of the price, charged by a vendor for cancellations and returns.

résumé Document in which job seekers outline their education, employment history, skills, and career goals.

Robinson-Patman Act Legislation containing a provision requiring that a merchant must charge all merchants the same price for a product.

Roth IRA Type of Individual Retirement Account into which one can invest any percentage of one's earned income without paying taxes on the interest it earns until one retires. Unlike a traditional IRA, contributions are taxed in the year they are made, rather than when the money is withdrawn.

sales associate Trained interior designer employed by a supplier to assist customers in the showroom to merchandise and make purchases.

sales tax Tax based on, and usually a percentage of, the total price of a purchase.

schematic design phase Stage of managing an interior design project during which a designer develops an initial design intent, or concept, and prepares a preliminary budget and schedule for client review.

scope-of-service analysis Detailed written enumeration of the services a designer is hired to perform.

selling Act of presenting the attributes and benefits of goods or services to individuals or small groups with the aim of convincing a prospect to make a purchase.

selling price Amount at which a designer offers a product for sale to a client.

severability In contract law, state of contract being able to be divided into separate legal obligations so that if one clause is breached or found to be unenforceable, the remainder of the contract remains in effect.

shadowing Technique for gathering project information that involves following people as they interact in spaces.

Sherman Antitrust Act Legislation aimed at curbing excessive commercial power by monopolies that interfere with smaller, less powerful businesses' abilities to compete in the marketplace.

slander Oral statement that is false and is found to have injured another person's reputation and from which that person is found to have suffered some form of damage.

sole proprietorship Business owned by one person that may operate in any commercially acceptable and viable manner an owner chooses.

specifications (specs) Document listing all details about the dimensions and nature of planned construction or modification of a physical structure and listing all materials that will be used.

staff position Job that provides support services to people in line positions. A person in a staff position usually reports to a person in a line position but is not part of the vertical hierarchy and does not supervise other employees. *See also* line position.

standard-form agreement Printed form with blanks that the parties fill in with the information requested.

standing Legal right to initiate a lawsuit because one is adequately affected by a matter in question, as when one is harmed or has suffered damage.

statement of cash flows A financial accounting document used to report the changes in amounts of cash available to a business through activities such as its operation, investment, and financing practices occurring within a specified, identifiable period.

statement of general conditions Document the client provides to bidders that includes information about the project such as the name of a client and the legal rights and responsibilities of the parties once the contract is awarded.

Self-Testing Exercises for Preprofessionals Program (STEP) A knowledge assessment and study skills workshop offered by local chapters of the ASID to prepare applicants for the NCIDQ exam.

storytelling Technique for gathering information for a project in which people are prompted to tell about their own experiences with using an item.

stress interview Type of job interview in which the interviewer uses a confrontational tone with the job seeker.

subcontractors Specialized service providers hired by a general contractor.

substantial completion Completion of a contract in a manner that differs, but not substantially, from what was initially bargained.

surety Third party, usually a specialized company or banking institution, that takes on the legal obligation to cover unbudgeted completion costs.

SWOT analysis Method of business decision making that assesses a problem or issue by identifying its **s**trengths, **w**eaknesses, **o**pportunities, and **t**hreats.

target market Those individuals and groups to whom specific products or services might appeal.

tender Document submitted by a service provider stating the formal price for completing a project.

termination Expiration of a contract, either because the agreed-upon performance has been completed or the parties to the contract agree in writing to end it.

theft by check Criminal offense of passing a bank draft that is not inadequately covered by funds with the intent to deprive another of property.

360-degree feedback An approach to evaluation in which colleagues situated in the organizational scheme above, below, and laterally to a worker (as well as the worker) prepare written statements describing their perceptions about the quality of work produced by that individual.

tort law Branch of law covering civil wrong, as opposed to criminal, other than breaches of contract.

total gross revenue *See* gross revenue.

trade discount Reduction offered to design professionals.

undue influence Exercise of influence over a party to a contract that is powerful enough to supersede the exercise of that individual's own free will; duress.

unfocus group   Technique for gathering project information similar to a focus group, but using a group made up of a wide variety of people.

unilateral contract   Contract that exists when one party shows acceptance through his or her actions, rather than through verbal agreement.

unjust enrichment   Acquisition of money or benefits that, in fairness, belong to someone else.

use tax   Tax imposed in place of a sales tax on goods purchase from out of state or over the Internet.

valid   Having legal weight; enforceable.

vendor   An individual or entity offering others goods or services for sale or retention.

vendor representative   Trained interior designer employed by a supplier to keep customers informed about products and services and to handle customer requests, problems, and so forth.

INDEX

academic institutions, 504. *See also* education

acceptance, 139–40, 225, 360

accommodation, public, 110, 145–46

accounting: financial, 15, 179, 181–83, 198–99, 315; managerial, 15, 179, 184–85, 198; and profitability, 31, 184

accreditation, 62–64. *See also* licensing; registration

acid test ratio, 187–88

active listening, 24–29

"acts of God" clause, in contract, 378

actual damages, 145

addendum, 442

administration: of business finances, 180–82; contract, 22–24, 329, 343–49, 371, 379, 435. *See also* business management

advertisement, 241, 243, 247–48; for employment, 484. *See also* marketing and promotion

advisors, 5, 14, 20, 32, 196. *see also* attorneys

advocacy, 70, 72, 82–83

affluence, 10

Age Discrimination in Employment Act of 1967 (amended in 1990), 222

agency, 16, 136

age of majority, 360

agreement, 411; antitrust, 158–59; designer-client, 269, 271, 274, 336; enforcement of, 137–38; mediation and arbitration, 377–78; written, 125–26, 128, 141, 195–96. *See also* contract

Alderman, Robert L., 341

amendment of contracts, 380, 382, 386–87

American Express, 193

American Institute of Decorators (AID), 60–61, 72

American Marketing Association (AMA), 240, 247

American National Standards Institute, 340

American Society for Testing and Materials (ASTM), 340

American Society of Interior Designers (ASID), 19, 31, 55, 62, 506; careers list of, 37; code of ethics, 90–91, 94–95, 96, 98–99, 109–12, 113–15; membership requirements of, 70–72; Web site, 25

Americans with Disabilities Act (ADA), 1992, 145, 498

analysis: existing condition, 73–74, 82; marketing, 240; SWOT, 17–18, 37–38; variance, 208

"Analysis of the Interior Design Profession" (1998), 15

Ankerson, Kathy S., 339, 341

antitrust law, 158–60

application costs, 269, 270

arbitrator, 377

architecture, 123, 504

articles of incorporation, 135

ASID. *See* American Society of Interior Designers

Associated Artists, 59

attorney (legal counsel), 69, 78, 307, 316, 444–45; and proposed contract, 366, 382. *See also* law and business

attorneys (legal counsel): and finances, 199–200

autonomy, 88

balance sheet, 183

Baldridge, Joy, 249

behavioral interview, 469

behavior mapping, 277

Bellman, Geoffrey M., 10

Bentham, Jeremy, 90

Better Business Bureau, 169

bidding, 433; competitive, 338–39, 344, 435–42

bilateral contract, 140

billing and collection procedures, 32, 297, 300, 315–17. *See also* fee for service; pricing

bodystorm, 277

bonds, 510

brainstorming activity, 36–38, 39–40

breach of contract, 144–45

bribe, 92

Brint, Steven, 9

budget, 28–29, 31, 194, 403–4, 417; constraints of, 273; estimates, 332; marketing, 240–41; project manager and, 330; proposed, 350–51, 365

business, 8–9, 10–11, 247; developmental stages of, 223–24; domains of knowledge for, 117; organization of, 13–14, 130, 385; ownership of, 10, 124, 377; starting new, 200

business cards, 253–55

business entity: corporation, 124–25, 130–31, 134–35, 385; limited liability company (LLC), 135, 385; sole proprietorship, 124–25, 127–28, 130

business finances. *See* finances

business management, 209, 210–36, 212; decisions in, 220–25; functions of, 213–16; introduction to, 211–12; objectives of, 212–13; policies and procedures in, 225–26; practices portfolio, 210–11; strategies-in-action projects, 228–36; in teams, 227; and workers, 216–20

business plan, 35, 78–79, 189, 190, 202; brainstorming, 36–38, 39–40

buy-in, client, 277

California: contract law in, 143, 383; licensing and certification in, 62, 69

cancellation of orders, 404

capacity, 360

career, 453–54, 497–521; contract case study, 520–21; developing, 17, 32, 504–10, 513; installation forms, 517–20; objectives of, 497–99; options for, 499–504, 507; project planning, 511–17; strategies-in-action projects for, 511–21. *See also* profession; employment; work life

carrying costs for services, 246

case law, 139. *See also* common law